GLOBALIZING AMERICAN STUDIES

Globalizing American Studies

EDITED BY BRIAN T. EDWARDS
AND DILIP PARAMESHWAR GAONKAR

The University of Chicago Press :: CHICAGO AND LONDON

BRIAN T. EDWARDS is associate professor of English, comparative
literary studies, and American studies at Northwestern University.
DILIP PARAMESHWAR GAONKAR is associate professor of rhetoric
and public culture and director of the Center for Global Culture and
Communication at Northwestern University.

The University of Chicago Press, Chicago 60637
The University of Chicago Press, Ltd., London
© 2010 by The University of Chicago
All rights reserved. Published 2010
Printed in the United States of America
19 18 17 16 15 14 13 12 11 10   1 2 3 4 5

ISBN-13: 978-0-226-18506-4 (cloth)
ISBN-13: 978-0-226-18507-1 (paper)
ISBN-10: 0-226-18506-0 (cloth)
ISBN-10: 0-226-18507-9 (paper)

Library of Congress Cataloging-in-Publication Data

Globalizing American studies / edited by Brian T. Edwards and Dilip
    Parameshwar Gaonkar.
        p. cm.
    Includes index.
    ISBN-13: 978-0-226-18506-4 (cloth : alk. paper)
    ISBN-13: 978-0-226-18507-1 (pbk. : alk. paper)
    ISBN-10: 0-226-18506-0 (cloth : alk. paper)
      ISBN-10: 0-226-18507-9 (pbk. : alk. paper) 1. United States—Study
and teaching. 2. Exceptionalism—United States. 3. Americanists—
Philosophy. I. Edwards, Brian T., 1968– II. Gaonkar, Dilip
Parameshwar, 1945–
E169.1.G545 2010
973.071—dc22

                                          2010018370

CONTENTS

ACKNOWLEDGMENTS

"Globalizing American Studies" names not only this book, but also an ongoing project at Northwestern University that has so far hosted three major symposia, occasional lectures, and a workshop. Some, but not all, of the pieces included here were first presented and developed under the auspices of this project. We would like to thank the many people who have helped with the various aspects of this project.

We thank first the organizations that provided the financial support for the project when it was only an idea and a string of words. At Northwestern, the Center for Global Culture and Communication, an initiative of the School of Communication; the Weinberg College of Arts and Sciences Dean's Office; and the Roberta Buffett Center for International and Comparative Studies provided substantial funds over several years that allowed us to invite and host more than thirty scholars from the United States, Europe, the Middle East, and North Africa. Daniel Linzer, Andrew Wachtel, Barbara O'Keefe, Sarah Mangelsdorf, Hendrik Spruyt, and Brian Hanson, who directed or lead these entities, were continually supportive of the Globalizing American Studies (GLAS) project both financially and intellectually. Along with our colleagues in rhetoric and public culture, English, and American studies, they make Northwestern a vibrant place within which to develop new ideas.

We thank all of those scholars who presented their work at Northwestern under the auspices of this project for sharing their research, intelligence, and critical acumen with audiences and participants at the GLAS symposia, workshops, and occasional lectures. A grant from the Carnegie Corporation of New York allowed Brian Edwards to visit American studies programs and symposia in the Middle East; some of the research from these trips makes its way into the final chapter of this book. He would like to thank his hosts in Fez, Morocco; Tunis and Sfax, Tunisia; Cairo, Alexandria, and Minufiya, Egypt; Tehran, Iran; Beirut, Lebanon; and Hyderabad, India, for their welcome, their invitations to lecture or lead seminars, and their generous hospitality. He especially thanks students and faculty at all these locations for their probing and generative questions and comments.

We thank two Northwestern graduate students in particular for their assistance: Amber Day, for her energetic organizational work at the three GLAS symposia, and Nathan Leahy, for his intelligent research assistance on the introduction and his help in preparing the manuscript for production. The two anonymous manuscript reviewers commissioned by the University of Chicago Press provided brilliant and detailed advice on the introduction and each of the chapters, which helped us all make this a better book. Late in the game, audiences at the University of Chicago (the Scherer Center for the Study of American Culture), Northwestern University (the American Cultures Colloquium), and the University of Wisconsin, Madison, commented on drafts of the introduction, offering us the opportunity to hone and clarify our argument.

At the University of Chicago Press, Alan Thomas, editorial director for the humanities, acquired the manuscript with enthusiasm, made numerous suggestions that improved its structure and content, and moved it through the review and approval process efficiently. Randy Petilos, assistant editor, guided this book into production with talent, timeliness, and good humor. Carol Saller, senior manuscript editor, took the reins on the later stages of production. Kathy Gohl was a consummate copy editor. And Siobhan Drummond produced the index with intelligence and care. All of them have our gratitude.

Finally, we would like to thank the contributors to this volume for their hard work writing, presenting, and revising their chapters; for their patience as we developed the book; and for the privilege of publishing their work in this volume.

INTRODUCTION:

GLOBALIZING AMERICAN STUDIES

Brian T. Edwards and Dilip Parameshwar Gaonkar

THE SPECTER OF AMERICA

Until now, American studies has been conducted under the shadow of the American Century, an epistemological framework and a period of time that have, it seems, drawn to a close.[1] Emerging contemporaneously in the early days of World War II and finding their earliest fruition in the postwar settlement, American studies and the naming of the so-called American Century both drew on and solidified the mythology of American exceptionalism that had been written into the fabric of the nation well before its actual founding, as far back as the famous call for a city on a hill uttered by the Puritan John Winthrop in 1630.[2]

The roots of both American studies and the understanding of the twentieth century as the "American Century" can be found earlier in the twentieth century. It seems clear, however, that the particular configuration of American exceptionalism that took hold with Henry Luce's 1941 *Life* magazine editorial "The American Century"—which both placed the United States in a line of great empires and distinguished it from predecessor formations—had great influence on how scholars, students, and citizens would think about the relationship of American culture, society, and the emergent global power status of the United States.[3] The myth of an American Century and the mythology of American exceptionalism sustained each other through subsequent decades, even though American studies scholars grappled with them both repeatedly and attempted to free themselves from these narratives by identifying and critiquing their limitations and occlusions. The irresolvable debate over American exceptionalism, with both the insight and blindness that it brings in its wake, seemed to its proponents to have been vindicated by the triumph of the American Century. Its critics, despite themselves, were often caught up in the powerful hermeneutics unleashed by the exceptionalist thesis itself.

What is the lure of the exceptionalist thesis? Exceptionalism is traditionally recognized as the logic by which American society and the nation itself are seen to be unique. By extension, exceptionalism demands of those who would study the United States both from within and from without a special hermeneutics. Such a strategy, while privileging complexity in analysis sought by "close reading" or by "historicism," simplifies the work of the critic by obviating comparative analysis. This methodological paradox prefigured within the exceptionalist thesis has given rise to an interpretive tradition that is simultaneously resilient and obdurate.

In the chapter following this introduction, Donald Pease, arguably the most perceptive and tenacious critic of the exceptionalist hermeneutic, gives a nuanced reading of its resilience and obduracy even as he tries, yet again, to deconstruct it. He begins by posing a decisive question: Is American studies possible after American exceptionalism? Pointing to the historical complicity between the two, Pease shows how the latter enables the former. In his historicization of the logic(s) of American exceptionalism, Pease comes close to disavowing the possibility of a postexceptionalist American studies. He concludes, however, by proposing a comparative analysis of "imperial state exceptionalisms," a more accurate rendering of American exceptionalism as derived in his essay.

Pease claims that Americanists, both U.S.-based and non-U.S.-based (the latter hitherto dominated by European Americanists), are held captive by the exceptionalist thesis. For Pease, this captivity is particularly evident in the work of those who have sought to dismantle exceptionalism as the logic by which a revised American studies might function. Pease begins by offering a detailed account of three responses (by Djelal Kadir, Amy Kaplan, and Daniel Rodgers) to President Bush's warrant for a State of Exception in the long aftermath of the events of September 11, 2001; each seems to offer avenues out of the perpetual bind gridlocking a putatively postexceptionalist American studies, yet each commits the very error it denounces.

Pease suggests that we understand Bush's State of Exception, as advanced through the documents *The National Security Strategy of the United States of America* and the declaration of a "Global War on Terror," as a disavowal of the American exceptionalist thesis (which had proclaimed American difference in characterizing previous interventions in the global realm, such as Wilson's "making the world safe for democracy") and a more confident reassertion of the American Imperium.[4] Asking why Bush should disavow the very psychosocial logic by which the state had interpellated its citizen-subjects into a conceptual framework that both constituted and excluded America's Others (whether domestic or international), Pease ultimately shows the inescapability of the exceptionalist logic—even when it is disavowed.

For Pease, the primary link is between American exceptionalism and American imperialism, although the former continually mutates in his historicist account under the pressures of a rapidly changing world propelled by capitalist modernity. From the early republic and Jefferson's "Empire for Liberty," through the mid-nineteenth century's Manifest Destiny until Theodore Roosevelt's characterization of the United States as "leader of the free world" at the dawn of the twentieth, to the moment in the twenty-first century when President Bush disavowed it, the putative exceptionalism of America authorizes a series of exceptions made by the state. And these "states of exception" are always seen, in Pease's account, in relation to the international antagonists of the United States, even when their referents were domestic. Thus, internal colonization and "ethnic cleansing" of Amerindians, for example, should be seen in the light of American conflict with European imperialism in the early nineteenth century, setting a pattern that would be modified and rewritten through the nineteenth and twentieth centuries.

Pease shows how consolidation of the term "American exceptionalism" during the cold war reincorporated varying strands that had operated in independent historical registers and rendered that logic as transhistorical. In the cold war, American intellectuals took a now explicit term, "exceptionalism"—uttered by none other than Joseph Stalin in the 1920s to describe the American Communist Party's alleged heretical deviation—and turned it into the ground on which American studies as an institution was built. That academic formation would be exported via the Marshall Plan and other post–World War II economic development projects to Europe and elsewhere (including Hyderabad, India, which Brian Edwards discusses in chapter 11), and hence it prepared the terrain for an international American studies that could only be seen by U.S.-based Americanists as secondary or derivative, given the asymmetrical access to resources.

Thus when Pease takes as a starting point Djelal Kadir's 2004 inaugural address to the International American Studies Association (IASA)[5]—an address that explicitly responded to the Bush doctrine—he shows us how the terms by which Kadir attempted to escape the rhetoric of American "exception" reverse upon themselves. Kadir countered Bush's version of exceptionalism by claiming that non-U.S.-based Americanists could play a critical role dismantling it. Although Pease finds much to agree with in Kadir's statement, he differs on two key points. First, by simply noting that Kadir resorts to a "good exceptionalism" ("the American Dream," "authentic America") to combat "bad exceptionalism" (the Bush regime), Pease makes the tenacious hold of exceptionalism apparent: "Kadir had in effect guaranteed the Americanness of the International American Studies Association by reinstituting the American exceptionalism that the Bush administration had abandoned." Second, and more important, is that Kadir understands Bush's State of Exception as a new—and thus exceptional—formation ("paradigm-altering," in Kadir's construction, because of its shift from earlier, more limited uses of the term to a now planetary scale). In fact, the U.S. state, both in domestic and international spheres, has often relied on a series of states of exception to justify its actions. It follows for Pease that in those moments, particularly after the institutionalization of American studies, U.S.-based Americanist scholars acquiesced with those exceptions either by ignoring them or dismissing them as inconsequential. This is the historical and continuing complicity between American exceptionalism and American studies that Pease critiques.

Pease's magisterial essay may be seen as a cleansing gesture rather than a substitutive gesture. Pease does not expect the whole of American studies to devote itself to his program of the comparative analysis of "imperial state exceptionalisms." For Pease, American studies is so deeply compromised and contaminated by the exceptionalist interpretive tradition that one has to go through a cleansing process before relocating and renewing American studies. Even the other two critical responses to Bush's recourse to a semipermanent "state of exception"—by Amy Kaplan, a formidable critic of American exceptionalist imperialism and by Daniel T. Rodgers, the most influential postexceptionalist historian—are unable to free themselves fully from the spell of the exceptionalist logic. To be sure, Pease is relentless, and his transformative essay perhaps threatens to kill American studies as we know it; his hope, however, is that it may renew it. The cancer of American exceptionalism is so malignant that it can only be cured by the *pharmakon* he administers.

It seems clear that American exceptionalism has served as an enabling matrix for American studies, especially given that in many ways American exceptionalism preceded American studies as an academic discipline. The question is whether American exceptionalism has always already been implicated in some sort of imperial formation, as Pease argues, with the American Century serving as the most recent incarnation of that imperial strand. This historical question, which Pease argues with considerable precision and force, need not, however, be the starting point for this introduction. If American exceptionalism was always implicated in American imperialism, so long as American imperialism does not come to an end, neither will some versions of American exceptionalism invoked to sustain that imperialism come to an end. In this we agree with Pease. But the question we ask is the following: What happens to American studies

when the American Century—which can be variously described, including as an imperial formation, but which always refers to a particular logic
of the circulation of capital, signs, texts, and (cultural) goods—comes to
an end or enters its *longue durée*? If the American Century in the Lucean
sense is coming or has come to an end, then we expect that the particular
link between American exceptionalism and American studies is bound to
change, if it has not already changed.

The exceptionalist thesis has made possible many sophisticated readings of American history, literature, and society. It provides a basic interpretive grid for what we identify in this volume as the vernacular tradition in American studies. This, the dominant strain for several decades, has
provided not only key works in the field but the periodization by which
American studies organizes itself (for example, Puritan New England as
the foundational moment of American society; the American Renaissance
as the fount of American culture; and the civil rights movement as a domestic instantiation of progress that might model similar movements for
communities organized around ethnicity or sexuality).[6] It is not just the
fecundity of the exceptionalist thesis, but the cunning of the tradition that
has been erected on that thesis, that has been difficult to disavow.

The American Century cannot be critiqued out of existence, even if
it renews itself in the guise of a decentered empire, as Michael Hardt and
Antonio Negri would have us believe.[7] Instead, it can only come to an end.
We need to come to that time when American exceptionalism has to stand
alone, in the multilateral world of the global. Indeed, we believe that we
have come to that time, or nearly so. Therefore we suggest that the closing
of the so-called American Century, less as unit of time than a decided shift
in global conditions, signals the weakening of the long and enduring myth
of American exceptionalism. American studies, as a result, must yield to
a context within which such a formation—of America's special place and
role in the world—requires the bracketing of fictions that can no longer
be sustained.

The complexity and the challenge are enhanced by the recognition
that we are not truly at the end of the American Century but in its twilight. The light that is set on American studies from this perspective offers
a series of refractions as well as (only) a dim visibility. In that twilight, new
formations are not yet manifest; perhaps they are not born. We don't yet
know what to expect, nor what the new formations will look like. People
today talk about the "new Europe," the Asian century. Even Luce's own
Time magazine had a special issue titled "The Chinese Century" (January 22, 2007), echoing a cover story by the same name in the *New York*

Times Magazine (July 4, 2004). Many others institutionally located within American studies have turned toward the hemisphere as a more appropriate formation. On the West Coast, the movement toward Pacific Rim studies has emerged with force, as has a coincident interest in borderlands. We are all studying dying formations, with their archives simultaneously ossifying and fragmenting. We are struggling to decipher the new formations as they emerge from the debris of eroding traditions and worlds.

What prevents us from studying America as a new phenomenon, one among many? The essays collected in this volume propose a series of answers to and cases that address this question; they encourage us to locate the roots of the multilateralism that may already exist in literature and Americanist scholarship, conscious of the contingency of "America" within global circulation. Essays collected here, such as Brent Hayes Edwards's piece on Ralph Ellison or Kate Baldwin's comparative approach to cold war womanhood, or Claudio Lomnitz's transnational perspective on border crossings between Mexico and the United States, locate for us texts and authors not entirely contaminated by the exceptionalist thesis. The chapters in this volume trace variously the emergent consciousness of America as one among many—even with all its imperial impulses—in an emerging multilateral imaginary. Hence, these essays posit a "spectral America" in various circulations, where "America" may lose its referent or exist only as a specter, against Kadir's ur-American address to the International American Studies Association. The multilateralism that these essays help us to locate and acknowledge is not appreciated in the field as constituted and imagined from within the United States—even when U.S. Americanists travel abroad—precisely because the sites wherein America is seen through a multilateral prism are weak (disciplinarily, conceptually, and fiscally, in the case of non-U.S. centers of American studies). More than anything else, it is the enduring prejudice of exceptionalism that leads even its most trenchant critics to believe that dismantling or reconfiguring the American tradition should nonetheless privilege what we call the vernacular tradition.

Thus the combination of American studies–American exceptionalism–American Century has served until now as an enabling interpretive matrix that has been able to contain a variety of contradictions, generated both internally by academic inquiry and externally by changing historical conditions. The resilience of this tripartite structure has enabled American studies to contain and defer disciplinary anxieties. We briefly defer the question of what sort of American studies emerges after the American Century by asking what sort of a disciplinary anxiety does our time—the end of the "American Century"—present?

DISCIPLINARY ANXIETY

Disciplinary anxieties are common. They are particularly acute among those interdisciplinary formations, such as American studies, which are prone to a reflexive process of perpetual self-marking and self-constitution in terms of five key elements: objects, methods, theoretical commitments, the assembling and securing of traditions, and political engagements. Such anxieties, prompted by habitual auto-critique, can be energizing as well as debilitating. The question that interests us here is whether American studies is inordinately more anxious than other multidisciplinary academic formations—which could be oriented around a geographical area (for example, Latin American studies) or thematically centered (for example, religious studies, postcolonial studies)—and whether that anxiety is more debilitating than productive. In the case of American studies, the last category—political engagements—involves both the interplay of contemporary politics of the United States and the field's relationship to the United States as a political entity. It is obvious that American studies has more than the usual share of politics. It is also clear, in the rapidly emerging institutional formations of American studies globally, that American studies scholarship frequently functions in an overdetermined political frame.

How are these disciplinary anxieties articulated? There are usually two discursive or narrative strategies that can be found within any given discipline. One tends to be resolutely metacritical; the other is a mixture of first-order critical-historical-theoretical practice as well as second-order (that is, metacritical) practice. These narratives might be further distinguished as the *founding narrative* and the *crisis narrative*. In each of these narratives, the five elements around which disciplinary anxiety revolves are differently configured.

The founding narrative is generally performative insofar as it is articulated in the course of a critical performance. Such is the case with foundational works of American studies by Henry Nash Smith, R. W. B. Lewis, Perry Miller, and the like, to whom subsequent American studies students and critics have so often turned as models for their practice as well as their metacritical commentary on what they were doing while they did it. In the latter case, prefaces, afterwords, and parenthetical remarks within these foundational texts often yield the decisive clues. So the founding narrative may not even be self-conscious at some level. It may be within the discussions by later critics who read and reinterpret these works as founding narratives, as in the case of Amy Kaplan's 1993 rereading of Perry Miller's preface to his 1956 *Errand into the Wilderness* (which we discuss later in the chapter), or before her, Gene Wise's 1979 reading of Vernon Parrington's *Main Currents in American Thought* (1927), or Alan Trachtenberg's 1978 reading of Henry Nash Smith's *Virgin Land* (1950).[8] Most often, the founding dimension of these founding narratives is related to the way such works reconfigure the object domain in terms of thematic unities, motifs, symbols, styles, and so forth. In the course of reconfiguring the object domain, such a founding text might also put forth implicitly a reading strategy and explicitly theoretical formulations (which may not necessarily be a full-blown theory, although it is sometimes the case, as with the "myth and symbol" school). In short, the effect is hybrid or ambiguous. That's why it comes to occupy the position of a founding text, containing within itself polysemous possibilities.

Regardless of how explicit they may be on such issues as topic, theme, reading strategy, and theory, the founding narratives' achievements remain singularly performative. Their impact is by and large holistic. They could be taken apart, broken down, criticized, in pieces, as succeeding generations do. Nevertheless they retain and cast an abiding spell as totalizing performatives.

Crisis narratives, on the other hand, tend to be discursive rather than performative. The crisis narrative is metacritical. It tends to be synoptic, looking after a broad set of internal critical practices against the background of a changing disciplinary landscape. At least in the case of American studies, crisis narratives seem to have emerged primarily from external impetuses, as opposed to the accumulation of anomalies, as in the case of Kuhnian paradigm shifts in natural sciences.

To see how this works, let us take for an example Amy Kaplan's famous deconstruction of Perry Miller's 1956 preface to his *Errand into the Wilderness*, itself a foundational text in American studies. Kaplan's essay "Left Alone with America" may be the most-cited essay in antiexceptionalist American studies work; indeed it appeared as the introduction to a key collection in the bibliography of the field.[9] In her reading of Miller's preface, Kaplan shows the tenacity of the exceptionalist thesis. Kaplan brilliantly exposes the ways in which Miller's own alleged discovery of his project within 1920s Belgian Congo allowed him to write out slavery as the central story of American expansion, visible in his decision to occlude Virginia and westward expansion as the key origins of American history. In Kaplan's astute account, Miller's downgrading of Virginia and the slave trade in turn enables the long repression of the African or Africanist presence within canonical American literature. (Her epigraph is of course from Toni Morrison's essay *Playing in the Dark*, which had been published the year before Kaplan's essay.) Kaplan locates Miller's error in his own "errand," highlighting the pun in the word, and focuses on the temporal and geospatial gap between his work on an oil tanker in the jungles of Africa as a young man, where he awakened to "the meaning of America" while participating in the economic exploitation of a colonial African nation, to the "security" of the American academy, where he would later explore the "uniqueness of the American experience" and create a pervasive model for American studies. In her essay, Kaplan proposes three paradigm shifts for new work in American studies, built around signal absences: the absence of the study of culture in historical accounts of American imperialism; the role of empire in the study of American culture; and the absence of American studies within postcolonial studies. The essay was and is a monument in the reconfiguration of American studies as it grappled with the end of the long cold war.

As we look back at Kaplan's essay from our vantage today, however, the image of Miller's return to America already prefigures every form of diasporic literature that would come to be a dominant strand in new Americanist reconfigurations—diaspora as a destination in and of itself. The diasporic writer's *return* and her *arrival* become, as with Perry Miller's errand in the jungle and his errand in the wilderness, two sides of the exceptionalist thesis. What is fundamentally absent here is the possibility of conceiving of America as a cosmopolitan node, or a turnstile in the global flows, where America is a pivotal but not the singular moment of arrival and departure. So, in the very process of dismantling Miller's exceptionalist "errand," Kaplan's reading unwittingly reinstalls exceptionalism. It dismantles the exceptionalist thesis, as articulated within what we call a vernacular tradition (of which Miller is a foundational figure), via Kaplan's cosmopolitan perspective, itself derived from Miller's own forgotten cosmopolitanism in her essay, *only to reinstall* the exceptionalism in the image of a return. The same might be said of her larger formulation: that the occlusion of culture in studies of American imperialism and of empire in studies of American culture might be redressed by the two fields' mutual consideration of one another. The force of Kaplan's cosmopolitanism in "Left Alone with America" is the way she refocuses her readers' attention on the triad occluded by Miller's dynamic (that is, that Africa is written out as a third term). Yet her famous paradigm shift remains caught within the dialectic of a dyadic arrangement.

Kaplan's reading is an example of a crisis narrative, and one that takes a founding narrative as its occasion. That Kaplan's crisis narrative—with its slippage back into an exceptionalist logic regarding the diasporic—has become something of a foundational narrative for putatively antiexceptionalist American studies motivates (or prompts) our earlier argument about the ineluctable relationship between American exceptionalism and American Century-era American studies. Kaplan remarks in her essay that she reads Perry Miller's comments about the relationship of *Errand into the Wilderness* to the Belgian Congo, "even though his model for American studies has in many ways been superseded." She does so, she explains with some noticeable anxiety, because "the imperial dimensions of his founding paradigm have yet to be fully explored and still remain in place today" (5). Founding texts such as Miller's frequently become allegories for the entire tradition. Although there may be exceptions, their structure—if one were to follow Hayden White's schema—is often metaphoric.

Our point in distinguishing between founding and crisis narratives is twofold. First, we note that founding narratives are ubiquitous within American studies. Such narratives wherever they occur are always partially aimed at alleviating disciplinary anxieties. These anxieties may exist and present themselves in a routine fashion at any given moment, or they become manifest in times of crisis, and these crises can be implicit and long developing, or they are explicit and public. Perhaps the best way to enter into this discussion is to engage a specific problem in which crises are explicit and manifest. This method is useful in the case of American studies because the field's very constitution occurs at a moment of historical crisis, namely, the foundational moment during World War II and its immediate aftermath, as Americans grappled with the newly emergent global supremacy of the United States and what that status might mean for the history of American culture and society that had preceded this moment. Since discussions of American studies are marked by a great deal of explicit discourse about its mission, its location, its tradition, and so forth, we are led to another way of mapping the crisis, one we have pursued in our research for this collection: mapping the crisis in the explicit statements about the field rather than routine practice.

It seems every major historical or epistemological crisis sooner or later produces two sets of discursive responses—an ASA presidential address at the annual gathering and an anthology with an introductory statement. Although there is some important gap between the two forms, one can map fairly consistently how each key crisis moment has elicited a forceful response from the presiding president of the ASA, accompanied by highly generative responses. These discursive responses propose strategies of containment and suturing devices. Such crises can be generative in two senses. First, most of these crises expand the object domain, but this expansion has to be done in such a way that the disciplinary borders are not rendered too porous that they do not wholly disfigure the canon. Second, the crises initiated by new theories or new methodologies and reading strategies can be generative insofar as they enable reading the object domain (especially the canon) in a new and transformative way. This happened in the case of feminist theory, for example, in its impact on American studies as signaled by Ann Douglas's monumental *The Feminization of American Culture* (1977); or in the case of queer theory a decade later, as signaled by Eve Sedgwick's influential rereading of Melville's "Billy Budd, Sailor."[10] Such crises not only expand the object domain but also deepen the hermeneutic, interpretative tradition.

These dramatic moments include the following, to name the major ones: the recognition of African American literature and history as worthy of scholarly research and consideration; the development of (second-wave) feminist theory; the arrival of poststructuralist literary theory in English departments; the multicultural explosion in the 1980s and 1990s; and the acknowledgment of diaspora as a category of experience that undoes an earlier focus on immigration/emigration. If we focus on these, we see the following clearly: the expansion of the object domain, with all the attendant problems regarding canon; and a dramatic change, transformation, or augmentation of reading strategy or method. We can readily see this pattern in the presidential addresses of a number of past presidents of the ASA, such as Patricia Nelson Limerick or John Higham, as they negotiate the challenge of multiculturalism in the pages of *American Quarterly*, or Mary Helen Washington as she negotiates the challenge of race studies, or Shelley Fisher Fishkin as she engages the transnational turn in American studies, or, earlier, Steven Watts negotiating poststructuralist theory.[11] We don't have the space here to read these in detail as Pease does in deconstructing the president of yet another organization, or as Wai Chee Dimock does in her reading here of Janice Radway's presidential address, but it is not surprising that Pease or Dimock would choose metacritical crisis narratives, because it is precisely here that disciplinary anxieties are negotiated. If we compared these to the presidential addresses of other academic organizations, we venture that none would demonstrate the degree of anxiety about crisis management as these addresses do. This is also true about the introductions to critical anthologies in the field, which are geared to signal, mark, and address these crises, and which have been amazingly influential in directing the agenda of research.

In Caroline Levander and Robert Levine's introduction to their critical anthology *Hemispheric American Studies* (2008), for example, the crisis of transnationalism for American studies provokes an engagement with a founding narrative (in this case, an influential literature anthology), followed by an anxious vacillation between expanding and rejecting the national frame for organizing American literary studies. Levander and

Levine begin their introduction provocatively. Taking on the influential two-volume anthology *American Literature: The Makers and the Making*, edited by Cleanth Brooks, R. W. B. Lewis, and Robert Penn Warren at Yale in 1973, Levander and Levine detect an intellectual scandal at the heart of the Yale project, namely, that Brooks, Lewis, and Warren's division of American literature in their collection bifurcated U.S. writings into the national and the "nonliterary." For Levander and Levine, this is a scandal because texts by African Americans and Native Americans were relegated by Brooks et al. to "literature of the non-literary world," a categorization Levander and Levine correctly denote as "oxymoronic." The two, however, derive a positive potentiality from Brooks et al.'s editorial decision: "perhaps the editors were simply prescient in relegating [Frederick] Douglass to their non-national grouping." Noting Douglass's fascination with Haiti as "the only self-made Black Republic in the world" and his championing of the Haitian revolution, Levander and Levine suggest that Douglass's more recent "relocation from the margins to the center of American literature anthologies should necessitate a rethinking of both the national and the literary."[12]

Levander and Levine are surely correct to note the impulse of what we call the *vernacular* tradition to absorb the challenge of a figure such as Douglass. But the lessons they draw from this point demonstrate a repetition (through expansion) of an exceptionalist frame rather than a rejection of it. The conclusion they draw is that the "national frame" of the United States is constituted by "complex ruptures," as embodied, say, in Douglass's trajectory from a fugitive slave to an abolitionist orator/publicist to a diplomat, and yet endures recognizably with an "overarching shape and texture" (2). At the heart of their theoretical argument is that a *spatial encounter* with the various trajectories of literary authors emerging from or engaging with the United States—"complex webs of regional, national, and hemispheric forces"—has the potential to disrupt the more homogenizing singularity of "nation time," which they see embedded in the Brooks, Lewis, and Warren tradition of American anthologies.

Their spatializing framework, however, seems to us to fall back into the vernacular pattern of reincorporating that which should fall beyond its purview. Justified by "webs" and "forces," Levander and Levine's argument for the hemisphere as the terrain of interpretation does not "allow us to view the nation beyond the terms of its own exceptionalist self-imaginings," as they suggest, but rather allows for the expansion of the very model itself. The editors seem acutely aware of this problem, which they restate repeatedly in their relatively brief introduction. Indeed the word "beyond" is a clue: Levander and Levine repeat it twice in the same key sentence—their call to "move beyond the U.S. nation in American studies" (7)—and twice more again in a somewhat anxious repetition of the same construction a couple of pages later. They are of course cognizant of the perils of their position and wonder whether their own project might threaten "a neoimperialist expansion into the field of Latin American studies." Their answer to the question they raise, however, is to disavow the possibility of doing otherwise: "Hemispheric American Studies . . . complicates questions of the nation, and thus raises rather than resolves interpretive problems. [It] can be regarded as a heuristic rather than a content- or theory-driven method; it allows for discovery of new configurations rather than confirmation of what we think we already know" (9). Although we find much to agree with in their passing calls for comparative perspectives and focus on "bodies in motion," their disavowal of a more certain resolution and the privileging of "heuristic" solutions or methods are admissions of their own refusal to move beyond experiential spatial registers.

This is not the place for a full-scale reading of either Levander and Levine's introduction or their anthology that follows, which contains essays that we may ally with our own project (although we would frame them differently, as should be clear, and dispense with the idea of expanding the national framework spatially to the hemisphere, a model that after all imagines contiguity). Rather, our more restricted point is that *Hemispheric American Studies* responds to a crisis moment, as other influential anthologies have done in earlier disciplinary crises, with an anxious and metacritical statement that engages a founding narrative as a way to mark a rupture that it would seek to suture. Our own anthology is not likely to be a radical exception to this pattern. All we can hope to do is to proceed with a heightened reflexivity in contributing to this genre.

Our second objective in distinguishing between founding and crisis narratives is to set the stage for our distinction between the vernacular and cosmopolitan traditions in American studies. We align the founding narrative with the vernacular tradition, and the crisis narrative with both vernacular and cosmopolitan traditions. We move into an explication of the cosmopolitan tradition because this tradition (which has several different strands) exceeds all the available crisis narratives. As a result, we must take up the cosmopolitan tradition on its own terms. What we mean here is that the founding narratives and the vernacular tradition have a close affinity, and in many ways they prefigure the tripartite structure discussed in the first section of this chapter. The crisis narrative, on the other hand, while trying to undermine the tripartite structure, oscillates between the vernacular and the cosmopolitan perspectives. On the surface, the crisis narrative may show a strong affinity with the cosmopolitan tradition, but it is rarely capable of resisting the gravitational force of the vernacular tradition due to the privileging of the object domain. This element was key in our critique of Kaplan's critique of Miller.

The one prevailing "method" of American studies has been, from the start, its interdisciplinarity, which is not nor ever has been disassociated from the national narrative of American diversity, or *unity within diversity*. To this day, American studies scholarship is valued on the grounds achieved by Vernon Parrington so early on in his 1927 magnum opus *Main Currents in American Thought*: its ability to organize, fuse, and weave together material from surprising or overlooked arenas or archives into a powerful argument or reading. The object domain of American studies has changed over the decades, but the question of the meaning of those objects, despite disciplinary debates, has remained consistent. Even in their critique of the progenitors or presumptions of the field, those who seek to break free of the exceptionalist thesis generally replicate and reproduce the multidisciplinary ethos and style valued within the field. It is no accident that American studies scholarship often reaches larger publics than that in contiguous fields: it is often pleasurable to read and surprising in its connections and resolution of disparate problems.

The most dominant trope within American self-understanding has been metaphor rather than metonymy—that is, a substitution based on similarity rather than on contiguity or something associated with the object.[13] Within what we call the *vernacular strand* of American studies, the metaphor is the transposition of the exceptionalist thesis itself. The metaphoric unity of America is a distinctive contribution of the vernacular tradition in American studies, and even functions within the resistant strand of American studies. One can easily move from Whitmanian prosaics for American democracy to the most radical critiques of American oppression, and find in a variety of ways a reinscription of exceptionalist "unity" wherein things can remain the same.[14]

What we call the *cosmopolitan strand* of American studies, in contrast, rejects the metaphoric unity of American experience, and in its place metonymically focuses on the differential placement of America abroad. It does so not only because its American interests are so variable as "America" in its various guises traverses other spaces (initially the colonial spaces of other regimes, to the postcolonial spaces under the sway of cold war concerns, and now in a new world order of imperial formation). There is a fragmentedness in the figure of the American abroad that carries over to the figure of America or American forms abroad.

What do we mean? The American abroad initially has to negotiate with other forces that are unfamiliar, from Mark Twain's and Henry James's innocents abroad to experiences by figures as diverse as James Weldon Johnson, Josephine Baker, Paul Robeson, and Richard Wright of different racial formations in Europe or Soviet Russia, to Paul Bowles's or U.S. Foreign Service officers' encounters in the 1940s with colonial or postcolonial governments and forces. The American abroad experiences a multilateralism, so his or her report back home cannot have a unity in the way that vernacular reports, even in their diversity and multiplicity, seem to.[15] In contradistinction to this fragmented quality of America as it travels abroad— the specter of America—is the relative continuity of the political tradition in the United States, the contiguousness of the territory, the progressive strengthening of the political regime, and its ideological grounding in a liberal imaginary, as elaborated by Louis Hartz in 1955.[16] The integrating forces in America (economy, technology, infrastructure, media) contribute no less to the concept of unity, even though they may seem to go against some aspects of American exceptionalism.

We must therefore focus most of our energy on the struggles within the cosmopolitan tradition. It is here that we come to the distinction between Americans abroad and the specter of America abroad, as mediated by the externally motivated crises provoked by the recognition and development of fields such as diaspora studies, hemispheric studies, and transnational studies. What is important to notice here is the way the cosmopolitan perspective deconstructs in the course of negotiating these challenges, unlike the vernacular perspective, which incorporates and strengthens itself in negotiating the challenges of the African American, feminist, multicultural, and, slightly later, diasporic moments.

One way to unpack the tripartite dialectic of American Century-American studies–American exceptionalism with which we began is to review it in the light of alternative perspectives of the vernacular and the cosmopolitan. The vernacular perspective configures object, method, theory, tradition, and politics in a particular way, although the object domain has been historically variable and expansive. In literary studies, at least, it begins by discussing (but also naming and reordering) the classic texts. Out of this process of critical rereading, the best-known crises have been successfully negotiated and absorbed. The field has also incorporated different genres, from studies of the classic novel, masterpieces of prose, both historical and sociological, and analyses of popular culture (for example, Constance Rourke's classic *American Humor* [1931], and Janice Radway's *Reading the Romance* [1984]). Through many decades, the trajectory was to refine the American exceptionalist thesis through extensions or elaborations of Frederick Jackson Turner's 1893 frontier thesis (for example, David Potter's *People of Plenty* [1954], and Richard Slotkin's trilogy, *Regeneration through Violence* [1973], *The Fatal Environment* [1985], and *Gunfighter Nation* [1992]), especially as we reach into the American Century and the founding of American studies, even though world historical events contributed to the making of the "American Century." One of the questions that remains to be answered is whether there are any strands—palpable or discernable—within the vernacular tradition which are fundamentally subversive of the exceptionalist mythology or resist the anointment of the American Century. These shadows of an emergent multilateralism are apparent throughout the contributions to this volume.

Let us be more precise. When you shift from the vernacular to the cosmopolitan perspective there are two variants. Within the first variant are two further substrands: one is the cosmopolitan readings of America, starting with the French trajectory from Tocqueville to Jean-François Revel to Jean Baudrillard to Bernard-Henri Lévy, who wrote about America from the position of cosmopolitan outsider.[17] These cosmopolitan works were pulled into the gravitational field of "America" by the vernacular tradition and thus disempowered of their potential to disfigure it. (Pease shows how this process worked for Tocqueville, tracing the incorporation of the Frenchman's nineteenth-century study into the arguments of cold war consensus historians Arthur Schlesinger, Jr., and Henry Steele Commager, and the centrality of Tocqueville to the arguments of Daniel Bell and Louis Hartz.) The French, of course, are not the only "cosmopolitan readers" of the American saga; there are other European variants, including the British variant, which is fairly distinguished, starting with Edmund Burke's eighteenth-century reading of the American character. What is less known, however, are the interpretations of America produced by cosmopolitan readers from the global south and from the colonized countries—a research topic very much in need of attention.[18]

Conversely, we place the American abroad, whose trajectory begins perhaps with Benjamin Franklin in Paris and runs to include Henry Adams, Twain, Henry James, Gertrude Stein, James Baldwin, among others. Such writers initially reflected on what it meant to be an American abroad, with a frequently European template against which to reimagine Americanness. But in their works—say Hemingway's or Stein's or Wright's on Spain and France, or the Bowleses' or William S. Burroughs's on Morocco—there was the possibility of a different configuration. Future work might ask to what extent this strand has also been pulled into the gravitational field of the vernacular, and to what extent work such as this is a predecessor to the diasporic literary imagination, in which expatriate U.S. literature reverses the image of someone coming to the United States and writing about their experience. (The signs of this configuration are strong, as in Maxine Hong Kingston's character Wittman Ah Sing.)[19] An intellectual such as Fareed Zakaria, whom we discuss later in this chapter, brings together these two patterns: the latter-day diasporic equivalent of Tocqueville, but a Tocqueville already incorporated by the vernacular tradition.

The question is whether in either of these two strands there is anything that is subversive of that which would become the tripartite mythology. This topic has been inadequately explored in part because the European reading of America and the American presence in Europe have been privileged, which has made it difficult to identify more subversive elements. Although there are many such figures available—both those who have been written out or ignored (as in Claudio Lomnitz's piece)—most have been misread according to the Eurocentric perspectives still underwriting American studies approaches to expatriate literature (Brian Edwards's rereading of the work of Paul and Jane Bowles, through use of a Moroccan Arabic-language archive, has struggled against this imperative).[20]

Now we elaborate on another variant within the cosmopolitan. This strand is fundamentally recalcitrant to the tripartite mythology. If we want to call the present a global or multilateral moment, we want also to argue that this characterization is fundamentally recalcitrant to the tripartite mythology. Whether such a moment may in the foreseeable future dislodge the hold of the mythology within the vernacular tradition is not the point. The issue is whether American studies can be more than an area studies (or latter-day "civilization studies").[21] What we want to ask is this: how might one imagine a truly alternative perspective, not to displace it but, as we argue later, to provincialize the vernacular tradition? We say that such a perspective is a multilateral one, even a global one.

The key to this strategy is to think of America as a collective agent abroad, collective but not unified by the ideology of exceptionalism. Rather, it is fragmented by the materiality of the capitalist project to which America has become committed, perhaps unbeknown to its own (imagined) soul. This is America global. America global becomes global only by diluting the vernacular, and by substituting "America" for the global. Whether that substitution can be reduced to things such as an "empire without colonies," or a hegemonic imperium, might be secondary to figuring out *how to read the archives of America abroad.* What is the American trace abroad, and how does that trace return to haunt the American vernacular? Innocence can never return. The destination of the immigrant and the return of the native, on both sides of the Atlantic Ocean, on both sides of the Pacific, have been suspended. America is no longer a destination, even though it may seem so to many people, as it may have been in the nineteenth and early twentieth centuries. Nor is there the possibility for the diasporic "American" to return to what has been left behind, as was already apparent to Henry James in the first decade of the twentieth century, when he returned after long absence from the United States to write *The American Scene* and found himself looking down at the hubbub of Ellis Island with the shock of the lack of recognition.[22] James, having returned to New York, thinking that his comprehensive vision could comprehend all visible things, recoiled in the acknowledgment that there are currents that may be seen but not grasped by even a Jamesian cosmopolitanism. This is our project.

VERNACULAR AND VERNACULAR REDUX

Let us juxtapose—apparently at random—another foundational text in American studies, R. W. B. Lewis's *The American Adam,* and a recent nonacademic text, Fareed Zakaria's *The Post-American Century*. The latter at first blush seems to be allied with our own project. The goal is twofold: first, to demonstrate how the logics of the vernacular tradition travel and underwrite themselves in surprisingly powerful ways outside American studies proper, even among those not within their gravitational field; and second, to show how one may move beyond such logics, which we take up in the final two sections of this essay.

The American Adam was published in 1955, when Lewis was a professor of English and American studies at Yale.[23] The argument of the book is familiar to those versed in American studies: there is an "Adamic theme" running through the classic texts of Emerson, Thoreau, Hawthorne, Melville, Henry James, and others. According to Lewis, the Adamic theme appears or operates differently within poetry, criticism, and fiction of the nineteenth century, but whatever the stance the text takes toward an America perceived variously as innocent (for Whitman) or fallen (for Hawthorne), the theme may be identified. In his identification of a theme across diverse genres and manifestations of culture, Lewis allied himself with the academic approach that Parrington had initiated. In this respect, *The American Adam* was legible as a work in the American studies vein. But there is more.

In poetry and criticism, Lewis's argument goes, the American author claims his literary space within the "shaggy and unshorn" America (quoting Longfellow, 79); in American fiction, he experiences the world "as it is," as a new Adam. For Emerson, for example, the project is "the refreshment of the word: so that it might utter the Adamic secret and contribute thereby to the Adamic career" (77). And this Emersonian call—to be heeded by diverse American poets—was to be in the service of the nation:

"It was to be a poetic equivalent of the life for which it would also be a revelation, providing, like *the* Revelation, some clues by which to plot a course of actual conduct" (77). For American fiction, less inclined toward the "refreshment of the word" and tending to narrate stories of individuals moving through space, the Adamic theme could be located in that very collision: "American fiction grew out of the attempt to chart the impacts which ensued, both upon Adam and upon the world he is thrust into. American fiction is the story begotten by the noble but illusory myth of the American as Adam" (89).

Although his study focused on the nineteenth century, Lewis identified the Adamic theme in what he considered to be the greatest twentieth-century American literature up to his present. In a brief epilogue, he calls his present moment the "age of containment," a phrase that would stick.[24] For Lewis, however, "the indestructible vitality of the Adamic vision of life" (198) remained "uncontained." Those quiet Americans—and ugly Americans—might thus be summoned to sustain the Adamic vision through the prosaics of cold war.

All of this—from the idea of the "new man" from Hector St.-Jean de Crèvecoeur, to the American as "new Adam" from Whitman—is of course classic exceptionalism, an alluring admixture of memory and desire to project a national fantasy. In that occlusion, Lewis relied heavily on Emerson's binaristic oppositions—"the party of the Past and the party of the Future," or the parties "of Memory and Hope, of the Understanding and the Reason" (7). What is of consequence, almost revelatory, in Lewis for our purposes is not so much his version of American exceptionalism, but how he developed it through *method*, a method at the heart of American studies. For Lewis, those "special complexities, the buoyant assurance, and the encircling doubt of the still unfolding American scene" (198) did not by themselves constitute what is exceptional. Rather, they had to be identified by a critical method specially attuned to analyzing them in their complexity, even as they continue to "unfold."

Lewis's crucial prologue—"the myth and the dialogue"—advances the methodological argument:

> I want, first, to suggest an analogy between the history of a culture—or of its thought and literature—and the unfolding course of a dialogue: a dialogue more or less philosophic in nature and, like Plato's, containing a number of voices. Every culture seems, as it advances toward maturity, to produce its own determining debate over the ideas that preoccupy it. . . . The debate, indeed, may be said to *be* the culture, at least on its loftiest levels; for a culture achieves identity not so much through the ascendancy of one particular set of convictions as through the emergence of its peculiar and distinctive dialogue. (Simi-

larly, a culture is on the decline when it submits to intellectual martial law, and fresh understanding is denied in a denial of further controversy.) . . . Or to put it more austerely: the historian looks not only for the major terms of discourse, but also for major pairs of opposed terms which, by their very opposition, carry discourse forward. (1–2)

Although Lewis perfunctorily concedes that every culture as it matures tends toward a culture of debate/dialogue, the reliance on antimony, opposed terms, and the debate over them as the key to understanding national "identity" is presented as distinctively American (in the absence of a comparative frame). This rendering of Americanness as dialogic, easily translatable into the idiom of liberal pluralism, which would privilege process over substance (the "just" over the "good"), was destined to become far more consequential than the particulars of Lewis's now outmoded sense of American innocence. Although Lewis's book could only be taught today as a document in the history of the field, it would be eminently possible to have the paragraph just quoted serve as a methodology in most of what happens in the current work in the field.

In its focus on the debate over culture (and marking debate as the very structure of American culture, and its absence as "intellectual martial law"), we associate Lewis's method with Gerald Graff's argument for "teaching the conflicts" in his 1992 work *Beyond the Culture Wars: How Teaching the Conflicts Can Revitalize American Education.* In the method and logic Lewis promulgated in *The American Adam,* American studies, which generally takes an oppositional stance toward mainstream American values and social politics, finds its critical starting point. The conflicts and oppositions that mark much of American history and society are critical loci of much of American studies conducted within the now flexible borders of the American framework—be they the continually contested borders of the United States or the various extended groupings (hemispheric, transatlantic, and the like) that now animate new work. Yet as Alan Filreis, an important American studies scholar of the cold war, pointed out in his review of Graff's book, the cold war context for such an argument runs deeply through a position such as Graff's and asks us to reconsider the logic of what seems to be a "conflict" position emerging from the left, namely, that "intellectual extreme opposites 'need' each other to make their positions meaningful."[25] In Filreis's characterization, this conflict position is a binarism that Filreis allies to the anticommunist and antianticommunist debates of the 1950s. There is much insight in Filreis's point. We must go even further, since one could extend the binarisms of the early cold war to an apparent engagement with the rest of the world that fell outside the U.S.-Soviet/capitalism-communism epistemologies of that period, within which Lewis and Graff alike were caught, even though Graff was writing in its twilight. As we will show, however, most clearly in the case of Fareed Zakaria, opening up the frame to a larger perspective does not eliminate binarism.

Lewis's invitation to focus on the debate over cultural identity as a way to understand and chart it leads to an incessant replication—from "teaching the conflicts" classrooms to democratic deliberation in the public sphere, both eminently exportable—and the subsequent reification of the idea of debate itself. That such an ontologized method emerged from *The American Adam* in tandem with the argument about the "new Adam" is important. Lewis's new approach to understanding American complexity— the crossing, fusing, and defusing of dissonant voices—emerged as the *methodological* "new Adam." Thus, Lewis's method is more than an elegant and optimal way to enter and to decipher the "special complexities" of the American soul; it *is* the American soul, dialogic and democratic. For Lewis, this approach would require repositioning the great bard of democracy, Whitman, in the service of the method:

> The American myth, unlike the Roman, was not fashioned ultimately by a single man of genius. It was and has remained a collective affair; it must be pieced together out of an assortment of essays, orations, poems, stories, histories, and sermons. We have not yet produced a Virgil, not even Walt Whitman being adequate to that function. *Leaves of Grass* (1855) did indeed set to a music of remarkable and original quality many attitudes that had been current for several decades. . . . But *Leaves of Grass* is scarcely more than a bundle of lyrics which gives us only one phase of the story imbedded in the American response to life; to round it out, other writings had to follow. (4–5)

To write about Whitman in this vein, particularly on the centenary of the first edition of *Leaves of Grass,* was a radical gesture. In place of the close investigation of the individual work, Lewis's proposal was that the investigation of the fabric of dialogue emerging from many individual works *was* the work of American studies, and a major reason that *The American Adam* is a foundational text of American studies. Lewis's critical work deposes Whitman's Adamic voice from its centrality, and originality, and replaces Whitman with the critical work that gathers a Whitmanian unity in diversity.

What happens when this dialogic method, conceived within American studies, goes public, goes global? Consider what President Obama, the most rhetorically gifted proponent of American exceptionalism in recent times, said in his widely watched (thanks to YouTube, Facebook, and an assortment of Iranian blogs) video address to the Iranian people on Nowruz 2009 (Iranian New Year). This video address discloses the power and cunning of the exceptionalist thesis far better than does Obama's eloquent but routine invocation of the exceptionalist trope, in his Grant Park (Chicago) speech on the night of his election, to account for and celebrate his historic victory, with Oprah Winfrey and Jesse Jackson visibly in tears in the audience. (In a similar vein, even Obama's opponent John McCain and his predecessor George W. Bush celebrated his victory with recourse to the exceptionalist trope, though without the tears.) Unlike the inaugural trope of the Grant Park speech, open to empirical questioning—"If there is anyone out there who still doubts that America is a place where all things are possible; who still wonders if the dream of our founders is alive in our time; who still questions the power of our democracy, tonight is your answer"— the governing trope of the video address is more serviceable and almost irrefutable. It is a call for dialogue within difference, and an invocation of a sense of "shared humanity" despite antinomous positions: "In this season of new beginnings I would like to speak clearly to Iran's leaders. We have serious differences that have grown over time. My administration is now committed to diplomacy that addresses the full range of issues before us, and to pursuing constructive ties among the United States, Iran and the international community. This process will not be advanced by threats. We seek instead engagement that is honest and grounded in mutual respect."[26] The antinomy between Iran and the United States—on diplomatic or state level—is reimagined as containable within "clear" and "honest" dialogue. Obama goes on to suggest that this newly reimagined dialogue of antinomous poles can lead to a peaceful future, but tellingly it is a "future that *we* seek" (emphasis added): "So on the occasion of your New Year, I want you, the people and leaders of Iran, to understand the future that we seek." Note the shift from "your" to "you" to "we" in the sentence. Obama continues: "It's a future with renewed exchanges among our people, and greater opportunities for partnership and commerce. It's a future where the old divisions are overcome, where you and all of your neighbors and the wider world can live in greater security and greater peace." What's American about this future is not simply that "we seek" it, but that it re-embraces the very debate that Lewis had identified as a method, as an American solution. Obama's conclusion is in this regard telling and even chilling: "I know that this won't be reached easily. There are those who insist that we be defined by our differences. But let us remember the words that were written by the poet Saadi, so many years ago: 'The children of Adam are limbs to each other, having been created of one essence.'"

Obama recasts the idea of ineluctable difference in a new framework: one of discussion, engagement, "commerce" that can admit, embrace, and master difference. The pronominal movement from "your" and "you" to "we" is reversed in the address's concluding line by moving back to a "your": your poet Saadi. Yet Obama's quotation from Saadi, the thirteenth-century Persian poet, is more than an apparent dialogue on Iranian terms, in Persian language (although he quoted Saadi in translation, Obama closed with a holiday greeting in good Persian). The quotation of Saadi is of course a line that sounds particularly Emersonian or Whitmanian given our discussion in this section. Saadi was indeed a poet particularly important to Emerson, one Emerson read (in translation), wrote about, and even dedicated a poem to ("Saadi" [1842]).[27] Obama's quotation of Saadi is a quotation filtered through Emerson and Whitman and returned back to Iran as a lesson learned from its own tradition informing a future that "we" Americans—new Adams, children of Adam—seek.

Returning to R. W. B. Lewis as paradigmatic, we find it is this debate—with constructed binaristic sides pro and contra, as if two positions could contain everything—that liberal Americans export as exceptional. (See Kate Baldwin's contribution to this volume on the ways in which the Nixon-Khrushchev "kitchen debate" in 1959 may profitably be seen from a comparative perspective, one that interrupts Americanist understandings of the very "kitchen" itself as domestic, feminized space.)

In the same way, for President Obama or for public intellectuals such as Fareed Zakaria, both of whom announce and prepare us for the coming of a "post-American world," the American voice remains preeminent in the dialogue of nations. It is the voice that recognizes and resonates with other voices, for it is the voice of reason itself forged within an ongoing internal dialogue. As opposed to a room full of voices that do not connect, which are cacophonic (as they are in some American versions of the United Nations), the American voice—in the very act of enunciation—sets the protocols for deliberation and debate drawn from the long career of the United States as a democratic nation, and more so a democratic culture. What is impossible from such a position is to imagine that the American voice could just be one among many, one that could as easily not be heard or not resonate in certain parts of the world. Privileging America as the sounding board, America always the mediator even within a "post-American world," cannot recognize a world within which the voice does not echo back. In this national fantasy of the global, as in the old image of RCA Victor, "his master's voice," the world listens when America speaks. America is both the primal speaking subject and the ultimate addressee, the essence of sovereignty in the dialogic mode.

What if this is no longer the case as the American Century draws to a close? Even among the critical or oppositional strand of American studies, it is difficult if not impossible to imagine this lack of resonance. Thus important studies of "circulation" (especially, in this collection, the chapters by Larkin, Thompson, Sakai, and Brian Edwards) are misread if readers do not perceive the ways in which the circulation of an American voice or form may be diverted off pathways imagined by the logocentric power.

Let us now turn briefly to Fareed Zakaria's 2008 best seller *The Post-American World*.[28] (Intriguingly, in May 2008, while on the campaign trail, Barack Obama was photographed holding the book, with his finger marking a page about halfway through.)[29] Zakaria, we need hardly say, is not someone associated institutionally with American studies. Since 2000, he has been editor of *Newsweek International* (thus overseeing its international editions, with a readership estimated at 24 million), former managing editor of the stalwart *Foreign Affairs,* a regular columnist for the *Washington Post* and the domestic edition of *Newsweek,* and now host of a weekly CNN television program on foreign affairs. Zakaria has made his name from widely circulated opinion pieces on the changing world order, from his best-selling book *The Future of Freedom* (2003) to his *Newsweek* cover story "Why They Hate Us" (October 2001), published in the immediate aftermath of the events of September 11. Rereading *The Post-American World,* his latest and possibly most influential text, less than a year after its initial publication, much of it seems embarrassingly wrong. For example, Zakaria spends much of his long second chapter ("The Cup Runneth Over") discussing the apparent paradox that despite the palpable increase in global violence, the global economy is stable. (He argues too that in fact "the times we are living in [are] ... in historical context, unusually calm" [10]). Even after the devastating global financial crisis of 2008, which continues to reverberate, Zakaria blithely issued "A Capitalist Manifesto" in *Newsweek* (September 20, 2009). It is not for this undoubtedly influential Pollyanna-ish argument about global markets and global violence, however, that we are interested in *The Post-American World*. Rather we are interested in the way that, even while exposing a part of the world that departs from the American Century (what he calls "the rise of the rest"), Zakaria underwrites precisely the logocentric Americanist vision of the unknown world he would seem to be undercutting. Zakaria discusses how the rise of newly powerful economic nations (China, India, Brazil, Russia, among others) is completely changing the way the world works in every respect, from security concerns to energy and ecology to religion and media—and the very future of liberal democracy. But Zakaria invariably speaks from the American vantage point: "The irony is that the rise of the rest is a consequence of American ideas and actions. For sixty years, American politicians and diplomats have traveled around the world pushing countries to open their markets, free up their politics, and embrace trade and technology. . . . We counseled them to be unafraid of change and learn the secrets of our success. And it worked: the natives have gotten good at capitalism. But now we are becoming suspicious of the very things we have long celebrated" (48).

This argument is not motivated simply by the rhetorical requirement of addressing a predominantly American readership, including the once and future president Barack Obama. More than anything else, Zakaria's mindset motivates the argument. Even in a multilateral world, the United States remains paradigmatic. The changing world is not just perceived as a challenge that the United States must master in order to remain preeminent, a notion common to any foreign policy thinking; the implicit assumption is that if the United States cannot master the changing world, perhaps no one can. In other words, the way the United States masters the coming of the post-American world must be exemplary—the most rational, most ethical, most portable. Thus, having initiated its own "post," the United States must teach the rising rest the protocols for engaging the post–American Century. This conviction is Adamic narcissism. If the Japanese mastered ecology, that mastery would not be portable. If Indians mastered the challenge of religious difference, such would not be portable. If Brazilians mastered multiculturalism, that is not portable. If Europeans mastered equitable social distribution, it is not portable. The only way anything is portable, hence universal, is if it is shaped in the United States and succeeds in other "virgin" lands. This impulse is yet another version of American exceptionalism.

We cannot undo or even deconstruct the vernacular. We can only provincialize it.

PROVINCIALIZING THE VERNACULAR

What is preventing us from seeing the new global order as it emerges except through an American cast of vision? What is preventing a multilateral approach from taking root in American studies? A multilateral approach, we want to clarify, does not mean looking at American studies from every possible angle, but rather from the perspective of shifting critical nodes: Japan (Naoki Sakai), Bombay (Brian Larkin), Cairo and Tehran (Brian Edwards), Mexico (Claudio Lomnitz), Moscow (Kate Baldwin), Damascus (Elizabeth Thompson).

To provincialize the vernacular is not easy. The vernacular has an uncanny ability to resist the appearance of being made provincial, as evident from its capacity to draw into its gravitational field so many themes and insights generated by the cosmopolitan tradition.

Tropes of both return and arrival can be absorbed fairly well within the vernacular tradition. Of course that tradition became richer as it responded to these returns and arrivals, but it is notable and striking that critical attention to the diasporic figure did not palpably subvert or challenge the exceptionalist thesis. The diasporic figure, as reconfigured within an American studies perspective, could in fact be made to underwrite the American Century thesis: the most complex fruition of unity within diversity, playing out Luce's idea that the entire century might be listed under the column of the American. Diaspora studies, suitably permitted to articulate their angst, as encountered by American studies, could then become yet another strand of multiculturalism. By privileging the trope of America as destination, the vernacular incorporation of diaspora reinscribes the unique path of American democracy from political resistance (against Britain) to socioeconomic redistribution (from the Square Deal to the New Deal to the War on Poverty) to recognition of cultural and other identities of difference.[30]

Within the new formation that we attend to, however, diasporic subjects who arrive in the United States do not come to "America" as a (final) destination but rather to the United States as a holding place. If we think of America not as terminus but rather as node through which people are passing, as we alluded to earlier, the enigma of arrival in America is of less interest than it appears within many American studies engagements with the various diasporas traversing the United States. Rather, *passing through* should command greater attention. "America" is after all—before all—a node in the global circuit, arguably the most important of nodes in the global circuitry. This characterization is not to underestimate the major role that the United States plays in present geopolitical arrangements but to recast it among a proliferating set of trajectories, national, subnational, and regional, that make up the present global matrix. (With the use of *nodes*, we are nodding toward earlier terms for this insight, including *alternative modernities*, *global cultural flows*, and the *circulatory matrix*.) The vernacular tradition is unable to consider America as node; perhaps it should not. To an extraordinary extent, too, though, much work in what we have called the cosmopolitan strand of American studies has conceived of its own work in terms of return, return of the prodigal, return to the shining city, or a deliberate exile, as in Amy Kaplan's crucial reading of Miller. This blindness that privileges return as against passing through is embedded in a complex interpretive tradition that can and does produce insight and is likely to continue to do so.

Hence, at one level the two traditions within American studies will continue, evolve, and productively engage each other—the vernacular and the cosmopolitan in its three or four different strands. From now on, however, they will have to be carried out under the shadow of what we call "America global." What escapes the vernacular tradition is precisely that collective agent—America global—that is, America as the agent of capitalist modernity. It is not as if within the vernacular and cosmopolitan traditions the theme of American capitalism has not been addressed. There is a distinguished critical tradition of the American Left that has done so. The idea, however, that America global as a collective agent traverses the globe as an agent of capitalist modernity leaves behind traces that have no legibility within the protocols of reading associated with either the vernacular or the cosmopolitan tradition. Not only does America global refuse the lure of the hitherto successful recuperative logics of the vernacular tradition, but increasingly this "America" casts an overwhelming shadow. It is this shadow that we need to study and engage. Unlike Americans themselves, who may return, America itself does not return. Nonreturn is the enigma of America global.

The aesthetics of the multilateral are difficult to grasp. Its archive is vast and disfigured—disfigured both by its vastness and by a metonymic dispersal that resists unifying metaphorization, and even allegorization. It is an archive that is accumulating at a staggering rate. Its seemingly endless horizons—moving from the republic of letters to cyberspace; interspersed within spaces, structures, and communities, both local and global; inscribed, staged, and circulated, physically and digitally—are clearly far removed from the usual purview of Americanists. This archive is not just the standard archive of cultural studies—music, cinema, television, advertising, and the like. It also includes physical spaces marked as American, even when only their form originates in the United States (big box stores, shopping malls, the American-style campus, the cybercafé); spaces of public deliberation such as the call-in show and the Internet chat room; and a global English increasingly illegible to Americans, propagated in small business institutes around the world and in the absence of principles for codification and canonization.[31] One can imagine the American studies scholar running for cover against the avalanche of this archive. Stubborn disciplinary prerogatives of American studies have not prepared the current generation of U.S.-based Americanists for this avalanche: (1) the simple but profound blindness caused by the monolingualism or at best the bilingualism of American studies, as signaled in Wai Chee Dimock's chapter here; and (2) until recently, the lack of credentialing from Americanist research in "foreign" archives—which is still only nascent and generally discouraged. Further, America global is often agentless, or sheds its agent (perhaps, a version of strategic deessentialism) as it circulates and becomes the logic of the global structure itself: a sort of second nature making critique difficult. A recognizably American form in circulation—a McDonald's in Moscow or Hong Kong (to take the classic example of globalization studies); a Chicago Bulls T-shirt worn on the streets of Fez or Dakar; a cybercafé in Tehran; the Hollywood "look" in a Moroccan film; a doughnut in Cairo or a muffin in Paris—is taken as a sign that globalization equals Americanization and vice versa. These figures of "America abroad," now detached from those generations of "Americans abroad" as commodities and the forms that are associated with them (looks, types, and so forth), move with rapidity and abstraction across multiple national boundaries. But this very abstraction—the key component in precisely what aspects of American culture circulate globally—demonstrates the potential of disentangling America as global culture from America as exceptional empire. Here we signal the danger of replacing American self-misrecognition with the other's misrecognition of America as mediated through global mass culture. Just as the image of America abroad through the global circulation of images from media might be misidentified as the America encountered at home, the fear here is not so much that *Baywatch* will be misidentified as Virgin Land but rather that commercial America, which is really no longer America, will be misidentified as what remains resolutely the liberal multicultural America.[32]

One ought not to mistake America abroad as simply American popular culture, which in some ways is no longer its own anyway. At the other end of the popular-intellectual culture spectrum, America abroad includes a wide range of American studies centers, sometimes partially or wholly funded by the U.S. state itself, but increasingly fully funded by foreign states or entities. The explicit study of America abroad, however, is not limited to the academy; nor is all of this America culled from popular culture. Scholars, intellectuals, politicians, and business entrepreneurs across the world study U.S. political systems, business models, legal systems, and the rest. (See Brian Edwards's discussion, in chapter 11, of the Osmania University College of Commerce and Business Management and its interest in American studies.) This trend also gives us a clue as to what we mean by "multilateral." It is inconceivable to study bilateral mutual representations of Japan and the United States, China and the United States, as once was proposed by proponents of the interculturalist approach (influenced by the bilateral model of cultural exchange). What we need to understand now is the way in which some pivotal sites (although it is not easy to settle on which those would be), or geopolitically critical adversarial sites (for example, Tehran), focus a detached regard back on America "global." Nor is it settled that history and literature will be the privileged sites for engagement emerging from those sites. One of the consequences of multilateralism is that, unlike the American studies vernacular tradition, the global thrust is toward horizontality rather than verticality, or spatiality rather than temporality, although with a disconnect unlike that to which the "hemispheric" model was too beholden. In other words, the multilateral perspective of those who regard the United States from without tends to see the United States horizontally in terms of its place and its interests in the world rather than vertically as an agent constituted and galvanized by a distinct set of historically sedimented institutions and ideologies. None of these perspectives maintains a singular or binary gaze but rather a regional and ultimately multilateral perspective back on America. (It could be, paradoxically, that the American studies centers that Edwards visits tend to be the least multilateral in their regard of American culture, and that they tend toward a more binaristic comparison of American culture and history with their own.)

In the vernacular strand of American studies, unity has been ontologized and historically located, as if unity was always and already a destiny of difference. In many ways, that kind of centrifugal metaphor—becoming one of many—has been overwhelmed by the global or "postnational" moment. Yet no national imaginary resists this movement as much as the American, which is less a reinvocation of American exceptionalism than a suggestion of how much Americans feel they stand to lose by acknowledging the postnational or multilateral configuration. America resists this movement by attempting to replicate around the world, whether through commerce, culture, or geopolitics, its own fantasy of a dialogic nation, of a democratic culture that simultaneously entertains and masters discordant and dissonant voices. To invite everyone to subscribe to the dialectic of one among (and out of) the many, the way America has, and to resist acknowledging alternative cultures of democracy and plurality such as the Indian and Iranian forms of democratic self-governance are potent examples. This is done, this message propagated, without recognition that the American way of being one among many, marking and effacing difference, has undergone a radical transformation. We hang on to it only by an excessively ontologized ideological projection of a form, a method divorced from ethical substance.

The United States as it engages the world does not always do so as a dialogic partner, even as a dominant dialogic partner. In this mode, American studies and "the United States" may be less distinguishable than elsewhere, which is evident from the way the Bush administration conducted itself, of course. Still, the benign face of the Obama administration as a dialogic partner could commit precisely the error of binarism, which we referred to in the previous section. As pointed out earlier, however, America abroad does not present itself as a speaking subject but as the agent of capitalist modernity, continuously distancing itself from the traditional ideals and values (and even illusions) of the foundational principles of the nation. What is noteworthy today is that the American presence in "developing" countries is not marked so much by its role as a democratic teacher or a Socratic midwife of modernity, nor even primarily as a hegemonic military power, but rather as a commercial/economic/financial force—both as successful model and, more recently and at the time of this writing, as a pitiful financial giant addicted to consumption and indebted to everyone. As a capitalist agent, America has saturated the globe with a variety of artifacts, attitudes, styles, forms, and modes of being in the world, which may or may not represent "the American soul." That is America abroad, which now casts a formidable shadow over both the vernacular and the cosmopolitan tradition, over both the American Adams at home and American innocents abroad. This shadow makes the diasporic imaginary impossible for both the American-born and those who would be Americans. In every respect, be it object domain, method, or theory itself, let alone politics, America abroad appears to be incomprehensible.

The intellectual sensibility that would have to mark American studies in what purports to be a moderately long transitional phase is a final version of what we've called the "transnational" moment or strand within the cosmopolitan tradition. Core methodological practices and the selecting and reading of objects within the vernacular tradition will continue as they always have, unperturbed perhaps. The peripheral topics within the vernacular tradition, however, particularly those such as diaspora studies, would have great difficulty making sense within the vernacular tradition except as an arrival within the vernacular center or as a negotiation between two places: "home" and the "new home." The challenge of the transnational, which is destined to emancipate the diasporic from the spell of the vernacular and in the process reposition the cosmopolitan, is something that can no longer be deferred. That emancipatory work, however, has to be carried out by those who have caught the archive fever, the debilitating pandemic of the post–American Century.

DISFIGURING THE ARCHIVE

We are not advocating that those who work under a globally conscious "American studies" focus their attention solely on the transnational figure, the scene of multinational finance capital, or the traveling figure per se. Rather, we are trying to *derive* from this figure and the experience of non-return (America as node) a sense of the fragmentary aspects of America, and from that sense a method or a call for an approach to the study of "America" in its many fragmentary guises. The experience of America abroad, be it for a native-born American or a diasporic American or for the rest, is necessarily fragmentary. At least here, the object prefigures the subject. The subject, as if by sheer act of the will, can no longer reappropriate and reconfigure America. It defies full comprehension, easy totalization; its inflationary archive, no longer bridled by the print-mediated canon, swerves and deflects. America is not exactly a floating signifier, although one is tempted to think of it in these terms (as Baudrillard does in *Amérique* and his other works that address the American fragment). America is a kind of material trace, an emanation. America's presence is felt through a series of interventions—military and diplomatic, in culture and commerce, science and technology, ideas and ideologies—which leave these traces. So, for example, in Brian Larkin's contribution to this collection, we detect the traces of a now dormant debate sparked elsewhere—in British colonial India—by an American cultural/commercial form (Hollywood cinema), ostensibly outside the legibility of the vernacular Americanist tradition. How dormant is that debate? How much more illegible and misrecognized is that debate among the putative Americanists when it is refashioned as Jihad vs. McWorld or as the Clash of Civilizations? The British colonial anxieties about representing the vulnerabilities of everyday "whiteness" before the native/colonial eyes are today allegedly replaced by the anxieties of the native, turned fundamentalist, about succumbing to the seductions of the multimediated everyday "whiteness" of television programs, from *Dallas* and *Baywatch* to *Beverly Hills 90210* and *Sex and the City*. Similar quandaries and situations are described and analyzed in Naoki Sakai's and Elizabeth Thompson's contributions to this collection; they are all perhaps mutually illegible but more powerful in their juxtaposition.

What do these case studies signal in terms of a research protocol, or a method by which to reimagine "American studies" itself? In some ways, the contributions collected here are a partial answer to this question, although we have learned from them and they did not proceed from these considerations but rather have been operating in their own spheres of interest, disciplinary and extradisciplinary frames.

The scholars in this volume provide alternative models of inquiry and interpretation for the next generation of transnational cultural studies work and are developing new paradigms about the circulation of public forms which are pushing the boundaries of fields such as media studies,

African American studies, gender studies, and American history. In multiple ways they address questions of globalization, global culture and diaspora, alternative modernities, and cosmopolitan forms and are not constrained by the paradigms in the various fields in which they were trained or within which they work. The contributors include faculty from departments of English, history, anthropology, Asian studies, comparative literature, women's studies, rhetoric, and American studies; all also have multiple affiliations with a diverse range of departments, such as African studies, Middle East studies, Latin American studies, African American studies, Asian American studies, gender studies, and media studies. This group is not one whose members would ordinarily find themselves classified together; it is, however, a group of scholars who are exceptionally dynamic in their scholarship and their mode of scholarly presentation.

The essays included in this volume, except for those by Kariann Yokota, Donald Pease, and Claudio Lomnitz, refer wholly to events of the twentieth century, the period of time during which the tripartite structure of American studies, American Century, and the exceptionalist thesis was coming to the fore. Even in the period of that emergence and consolidation one can detect the destabilizing presence of multilateralism.

To begin with, in the late eighteenth century, the British Empire had set in place complex circuits of exchange of goods, people, ideas, and ideologies, of which colonial America and the newly independent America were a part. Kariann Akemi Yokota's account of a newly independent but intellectually insecure America trying to acquire cultural capital in Scotland demonstrates a multilateral strategy on the part of individual, elite Americans—one matched by the methodological strategy of the cosmopolitan scholar herself. What is distinctive about Yokota's essay, "Bodies of Knowledge," is its concern with the movement of people—more precisely, the mobility of individuals in the world of medicine and those who aspired to enter this world during the colonial and early republic period. Characterized as bearers of scientific knowledge, these elites enter and try to negotiate a transatlantic matrix marked by what Yokota calls the geography of value. The putatively neocolonial relationship with Britain turns out not to be a relationship with Britain primarily but rather with Scotland. The operation of this geography of value cannot be grasped in any bilateral sense. The perceived superiority of Scotland's scientific knowledge versus that of the subordinate United States shows American science in need of supplementation. In fact, as Yokota shows us, supplementarity was already in play in the relation of England and Scotland, with the latter deemed inferior and peripheral to the British imperial center. In Yokota's essay, the human body and mind are the privileged bearers of national identity.

Exchange between the United States and Scotland occurs primarily in the mode of human bodies traveling back and forth across the ocean, and secondarily in the movement of texts (such as maps and books of geography) and material cultural in motion. Yet what is interesting is that individuals on both sides of the Atlantic (in Scotland and the United States) as well as institutions (the College of New Jersey, later Princeton) are engaged in taking advantage of or leveraging this particular matrix of exchange while realizing fully that it is a multinodal matrix. Yokota maps with great diligence a perfect model of exchange: two physicians from either side of the Atlantic (David Hosack and John Maclean) make correct sets of moves and benefit greatly from the evolving geography of value. At the same time, she also elicits the pathos of two individuals—a fake (Benjamin Barton) and a son (James Rush). Both are successful in taking advantage of the exchange value of Scottish prestige, but both question or subvert the legitimacy of the exchange with considerable unease. Even for the elite, the geography of value is not transparent, and neither is the imperial hierarchy. The value is not oppositional, nor does it have only two poles. Rather, it is already triangular. Multilateralism is not new.

Brent Hayes Edwards's essay "Ralph Ellison and the Grain of Internationalism" continues to privilege the human agent as the bearer of national identity. As Edwards points out, however, not only is Ellison *not* an ideal, unified national subject, but the world he encounters turns out *not* to be made of well-contained national units or cultures or even ideologies. What Ellison encounters is not, to use the distinction Claudio Lomnitz makes later in the collection, the bilateralism of internationalism, but the multilateral model of transnationalism. Not only is Edwards's essay successful in its effort to rethink a major American author in terms of his relationship to the international, but it explains how previous critics have misread those impulses within Ellison's work precisely because of a failure to think beyond binaries when conceiving of the relationship of the individual American to the international. Of course Ellison is not any old case study; he is, rather, perhaps the most crucial U.S. author of the twentieth century whose thinking about and negotiation with that problem is arguably richest. Edwards anchors his reading of Ellison's work in the wartime 1940s, when the relationship between the United States (and its constituent peoples) and the world (and its peoples) was in radical question, a momentous period too often given short shrift. The essay describes the place of Ellison among Afrocentric, nationalist, and naively patriotic positions. When Edwards describes the shift from the Ellison of "unity in diversity" to the later Ellison who argued for "identity of passions," he opens up a second phase of Ellison. In the final turn in the essay, Edwards points to Ellison's late work (particularly, the unfinished novel *June-teenth*) and suggestively calls it a "postcolonial failure." Here Edwards signals his judgment that anticolonial internationalism of the 1940s and 1950s and nascent globalization of the 1960s and 1970s outran Ellison's ability to formulate it. Edwards's suggestion that we think through the "grain" of Ellison's radical internationalism, as his essay does so power-fully, therefore forces its readers to adjust the terms and methods of analysis for American literary studies.

Kate Baldwin, in her essay "Cold War, Hot Kitchen," grapples with a wayward cosmopolitan text: the kitchen as cipher for cold war female domesticity. In Baldwin, we are confronted with the familiar binarism of the cold war, yet the texts she discusses—both social and literary—and her very method itself work to deconstruct that binarism. Building on her work in *Beyond the Color Line and the Iron Curtain*, this essay brings together a comparative focus on Soviet and American notions of diversity and captivity, focused around two less familiar texts, novels by the African American writer Alice Childress and the Soviet author Natalya Baranskaya. Baldwin's texts are not haphazardly chosen and reflect deeply on the conditions of the other: her object domain is clearly signaled and works outside the prerogatives of the vernacular tradition from the start. The central thematic play in Baldwin's essay is that of notions of diversity and captivity, at the heart of the cold war tensions and misapprehensions between Soviets and Americans. For example, the American kitchen, as represented by U.S. vice president Richard Nixon in his famous 1959 "kitchen debate" with Soviet premier Nikita Khrushchev in Moscow, offered a diversity of choices (products) that turn out to reveal, in Baldwin's reading of Childress, a multilayered captivity (to the market/domesticity/race). Similarly, Baldwin's reading of Baranskaya shows how the much vaunted diversity of professional opportunities open to Soviet women are equally implicated in varied forms of captivity (to career/domesticity/gender). Interestingly, Baldwin spins the diversity/captivity theme through a reconsideration of the DuBoisian notion of double consciousness, skillfully staging a differential Soviet and African American engagement with that protean notion to discern possible venues of transnational affiliations triggered by gender trouble and its aftermath. Du Bois's description of veiling (at the heart of his own notion of double consciousness) may then be regarded as paradigmatic case of captivity in diversity, and Baldwin's essay moves in a direction of identifying what may be the articulations of a diversity without captivity. Baldwin's most intriguing claim seems to be that arriving at a notion of diversity *without* captivity signals a multilateral consciousness.

For her that consciousness would always already be preceded by a feminist consciousness.

The chapters of the next section move beyond the orbit of Americans abroad, beyond the privileging of human agency. On the surface, Claudio Lomnitz's "Chronotopes of a Dystopic Nation" seems to revolve around six individual cases, but those profiles are dominated by the space and act of border crossing. Lomnitz prefigures and characterizes that emergent, yet fugitive, space not as a space between nations but a space made possible by the movement of capital. It is the space of emerging tension, which Lomnitz presciently places as early as the 1890s, between a bilateral internationalism that aligns a hegemonic United States with a subservient Mexico, and their respective emissaries, and a borderland transnationalism that dynamically fuses a varied cast of characters, interests, ideas, and images—all made possible and mobilized by capital. If James Creelman is producing a cultural imaginary of internationalism, John Reed and John Kenneth Turner are already tracing the pathways and byways of capital and the multilateral positionalities to which it gives rise, which cannot be easily subsumed as either Mexican or American. Here we have a multilateralism emerging that is not a product of the visible presence of the third or fourth nation but of that ubiquitous and protean third player in the relation of all nations: capital.

If the idiosyncratic individuals profiled in Lomnitz's essay are the bearers of this multilateralism, Naoki Sakai's "Transpacific Complicity and Comparatist Strategy" explains the paradoxes of jingoistic nationalism in postwar Japan, especially since the 1990s (coinciding with prolonged economic slide and stagnation), as consequences of a multilateral strategy. The key to this paradox is that at one level Japanese nationalism feeds on anti-Americanism, especially on the remnants of the Occupation as symbolized by article 9 of Japan's constitution, which forbids Japan from having its own defense forces, something that was subverted from the beginning with U.S. approval. Sakai convincingly shows that this rhetoric of "anti-Americanism" functions as distraction and displacement, both historically and in the present. This is in part because contemporary Japanese identity, especially its reconfiguration from a universalist empire to a culturally bound ethno-nation, was forged during the occupation years by a loose collaboration between Japanese conservatives and the U.S. military and foreign policy establishment, aided by the "area studies" scholars committed to imagining the world in terms of discrete national/cultural units. Japanese conservatives—simultaneously the custodians of an earlier form of Japanese imperialism and the proponents of a newly emerging nationalism—take shelter under American imperial nationalism in a manner that gestures toward a transnational strategy. This strategy, more than anything else, allows Japan not simply to negotiate its subordinate relationship to the United States but more importantly to negotiate a relationship with its former colonies—increasingly with the emerging giant next door, China. As Sakai describes it, this strategy works at so many levels—ideologically and materially, insofar as it facilitates a fabulously successful export economy while absolving Japan from the necessity of coming to terms with its imperial/colonial atrocities before and during World War II—that to imagine this conjuncture in northeast Asia as if it were a legible effect of American imperialism and its bilateral arrangements seems completely erroneous. Japan is clearly operating with a multilateral strategy, perhaps an unsavory one. Such, alas, is sometimes the cramped space of multilateralism.

As we move back to the essays by Brian Larkin and Elizabeth Thompson, the human agents are beginning to be progressively effaced. The America in motion is here represented by its cultural products: the movies. For that America, even as it traverses spaces dominated by other colonial powers, the efficacy of America abroad is no less powerful than was the efficacy of Americans abroad, be they Gen. MacArthur or James Creelman or John Reed, or (through their novels) Ralph Ellison or Alice Childress. As indicated earlier, Larkin shows how the British colonial authorities were anxious that commercially motivated representation of whiteness staged and circulated through the Hollywood film would shift and imperil imperial hierarchies and colonial relations in unexpected ways. Because colonial audiences viewed popular films even before the films opened in London, for Larkin "London could be viewed as [as] much of a periphery as Bombay," and Hollywood linked "racially and geographically disparate peoples." Larkin's account thus focuses on more than representations of Britishness per se. There are compelling moments in his essay where British anxiety about *American* representation of Britishness, or class, or "Western civilization," is enunciated in ways that challenge or put in a different light the question of anxiety over whiteness. And "whiteness" may in turn merely be the word for something different, less locatable at the time—namely, that which was emerging from America onto the world scene. That is, according to the anxious colonial British, there was a sense that American understanding of (Western) "civilization" was a spin or swerve of "civilization" or culture (in Arnoldian terms) moving in a lamentable direction. We see in Larkin's essay how American cultural production could destabilize other binary relations of imperial internationalism. So if American movies can destabilize bilateralism, might it not be the case that Bollywood was always already destabilizing America's relationship with Pakistan, Nigeria, and even Iran or Afghanistan?[33]

In a similar way, Thompson's rendering of the audience's reception of *Gone with the Wind* in Damascus in the early 1940s reiterates in a different context what is now a commonplace of cultural studies—that there are dominant readings, as well as resistant readings and subversive readings, of canonical as well as popular texts. The point here is that even if *Gone with the Wind* was not read in Damascus as it was read in Dallas or Chicago, the film was no less commercially successful or ideologically compelling. As Thompson mobilizes Miriam Hansen's notion of Hollywood as "global vernacular," it is conceivable that precisely this ability to be abstracted and yield different sets of meanings is what made the film successful in Damascus in the first place. It is conceivable that America, with all its contradictions of race, geography, and gender, was not seen necessarily in Damascus as a neat overcoming of contradictions but rather as a dispersal of tensions, a metanomic text rather than a metaphoric text, not about a particular nation, but about a love story—and an unfulfilled one at that. Posing her work here as a "first step toward a history of Middle Eastern movie spectatorship," Thompson—in an essay rich in archival research—proceeds to overturn common wisdom about Arab responses to American culture, an as yet unwritten cultural history. (This history is suggested again in the book's final chapter, which ends in Cairo in the wake of Obama's victory, when hip-hop music has become a key cultural form.) As she does so, Thompson draws out the tensions felt in the transition from the colonial era to the American Century, between the notions of "universal humanism and particularist religious and national identities." Her work provides a forgotten debate that prefigures much that follows half a century later.

The final section is made up of three chapters in which "America abroad" completely overpowers Americans abroad in any sense. Starting with Wai Chee Dimock's critique of nation as a container, in her essay "War in Several Tongues," the opposition to privileging a single language or genre is underlined. We are already moving toward an archive with multiple trajectories. As Wai Chee Dimock reads the terrain of wars, arguably the most important locus for staging, as well as deconstructing, American exceptionalism and the American Imperium, she notices that archives of wars are composed from more angles and standpoints than those of losers and winners, as the traditional account has it. Dimock reads a wide range of texts, from Niven and Pournelle's *Inferno*, which reverses the roles of Mussolini and Churchill, to Vonnegut's *Slaughterhouse-Five*, which represents the bombing of Dresden by an American ally from the point of view of an American POW. In between are detours through the *Iliad* and other texts: the archive of war cannot be stabilized—that stabilization is so crucial to the legitimation of empire, even an exceptional empire. How can we continue to maintain the distinction between the hegemon and the subaltern in a bilateral mode? It is not that there are no hegemons, not that there are no imperial impulses and formations, but they are working in a field made up of differential sets of players. On this terrain, there are bullies, there are hooligans, there are criminals, there are saints, citizens and soldiers, guerillas and revolutionaries—every conceivable agent of every conceivable utopia and dystopia, from liberal to republican and from anarchist to socialist. So John Reed, seen again in this light, doesn't belong to America; nor does he belong to Mexico, or the Soviet Union. He is not the agent of bilateral international relations but a figure of the transnational, elusive and mobile, a self-deconstructing figure.

The final two essays disclose two potential strategies for coping with transnationalism and multilaterality. Things get complicated as we get into less canonical texts, as we do with Ali Behdad and Juliet Williams in their essay "Neo-Orientalism," as they begin to treat ephemera such as Azar Nafisi's *Reading Lolita in Tehran*—a book temporarily canonized by the U.S. publishing establishment and American readers. Composed for the West, ostensibly by a native intellectual to justify to the West why it was correct to promote a singular notion of modernity, *Reading Lolita in Tehran* invariably poses gender as a key ingredient; but race and class lose their efficacy in the age of mobile capital. Nafisi's influential text—as well as those by others who would mirror her strategy—is an act of reproducing, reconstituting, and stabilizing the rest for the West, a practice deconstructed by Behdad and Williams; it is an attempt to recuperate a singular national perspective against the grain of transnationalism. Nafisi, predictably, reads modern classics—the canon, however subversive a canon—and shifts the location from the byways of America traveled by Humbert Humbert to Tehran, suggesting that the ideological burden that Nabokov's *Lolita* bears with respect to gender can be as efficacious in Tehran in the late twentieth century as it was in America during the cold war. (That *Lolita* was written by a Russian émigré was key to its celebration, once its "obscenity" had been negotiated within the constricting gender field in 1950s America.) Nabokov's is an internally dense and polysemous text that carries with it the ideology of Western modernity as mobility. Here, once again, we see that for those overdetermined Americans like Nafisi and Zakaria, whether native-born or naturalized, Whitman's *Democratic Vistas* is always and forever portable. In the reception of Nafisi's text (we are surely passing through inflationary times in literary appreciation), we are tempted to think that Nabokov's Gender Vista is also portable; we return to "the classics," as the book blurbs put it, and away from a more destabilizing Iranian perspective on the United States.

The opposite strategy emerges in Brian Edwards's concluding essay, "American Studies in Motion," namely, how "the rest," or the global South, is assembling its archives about the United States, primarily from the jetsam and flotsam of popular culture, business reports and news, and bureaucratically generated foreign policy papers and memorandums—and how it tries to make sense of that disorganized and proliferating archive almost exclusively from a strategic and presentist point of view. It is not as if there is no access to Whitman, or *Moby-Dick*, but rather that the allegory of *Moby-Dick*—so central to American self-fashioning during the cold war— has restricted appeal and resonance. The cultural forms and objects so lovingly nurtured within the vernacular tradition do not travel well abroad. What matters instead, as Edwards discovers during his visits to Tehran, Hyderabad, and Cairo, are the inexhaustible offerings from commercially driven American popular culture, the distorted mirror of American soul and style, character and beauty, humor and bravado. Here is where the American promise is branded and betrayed repeatedly, without any anxiety about the representations of "America," so unlike Larkin's account of the British colonial anxiety over representations of "whiteness." In the new semiotics of America global, the signifiers let loose by popular culture are not tethered to an imaginary master signifier called America. In the absence of such a master signifier or master narrative, central to the constitution of both the vernacular and the cosmopolitan traditions discussed earlier, the American archive begins to splinter and disseminate. What is "America" is constituted from a jumble of such fragments. Now everyone can and does know America, everyone is an Americanist. For each Nafisi telling her tale of Iran, there are a thousand and one counterparts abroad reciting their tales of America.

These are all transitional pieces. *Globalizing American Studies* is an interim report, not a promissory note. It is not designed to recuperate or redirect the whole of American studies. The installed capacity of American studies in the U.S. academy is formidable. The contingent history of its formation, along with its political entanglements and cultural longings, cannot be reversed by a singular act of critical will. There are, however, intimations of a shift in the global imaginaries prompted by the closing of the American Century—new vistas are opening, the old pathways are falling into desuetude, and there is a bend, a fissure in the American self-image. The essays collected in this volume are variously trying to locate American studies within that emergent global imaginary—characterized in this introduction as transnational and multilateral—whether or not that is the formation they are consciously addressing. While pursuing their inquiry, in the most potent of moments, the authors of these essays disclose new possibilities for the constitution of objects, methods, theorizing, and political engagement, without reverting to the received traditions and idioms of American studies. It is our modest hope that *Globalizing American Studies* does not leave the world of American studies exactly as it finds it. A crack in the mirror, the opening of a critical aperture, is all we seek.

Notes

Globalizing American Studies is the product of a project founded at Northwestern University in 2004 which has since grown to encompass three large symposia, a lecture series, and an international network of scholars. Much interesting work has emerged from this project by young scholars who have since risen to increased prominence and by more senior scholars working in a variety of fields and national locations. From the start, we have had an eye to pulling out some of the best work in the interest of making a collective and powerful statement that would move discussions about the transnational turn in American studies beyond the current impasse and intimate, if not fully enunciate, new trajectories by exemplary critical performances. Our collaboration as coeditors who approach the question from different angles—one of us has been engaged in critiquing the limitations of American studies from within the field; the other is outside of American studies, with wide experience in paradigms of transnational cultural studies—has led us to embrace the work of a collection of scholars who might not normally see themselves grouped together.

   1. When we use the term "American studies" in this introduction, we are referring for the most part to the interdisciplinary formation that calls itself by this name in the United States, including academic departments and programs, journals, conferences, and associations (including the American Studies Association and its regional associations). We are to a lesser extent referring to nonacademic invocations of the field of American studies in the past decade. The U.S. State Department has in the past decade encouraged a largely national supremacist version of "American studies" through the sponsorship of new Fulbright initiatives in "U.S. studies" and publication of an online journal called *eJournal USA* (formerly called *Society and Values*; http://www.america.gov/publications/ejournalusa.html), complete with Arabic and Farsi translations. Unless we specify otherwise, we are not in this introduction discussing international American studies programs outside of the United States. For a discussion of different instantiations of such international American studies programs and initiatives, see chapter 11 in this volume.

   Although it has intellectual roots that precede the 1940s, American studies as an institutional formation did not come about until the World War II years. In 1940, Henry Nash Smith (1906–1986), a commonly named founder of the field, was awarded the first Ph.D. in the history of American civilization by Harvard University for a dissertation titled "American Emotional and Imaginative Attitudes toward the Great Plains and the Rocky Mountains, 1803–50." (In 1933, A. Whitney Griswold—who would go on to be president of Yale—wrote a Ph.D. dissertation titled "The American Cult of Success," at Yale's then new Department of History, the Arts, and Letters; Griswold's is sometimes claimed to be the first "American studies-like" Ph.D. ever granted, and a precursor. See Gene Wise, "'Paradigm Dramas' in American

Studies: A Cultural and Institutional History of the Movement," *American Quarterly* 31, no. 3 [1979]: 305.) In the wake of World War II, fueled by the impulse to understand the new superpower status of the United States, and in the wake of the social foment of the 1930s, many programs developed around the United States. The programs at the University of Minnesota and Yale University were particularly important and well funded, and are often named as pioneering departments. By 1947, according to Gene Wise, there were more than sixty institutions offering undergraduate majors in American studies, with fifteen of them offering an M.A. or Ph.D. Simultaneously, the U.S. academy was witnessing the establishment of area studies programs, a state-sponsored effort to establish knowledge of other parts of the globe necessary for a newly emergent superpower. Despite the contemporaneity of these initiatives, American studies has not generally been considered an area studies program within the United States. (See Paul Bové, "Can American Studies Be Area Studies?" in *Learning Places: The Afterlives of Area Studies*, ed. Masao Miyoshi and Harry Harootunian [Durham, NC: Duke University Press, 2002], for a speculative consideration of this question.)

Today, it is difficult to find a major accredited college or university that does not offer at least a B.A. in American studies, with many offering M.A.'s and Ph.D.'s in the field. These programs do not always take the name "American studies" proper, which sometimes leads to confusion. Harvard's and Brown's programs carry the name "American civilization," which seems an antiquated term to many in the field today. At the other pole, New York University's new flagship Program in American Studies emerges from the Department of Social and Cultural Analysis. Graduates of these programs may move in a variety of professional directions. An undergraduate degree in American studies is generally seen as a generalist liberal arts or humanities degree, and not necessarily training for any particular profession. Undergraduates drawn to a major in American studies are often interested in politics (from a conservative or liberal position), communications, or social justice. Conversely, those who pursue graduate degrees in American studies generally pursue academic careers and sometimes curatorial work at museums.

Within the field, the primary scholarly organization is the American Studies Association (http://www.theasa.net/), with approximately 5,000 individual members, and 2,200 library and institutional members, as well as active regional subchapters. Founded in 1950, the ASA is large and inclusive in its scope and activities, although its leaders tend to be at or near the cutting edge in pursuing questions about internationalizing the field and its membership. The ASA holds a large annual meeting (generally a weekend in October or November) at varying locations, frequently returning to Washington, DC. Several days of simultaneous sessions, as well as a large book exhibit, ensure that there is no common point of view. Meetings follow published themes, although this is not often apparent from the panels themselves. *American Quarterly,* the official journal of the ASA, is a peer-reviewed quarterly distributed to all members of the organization and a respected venue for new scholarship and book reviews.

2. "For we must consider that we shall be as a city upon a hill. The eyes of all people are upon us" (Winthrop, "A Model of Christian Charity," 1630).

3. Henry Luce, *The American Century* (New York: Farrar and Rinehart, 1941). The essay was originally published in the February 1941 issue of *Life.*

4. *The National Security Strategy of the United States of America* (Washington, DC, September 2002), http://georgewbush-whitehouse.archives.gov/nsc/nss/2002.

5. In 2000, at a meeting in Bellagio, Italy, the International American Studies Association (IASA) was founded by Djelal Kadir (professor of comparative literature at Pennsylvania State University) and twenty-two other Americanists from the United States, Europe, and Asia. IASA has since held four world congresses (at Leiden, Netherlands, 2003; Ottawa, Canada, 2005; Lisbon, Portugal, 2007; and Beijing, China, 2009) and scheduled another (Rio

de Janeiro, Brazil, 2011). The association also publishes a peer-reviewed online journal, *RIAS* (http://iasaweb.org/rias/). The core of the association's mission is international and comparative perspectives on American culture and society; it has established partnerships with many international American studies associations around the globe and reached out to non-U.S.-based scholars in the field. Its leadership, however, has remained American or British, although its executive committee members are fairly well distributed in terms of national origin and professional location.

6. In the case of the civil rights movement, the alternative of course is to see the interrelationship of cold war geopolitics and domestic race relations, and to link the U.S. civil rights movement with the decolonization of Europe's empires. A rich body of work has recently emerged which points us in this direction, including Vijay Prashad, *Everybody Was Kung Fu Fighting: Afro-Asian Connections and the Myth of Cultural Purity* (Boston: Beacon Press, 2001); Kate A. Baldwin, *Beyond the Color Line and the Iron Curtain: Reading Encounters between Black and Red, 1922–1963* (Durham, NC: Duke University Press, 2002); Thomas Borstelmann, *The Cold War and the Color Line: American Race Relations in the Global Arena* (Cambridge: Harvard University Press, 2003); Brent Hayes Edwards, *The Practice of Diaspora: Literature, Translation, and the Rise of Black Internationalism* (Cambridge: Harvard University Press, 2003); Nikhil Singh, *Black Is a Country: Race and the Unfinished Struggle for Democracy* (Cambridge: Harvard University Press, 2004); Bill V. Mullen, *Afro Orientalism* (Minneapolis: University of Minnesota Press, 2004); and Vijay Prashad, *The Darker Nations: A People's History of the Third World* (New York: New Press, 2007).

7. Michael Hardt and Antonio Negri, *Empire* (Cambridge: Harvard University Press, 2000).

8. Amy Kaplan, "Left Alone with America," in *Cultures of United States Imperialism*, ed. Amy Kaplan and Donald E. Pease (Durham, NC: Duke University Press, 1993), 3–21. Wise, "'Paradigm Dramas' in American Studies," 293–337. Alan Trachtenberg, "Myth, History, and Literature in *Virgin Land*," *Prospects* 3 (October 1978): 125–33.

9. Kaplan, "Left Alone with America," 3–21.

10. Eve Kosofsky Sedgwick, *The Epistemology of the Closet* (Berkeley: University of California Press, 1990).

11. Henry Nash Smith, "Can 'American Studies' Develop a Method?" *American Quarterly* 9, no. 2, pt. 2 (Summer 1957): 197–208. Gene Wise, "Political 'Reality' in Recent American Scholarship: Progressives versus Symbolists," *American Quarterly* 19, no. 2, pt. 2 (Summer 1967): 303–28. Robert Sklar, "American Studies and the Realities of America," *American Quarterly* 22, no. 2, pt. 2 (Summer 1970): 597–605. Linda K. Kerber, "Diversity and the Transformation of American Studies," *American Quarterly* 41, no. 3 (September 1989): 415–31. Steven Watts, "The Idiocy of American Studies: Poststructuralism, Language, and Politics in the Age of Self-Fulfillment," *American Quarterly* 43, no. 4 (December 1991): 625–60. (Watts's paper was delivered as a presidential address to the Mid-America American Studies Association, not the annual meeting of the ASA.) Responses to Watts by Barry Shank and Nancy Isenberg were published in *American Quarterly* 44, no. 3 (September 1992). John Higham, "Multiculturalism and Universalism: A History and Critique," special issue on Multiculturalism, *American Quarterly* 45, no. 2, (June 1993): 195–219. Higham was a former ASA president; this article, however, is not a presidential address but the cornerstone of the issue's symposium on multiculturalism. Patricia Nelson Limerick, "Insiders and Outsiders: The Borders of the USA and the Limits of the ASA: Presidential Address to the American Studies Association, 31 October 1996," *American Quarterly* 49, no. 3 (1997): 449–469; Mary Helen Washington, "Disturbing the Peace: What Happens to American Studies if You Put African American Studies at the Center? Presidential Address to the American Studies Association, October 29, 1997," *American Quarterly* 50, no. 1 (1998): 1–23. Stephen H. Sumida, "Where in the World Is

American Studies? Presidential Address to the American Studies Association," *American Quarterly* 55, no. 3 (September 2003): 333–52. Shelley Fisher Fishkin, "Crossroads of Cultures: The Transnational Turn in American Studies: Presidential Address to the American Studies Association, November 12, 2004," *American Quarterly* 57, no. 1 (March 2005): 17–57. Emory Elliott, "Diversity in the United States and Abroad: What Does It Mean When American Studies Is Transnational?" *American Quarterly* 59, no. 1 (March 2007): 1–22.

12. Caroline F. Levander and Robert S. Levine, "Introduction: Essays beyond the Nation," in *Hemispheric American Studies*, ed. C. Levander and R. Levine (New Brunswick, NJ: Rutgers University Press, 2008), 1–2.

13. Here we are following Hayden White's reflections in *Metahistory: The Historical Imagination in Nineteenth-Century Europe* (Baltimore: Johns Hopkins University Press, 1973). According to White, historiographic imagination (by implication also literary, philosophical, and any other writerly imagination) is tropologically structured in its prefiguration of the object domain. In singling out the four master tropes—metaphor, metonymy, synecdoche, and irony—White draws on the work of four multidisciplinary scholars: Stephen C. Pepper, Kenneth Burke, Northrop Frye, and Karl Mannheim. The resulting synthesis is highly suggestive and useful in mapping disciplinary imaginations, trajectories, and crises in terms of the five key elements we have identified earlier—objects, methods, theoretical commitments, interpretive traditions, and political engagements.

14. Although it didn't take place explicitly within the scope of American studies but crossed over into it, the controversy surrounding Joseph Massad's argument against the "gay international," in his *Public Culture* article and book *Desiring Arabs* (Chicago: University of Chicago Press, 2007), offers a powerful example of this tendency to reinscribe an exceptionalist understanding of American forms of sociality—here of sexuality or "queerness"—that remain bound within a delimited frame. Joseph Massad, "Re-Orienting Desire: The Gay International and the Arab World," *Public Culture* 14, no. 2 (Spring 2002): 361–85. For the response, see Arno Schmitt, "Gay Rights versus Human Rights: A Response to Joseph Massad," *Public Culture* 15, no. 3 (Fall 2003): 587–91.

15. This seems to us a Saidian point.

16. See Donald Pease's forceful critique of Hartz's consensus account in chapter 1 of this collection.

17. Jean-François Revel, *Without Marx or Jesus: The New American Revolution Has Begun* (Garden City, NY: Doubleday, 1971), a translation of *Ni Marx, ni Jésus* (Paris: Robert Laffont, 1971); Jean Baudrillard, *Amérique* (Paris: Grasset, 1986); Bernard-Henri Lévy, *American Vertigo: Traveling America in the Footsteps of Tocqueville* (New York: Random House, 2006), a translation of *American Vertigo* (Paris: Grasset et Fasquelle, 2006).

18. For this reason, Brian Edwards has suggested the inclusion on the American literature syllabus of Saudi writer Abderrahman Munif's Arabic-language novel *City of Salt*, with its critique of U.S. oil interests at the dawn of U.S. involvement in the Persian Gulf. See Brian T. Edwards, "Preposterous Encounters: Interrupting American Studies with the (Post) colonial, or *Casablanca* in the American Century," *Comparative Studies of South Asia, Africa and the Middle East* 23, nos. 1–2 (2003): 70–86.

19. Maxine Hong Kingston, *Tripmaster Monkey: His Fake Book* (New York: Knopf, 1989).

20. Brian T. Edwards, *Morocco Bound: Disorienting America's Maghreb, from Casablanca to the Marrakech Express* (Durham, NC: Duke University Press, 2005).

21. Vicente Rafael has, in fact, argued that area studies were initially modeled after "civilizational studies" and later came under the generalizing/universalizing model of the social sciences preoccupied with the study of modernity. Vicente L. Rafael, "The Cultures of Area Studies in the United States," *Social Text* 41 (1994): 91–112.

22. See Alan Trachtenberg, "Conceivable Aliens," chapter 2 of *Shades of Hiawatha: Stag-*

ing Indians, Making Americans, 1880–1930 (New York: Hill and Wang, 2005), for a reading of this scene.

23. R. W. B. Lewis, *The American Adam: Innocence, Tragedy and Tradition in the Nineteenth Century* (Chicago: University of Chicago Press, 1955).

24. See, for example, Alan Nadel, *Containment Culture: American Narratives, Postmodernism, and the Atomic Age,* New Americanists series (Durham, NC: Duke University Press, 1995).

25. Alan Filreis, "Conflict Seems Vaguely Un-American: Teaching the Conflicts and the Legacy of Cold War," *Review* 17 (1995): 155–69.

26. Videotaped remarks by President Barack Obama in celebration of Nowruz, March 20, 2009, http://www.whitehouse.gov/nowruz/.

27. For Emerson, Saadi inspired a sense of poetic independence: "What a contrast between the cynical tone of Byron and the benevolent wisdom of Saadi!" Ralph W. Emerson, introduction to a translation of Saadi's *The Gulistan, or Rose Garden* (1865), as quoted in F. O. Matthiessen, *American Renaissance: Art and Expression in the Age of Emerson and Whitman* (New York: Oxford University Press, 1941). Matthiessen's is of course another of the foundational texts in American studies.

28. Fareed Zakaria, *The Post-American World* (New York: Norton, 2008).

29. See http://papercuts.blogs.nytimes.com/2008/05/21/what-obama-is-reading.

30. See Charles Taylor, "The Politics of Recognition," in *Multiculturalism: Examining the Politics of Recognition,* ed. Amy Gutmann (Princeton: Princeton University Press, 1994).

31. On call-in programs on al-Jazeera, see Marc Lynch, *Voices of the New Arab Public: Iraq, al-Jazeera, and Middle East Politics Today* (New York: Columbia University Press, 2005). On Hollywood as global "vernacular," see Miriam Hansen, "The Mass Production of the Senses: Classical Cinema as Vernacular Modernism," *Modernism/Modernity* 6, no. 2 (1999): 59–77. For a reading of the circulation of a Hollywood "look" or "style" into recent Moroccan cinema otherwise unconcerned with the United States, see Brian T. Edwards, "*Marock* in Morocco: Reading Moroccan Films in the Age of Circulation," *Journal of North African Studies* 12, no. 3 (2007): 287–307.

32. The reference to *Baywatch,* of course, is to the frequently republished comments, by its star David Hasselhoff, that the broadcasting and popularity of *Baywatch* in Iran was helping its women's movement. Bill Carter, "Stand Aside, CNN. America's No. 1 TV Export Is—No Scoffing, Please—'Baywatch,'" *New York Times,* July 3, 1995. See H. Temourian, "Iran Bans Baywatch with Purge on 'Satan's Dishes,'" *Sunday Times,* April 23, 1995. See also Thomas Friedman, "Of Body and Soul," *New York Times,* June 9, 1997; reprinted in T. Friedman, *The Lexus and the Olive Tree: Understanding Globalization* (New York: Farrar, Straus and Giroux, 2000), 67–68.

33. The press observed that after the defeat of the Taliban in Afghanistan, one of the first products to return to the streets, along with cosmetics, were trading cards of Bollywood movie stars.

PART I

ONE

American Studies after American Exceptionalism?

Toward a Comparative Analysis of Imperial State Exceptionalisms

Donald E. Pease

AMERICAN EXCEPTIONALISM(S) IN AN EXTENDED FIELD: THE INAUGURATION OF INTERNATIONAL AMERICAN STUDIES

In "Defending America against Its Devotees," the presidential address that he delivered at the Inaugural Congress of the International American Studies Association at Leiden, Netherlands, on May 22, 2004, Djelal Kadir represented the members of the newly formed association as united in their repudiation of the Bush administration's global strategy for planetary dominance "that ratified a version of American exceptionalism."[1] The specific targets of Kadir's denunciation were the members of the Bush administration responsible for the construction of two epochal documents, *The National Security Strategy of the United States* and the declaration of a "Global War on Terror," which had turned U.S. global dominance into American exceptionalism's new raison d'être.[2] According to Kadir, this new rationale had also effected a new paradigm in American studies, whose pedagogy was encapsulated in Bush's twinned doctrines of preemptive strikes and full-spectrum global dominance. He explained that the combined operations of these doctrines had resulted in the installation of the United States as a State of Exception in the international order, and that it showed little interest in seeing itself through the eyes of the world it sought to dominate. After he characterized Bush's new national defense strategy as the "21st century's Monroe Doctrine on a global scale" (144), Kadir concluded that its enactment "may well prove a watershed for American culture and paradigm-altering for American Studies" (135).

Whereas the Bush administration had installed seemingly insuperable obstacles in between the state's policies and the people's understanding of them, Kadir described the mission of the IASA as a collective effort to break down these epistemological barriers by producing formations of knowledge about America that would undermine this new paradigm. To accomplish this mission, Kadir enjoined the members of the International

American Studies Association to scrutinize the significance of this paradigm shift by undertaking a "revisionary self-understanding" of American studies programs across the globe that would entail examining "what these changes mean and articulating their implications for our curricular and investigatory endeavors" (145).

Kadir specifically recommended that international americanist scholars construe these new policies as symptomatic case studies that would comprise the investigative and curricular subject matter of the new field of study. Then he exhorted international americanist scholars to reread the historical archive within a larger context than that which had been circumscribed by the disciplinary parameters of the field instituted by U.S. americanists who had been "trained under the auspices of the Marshall Plan and the Cold War" (143). "We, as Americanists, need to worry about those asymmetrical frames that define our own subject agency, institutional instrumentality, discursive strategies, all of which are part and parcel of the formative complex and transformative thrust that goes by the field designation of American Studies" (141).

When he described the Bush administration's policies as "paradigm-altering," Kadir tacitly characterized Bush's governmental apparatus as the meta-agent of a new American studies, and he conceptualized the doctrines of preemption and global dominance as the core tenets of this new state pedagogy. Kadir described Bush's practices of state governance as inaugurating a new paradigm of U.S. American studies so as to call attention to the "disciplinary exceptionalism" of U.S. American studies. In Kadir's estimation, American exceptionalism did not merely refer to a specific form of knowledge; as the organizing logic of the field's paradigm, American exceptionalism regulated the forms of the knowledge that could be produced about the United States. As the disciplinary medium through which American exceptionalism was regulatively transmitted across the globe, U.S. American studies was construed by Kadir as itself an extension of the state's govermentality: "American Studies is, indeed, very much a *discipline* in the strongest Foucauldian sense of governmentality. It is so to the point of having disciplined the practitioners of American Studies to deny that their practices form and are formed by a discipline" (147).

After World War II, its status as a form of cultural diplomacy positioned U.S. American studies scholarship within an extraterritorial space that exempted it from subordination to "foreign" knowledge productions about the United States and that rendered U.S. American studies scholars immune to the scholarly influence of "non-American" students of American studies. At the conjunctural moment in which nation-states and newly decolonized regions were determining their individual and collective relationship with the cold war's drastic reorganization of global political and economic processes, U.S. American studies scholars encouraged their international clientele to resort to an American reference in conducting their intranational debates over the role of the state and the rule of law, immigration policies and migrant populations, the underclass and the welfare state, as well as questions of minority rights.

When it worked in tandem with the Marshall Plan, U.S. American studies was a scholarly field as well as an international movement that functioned as a cultural diplomacy extension of U.S. international policy. U.S. American studies referred at once to a restricted area of scholarly inquiry as well to the agency responsible for the propagation of a generalizable symbolic economy. As an area studies program, American studies supplied an interdisciplinary methodology for studying the literature, history, politics, and territorial geography of the United States. As an agency that legitimated processes of Americanization worldwide, American studies also instructed international scholars in how to deploy the field of American studies as an encompassing medium of acculturation (*translatio studii imperii americani*).[3]

The discourse of American exceptionalism monitored how American culture was studied, and it regulated these processes of translatability. Stipulating that the nation's uniqueness required that the U.S. state remain apart from the national cultures whose processes it regulated, American exceptionalism installed an asymmetrical relationship between international scholars and U.S. americanists. By setting vertical operations into motion that presupposed a hierarchical relationship between the U.S. culture to be translated and the national cultures translating it, the discourse of American exceptionalism deployed this asymmetrical relationship between international scholars and U.S. americanists to regulate these interactions. When engaged in a dialogue about American culture with an international scholar, a U.S. americanist could act at once as a dialogue partner and as the agent who controlled the discourse through which the dialogue was initiated, its terms defined, its concepts interpreted, and its disputes resolved.

American studies scholars within the international community, however, never identified themselves as docile recipients of U.S. americanists' scholarship. International scholars in American studies devised methodological "tool kits" that enabled them to design versions of American exceptionalism that isolated aspects of American history and political society suited to the particular ideological needs of the nation-states in which they practiced. In selectively adopting the discourse of American exceptionalism to their own research protocols and ideological purposes, international americanists wielded American studies as a double-edged sword. When they held up what they found exemplary about U.S. political culture, international americanists fostered changes within their own national cultures. But when they isolated what they found either pernicious or unassimilable about the American way of life, these scholars did so to ward off U.S. cultural imperialism.[4] After World War II, American studies scholars in Europe in particular devised paradoxical scholarly representations of American exceptionalism as a democratizing countermodel to European political norms that inspired resistance to political repressions within their home countries; they also negatively described American exceptionalism as the ideology of a global hegemon whose imperial ambitions they subjected to critique.[5] Each national American studies association thereby particularized its knowledge about America through the practicing of an alternative American modernity.

Despite the fact that international americanists produced innovative scholarship about the United States, the terms of comparative analysis formulated within the territorial United States reduced americanist scholarly works produced outside of U.S. borders into pale reflections of U.S. americanists' scholarly prerogatives.[6] Insofar as American exceptionalism installed an americanist frame of reference designed to promote the transformation of the international scholar's native culture, it recast the international scholar into a secondary participant in the American way of life. Feeling diminished by terms of comparison whose grounds were outside of their control, internationalist americanist scholars felt insulted by a field of scholarship that transposed the structural similarities between U.S. and international American studies into the occasions to reassert U.S. geopolitical dominance.

In inaugurating the International American Studies Association, Kadir aspired to redress this imbalance in the intercultural dialogues between U.S. and international americanists. Throughout his address, Kadir urged the members of the International American Studies Association to undertake critical reassessments of their previous relationship to U.S.-based American studies so as to construct a range of scholarly alternatives.

As these observations indicate, Kadir directed his critique primarily against the globalization of U.S. American studies. After describing the Bush administration's global dominance as the new paradigm for U.S. American studies, Kadir criticized U.S. American studies' engulfing of every national American studies association within its encompassing vantage point. Kadir insisted that the status of American studies as an international field should oblige americanist scholars outside the United States to resist the reabsorption of their scholarship into the globalizing agendas of U.S. American studies, and he urged the international scholars in the IASA to view America from national points of view that remained ineluctably "nonamerican": "The internationalization of the term 'America' as referent for the whole hemisphere helps us to understand what non-Americanized Americanists, or those scholars and historians worldwide who have studied and written on America as a global phenomenon have always understood: that the ideologically circumscribed reduction of America, and of American Studies, to the United States screens out history's documentary archive that could help understand what is occurring presently on a global . . . scale" (143).

The changes that Kadir called for were more specifically designed to effect a shift in the "disciplinary exceptionalism" of American studies that would undermine the recent "cultural turn" in U.S. American studies in particular. Kadir phrased this reorientation in terms of a series of irreversible transitions that would move America *from* the originator and propagator of its own epistemic paradigms *to* the recipient of knowledge production constructed about America globally, that would displace America *from* a national object of devotion *to* an international object of secular criticism, and that would uproot U.S. americanists from their privileged positions as the proprietary agents of American studies and reposition them as the targets of a "passive revolution" (136–37). The constellation of scholarly interests that this revolution disassembled would instigate a wholesale realignment of the disciplines within the field of American studies, enabling political science and international relations, economics, demographic analyses, and informational technologies to supplant U.S. literary studies and U.S. cultural studies as the primary architects of americanist scholarly and pedagogical agendas.

Notwithstanding the revolutionary rhetoric at work in Kadir's address, however, the IASA did not in fact institute a radical break from the tenets of American exceptionalism. Rather than condemning it in all of its iterations, Kadir displayed contradictory attitudes toward different versions of American exceptionalism. The vantage point from which Kadir criticized Bush's State of Exception depended on assumptions concerning American exceptionalism that Bush's new paradigm had supplanted but that the majority of the membership of the IASA had endorsed. The good exceptionalism that Kadir recuperated supplied him with a set of ideological themes ("the American Dream," "Immigrant Nation," "the American Way") that authorized his critique of Bush's bad version of American exceptionalism as contradictory to those collective representations. Each of the irreversible turning points that Kadir installed in his convocation address presupposed the use of these exceptionalist attributes for their decisive force.

Indeed the keynotes of Kadir's address recalled the governing tropes of American exceptionalism so as to mobilize the IASA's opposition to Bush's "wayward" foreign policy. "Americanists, especially those of us intellectually molded by 'the American Dream' and formed in 'the American Way,' are urgently confronted by what the majority of the world considers a wayward America that would have its way, no matter" (137–38).

The IASA emerged, at the moment of a decisive paradigm shift that had resulted from the massive destabilization of cold war American exceptionalism, as the field-constituting discourse. Arguably, the national and regional associations within the International American Studies Association were formed out of the different significations that their memberships had assigned to American exceptionalism. Kadir's talk set Bush's State of Exception in a relation of opposition to the disparate American exceptionalism(s) espoused by the members of the International American Studies Association. Although he condemned Bush for inaugurating a wayward version of American exceptionalism, Kadir had in fact founded IASA through the retrieval of core themes, events, texts, and personalities that renewed what he considered to be the geopolitically correct exceptionalist convictions that the United States had ostensibly betrayed after September 11, 2001. "The United States of America, then, to the extent that one can identify a nation with its government at the moment, has turned away through its governmental policy from all that we have been taught to value as the best of that America" (147).

Since the Bush administration had undertaken the malicious undermining of them, the President of the IASA felt obliged to reinstate the core tenets of good old-fashioned American exceptionalism as the basis for the Americanness of the newly formed organization. Insofar as all of the international americanists whom Kadir addressed had depended on homegrown versions of American exceptionalism to articulate their field identities, Kadir, in his keynote address, went about the business of rededicating those identities to the exceptionalist precepts undergirding the newly internationalized field. When Kadir thereafter hegemonized the IASA's overall project, he did so from the perspective of an "authentic America" that refused Bush's redefinition of America as a State of Exception: "Our most urgent task . . . is to be sure to differentiate between America and the governing regime of the United States of America. Regimes are ephemeral events, with global repercussions, certainly" (138).

Without American exceptionalism as the general form of describability underpinning his manifesto, Kadir might not have felt authorized to represent the absent fullness ("Authentic America") that he believed U.S. American studies was now lacking. Kadir had in effect guaranteed the

Americanness of the International American Studies Association by rein-stituting the American exceptionalism that the Bush administration had abandoned. In her response to Kadir's address, "The Tenacious Grasp of American Exceptionalism," Amy Kaplan, who was then president of the U.S. American Studies Association, endorsed Kadir's call for international perspectives. Her endorsements, however, assumed the form of a revision of Kadir's critique of Bush's State of Exception:

> The Bush administration is committed to shoring up American national boundaries through juridical, covert, and discursive means, at the same time that it violates international law and turns the rest of the world into a space of porous and violable borders for its own exercise of power. This division between the United States and the world can be seen in the embrace of two new terms in U.S. public discourse, which have become predominant since September 11, 2001: the empire and the homeland. In a dramatic turn away from the disavowal of its own imperial history, the embrace of empire across the political spectrum celebrates and normalizes U.S. global dominance as an inevitable process. The notion of the homeland, with its nativist connotations, works to protect a sense of domestic insularity, always under attack yet cor-doned off from the threatening outside world.[7]

Following her qualified endorsement of his mission statement, Kap-lan proceeded to fault Kadir for the unintended consequences of his re-claiming exceptionalist assumptions: "Condemning the U.S. for failing to measure up to its own highest standards may have some strategic value in public debates, but this approach is both insular and exceptionalist, as it implicitly makes the U.S. the bearer of universal values" (156). Upon repu-diating the exceptionalist perspective that she found evidenced in Kadir's reconfiguration of the field, Kaplan went on to mount a critique of Kadir's proposal from the perspective of the U.S. cultural studies that had been the principal target of Kadir's disciplinary critique. Despite his "exhilarating call for a momentous paradigm shift," Kadir's continued indebtedness to American exceptionalism led him to resuscitate the most "traditional para-digms" of American studies, "the Euro-American white male canon, even for those he calls upon as critics and outsiders" (156). Kaplan detected a comparable gendered hierarchy informing the distinction that Kadir ad-duced between "hard" political science and "soft" cultural studies, as well as a masculinist bias in the "base and superstructure" matrix of his anal-ysis. "Why relegate ethnic studies to the 'cultural' and exclude it from the political and international?" Kaplan wondered, when the "most important work in ethnic studies today shows that culture and politics, the national and international, are inseparable from one another" (156).

Having designated Kadir's recidivist allegiances to American exceptionalism as the agency primarily responsible for the shortcomings in his
international perspective, Kaplan nevertheless discerned an emancipatory
potential in the IASA that Kadir had failed to tap: "I would add that the
project of international American studies has the potential to undo the tenacious paradigm of American exceptionalism, the paradoxical claim of
the United States to uniqueness and universality at the same time" (154).
Kaplan specifically promoted an interdisciplinary project that would involve international americanists in comparative studies of empires and
their legacies as one way to release the IASA from the prison of American
exceptionalism.

Although it operates below the threshold of Kaplan's substantive formulations, a version of American exceptionalism is discernibly at work
in the proprietary attitude from which Kaplan magisterially formulated
her critical response to this "non-American" americanist; it is also tacitly
underpins the specific alternatives to American exceptionalism that she
proposed as remedies. When Kaplan shifted the terms of her response
from a description of what Kadir's address had done in order to articulate
prescriptions concerning what the members of the IASA should instead
do, Kaplan took up the extraterritorial space that the cold war had opened
up for the U.S. American studies scholars who served as the field's cultural
diplomats. As the president of the American Studies Association, Kaplan
positioned herself within this site when she exercised the quasi-legislative
power to pronounce upon what international americanists should and
should not do.

In his critique of U.S. cultural studies, Kadir represented resentments
at the "disciplinary exceptionalism" of U.S. American studies that were
widely shared within the international community. When Kaplan recommended prescriptions concerning the future scholarly agendas of international americanists, she presupposed the structure in dominance of U.S.
americanists' relations of knowledge production. In conducting her critique of Kadir's initiatives from (inter)disciplinary perspectives formulated
within the field of American cultural studies, Kaplan tacitly presupposed
that the relations of knowledge production that were then prevalent in
U.S. academic institutions could (and should) be universalized as the normative scholarly attitude of americanist scholars worldwide.

The political and socioeconomic formations responsible for the emergence of the IASA as an international project, however, included heterogeneous modes of knowledge production. In the papers they presented
at the First Congress of the IASA, held in Leiden in 2003, some of the
members of the International American Studies Association adapted the

research protocols developed within American cultural studies to fit their own scholarly agenda. Others represented their disciplinary and interdisciplinary agendas as incompatible with U.S. models.

Rather than formulating a critique against Bush's State of Exception, Kaplan instead targeted the exceptionalist convictions that informed Kadir's choice of Leiden as the location for the founding of the IASA. In his inaugural address, Kadir had described Leiden as especially well suited as the foundational site for the IASA because it was "from this ground where the Puritan pilgrims surveyed the Western horizon for some twenty years and sailed toward it nearly four centuries ago" (137). In her response, Kaplan asserted that it was Kadir's allegiance to American exceptionalism that inspired him to choose Leiden as the scene of origin for the IASA:

> Let's start with the Puritans, one of the powerful origin myths on which exceptionalism relies. . . . An international approach to the Puritans would contextualize this small community of migrants in the context of world trade, commerce and competing imperial projects in the 17th century. At the same time that some Puritans were looking toward the new world from Leiden, the Dutch West India Company was chartered in the Hague to have a trade monopoly, which included parts of West Africa, the "Gold Coast," islands in the Caribbean, the Americas on the Atlantic and Pacific coasts, Portuguese possessions in Brazil, and part of the Atlantic slave trade. To place the Puritan mission in this wider context of mercantilism, colonialism and the slave trade among the British, Dutch, Portuguese, and Spanish empires would invite a truly international effort that would decenter the United States as the teleological object of study, even during the colonial period. (157)

This series of observations supplied Kaplan with historical warrant for declaring "the need for international American Studies to be involved in collaborative comparative studies of empires and their legacies, so that even the study of the American empire doesn't simply reproduce an imperial insularity" (158).

The standpoint from which Kaplan conducted her critique of Kadir's recovery of the ethos of American exceptionalism drew on her prior characterization of the Bush administration's dramatic abandonment of it. According to Kaplan, Bush's abrogation of American exceptionalism was evidenced in its "dramatic turn away from the disavowal" of the nation's own imperial history and in his "embrace of empire across the political spectrum" (154). Kadir founded an International American Studies Association on the retrieval of a version of American exceptionalism that Bush's State of Exception had repudiated. After Kaplan revised Kadir's critique of the Bush administration with the observation that Bush's imperialism was no longer in need of this exceptionalist ruse, however, she proceeded to place Kadir *within* the tenacious grasp of a version of American exceptionalism from which the Bush administration had already extricated itself.[8] Did not the Bush administration's refusal to disavow its imperial ambitions constitute a case study in how to emancipate American studies and U.S. culture from the tenacious grasp of the version of American exceptionalism that Kaplan had invoked in her critique of Kadir? In no longer finding it necessary to disavow the imperialism that the United States was in fact practicing, had not the Bush administration rendered the U.S. Imperium more or less comparable to other imperial ventures in world history? But if the Bush administration had already rendered U.S. imperialism more or less comparable with the imperial adventures of the Roman, British, Spanish and Portuguese empires, why should the membership associations of the IASA want to become "involved in collaborative comparative studies of empires and their legacies"? Since the Bush State of Exception inaugurated an American imperial formation that did not require the discourse of American exceptionalism for its legitimation, would not the comparative analysis of empires ignore the drastic alteration of the paradigm of American exceptionalism that Bush has inaugurated?

A vast complex of ideas, policies, and actions is comprehended under the phrase "American exceptionalism." And the disparate significations of this complex are neither compatible nor derived from a shared semantic source. Three separate uses of the term seem to be at work within these disparate iterations. The State of Exception that Kadir condemned the "devotees" in the Bush administration for having inaugurated in declaring a global war on terror possessed a meaning and function that was different from the American exceptionalism that Djelal Kadir resuscitated to inaugurate the International America Studies Association. And both of these uses differed from the American exceptionalism out of whose tenacious grasp Kaplan aspired to emancipate americanists worldwide.

Kadir characterized Bush's State of Exception as "bad" because it lacked the ideological justification of the good American exceptionalism embraced by the member organizations of the IASA. Unlike Kadir, Amy Kaplan regarded Bush's State of Exception as a variant of U.S. imperialism that was incompatible with American exceptionalism insofar as it was lacking the psychosocial structures through which that discourse had facilitated the disavowal of U.S. imperialism. In aspiring to release international American Studies from the tenacious grasp of American exceptionalism, Kaplan directed her critique against Kadir's selection of American exceptionalism as a weapon of resistance. Kaplan buttressed this critique by advocating a scholarly agenda that would undermine Kadir's residual attachments to U.S. American exceptionalism by undertaking a comparative analysis of empires. But as Ann Laura Stoler has observed, a U.S. americanist scholar cannot conduct the comparative analysis of empires that Kaplan has recommended without recognizing that "discourses of exceptionalism are part of the discursive apparatus of empires themselves." According to Stoler, all "imperial states operate as states of exception that vigilantly produce exceptions to their principles and exceptions to their laws." "When viewed from this vantage point," Stoler adds, the United States is a quintessential empire, "a consummate producer of excepted populations, excepted spaces, and its own exception from international and domestic laws."[9]

Kaplan believes that comparative analysis would remove the United States from its claims to uniqueness and insularity. But since exceptionalism constitutes the means whereby every empire has universalized the uniqueness of its colonial practices, the comparative study of empires would require the production of criteria that would ultimately lead Kaplan to rediscover that it is American exceptionalism that differentiates the U.S. imperial formation from those of the European imperial powers. In the eighteenth, nineteenth, and twentieth centuries, each of the imperial nations with which Kaplan would compare U.S. imperialism had developed its own version of exceptionalism. These disparate discourses of exceptionalism supplied each of these imperial nations with the justificatory criteria they needed to formulate and manage their population's understanding of the contradictory relationship between imperialism and nationalism and racism as they undertook colonial projects in the New World.[10] The comparative study of empires that Kaplan has proposed might indeed supply the analytic frames of analysis required to differentiate the Italian, French, German, Spanish, Dutch, British, and Portuguese imperialisms from the American rendition. But this comparativist project would not extricate scholars from the tenacious grasp of American exceptionalism so much as it would explain the contestable geopolitical terrain in which it was set to work.

The version of American exceptionalism from out of whose tenacious grasp Kaplan wanted to release the IASA was fashioned at the outset of the twentieth century—a historical period in which the sheer volume of trade, financial transactions, and commercial enterprise first brought what is presently referred to as globalization into stark visibility. In her critique of Kadir's address, however, Kaplan has ignored the ways in which the geopolitical strategies that prevailed at the turn of the twentieth century— when the diffusions of nationalism, colonialism, and large-scale wars constituted interrelated ways of regulating and controlling global processes—

were profoundly different from the economic assumptions in play at the turn of the twenty-first century, which characterized nation-states and imperial warfare as inefficient technologies of management.[11]

At the turn of the twenty-first century, the market ideology propagated by the neoliberal global economy instituted a negative relation to nation-states and installed forms of governmentality that redefined political governance in terms of self-regulating processes that required technical rather than political solutions.[12] Lacking any alternative to which it needed to stipulate itself as the exception, the neoliberal imperatives—rule of law and deregulated markets—that underpinned the twentieth-century discourse of American exceptionalism have, at the outset of the twenty-first century, become the planetary norm.

Both Kadir and Kaplan needed some version of American exceptionalism to critique in order to conduct their critiques of U.S. imperialism. Yet both of their critiques resulted in the reinstallation of some version of American exceptionalism in its place. But if the discourse of American exceptionalism is possessed of sufficient elasticity to enable different versions of American exceptionalism to return through the very antiexceptionalist and postexceptionalist frameworks that Kadir and Kaplan have designed, is it not necessary to inquire how or whether there can be an American studies after American exceptionalism?

My effort to answer these questions supplies the rationale for the trajectory of the remarks that follow. I begin with a brief critical genealogy of American exceptionalism in which I try to explain the forces that overdetermine the relations among these disparate manifestations of it. My effort to analyze the problems that confront any effort to construct a field of American studies after U.S. exceptionalism then leads to a consideration of the arguments of Daniel Rodgers, who is perhaps the most convincing advocate of postexceptionalist American studies. At their conclusion, they return to the remedies proposed by Kadir and Kaplan and Rodgers to the Bush State of Exception, to the relationship the states of exception and the discourse of exceptionalism bear to the future disposition of the field of American studies.

AMERICAN EXCEPTIONALISM(S):
A BRIEF CRITICAL GENEALOGY

The term "American exceptionalism" found its way into the scholarly lexicon in the late 1920s, when Joseph Stalin deployed it to accuse the Lovestoneite faction of the American Communist Party of a heretical deviation from Party orthodoxy.[13] The Lovestoneites drew Stalin's condemnation for having claimed that economic developments in the United States differed from those in Europe, and that these differences explained why the United States had not yet arrived at the point of the economic collapse that then plagued European countries.

Stalin's use of the term as a heresy explains why exceptionalism was reappropriated as the key term within cold war ideology. Whereas Stalin had excommunicated the Lovestoneite faction for having described the United States as an exception to the laws of historical motion to which Europe was subject, cold war ideologues subsequently elevated American exceptionalism to a doctrine that explained *why* the United States was exempt from the incursions of Marxian communism. Daniel Rodgers has explained the historical rationale for this appropriation with characteristic clarity: "Extracting 'exceptionalism' from Communist party jargon, scholars moving centerward from the anti-Stalinist left injected it into the central vocabulary of American social and political science. An absence— the relative failure of socialism in the United States—became the defining point of the nation's history, a ratification of the special dispensation of the United States in a revolutionary world where Marx still tempted."[14]

If the doctrine installed American exceptionalism as a transhistorical model, however, specifications of the doctrine's content have changed with historical circumstances. Exponents of American exceptionality have placed in nomination various descriptions of the nation's world historical role. Candidates have included the "redeemer nation," "conqueror of the world's markets," and most recently the "global homeland state." Each of these designations distilled and summarized a very different form of governance, but each of these variations on the nation's exceptional place in the world order was derived from the conviction of the United States' unique role in world history.

If the doctrine of American exceptionalism derived its authority from the account of the United States' unique place in world history that it authorized, it drew its structure out of its difference from the social imaginaries that it attributed to Europe, the Soviet Union, and the so-called Third World. The exceptionalist paradigm described U.S. uniqueness in terms of what was putatively absent—a landed aristocracy that monopolized ownership of the land, a feudal monarchy, a territorial empire, trade unions, a society hierarchized in terms of class differences, and a deeply anchored socialist tradition—from U.S. history. Exceptionalist historians explained how the absence of class conflict in particular rendered the United States free from the revolutionary socialism that they described as the agency primarily responsible for the destabilization of Europe

Representations of the United States as an exception to norms of Europeanization also promoted an understanding of the United States as the standard for the future of democracy, which Europe should emulate. The doctrine, with its exception to the rule of European normalization, sustained an image of a Europe composed of states that could not find their reflection in the U.S. mirror. What the United States was lacking rendered it not merely different but also qualitatively better than the European nation-states, whose social orders were described by exceptionalist historians as having been devastated by Marxian socialism. American exceptionalism imagined a Soviet Empire that threatened to overthrow the world order through the spread of revolutionary socialism, and it represented Europe as especially susceptible to this threat.

Overall, American exceptionalism was a political doctrine as well as a regulatory ideal assigned responsibility for defining, supporting, and defending the U.S. national identity. But the power of the doctrine to solicit the belief that the United States was unencumbered by Europe's historical traditions depended on the recognition of European observers for its validation. In the transition from World War II to the cold war, U.S. consensus historians such as Arthur Schlesinger, Jr., and Henry Steele Commager cited Alexis de Tocqueville's nineteenth-century account of his travels throughout the United States as definitive verification of the doctrine of U.S. exceptionalism.

Observing that Tocqueville had found U.S. political society exceptional in lacking the feudal traditions that had precipitated the violent confrontations in France's moment of transition, Daniel Bell grounded his "end of ideology" thesis on this claim.[15] As an addendum to Bell's argument, Louis Hartz advanced the claim in *The Liberal Tradition in America* that the absence of class conflict from a liberal capitalist order had rendered impossible the emergence of socialism within U.S. territorial borders.[16] In thus eliminating from U.S. territory the socialist initiatives that Bell had excepted from its history, Hartz in effect deployed *Democracy in America* to secure the nation's borders against the negative exceptionalism of the Imperial Soviet.

Hartz believed that the United States was an upwardly mobile society free from the class warfare that plagued Europe. In arriving at this thesis, Hartz described Frederick Jackson Turner's "frontier thesis" as the articulation a complementary representation of U.S. exceptionalism. Turner represented the frontier as the space on the map where the lingering European influences were removed completely through encounters with the inexhaustible wilderness that was promised to all the "Americans" who answered the call of the wild frontier.

After describing the national past as lacking the history of class antagonism that they posited as the precondition for world communism, American studies scholars cooperated with policymakers and the press in constructing a mythology of national uniqueness out of whose narrative themes U.S. citizens constructed imaginary relations to the cold war state. Events on a world scale were thereafter assimilated to this cultural typology that was made to translate them. Practitioners of the myth-symbol-image school of American studies endowed the texts, personalities, and events under their analysis with traits that corroborated exceptionalist assumption.

Whereas U.S. policymakers depended on the doctrine to authorize their practices of governance, historians and literary scholars turned the doctrine into the principle of selection through which they decided which historical events they would allow representation within the historical record and which literary works they would include within the U.S. canon. Examining the past became, for scholars who were steeped in exceptionalist convictions, a romance quest whereby they would understand the meaning of their "American" identity through their uncovering of the special significance the nation's institutions. In the early years of the cold war, proponents of the myth-symbol-image school of American studies constructed an image of the United States out of exceptionalist assumptions. Then they propagated this image throughout Europe and the newly decolonized world as a prescriptive model for the construction of political communities that would, like the United States in whose image they were to be remodeled, be defended against the incursions of Marxian socialism.

The state presupposed this doctrinal belief when it declared that its coercive power to make and preserve laws constituted an exception to the laws it enforced. In recasting Japanese internment camps, Operation Wetback, and the Vietnam War as "exceptions" to the norms of U.S. exceptionalism, for example, state policymakers removed these troubling events from the orderly temporal succession organizing the nation's official history.

If the doctrine of exceptionalism produced beliefs to which the state has regularly taken exception, the cold war state nevertheless needed the doctrine to solicit its citizenry's assent to its monopoly over the legitimate use of violence. In light of these contradictions, the relations between U.S. citizens' belief in U.S. exceptionalism and the state's exceptions may best be described in psychological terms as structures of denial. U.S. exceptionalism names the surplus element to the normative model of U.S. cold war governance; it also functioned as the superego supplement that enjoined U.S. citizens to disavow the existence of this extralegal force. By enabling U.S. citizens to disavow the state's exceptions that threatened their beliefs, the doctrine of exceptionalism regulated U.S. citizens' responses to historical events throughout the cold war era.[17]

Indeed the authority of the doctrine is discernible in its power actively to ignore the state's exceptions. It supplied its adherents with the absences they required to maintain their foundational beliefs. The doctrine was a composite construction that involved an alliance among cultural workers, the economic sector, and the state in refusing to acknowledge the realities of political domination. In this broad-ranging network of discourses, the doctrine has served as both an object of study and an instrument of rule.

The doctrine also shaped the contours of the academic field of American studies out of the prolonged debate conducted therein over whether the nation was a variation on or a deviation from European models. Whether and how it differed released a range of problems that delimited the scope of the field's inquiry. In restricting its understanding of U.S. culture to these standpoints, American studies in turn provided the discourse of American studies with an operational context determining how U.S. culture got taught, administered, and pronounced upon.

Exceptionalism and the state's exceptions to it at once required each other's operations, yet they were also set in opposition. The power of the state's exceptions became evident in what the discourse of exceptionalism was compelled to disavow. By way of its exceptions, the state includes instances of what the doctrine of exceptionalism had described as missing from the national history. The state thereafter exercised the sovereign power to produce the absence that exceptionalism has described as foundational.

The disavowal that was crucial to the production of the state's exceptions disclosed the willfulness through which the United States misrepresented its history as well as its place in the world. Official historians had fashioned their accounts of U.S. domestic policies out of the conviction that the nation was different from European imperial states in that it repudiated the acquisition of colonies. Disowning knowledge of the historical realities of imported slave labor, of overseas colonialism, and of the economic exploitation of refugees entailed exceptionalist historians' differentiating the U.S. government's domestic policies from the realpolitik of the international arena. But in their distribution of ethnic and "racialist" differences into hierarchical social rankings, U.S. immigration laws in particular have depended on stereotypes developed out of a residual colonial discourse. Moreover, throughout much of the nation's history, U.S. foreign policy has worked in more or less open violation of democratic ideals. The historical struggles of Asian, Hispanic, and Amerindian groups for recognition of their equal rights reveal linkages between domestic and foreign policies that U.S. exceptionalism effaced.

State historians have grounded the narrative through which they have ignored the contradiction between the nation's democratic ideals and subsequent imperialist practices in the discourse of exceptionalism. The historians' meta-narrative linked the United States' place in world history with a quasi-messianic national ideology. This ideology was believed to have originated in the Puritans' conviction that providential design had assigned them the unique world historical task of dispossessing Amerindians of their lands as the precondition for the redemption of their souls.

William Appleman Williams has described the dissociative reasoning through which historians have recounted the exceptionalist narrative succinctly: "One of the central themes of American historiography is that there is no American Empire. Most historians will admit, if pressed, that the United States once had an empire. They then promptly insist that it was given away. But they also speak persistently of America as a world power."[18] In between U.S. historians' admission of a U.S. colonial empire and their insistence "that it was given away," an entire imperial history becomes visible as what cannot become straightforwardly referential in the post–World War II exceptionalist meta-narrative.

As a result of the work of cold war americanist scholars, the discourse of American exceptionalism that had been formulated in the twentieth century as a bulwark against Soviet imperialism was retroactively applied to a series of disparate historical epochs, beginning with the Puritans. In the estimation of the founders of U.S. American studies, the Puritans were better suited than other colonial settlers to meet the needs of this invented tradition. When U.S. American studies scholars selected the Puritans' Exodus as the origin story for the tradition of American exceptionalism, they endowed the political fiction that America had inaugurated a new order for the ages (*"Annuit coeptis novus ordo seclorum"* "He has approved our undertakings") with the Puritans' representations of a divinely ordained "errand into the wilderness." The Puritans' mission thereafter became the theological matrix of the Reason of the Cold War State.[19]

Throughout the cold war, American exceptionalism was grounded in an anti-imperialist ethos that would overcome the aspirations to world domination of the Imperial Soviet. The U.S. americanists who invented this tradition selected collective representations from disparate historic epochs—Nation of Nations at the end of the eighteenth century, Manifest Destiny from the period of U.S. continental expansionism in the middle of the nineteenth century, Conqueror of World Markets from the period of extracontinental expansionism in the late nineteenth century—as more or less interchangeable manifestations of the cold war discourse of American exceptionalism. Each of these tropes was described as corroborative of the cold war's anti-imperialist ethos. If we add Empire for Liberty, however, the phrase that Thomas Jefferson invented to describe his policy of populating the western territories, an entirely different genealogy emerges, revealing that the United States of America has been in the process of imperial state formation from the time of its founding.

When Thomas Jefferson coined the phrase "Empire for Liberty," U.S. citizens had not yet arrived at an agreed-upon collective self-representation. In the early 1800s, the nation-state consisted of a series of commercial networks constellated around disparate endeavors that involved the capitalist expropriation and subsequent development of vast tracts of land. It was the continued presence of French, British, Spanish, and imperial formations within the northwestern and southwestern territories that provided Jefferson's phrase with its nation-making powers.[20] "Empire for Liberty" was invented to perform the rhetorical work of establishing the difference between Jefferson's democratizing policy of territorial expansion and Alexander Hamilton's federalist imperializing of these territories under a central government on the one hand, and the political work of liberating these territories from the dominions of the Spanish, French, and British empires on the other. In stipulating that the state's policies of expansionism were to be construed as exceptions to the acquisitional imperialisms of these European powers, Jefferson also meant the phrase "Empire for Liberty" to indicate that the expansion to the West was to result in the relative autonomy of the newly formed states in their relation to the federalist's imperium.[21] Jefferson thereby assigned the sources for dislocations in the domestic polity to an external threat, and he recast the conflict between democrats and federalists in terms of the antagonism between the U.S. Empire for Liberty and European imperial competitors.

"Empire for Liberty" supplied Jefferson with the discursive means of subordinating the sovereign democratic will of U.S. populations to the sovereign imperatives of the imperializing state.[22] The Empire for Liberty positioned the nation's citizen-subjects at the conjunctural site where these dual sovereignties—that of U.S. citizens and that of the state—diverged. The U.S. citizens who traveled west resolved this split in the state's favor when they exercised the state's sovereign power to subject the Indians they encountered on their way to the state's deadly force.

The phrase "Empire for Liberty" additionally established an antagonism between democratic imperializing nationalism and European imperialisms that enabled U.S. citizen-settlers to believe that it was not their violence but their mimesis of the violence of their European enemies that was responsible for realizing Jefferson's purposes. Jefferson described the westering of American liberty as the necessary means of extending the cause of freedom within geographies that were under permanent threat of being annexed by European imperial states. The exceptions that empowered Jefferson's implementation of the Empire for Liberty—allying with the French against Toussaint L'Ouverture in Santo Domingo, the policy of "peace through the medium of war" against the Barbary states, the recommendation of a policy of Indian extermination following the alliance of tribes with the British during the War of 1812—were explained in terms of Jefferson's efforts to produce definitive differences between U.S. expansive republicanism, Indian savagery, and European imperialist violence.

In the 1840s the U.S. population remained a loosely confederated agglomeration, many of whose members were more intimately connected with Atlantic and Pacific trade routes than with a collectively shared national purpose. Anxieties over perceived efforts by the British and French to obstruct the annexation of the western territories induced John O'Sullivan to conscript the phrase "Manifest Destiny" to a nationalizing mission. In O'Sullivan's opinion, this national purpose could only be revealed through the overcoming of the obstructions to expansion posed by the European empires that had remained shadowy presences within the western territories, where they had gathered "in a spirit of hostile interference against us, for the avowed object of thwarting our policy and hampering our power, limiting our greatness and checking the fulfillment of our manifest destiny to overspread the continent allotted by providence for the free development of our yearly multiplying millions."[23]

Manifest Destiny fostered the belief that the exceptions—the Indian Removal Act, the Wilmot Proviso, the Kansas-Nebraska Act—that the state had fashioned in annexing the western territories were the work of God's transhistorical providential design, which predestined the United States to supersede European empires as the world's dominant power. O'Sullivan described the individual's internalization of this "manifest" as formative of American freedom, and he encouraged U.S. citizens to believe that they realized this national mission by participating in the state's annexationist practices. The doctrine of Manifest Destiny additionally enabled U.S. citizens to interpret American logistical superiority in warfare as a divine sign of U.S. moral-cultural superiority.[24] Manifest Destiny thereafter translated the expropriation and annexation of Indian and Mexican lands into nation-consolidating expressions of U.S. opposition to British, French, and Spanish imperialism.

Law and war were the most effective instruments that the state had devised to involve disparate populations in the transhistorical mission of creating and maintaining the Imperial Republic. The state fashioned its exceptions at frontier sites where the law of war coincided with the force of law. According to Ann Laura Stoler, U.S. imperial formations were founded

on hierarchized variations of sovereignty and disenfranchisement and authorized by multiple and heterogeneous criteria for inclusion and exclusion. These contradictory criteria required constant juridical and political
reassessments.[25] Max Savelle has explained the criteria that the U.S. imperial state had invented to resolve these juridical dilemmas in terms of the
distinctions the state's jurists had drawn between U.S. imperial relations
and those of the European powers. In addressing questions concerning
the juridical authority through which the United States could justify the
conquest and settlement of Indian lands, the U.S. judiciary weighed the
relative merits of the legal fictions invented by disparate imperial powers:
"Spanish jurists contended that Indians constituted sovereign nations and
owned and possessed the land, the French also maintained that the Indians tribes were sovereign nations and that they were possessors of the
land and they must be treated as such, but the English maintained that the
Indians were subject peoples who occupied but did not own the land, and
who had placed themselves under the protection of the British king, and
who were therefore subject to that king's order."[26]

The United States displayed its mastery of the art of imperial governance through the construction of highly contradictory domains of jurisdiction wherein ad hoc exemptions from the law on the basis of race and
cultural difference resulted in the construction of exceptional spaces such
as the "domestic dependent nations" invented by Chief Justice Marshall in
Worcester v. Georgia (1832) and in the production of the stateless and kin-
less peoples who were brought into existence by Justice Taney's notion of
"natal alienation" in *Dred Scott v. Sandford* (1857). When Chief Justice Marshall described native tribes as "domestic dependent nations" voided of
the right to land that they neither colonized nor cultivated, he intended
that their condition of dependency be understood as the consequence of
their lands having formerly been targeted for expropriation by European
empires.[27] This benchmark decision, which turned native peoples into sur-
rogates for the European imperial powers to which the United States had
positioned itself in opposition, became one of the defining principles of
the U.S. imperial state. Manifest Destiny justified the state's policies of
Indian removal by representing them as alternatives to European strategies of imperial colonization. After they were represented as the bearers
of properties of alien imperial powers, Indians could not be nationalized.
They were instead converted into racialized aliens.

When coupled with the state's more broad-gauged geopolitical designs,
Empire for Liberty and Manifest Destiny enabled Jefferson and O'Sullivan
to describe America's policies of imperial expansion to the south and
northwest as having been forged as "exceptions" to British, French, and

Spanish imperialism. The U.S. citizens who participated in them described these imperial adventures as campaigns in the continuing war against European imperial aggression. The policy of expropriating Indians from their lands without the construction of colonies was reputed to be the chief distinction between U.S. and European imperial formations. Instead of colonizing the Indians, the United States, through its policy of Manifest Destiny, was to forcibly separate them from the land that Empire for Liberty had formerly defended against incursions from European imperialism.

The U.S. state's exceptions possessed no essence other than their complete negation of a foreign imperial formation. But the unity of the discourses in which these tropes were inscribed emanated from the racialized Other, onto which the discourse projected the contradictions internal to American exceptionalism. Indeed what galvanized U.S. citizens' shared sense of Americanness throughout the nineteenth century was the state's production of a racialized Other who was made to represent the continuing threats that French, British, and Spanish imperial powers were imagined to pose within the U.S. polity.

The state viewed Indians as negative exceptions to civil society. What putatively separated U.S. citizens from the state of Indian "savagery" was the civi-territorial compact that represented Indians in terms of what they lacked—law, government, property, husbandry, civility. The state's relegation of Indians to this status effected a biopolitical distinction that separated the national body politic from biologized indigenous populations. In relegating Indians to this condition of disposable bodies, the state turned the ethnic cleansing of Native Americans into the permanent civil war necessitated to accomplish the permanent purification of U.S. civil society. At the bar inscribing these dichotomies—citizen/savage, freeman/slave, securitized American/terrorizing subversive—there insisted a subracial, subhuman, subindividual other who had access to nothing but the negation that underpinned the power of the exception.

The American exceptionalism(s) engendered throughout U.S. history gave rise to two heterogeneous but co-constituting figures: the citizen-subject, who was empowered to speak the discourse and participate in the enactment of its rule; and subjugated and racialized Others, who lacked representation within the discourse but who were subjected to its rules. American exceptionalism(s) thereby installed a permanent division within U.S. citizen-subjects that dissociated the part that participated in the state's sovereign powers of subjection from the part that felt threatened by alien subjugating powers.

The decisions over who was to be included within the republic and who could not belong, however, required the state's constant reconfiguration of the relationships between U.S. citizens and the state's subjects. The sociopolitical categorizations that were invented to facilitate these decisions—resident alien, guest worker, naturalized citizen, citizen without voting rights—reflected disparate forms of assimilation and differentiation. The designers of the U.S. imperial formation created numerous exceptional spaces—Indian reservations, unincorporated territories, internal colonies, protectorates, transfer stations, detainee centers, trusteeships, possessions that belonged to the state but were not part of U.S. polity—to accommodate the disparate populations referenced by the state's categorizations. The juridical and political decisions that were responsible for the production and justification of these anomalous sites of exception determined who was and who was not included.[28]

The state's exception took place at the decisive moment of power in which the state intervened within the geopolitical realm to inaugurate an utterly different policy. Whereas the state's exceptions disarticulated the state's new policy from prevailing norms, the discourse of American exceptionalism rearticulated the state's exceptions to a recognizable praxis by deciding on which of the preexisting forms of knowledge could normalize this new state policy. As it opened up spaces that were at once discursive and political, the discourse of American exceptionalism infused a shared national vocabulary with different political meanings. When it did, the discourse of American exceptionalism provided the state's exceptions with the magical efficacy that operationalized them into transmissible protocols and significations.

The imperial nationalism mobilized under the aegis of Jefferson's Empire for Liberty gave way to the policy of anti-imperial nationalism that Manifest Destiny called for in the middle of the nineteenth century. Theodore Roosevelt introduced another decisive shift in the disposition of American exceptionalism at the turn of the twentieth century when he transformed the earlier discourses of Manifest Destiny and Empire of Liberty into the warrant for imperial policies that effected a massive reconfiguration of the U.S. relationship to world imperial formations. In the transitions from Jefferson's Empire for Liberty, to O'Sullivan's Manifest Destiny, to the outright imperial rivalry evidenced in Roosevelt's characterization of the United States as the "leader of the free world," the discourse of American exceptionalism underwent radical transvaluations that turned on the extremely different political rationalities that each of these core tropes assigned to the state's exceptions.

Roosevelt's discourse of exceptionalism produced an imaginary relationship to the Reason of State that refunctioned the exceptional spaces—

domestic dependent nations, unincorporated territories, protectorates, plantations—that had been devised to justify internal expansionism, during the epochs of the Empire for Liberty and Manifest Destiny, into models for the U.S. effort to acquire an "informal" overseas empire at the turn of the twentieth century. Roosevelt construed imperial expansion to be an aspect of the state's strenuous exercise of self-governance which would permit the United States to control the international marketplace. Roosevelt's conceptualization of imperial conquest involved a dual orientation that included "an internal conquest of the self, a regeneration, as well as an outward charge to purge and uplift the conquered spaces and peoples themselves."[29] In keeping with this policy of dual conquest, Roosevelt instructed the U.S. citizens and soldiers under his tutelage that in exercising rule over native others, they were in fact practicing a form of liberal self-governance.

In setting the U.S. abnormal colonization policies to the work of extracontinental expansion, Roosevelt turned the exceptions at work in Jefferson's imperial nationalism and O'Sullivan's nationalist anti-imperialism inside out. The policies Roosevelt set into place reduced Puerto Rico, the Philippines, Cuba, and Guam into the extraterritorial analogues to "domestic dependent nations," and he converted the figure of the American frontiersman into the wardens of these protectorates. Julian Go has described Roosevelt's composite imperial state formation as a form of "Manifest Exceptionalism" whereby the United States "would discipline the colonized in the lessons of liberal self-governance ... and as Puerto Ricans and Filipinos learned their 'lessons,' American control would devolve and the colonized would eventually receive full self-government."[30]

Yet insofar as he turned the insular projects of Jefferson's Empire for Liberty and O'Sullivan's Manifest Destiny in an outward direction, Roosevelt abandoned the history of U.S. isolationism. His wholehearted endorsement of U.S. imperial power aroused fears concerning America's "fall" into the world of European imperial powers from whose rivalries its isolated geography had formerly exempted it. Roosevelt characterized American freedom as the right to impose the American sense of rights onto whomever the state wanted—by whatever means necessary.[31] After boasting that the United States had always been about subjugation and displacement, Senator Henry Cabot Lodge concurred with Roosevelt's perspective when he proudly pointed to "a record of conquest, colonization and territorial expansion" unequaled by any people in the nineteenth century: "We do not have to go the Luzon in the Philippines for American barbarities. . . . If no more territory was to be taken because it was contrary to American principles we might as well give New Mexico back to the Apaches."[32]

As this brief genealogy indicates, American exceptionalism is not reducible to the articles of a credo, and it endorses neither a preexisting ideology nor a structure of feeling. Throughout U.S. history, the state installed exceptions to the nation's norms so as to obtain an advantage in the competition with other imperial state formations. The versions of American exceptionalism under discussion in this genealogy mediated the contradictory relationship between the United States as an exemplary republic and the United States as a rapacious imperializing power. One version of exceptionalism gave way to an alternative as a result of the performative power of a paradigmatic trope that reconfigured its significations by seizing on different elements in earlier discourses and infusing this vocabulary with different political meanings so as to reconstitute the discourse for different political ends. From the eighteenth century to the present, the discourse of American exceptionalism linked the state's exception with core terms—Empire for Liberty, Manifest Destiny, leader of the free world, liberal anticommunism, global homeland state—that supplied an exemplary paradigm against which the validity or reality of a state action was measured. The paradigmatic force at work within each of these disparate exemplars of American exceptionalism exercised the power to install definitive breaks from settled convictions so as to hegemonize an alternative common sense and to communicate a different structure of feeling about the United States' purpose and place in the world. Overall the disparate historical iterations of American exceptionalism consisted of heterogeneous configurations of the U.S. population's paradoxical relationships to war and law in which state racism, state colonialism, state imperialism, and state nationalism have constituted separate but interdependent episodes.

CAN AMERICAN STUDIES EXIST AFTER AMERICAN EXCEPTIONALISM?

If the state's exceptions can only be successfully implemented after the discourse of American exceptionalism has effected the reorganization of the discursive order, why did Bush inaugurate a State of Exception that would do without the hegemonizing discourse of American exceptionalism?

In my earlier remarks about this conjunctural site, I discussed the ways in which Kadir's and Kaplan's critiques of Bush's State of Exception led them to reinstate some version of American exceptionalism rather than to answer this question as to why or how or whether the Bush State of Exception had done without it. Before attempting to answer this question directly, I need to turn to a U.S. americanist scholar who has answered this question indirectly by supplying a historical explanation of why American studies should be practiced without recourse to American exceptionalism.

Daniel T. Rodgers, perhaps the most articulate of a growing cadre of postexceptionalist U.S. historians, has formulated the rationale for this collective endeavor with eminent clarity. The first impetus toward a postexceptionalist American history came, Rodgers observes, from the change that the globalization of political economy played in the collective experience of space: "Living within the global economy's powerful transnational forces and flows has dramatically shifted conventions about what lies inside and what lies outside . . . nations themselves exceed their borders." A comparable shift in the consciousness of time took place when "the great nineteenth century schemes of universal history unexpectedly ran out of steam."[33]

Rodgers apprises the disciplinary consequences of these changes in the planet's spatiotemporal coordinates with the following succinct formulation: "Albeit dogged with controversy, a postexceptionalist American history has come into view. One of the key historiographical events in this regard has been the fading away of the exceptionalists' imagined Europe and, with it, the imagined rules of other nation's histories. Throughout the modern world, economic integration and national particularization both proceed at once. The imagined central tendencies of history no longer apply. . . . In a world without rules, there can be no exceptions—only an infinite regress of differences" (25).

Rodgers described the global economic order as a world without rules in order to demonstrate the logical incoherence of any nation-state that would represent itself as an exception to global norms. In Rodgers's estimation, the geopolitical order organized around the logic of rules, norms, and exceptions was rendered obsolete by the unruly connectivities characteristic of the newly globalized order. And Rodgers understands himself under an obligation to situate U.S. history within this interconnected world so as to update it to fit the new reality.

There is great historical merit in Rodgers's argument. With the breakup of the Soviet Union and the formation of the European Union, the United States lost its threatening Socialist totalitarian Russian Other as well as its destabilized and dependent European and Third World Others. After the historical conditions that had formerly undergirded its assumptions faded into the historical past, the exceptionalist paradigm was unable to recoup the absences of these historical processes as signs of U.S. uniqueness. And after the United States lost the geopolitical rationale for the representation of itself as an exception to the laws of nations, it also lost the putative right to establish the rules for the global order.

According to Rodgers, with the disappearance of cold war relations that were grounded in its macropolitical dichotomies, a disremembered underside of American exceptionalism returned into the geopolitical arena. And since these multiple, interconnected, and heterogeneous processes were irreducible to stabilized oppositions, U.S. historians were under an obligation to respond to the changed conditions of the newly globalized world order by fostering a "postexceptionalist" understanding of the United States' embeddedness within transnational and transcultural forces rather than the reaffirmations of its splendid isolation from them (27).

Their effort to fulfill this obligation has led Rodgers and growing numbers of like-minded postexceptionalist historians to undertake a fundamental reshaping of accounts of the United States' place in world history. In the following passage, Rodgers explains why U.S. historians have undertaken this collective project: "With the collapse of the socialist monolith, American politics began to look more contingent disharmonious and unpredictable ... the U.S. answered less to unique historical necessities than to transcultural historical processes. The boundaries between the rule and the exceptions have shifted. ... As a consequence, the banished and censured parts of one's history threaten to return" (31).

Rodgers explains the insurgent postexceptionalist strain in contemporary U.S. americanist work as the effect of a sudden inflooding of these foreclosed dimensions of the U.S. past. According to Rodgers, it was this return of this previously foreclosed knowledge of the United States' interconnectedness that also rendered the conflict between exceptionalist and postexceptionalist americanist projects so acute. These emergent alternatives to exceptionalist history brought into consciousness a dark underside of American history and politics that the discourse of exceptionalism had disavowed.

The underside that postexceptionalist history exposed to full view included at once the knowledge of America's interconnectedness with the rest of the world along with knowledge of the mechanisms that had prohibited U.S. historians from revealing this knowledge. "Part of the work that all exceptionalist historical arguments do is to silence and marginalize parts of the nation's past," Rodgers explains apropos of these mechanisms; "by the very formulas constituting their construction they load parts of the national history elsewhere" (29). "The historical laws regulative of the rest of the world places 'our here' against 'their elsewhere.' ... Postulating a universal rule while holding one's own nature exempt from it, produces a here against an elsewhere, and a we against a universalized they in a world elsewhere" (23). "It was by way of this imaginative displacement that American historians were able to write about an American past that was free of racial and class tension so that they could thereafter see it so quickly in Africa or in Latin and South America or Russia." Rodgers concludes this line of thought by drawing the following historical lesson: "There has been and there continues to be generated much more inequality in the history of the United States than exceptionalist readings of its history and nature acknowledge" (33).

Here as well as elsewhere in his explanation of the rationale for a postexceptionalist history, Rodgers has attributed the state's activities to U.S. historians' accounts of them. It was not U.S. historians who marginalized or silenced or displaced entire populations. But U.S. historians were and are responsible for foreclosing recognition of the state's role in effecting these activities with historical narratives whose representations were regulated by the meta-discourse of American exceptionalism.

By describing globalization in terms of the return of the foreclosed underside of American exceptionalism, but lacking the bar of repression, Rodgers has ignored the role the repressive state apparatus historically played in imposing that bar. More specifically, Rodgers continues to disallow recognition of the fact that the state introduced the bar separating the here from the elsewhere and that the state has now relaxed the regulations at the boundaries so as to permit the more efficient flow of goods and capital. How can Rodgers endorse what he has called "a world of differences without rules" without recognizing that Bush's State of Exception has enforced set of regulatory norms that anchor these differences within the same neoliberal global order?[34]

Rodgers has also ignored the repressive role that the state continues to play in regulating the knowledge Rodgers represents as having been foreclosed. Why has Rodgers not explained how the neoliberal market ideology that had underpinned U.S. exceptionalism has become the planetary norm? And why has he has neither supplied an account of nor explained how the U.S. state's exceptions to the rules established its position of dominance within the global economic order?

Rodgers omits from his account of the underside of American exceptionalism any knowledge of the disparate colonial, expansionist, imperial projects through which the state had established regulatory control over these processes of interconnectivity. The disavowed underside of American exceptionalism also possessed the power to expose the acts of colonial violence and imperial predation that constituted the obscene supplement to the discourse of American exceptionalism. The geopolitical dispensation guaranteed by the discourse of American exceptionalism always depended on an unseen, disavowed political violence.

The international contests over control of the global economic order that began with the exploration of the New World in the fifteenth century required that the United States set its imperial ambitions into competition with that of other imperial state formations. During the cold war era, U.S. historians described America's global dominance as having been sustained by the United States' exemption from the laws of history that regulated the course of other nation-states across the globe. Throughout the cold war, the United States did indeed constantly produce exceptions to international rules that gave it an edge in the international marketplace. But U.S. historians consistently misrepresented the state's exception as signs of the United States' exemption from the historical laws that determined the historical destiny of the other nation-states on the planet.

Despite their absence from Rodgers account, these exceptions did not cease to exist after "globalization took command." Although the state's exceptions could not be included within the normative order of global capitalism, those exceptions—the broken Kyoto treaty, the regulations of the U.S.-controlled World Bank, the invasions of Iraq and Afghanistan—were responsible for the at times violent measures through which neoliberal values were universalized as the planetary norm. These state apparatuses did not set the rules of the newly globalized world order; they were also responsible for the invasive introduction of neoliberal market values in regions that adhered to values incompatible with the assumptions of the global marketplace.

Rodgers's work supplies an instructive illustration of Djelal Kadir's claim that as the disciplinary medium through which American exceptionalism was regulatively transmitted across the globe, U.S. American studies was itself an extension of the state's govermentality: "American Studies is, indeed, very much a *discipline* in the strongest Foucauldian sense of governmentality. It is so to the point of having disciplined the practitioners of American Studies to deny that their practices form and are formed by a discipline" (147). The discourse of American exceptionalism structured the vantage point from which U.S. historians represented what took place in the course of U.S. history, and it set the rules that established the interpretive norms that regulated how U.S. historians should interpret those representations. Rodgers complied with these regulations by persistently failing to recognize how the state changed the rules governing the global economic order, and how the state has enforced the rules that it has changed.

The absence of the need for this justifying discourse in the newly globalized world economy has inspired Rodgers to represent globalization as marking the end of American exceptionalism. Rodgers is indeed correct in his claim that globalization and American exceptionalism work according to very different logic. In arguing that the global order does not operate by the rules and laws that regulated economic processes during the cold war, Rodgers has, however, ignored a crucial dimension of the new dispensation. In the era of globalization, Bush inaugurated a global State of Exception so as to set and enforce rules that would regulate the unruly interconnectivities of global capitalism.

AMERICAN STUDIES AS THE COMPARATIVE ANALYSIS OF IMPERIAL STATE EXCEPTIONALISMS

In the course of these remarks, I have discussed four different accounts of the provenance of American exceptionalism within the field of American studies. All four of these accounts—those of Bush, Kadir, Kaplan, and Rodgers—have emerged at a historical moment in which the socioeconomic processes that accompanied globalization have supplanted the geopolitical rationalities that prevailed throughout the cold war. Bush's State of Exception placed the United States apart from the international laws and rules governing other nations, and he openly embraced imperial strategies in Iraq and Afghanistan. Kadir characterized Bush's State of Exception as "bad" because it lacked the ideological justification of the "American Way" embraced by the member organizations of the IASA. Whereas Kadir criticized Bush's State of Exception, Kaplan upbraided Kadir for having embraced the American exceptionalism that the Bush administration had left behind. In doing so, Kaplan turned American exceptionalism into an object of critique rather than the object cause of the field of American studies. Rather than ratifying a version of it or turning it into an object of critique, Rodgers explained that the economic and political processes associated with globalization had already rendered American exceptionalism utterly inoperative.

In their explanations of its workings, Kadir, Kaplan, and Rodgers have presupposed very different understandings of American exceptionalism. Since those assumptions also differ from my own, I should, in turning to a conclusion, formulate a definition of what American exceptionalism is and does. The American exceptionalism referenced throughout this account did not result from the universalization of a concrete national particularity, it did not endorse a view of U.S. history as overseen by a providential design that exempted the United States from the laws of universal history to which all other nations have been subjected, and it is not reducible to a mere deviation from a norm. Although at times it includes this psychosocial feature (especially during the post–Civil War era of the nineteenth century and during the cold war epoch of the twentieth), American exceptionalism has not always communicated an anti-imperialist structure of feeling.

American exceptionalism, however, has constituted a discursive relationship to the exceptions that the U.S. imperial state instituted throughout its history of struggles with other imperial state formations over the control of geopolitical order. More specifically, the discourse of American exceptionalism supplied the psychosocial structure through which U.S. americanists have disavowed the exceptions undertaken by the United States as an imperial state formation. In providing the discursive means through which individuals accomplished this structuring denial, the discourse of American exceptionalism propagated a way of practicing the disavowal of the state's exceptions as the American way of life.

In defining American exceptionalism as the discourse through which individuals have taken up an imaginary relationship to the real exceptions of the U.S. imperial state, I have designated the state's exceptions as constituting the core matrix of the discourse of American exceptionalism. In proposing that different discourses of exceptionalism were linked to different states of exception, and that these disparate exceptions were placed in the service of contesting the exceptions of other imperial states, I have also indicated that these states of exception were linked to questions of international law and international diplomacy.

Given this account of the relationship between the state's exceptions and American exceptionalism, why did the Bush administration institute an imperial state formation that did not require the structure of disavowal at work in the discourse of American exceptionalism? Bush's State of Exception did not require this structure of disavowal because it constituted *the Exception* to the discourse that proved its power to rule. After the attacks on the Twin Towers on September 11, 2001, Bush inaugurated a State of Exception that did not just change the rules and norms informing the United States' domestic and foreign policy, but it also changed the framework through which those rules and norms could be interpreted. As an exception to the exceptionalist norms that it propagated and enforced across the planet, Bush's State of Exception did not depend for its legitimacy on the hegemony of exceptionalist norms, and it did not require the discourse of American exceptionalism to disavow its status as *the Exception*. Bush's State of Exception instituted a version of American exceptionalism that was devoid of American exceptionalists.

Bush had instituted this State of Exception in a world in which two of the constitutive norms of American exceptionalism—rule of law and free markets—had become the planetary norm. To ensure that they remained the norm, Bush's State of Exception enforced the planetary conditions that rendered them normal. But in instituting exceptions to the norms of U.S. political governance, Bush's State of Exception also suspended the U.S. Constitution, which had defined the state's relationship with U.S. citizens in terms of shared sovereignty. The State of Exception operates in a sphere that is separable from the logics of the nation and that is irreducible to its terms. Bush's State of Exception suspended the laws that protect civil liberties and the meta-narrative frameworks through which citizens internalize these laws as ruling norm. The citizen as the agent of the sovereign power of "We the people" had no part to play in the State of Exception. Bush's State of Exception had in effect placed the state and the nation into two separate and mutually exclusive spheres. In relegating U.S. citizens to a "homeland" that it secured and defended against terrorist attacks, Bush's State of Exception repositioned the national community within the equivalent of the exceptional space that Chief Justice Marshall had called a "domestic dependent nation" in his 1831 ruling on the rights of the Cherokees. Rather than sharing sovereignty with the state, U.S. citizens were treated as denizens of a protectorate that the State of Exception defended rather than answered to.

Bush disassociated the State of Exception from the normalizing powers of the discourse of American exceptionalism because he wanted to render the state exempt from answering to its norms. In declaring the United States an exception to the rules and treaties governing other nations, the Bush administration redefined sovereignty as predicated less upon national control over territorial borders than upon the state's exercising of control over global networks. The United States did not want territory; it wanted to exercise authoritative control over the global commons—the sea and the air—in the interests of guaranteeing the free movement of capital, commodities, and peoples. It was the putative threats that terrorism and rogue states posed to global interconnectivities that supplied the United States with the planetary enemy that it required to justify its positioning of itself as the exception to the rules it enforced across the planet. By justifying the United States' monopoly over all the processes of global interconnectivity, the War on Terror enabled the Bush administration to arrogate to itself the right to traverse every national boundary in its effort to uproot the international terrorist networks and to defend the "homeland" against incursions of radical extremists.

From the eighteenth century through the cold war epoch, nationalism and imperialism contributed to global capitalism by dividing the globe into national and colonial enclaves. International capitalism appealed to the nation-state's powers of regulation and distribution. However, the economic demands of the global marketplace have redefined the state's mission, requiring that it downplay its obligations to the constituencies within a bounded national territory so as to meet the extranational needs and demands of global capital. The unruly capitalism that globalization has sponsored would strip nation-states of their regulatory powers and reinstate an earlier alliance between capital and the state that restricted the states to the role of protecting the local newly emerging regions and local outposts of the global economy.

In an era when market priorities have reshaped sociopolitical agendas, the nation-state's social and political commitments are perceived as impediments to the efficient functioning of the global marketplace. The state has aspired to exempt itself from its contractual obligations to the national community and to dissever its ties with every constituency except the entrepreneurial capitalists responsible for managing the global economy. Rather than representing the interests of the entire nation, this managerial elite, with its selective interests, has bifurcated nation-states into capitalist sectors that are integrated into the global capitalist order and into regions whose premodern economic practices are subjected to the exploitative forces of the capitalist sector.[35]

As we have seen, the state's exceptions introduced a void in political norms that the discourse of American exceptionalism normatively disavowed. After the state's exceptions were sutured to the discourse of American exceptionalism, U.S. citizens were supplied with a structure that enabled them to disavow this void in the normal order of things. In the status as supernumerary elements in the discourse of exceptionalism, however, the state's exceptions prevented its closure. Kadir, Kaplan, and Rodgers articulated their critiques of American exceptionalism after Bush inaugurated the State of Exception. Bush's State of Exception confronted all three of these U.S. americanists with the responsibility to come to terms with the state's exceptions voided of the powers of avoidance with which the discourse of exceptionalism had normatively supplied them. Each of their interventions can be understood in part as an effort to find a way to undermine the state's exceptions in the displaced form of criticizing the discourse of American exceptionalism through which they were disavowed. But each of their critiques of American exceptionalism also involves them in a direct or an indirect confrontation with a dimension of Bush's State of Exception

This conclusion assumes the form of a brief comparison of their responses; it also includes some general remarks about the interrelationships pertaining among the discourse of American exceptionalism, and American studies as a field. I begin with the observation that each of their criticisms of American exceptionalism turns on a blind spot to a dimension of the State of Exception. In calling for a wholesale dismantling of American exceptionalism, Rodgers fails to see that Bush's State of Exception has propagated and enforced exceptionalist norms across the planet. Kadir does not see that the versions of American exceptionalism ("the American Way," "the American Dream") that he would reinstate were themselves the outcomes of the state's exceptions. In advocating that the IASA extricate itself from American exceptionalism, Kaplan has failed to recognize that its member associations have emerged through and are reproduced out of their own version of American exceptionalism.

Despite these blind spots, the critiques of American exceptionalism by Kadir, Rodgers, and Kaplan have also enabled each of them to ameliorate one or another of the abnormal geopolitical conditions that Bush's State of Exception has produced. At a moment when the global homeland state has turned nations across the planet into U.S. protectorates, the members of Kadir's IASA have reasserted the rights of national constituencies to shape sociopolitical agendas. In his assessment of the ways that global economic processes have exceeded the nation-state's regulatory powers, Rodgers has called attention to extranational regional geographies and to the disparate practices of spatialization, as they are evidenced in diasporas, migrations, and borderlands, that require the formation of postnational regulatory agencies and international courts of justice. In calling for a comparative study of empires, Kaplan has acknowledged that interconnectivity is a fact of life in the global order, but she explains that this fact of life has emerged ridden with contradictions that have opened up questions concerned with scale and region. Neoliberal capitalism is incomprehensible without reference to colonialism as a form of economic exploitation and political domination. Indeed the vast inequities in the distribution of wealth have led some commentators to describe globalization as "invisible colonialism—the third phase of the Euro-American colonization of the globe."[36]

If, however, we supplement the comparativist analysis of empires that Kaplan has recommended with an explanation of the exceptions to international law and to the rationales of nation-states that disparate imperial state formations constructed to gain control over the globe's resources, the resulting model would link the transcultural models proposed by Rodgers and the nationalist framework that Kadir has advocated to the legacies of colonial modernity that Kaplan would restore to visibility. The "truth" of U.S. imperial state formation inheres in the exceptions that the state produced in its long contestation with European imperial formations.

When we recall that each of the nations within the IASA emerged out of the contestatory relationships among disparate imperial state formations from across the globe, the restoration of those histories of imperial exceptionalism formative can resituate U.S. American exceptionalism within this expanded field of imperial exceptionalisms. This work of historical comparative analysis would again make visible the wars and the laws through which the British, Spanish, French, Dutch, Italian, Portuguese, Incan, German, Chinese, Mayan, and Russian empires contested with the emergent American imperial state over control of the New World. These different exceptionalisms were linked to different states of exception, and these states of exception were linked to questions of international law and international diplomacy. In renegotiating the relationship with the New World and with each other, these imperial states felt a certain reverse effect on their own cultures and institutions, especially in the realm of diplomacy and international law that Max Savelle has described succinctly:

> Out of the colonial situation, there also arose the doctrine of the two spheres, that is, the idea that Europe had its own system of international law and custom, while the colonial world beyond the lines of amity—the North and South lines of the treaty of Tordesillas and the Tropic of Cancer—was a new and distinct sphere of international law, and relations and international treaties (unless they specifically mentioned the New World) did not apply. As a corollary to this doctrine the colonizing nations had earlier accepted the assumption that "might makes right beyond the line" and that there is no peace beyond the line.[37]

While the United States might not have existed as we know it without the exceptions normalized within the discourse of exceptionalism, a field of American studies can and I would argue should exist that is grounded in a comparativist model of imperial state exceptionalisms. This model would turn the state's exceptions as well as the structures through which the discourse of American exceptionalism has historically disavowed them into objects of analysis and explanatory critique—rather than as the paradigmatic form of americanist practice. One of the challenging areas of inquiry that this new field of American studies would be positioned to address pertains to the ways in which Bush's State of Exception would disallow the formation of any competing form of imperial state exceptionalism.

Notes

I delivered versions of this essay at the conference Globalizing American Studies organized by Brian Edwards and Dilip Gaonkar at Northwestern University in 2007 and at the 2007 European Conference of American Studies. A version of the essay, titled "American

Exceptionalism(s) in an Extended Field: The Inauguration of International American Studies," was published in the proceedings of that conference, *Conformism, Non-Conformism and Anti-Conformism*, ed. Antonis Balasopoulos, Gesa Mackenthun, and Theodora Tsimpouki (Heidelberg: Universitaetsverlag Heidelberg, 2008), 9–43.

    1. Djelal Kadir, "Defending America against Its Devotees," *Comparative American Studies: An International Journal* 2, no. 2 (2004): 135–52. Hereafter, citations to this article are in the body of the text.

    2. *The National Security Strategy of the United States* (Washington, DC, 2002), http://www.whitehouse.gov/nsc/nss.html.

    3. Richard H. Pells, *Not Like Us: How Europeans Have Loved, Hated, and Transformed American Culture since World War II* (New York: Basic Books, 1979), 105–11. I elaborate on this dynamic in a forthcoming essay titled "Guenter Lenz and the Transculturation of U.S. American Studies: An Unfinished Trans-Atlantic Negotiation."

    4. See Richard H. Pells, "The Europeanization of American Studies," in *Not Like Us*, 129–34.

    5. Guenter Lenz has proposed that the international scholars who accuse the United States of cultural imperialism "have to pursue the question of how far their own American studies programs, often founded as 'area studies programs' in the period of the Cold War, have been implicated in, and actively supportive of these imperial politics." Guenter Lenz, "Toward a Dialogics of International American Culture Studies: Transnationality, Border Discourses, and Public Culture(s)," in *The Futures of American Studies*, ed. Donald E. Pease and Robyn Wiegman (Durham, NC: Duke University Press, 2002), 481.

    6. Rob Kroes has observed the venerated tradition of European American studies that is almost never acknowledged by U.S. americanists:

> Whatever the precise academic and institutional history of the field, however, it can be argued that Europe has known a history of intellectual reflection on the United States that allows one to speak of European American studies . . . with its canon of great names, from Tocqueville to Sombart, from Bryce to Huizinga, from Myrdal to Pavese. It is in fact a tradition older than the one which in the United States emerged as the American Studies movement and which, after the war, became a model for many American Studies programs elsewhere to follow. Clearly, any program for a European approach to American studies should start from this recognition. European students of American history, society and culture should be trained in an awareness of these longer lines of European reflection on America, on its otherness, offering cultural counterpoints to Europe, as well as on its similarities and parallels. Only then can the American studies movement in the United States be seen as serving different existential needs, answering different questions of national identity, than the European reflection on America.

Rob Kroes, "Studying America in Europe: Four Vignettes and a Program," *Journal of American Culture* 20 (Winter 1997): 63.

    7. Amy Kaplan, "The Tenacious Grasp of American Exceptionalism," *Comparative American Studies: An International Journal* 2, no. 2 (2004): 154. Kaplan also characterized Bush's State of Exception as having abandoned the "disavowal of imperialism" that she has designated as the transhistorical psychosocial structure underpinning of American exceptionalism. But this affect structure in fact enjoyed a very restricted historical duration. From the time of its founding up to the outset of the cold war, the public demonstrated a range of affective responses ranging from the wholehearted embrace of imperial ambitions to their utter rejection. Hereafter, citations to this article are in the body of the text.

    8. Kaplan criticizes American exceptionalism for claiming to be at once unique and universal. As Étienne Balibar has observed, however, the paradoxical claim to universalize its

uniqueness is the constitutive matrix of every nationalist discourse. According to Balibar, "nationalism . . . is particularistic, inasmuch as it claims that national entities have different roots, that they must keep control over their own members, who belong to them in some strong sense, and that they must remain isolated from one another in order to preserve their identities." But nationalism as an ideology is also universalistic in at least two senses: "first nationalism supported the idea of formal equality . . . thus removing notions of castes, status groups and local privileges"; and second, in order to think of itself as exceptional, the "nation has to think of itself as immediately universal in its singularity." Étienne Balibar, *Masses, Classes, Ideas: Studies in Politics and Philosophy before and after Marx* (New York: Routledge, 1994), 193.

9. See Ann Laura Stoler, "Imperial Formations and the Opacities of Rule," in *Lessons of Empire: Imperial Histories and American Power*, ed. Craig Calhoun, Frederick Cooper and Kevin W. Moore (New York: New Press, 2006), 57. Edward Said observes that "every single empire in its official discourse has said that it is not like the others, that its circumstances are special, that it has a mission to enlighten, civilize, bring order and democracy, and that it uses force only as a last resort." Edward Said, *Orientalism* (New York: Vintage, 2003), xxi.

10. See Stoler, "Imperial Formations and the Opacities of Rule," 57.

11. Stephen Rosen, professor of national security and military affairs at Harvard's Olin Institute for Strategic Studies, makes the point that "the organizing principle of empire rests on the existence of an overarching power that creates and enforces the principle of hierarchy, but is not itself bound by such rules." Stephen Rosen, "An Empire, If You Can Keep It," *National Interest* 71 (Spring 2003): 53. Arif Dirlik discusses this process with great acuity in *Global Modernity: Modernity in the Age of Global Capitalism* (Boulder, CO: Paradigm Publishers, 2007).

12. "As a new mode of political organization, neoliberalism reconfigures relationships between the governing and the governed, power and knowledge, sovereignty and territoriality. Whereas neoliberalism is usually conceived as an economic doctrine with a negative relation to state power, a market ideology that seeks to limit the scope and activity of governing, it can also be conceived as a new relationship between governing and the knowledge through which governing activities are recast as non-political and non-ideological problems that need only technical solutions. Neoliberalism as a technology of governance is an active way of rationalizing, a way of governing and a form of self-government to optimize production." Aihwa Ong, *Neoliberalism as Exception: Mutations in Citizenship and Sovereignty* (Durham, NC: Duke University Press, 2005), 3.

13. Daniel Rodgers, "Exceptionalism," in *Imagined Histories: American Historians Interpret the Past* (Princeton: Princeton University Press, 1998); Ian Tyrrell, "American Exceptionalism in an Age of International History, " *American Historical Review* 96 (1991): 1031–55. J. Robert Alexander, *The Right Opposition: The Lovestoneites and the International Communist Opposition of the 1930's* (Westport, CT: Greenwood Press, 1981).

14. Rodgers, "Exceptionalism," 28.

15. Daniel Bell, *The End of Ideology* (Glencoe, IL: Free Press, 1960).

16. Louis Hartz, *The Liberal Tradition in America: An Interpretation of American Political Thought since the Revolution* (New York: Harcourt, Brace, 1955).

17. See Donald E. Pease, "Imperial Discourse," *Diplomatic History* 22 (1998): 605–15.

18. William Appleman Williams, *Empire as a Way of Life* (New York: Dell, 1980), 380.

19. Anders Stephanson, *Manifest Destiny: American Expansion and the Empire of Right* (New York: Hill and Wang, 1995).

20. Ibid.

21. Robert W. Tucker and David C. Hendrickson, *Empire of Liberty: The Statecraft of Thomas Jefferson* (New York: Oxford University Press, 1990), 17–21.

22. In a letter that he wrote to James Madison on April 27, 1809, Jefferson explicitly confirmed his sense that the U.S. Republic was ideally suited to acquire the standing of an empire: "I am persuaded no constitution was ever before so well calculated as ours for extensive empire and self government." Tucker and Hendrickson, *Empire of Liberty*, 140.

23. John O'Sullivan, "Annexation," *Democratic Review* 17 (July–August 1845): 5.

24. Technical and logistical superiority in warfare became culturally transmitted as a sign of moral-cultural superiority. European and American civilization morally deserved to defeat Indian savagery. Might made right. The expression of Anglo-Saxon freedom included the right of Anglos and Europeans to impose their sense of rights onto whomever they wished. It was the theme of the invasion of foreign nations inside a state that provided the basis for the genealogy. Out of the aristocratic narration of the nation and of its bourgeois variant we acquire two discourses—the struggle of race and the struggle of class.

25. See Stoler, "Imperial Formations and the Opacities of Rule," 57.

26. Max Savelle, *Empires to Nations: Expansion in America, 1713–1824*, Europe and the World in the Age of Expansion ser., vol. 5 (Minneapolis: University of Minnesota Press, 1974), 138–39.

27. In *Worcester v. Georgia* (1832), Chief Justice Marshall installed an underlying discourse of permanent war against occupying imperial powers that supplied the state with a permanent warrant for the fashioning of exceptions grounded in state racism. In a recovering of the memories of the unjust British state, the race wars that the state declared against Indians replayed the American Revolution in reverse. Marshall explained the rationale for his decision: "During the war of the revolution, the Cherokee took part with the British. . . . After its termination . . . the Cherokee nation is under the protection of the United States of America, and of no other sovereign whatsoever." *Documents of American Constitutional and Legal History*, ed. Melvin Urofsky and Paul Finkelman (New York: Oxford University Press, 2002), 1:258–60.

28. Stoler, "Imperial Formations," 55–56.

29. Stephanson, *Manifest Destiny*, 86.

30. Julian Go, "Imperial Power and Its Limits: America's Colonial Empire in the Early Twentieth Century," in *Lessons of Empire: Imperial Histories and American Power*, ed. Craig Calhoun, Frederick Cooper, and Levin W. Moore (New York: New Press, 2006), 208.

31. Ibid.

32. Stephanson, *Manifest Destiny*, 104.

33. Daniel T. Rodgers, "American Exceptionalism Revisited," *Raritan* 24, no. 2 (2004): 21–47. Hereafter, citations to this article are in the body of the text.

34. Dirlik elaborates on this dynamic in *Global Modernity*.

35. Aihwa Ong, in *Neoliberalism as Exception*, focuses on the active interventionist aspect of neoliberalism in non-Western societies where neoliberalism as exception articulates regimes of citizenship and sovereign rule. Of course the difference between neoliberalism as exception and exceptions to neoliberalism hinges on the normative order in a particular milieu of investigation.

36. See Dirlik, *Global Modernity*.

37. Savelle, *Empires to Nations*, 141.

TWO

Bodies of Knowledge

The Exchange of Intellectuals and Intellectual Exchange between Scotland and America in the Post-Revolutionary Period

Kariann Akemi Yokota

The time is come to explode the European creed, that we are infantine in our acquisitions, and savage in our manners, because we are inhabitants of a new world, lately occupied by a race of savages.

—*[Timothy Dwight], "An Essay in American Genius," 1787*

Americans must believe and act from the belief that it is dishonorable to waste life in mimicking the follies of other nations and basking in the sunshine of foreign glory.

—*Noah Webster, "On the Education of Youth in America," 1788*

David Hosack was an ambitious man. Born in New York during the waning years of British rule, he would go on to become a prominent physician and a pioneer of botany in America.[1] In 1789 Hosack graduated from the College of New Jersey (later Princeton University); he then received a medical degree from the University of Pennsylvania. Soon after completing his training he wed Catharine "Kitty" Warner and established a practice in Alexandria, Virginia.[2] Despite his new marriage and a growing patient base, the young doctor soon became restive: he feared that his professional life would begin to stall because of his lack of European training. Looking across the Atlantic, Hosack considered the possibility of furthering his career by continuing his education at the University of Edinburgh, which at the time was the British Empire's most prestigious medical school. For Americans who aspired to reach the pinnacle of their field, ultimate success was predicated on their ability to deftly traverse the transatlantic networks between America and Great Britain.

Whatever his misgivings about temporary expatriation and making the journey to the Old World—it was "painful" for him to "think of leaving my family"—in the end Hosack "took passage" to Europe. The eminent physician Benjamin Rush, himself a graduate of the Scottish university, described how many American physicians made the same choice in order to "pursue the stream [of knowledge] to its fountain in Edinburgh."[3] The

young doctor's decision was driven by the knowledge that American patients strongly preferred practitioners who had studied abroad. According
to a later account by his son, Hosack was "convinced that the distinction
which our [American] citizens at that time made between those physicians
who had been educated at home and those who had had additional instruction from the universities of Europe" would ultimately "prevent him
from the success he craved" unless he went abroad.[4] Americans wanted
caregivers who offered the benefit of the latest advances in Western medicine in the same way that they expected merchants to deliver the newest
fashions from London. Hosack's relatively humble origins increased his
need to succeed professionally. Considering how "little property I had reason to expect from my parents," he observed, his "chief dependence was
upon my own industry and unceasing attention to the profession I had
chosen as the means of my subsistence; my ambition to excel in my profession did not suffer me to remain insensible under such distinction."[5]

Hosack was an emblematic figure in the post-Revolutionary generation of American elites who accepted that ties to the British intellectual
establishment increased one's status at home.[6] His experience in Scotland
illustrates how he and other late eighteenth-century Americans exploited
the relationship of Great Britain and the United States, despite the asym-
metries in power between the nascent republic and the mother country.
Regardless of the strong drive for American autonomy, the client/patron
dynamic that characterized so many aspects of life in the new nation recalled the thirteen colonies' dependence on Britain. America's dramatic
exit from empire did not end this unequal relationship. Paradoxically, new
citizens spent the first years of their hard-won independence struggling to
remain connected to the complex circuits of material, economic, and cultural exchange set in place during the colonial period.[7]

As part of this effort to maintain the transatlantic links that were vital
to the survival of the young nation, early Americans assimilated, transported, and eagerly consumed institutionalized knowledge. Like confirmed
believers on an intellectual pilgrimage, students crossed the Atlantic to
worship at the feet of European academic authorities, who bestowed the
gift of knowledge upon them. As social theorists have argued, however, no
gift is entirely unconditional; if one cannot reciprocate in kind when given
an offering, then that relationship is marked as unequal. As Marcel Mauss
famously observed, gifts, which might seem "disinterested and spontaneous ... are in fact obligatory and interested."[8]

If Britons had the power to bestow their learning upon Americans,
what did they receive in exchange? Although individual motivations differed, in the main, serving as the definitive source of knowledge within

the transatlantic world allowed British institutions to maintain their cultural hegemony over the newly independent United States. In the post-Revolutionary years, Americans continued to arrive in Britain as supplicants. Upon their return, those who had enjoyed the privilege of an overseas education leveraged the superiority of the learning they had received. In this way, Americans themselves legitimized the continuation of European cultural dominance.

CALEDONIA'S PROMISE: SCOTLAND AS A CENTER OF AMERICAN REFINEMENT

Both Edinburgh and London represented important sources of refinement and learning, and Americans visited Scotland and England as part of the process of garnering cultural polish from their travels abroad. Cosmopolitan Americans who would have been aware of the English bias against Scotland must have wondered if they inhabited an even lower rung on the ladder of this cultural hierarchy. In his essay on the relationship between Philadelphia and Edinburgh during the age of the Enlightenment, historian Andrew Hook asserts: "There is no evidence that Philadelphians regarded Scottish culture itself as in any sense 'inferior'; on the contrary, respect and admiration for Scotland's cultural achievements clearly continued to grow in Philadelphia throughout the eighteenth century." Commenting on the nature of the cultural exchange between the two, he wrote: "There is no question as to which city was more likely to learn from the other."[9] The active recruitment of Scottish ministers, doctors, educators, scientists, artists, and even artisans and tradesmen throughout the nineteenth century underscores this belief.

This view of Scotland as a source of cultural sophistication contrasts with the English stereotypes circulating during this period. During the seventeenth and eighteenth centuries, Scotland held a relatively marginal position within Great Britain, with its people plagued by unflattering descriptions portraying the lower classes as rude and rough and its elites as provincial, grasping upstarts. The German author Friedrich August Wendeborn observed in 1791 that despite sharing the "name of Britons" after the Act of Union in 1707, the English "were more averse" to the Scots than to "foreigners."[10] This disdain was often manifested materially in the ridicule of Scottish clothing and cuisine, which were believed to reflect the society's lack of civility. Disparaging images commonly portrayed its people as wearing kilts and eating a crude diet of haggis, sheep heads, and oats, a grain that Samuel Johnson's dictionary proclaimed was used to feed horses in England.[11] Even elite lowland Scots who managed to overcome barriers and attain political and social success found themselves the target of some of the most virulent English diatribes. The Scottish origin of John Stuart, the third Earl of Bute, who was appointed prime minister under King George III, proved to be his Achilles' heel.

Despite English prejudice against the Scots, in relative terms the English view of Scottish provinciality could not be equated with American provinciality. In the wake of the Union of 1707, Scots were formally entitled to reap the benefits of membership in the British Empire. They proved enthusiastic partners in colonizing foreign lands and profited from overseas expansion. Known for their willingness to leave their homeland in search of lucrative opportunities, they comprised the vanguard of the British Empire, sending soldiers and enterprising adventurers to every corner of imperial settlement.[12]

Scots, particularly those who supported efforts to extend the empire, believed they shared a proprietary interest in the colonies that spanned the globe. This emphasis on the asymmetrical relationship between America and Scotland offers a different perspective from analyses that have generally emphasized their shared religious affinities and common peripheral relationship with England.[13] Although these factors strengthened the connections between the two societies, what contemporaries perceived as critical differences between Old World Scotland and New World America were equally significant. If they overemphasized the exceptional, distinctive nature of "Scottishness" in the late eighteenth century, they risked underestimating the extent to which Scots identified with a collective sense of a British identity. Historian R. J. Finlay makes this point when he observes how scholars' "efforts to reveal Scotland's ongoing particularity within the domestic British Union has narrowed perspectives that might reveal how these very same social components helped shape the wider Scottish imperial experience."[14] Moreover, cultural and class distinctions within Scotland allowed lowland elites to see themselves as different from "barbaric" highlanders—a differentiation similar to that made by American elites who distinguished themselves from the "unruly masses" in their midst, including American Indians, Africans, and poor whites.

As Hosack's life trajectory shows, traveling from the United States to Scotland and then back again was a worthwhile investment for those who wished to advance their professional and personal standing. Despite America's subordinate position in this system of transatlantic exchange, some individuals managed to leverage the system to their advantage, bolstering their careers as American physicians, naturalists, merchants, and men of letters by going abroad.[15] Those who were able to adroitly navigate the system and take advantage of the "added value" they accrued by going abroad perpetuated a system that fostered a belief in European superiority.

THE GEOGRAPHY OF VALUE AND
ECONOMIES OF RELATIVE LOCATION

Tensions and contradictions defined the American national project; the United States was culturally suspended during the interstitial period between the colonial ancien régime and the modern capitalist society that emerged over the course of the nineteenth century. During this time, American elites worked more assiduously than ever to maintain the privilege of British patronage that had been a natural benefit of their colonial status. While resentment about this inequity seethed during the colonial period, much of it remained subterranean. In the post-Revolutionary period it bubbled to the surface as a result of conflicts between this dependent position and national values extolling the value of independence.

James Rush's life story illustrates changes in the way American citizens felt about continuing cultural and intellectual dependence on Great Britain.[16] Born in 1809, Rush was an American citizen, and his identity as such was markedly different from that of his father, who was born in 1745, or even from that of David Hosack, who was born in 1769. James belonged to a generation whose members had never been colonial subjects. He traveled to Edinburgh after receiving his U.S. medical degree not because of an inner desire to gain the polish of a foreign education but because he was pressured by his family to follow his father's footsteps. He was given direct instructions to "to acquire that knowledge wh[ich] other countries furnish in greater abundance or with easier modes of attainment" than did his own.[17]

American men of learning in the post-Revolutionary period took a practical view of their travel to Great Britain just as their colonial counterparts had done. They saw these trips as an opportunity to gather as much knowledge as possible about their profession. The difference was that garnering this information was now understood as a way to establish American independence from Britain by learning how to replicate the cultural and economic institutions of the mother country. James was instructed by his father that, while visiting, he was to "be all eye—all ear—all grasp." He should "record every thing useful, especially where *numbers* are concerned in your journal. They will be choice new materials to work upon in promoting the happiness of your fellow citizens when you return."[18] Yet while emulation of a supposedly superior model held out the promise of equality, it also raised the specter of inferiority.

When attempting to imagine what it was like for a postcolonial American to arrive in Great Britain during the years after the Revolution, we must remember that although culturally much had remained the same (Americans continued to go overseas for polish and knowledge), other things had changed in the Anglo-American world. While obediently following the same itinerary of his successful father, who had taken the journey decades earlier, James reacted differently to symbols of monarchy. During his stay in England in 1768, a young Benjamin Rush had had the opportunity to view the king's throne. He eagerly convinced his guide to allow him to sit on it, where he perched in awe for a "considerable time."[19] In contrast, shortly after James arrived in Britain, he was "treated" to the spectacle of the celebration of King George III's coronation. He wrote to his father from Edinburgh that "I dont feel much enthusiasm on the occasion."[20] To his mother Julia Rush, James further related his alienation at the patriotic rites of the British nation: "I have just left the street where drums horns and bagpipes are contending for sway in the empire of sounds; and have shut myself up in my room to write to my Mother, were I an enthusiastic Britton and not an American spectator I might enter into the spirit of what I have seen this morning, and attempt to describe it— But my views all took the course of satire or censure."[21]

Although Benjamin Rush had found his time in Scotland to be enjoyable and among the most meaningful in his life, after a year at the University of Edinburgh, James was deeply disappointed with his experience. Frequent letters from his family in Philadelphia left James "melancholy" because they reminded him of the disparity between the reactions of father and son to the sights and sounds of Scotland. He wrote: "When I compare your stay in this country with mine, it gives a palsy to my mind, and in a fit of shame I almost resolve never to go home." In numerous letters, James constantly complained that his sojourn was a "waste of time" and money and that he was thinking of "putting up for the first packet that sails" back to America.[22]

James Rush's generation was caught in a bind that resembles the experiences of postcolonial subjects of later historical periods and geographic locations. While early Americans sought to lessen their dependence on Great Britain, they were aware that a complete disintegration of ties was neither desirable nor possible if the nation was to survive. As former colonials, Americans were both closer to Britain than was comfortable for a free people and farther away from what they still considered the center of civility than they cared to concede. At the same time, their physical proximity to Native Americans and African Americans made the construction and exaggeration of cultural distance all the more urgent. These concerns of positionality, with meanings that shifted relative to their place within preexisting colonial networks, again foreground the concept of the geography of value, which measured these distances between the new nation and the former mother country.

The value assigned to specific objects and bodies changed as they moved from one point in the transatlantic world to another, creating economies of relative location. Borrowed from geography, an economy of relative location can be distinguished from an absolute one, with the former concerned about relations with other economic landmarks, whereas the latter dictates value based on an established coordinate system of commercial latitude and longitude. That Philadelphia was 3,548 miles from London possessed greater value to the postcolonial elite than that the city was at 39.57N latitude and 75.10W longitude. Similarly, if an object was transported to a place where it was rare and its qualities were in demand, its value increased exponentially. Knowledge, embodied in individuals, could be carried from place to place in the same way. Like other valuable objects, the value of knowledge differed depending on the economies of relative location. An Old World education at an ancient university in Scotland, while valuable at its point of origin, was even more precious when taken to the New World, which lacked similar institutions.

Analyzing Americans' travels to Scotland and the recruitment of Scottish intellectuals to the United States demonstrates how the geography of value in the early national period defined the relationship of Scotland and America within the framework of the British Empire. Such a mapping illustrates how, at any given time, particular objects held different values at different locations. Related to this economy of relative location, the movement of these same objects from one place to another became a lucrative social and economic practice. By taking advantage of the differentials in value that their embodied knowledge had at different locations, both Americans and Scots engaged in profitably trafficking various goods and people across the Atlantic.

THE UNITED STATES, AN "UNTRODDEN FIELD" FOR CIVILIZED KNOWLEDGE

It is significant that Hosack did not originally plan on earning another formal medical degree in Edinburgh. Having already earned a degree in America, he thought that traveling to Britain was enough to earn him the reputation he desired because the experience would differentiate him from the majority of his fellow Americans and bestow on him the distinction of cosmopolitan discernment and knowledge. From extant transatlantic letters, it is clear that nonprofessional polish was also an integral part of what American upper-class physicians hoped to acquire while in

Europe. Hosack's biographer supports this view: "His major aim was . . . to return . . . with the added prestige of having studied at Edinburgh and London with whatever that might mean in the way of the latest and best available medical information." As part of this effort to increase his personal value, Hosack "did not neglect to add 'polish' by attendance at the theater and by whatever contacts with the eminent were possible."[23]

These efforts at improvement were not without their drawbacks. Overseas Americans often experienced the discomfort of realizing their own provinciality and ignorance.[24] Back home in America, Hosack had considered himself a cultured gentleman in large part because of his acquisition of imported books, paintings, portrait busts of friends, and a wine cellar. His painful moment of provincial reckoning occurred during an otherwise pleasant afternoon wandering through the gardens of Blackford, the estate of the Scottish Dr. Alexander Hamilton, located near Edinburgh. During the course of the day, it became obvious to him, and worse yet, to those around him, that the young American could contribute nothing to their polite conversation: "mortified by my ignorance of botany with which other guests were conversant, I resolved, at that time, whenever an opportunity might offer, to acquire a knowledge of that department of science."[25]

The same man who spoke those words would become the founder of the first botanical garden in the United States, which he named Elgin Gardens, in tribute to his parents' hometown in Scotland and to his own experience there.[26] Although Hosack was embarrassed by his lack of botanical knowledge while in Europe, when he returned home his ownership of the precious specimens he had acquired there (which, ironically, were dried plants from America, collected by European scientists), books, and lecture notes made him an undisputed expert in what he described as the "as yet untrodden field [of botany] in this country."[27] And so it came to pass that Hosack not only became one of the most successful physicians of his generation, but he also earned recognition among his countrymen as one of their most distinguished botanists.

The politics operating in the Anglo-American scientific networks during the postcolonial period were complex. For decades into the nineteenth century, Americans felt the enduring pull of Europe, which they continued to believe was the center of knowledge production. Many learned Americans derived "great satisfaction" from the fact that Europeans such as the noted English naturalist Thomas Nuttall showed an interest in the United States. Publication of scientific studies of previously unexplored American territory and the plant, animal, and human life found there put the nation on the map both literally and figuratively.[28] Scottish naturalist Alexander Wilson came to America to study bird life. He compiled the majestic *American Ornithology,* which was published in nine volumes in Philadelphia between 1808 and 1814.[29] The popularity of these studies worked to the advantage of struggling American naturalists by raising and renewing European interest in America.

Americans' dependence on Europe was material as well as intellectual; they looked overseas for more than a first-rate medical education. They also imported books containing the latest Enlightenment scholarship. Such volumes provided a transportable container allowing a provincial audience to consume European knowledge from the comfort of their own hearths. These distant members of the transatlantic world even sent away for geographic information about their own country. They looked to others to learn about themselves. Geographies were extremely popular in eighteenth- and nineteenth-century society. They were part of the Enlightenment impulse to learn about the world around us. One of the most popular works of the period was the *Geographical, Historical, and Commercial Grammar* by the Scottish author William Guthrie. Although this graduate of the University of Aberdeen wrote several tracts, this work by far was his best seller. The book, which became known simply as Guthrie's *Geography,* outlived its author by several decades, with "new and revised" editions coming out steadily for over fifty years after his death in 1770.[30]

Objects easily outlast fragile human bonds. In the case of imported geographies, their exercises, texts, and maps reflected political formations that were no longer valid. In 1784, the year the Paris Peace Treaty granted America its independence, Guthrie's text had been established as one of the most widely used books in the classrooms and homes of Americans. Surprisingly, more than a decade after the Revolution, this popular text did not acknowledge the sovereignty of the new nation. As one scholar observed, the map in Guthrie's *Geography* reflects British political interests by enlarging the size of Canada and making the United States appear smaller.[31]

Guthrie's work and many others like it taught children to orient themselves in the world from a position that placed Great Britain at the center of the empire and America at its periphery.[32] They presented readers with a particularly British view of the world. The textual tour of the globe started "at home," which was assumed to be Great Britain. It then gradually moved outward in widening concentric circles, going from the English provinces, Wales, Scotland, and Ireland, to other "civilized" western European nations. Increasingly exotic locations, including the wilderness of North America, were introduced as one moved farther out from the center.

Along the way, the author presented pro-British descriptions, such as the statement that the "United Kingdom of Great Britain and Ireland" was "unequalled" in "her wealth, the value of her manufactures, and the extent of her commerce." American readers learned about the "intelligence and industry of [Great Britain's] inhabitants, the excellent form of her political constitution, the just administration of her laws, and the independence arising from her insular situation," which "combine to render her an object of admiration to all other nations." In juxtaposition to the vast continent of North America, the author observed that Europe was the "smallest of the grand divisions or quarters of the world," but it was "inhabited by an active and intelligent race of people."[33]

Until they produced domestic geographies, Americans had to teach their children geography from the biased perspective of the mother country. The Rev. Jedidiah Morse was among the most vocal critics of this dependence, calling it a "disgraceful blot upon our literary and national character." In a preface to one of his books, Morse asserted that it was not acceptable "to receive the knowledge of the Geography and internal state of our own country, from a kingdom three thousand miles distant from us—to depend on foreigners, partial, to a proverb, to their own country, for an account ... of the American States."[34] For him, imported geographies were unsuitable for educating a new generation of free-born American citizens.[35] His would be instead "an American geography" titled *Geography Made Easy* and published in 1784.[36]

Despite his call to end dependency, Morse was unable to escape from his reliance on Old World sources. He patterned *Geography Made Easy* directly after Guthrie's text, as well as after Englishman Richard Turner's *A New and Easy Introduction to Universal Geography* written four years earlier.[37] In a letter to a European correspondent, Morse conceded that much of his book, including layout, structure, and even content, was taken from British models: "When I adopted my plan, Guthrie's was in high repute and it was in a manner necessary to adopt his plan."[38] Morse's conundrum articulates a recurring theme in American culture during the interstitial period between colonial dependence and national independence: citizens were caught between the urge to innovate while also feeling the need to adhere to European standards and traditions, which conferred legitimacy on the bearers of this knowledge.

As a result of the confusion, objects were sometimes created that contained conflicting messages. For instance, many American maps of this period adopted a confusing system in which both Philadelphia and London were listed as prime meridians. This compromise allowed American authors to pay tribute to the nation and to pay homage to the enduring intellectual dominance of London.[39]

Morse protested the short shrift Americans were given by British authors. In the preface to a later edition of his work, he attacked the "deficiency" and "falsity" of Guthrie's statements about the United States of America. He spoke against the long-standing practice of turning to the mother country for self-definition: "It is not to be supposed that European Geographers should be as well acquainted with America as with their own country. Accordingly, we find that their accounts of the United States are not only very concise, but very inaccurate. To attempt to give American youth a knowledge of their own country from these imperfect and erroneous sketches, would be as fruitless as absurd; it would be to instill into the minds of Americans, British ideas of America, which are far from being favourable or just."[40] Betraying an almost painful determination to make his case, Morse counted the pages the Scottish author had devoted to America in his book. Although such actions were petty, he was correct in thinking that his country was being slighted. The numbers are revealing. In the third edition of the *Geographical Grammar*, Guthrie devoted 440 pages to Europe and only 116 pages to America. The sections on Asia and Africa were even shorter, with 32 pages and 26 pages, respectively. Asia was depicted as a semifeudal society based on luxury and effeminacy, similar to medieval Europe.[41] Societies on the continents of America and Africa were seen as even less developed, with Native American tribes defined as living in the pre-agricultural pastoral stage.[42]

Despite his nationalist sentiments, Morse did not hesitate to borrow from the British when convenient and did so with a complete sense of entitlement: "to import from Europe all their literary works, and their mechanical, nautical and Geographical improvements and discoveries, is highly useful and proper."[43] And import he did. The second edition of his geography, titled *American Geography* and published in 1793, added a volume devoted to the "Eastern Continent"; it was compiled from items in Guthrie's *Geography*—the same book Morse hoped to push out of American classrooms. The new edition was massive, and its two octavo volumes totaled more than sixteen hundred pages. To match its expanded size, the edition's title was transformed from *American Geography* into *The American Universal Geography, Much Enlarged with a Second Volume on the Eastern Hemisphere*.[44] Despite the pretentious title, the book was basically British text placed between new American boards. Its publisher, Thomas and Andrews, even had to import special type from Great Britain to print Morse's edition. Yet Morse claimed his work was better suited to American tastes and needs than were European books because it was an American book.[45]

In an effort to resist British intellectual hegemony, Morse urged Americans to achieve cultural independence through, among other things, choosing to purchase his geography rather than the British alternative. Appealing to patriotic pride, he described how before the Revolution, "Americans seldom pretended to write or to think for themselves. We humbly received from Great Britain our laws, our manners, our books, and our modes of thinking; and our youth were educated as the subjects of the British king, rather than as citizens of a free and independent republic." He warned that the "propriety of importing any of our school books from Great Britain, unless they are previously modified and adapted to the genius of our republican government, is very questionable; as we otherwise run the hazard of having our children imbibe from them the monarchial ideas, and national prejudices of the English."[46] Yet Morse placed a printing order for 5,000 copies of every map that appeared in Guthrie's geography text.[47] The fact that this substantial order of Guthrie's maps would have provided the correct number needed for a reprint of Morse's geography hints at a possible motive. The quality of Morse's maps had been publicly criticized, which was especially damning for a geography book.[48] Despite his patriotic exhortations to end American dependence on British works, Morse appears to have been prepared to insert Guthrie's maps into the pages of his own volume.

For American readers, Guthrie's popular book represented the authoritative view of the empire. What they did not realize was that from the vantage point of the British Isles, the book clearly reflected Guthrie's Scottish identity. Within the universe of British geographies, English works that assumed an Anglocentric and Anglican point of view dominated. As Mayhew argued in his essay, Guthrie's *Geography* reflected the outlook of moderate thinkers of the Scottish revolution who supported moderate Christian beliefs.[49] When placed in the schema of relative value, the meaning of Guthrie's book changed.

DESPERATE TO "SUPPLY THE DEFICIENCY": AMERICAN SCIENCE AS A MATERIAL PRACTICE

American physicians and botanists struggled with their material, social, and intellectual marginality, which forced them to depend on Britain decades after the formal political break. Lacking the institutional support and domestic funding enjoyed by their British counterparts, they often appealed to the British for sympathy with their deprivation when asking for assistance. It was crucial for the continuation of their work to maintain transatlantic networks. In their correspondence they used familial metaphors describing British patrons as "elder brethren" who were being entreated to bestow favors upon their younger, poorer, and less fortunate

American siblings. In 1811 Waterhouse lamented, "Our elder brethren in Europe know not the difficulties that the first settlers in science have to encounter." The pleas for help called on British sympathy and concern in language employed by Americans engaged in nonscientific activities as varied as missionary work and art. "No one in Europe," wrote Stephen Elliott to a friend in London in 1825, can "appreciate correctly the difficulty of the task in which I have engaged. The want of books, the want of opportunities for examining living collections or good herbaria, the want of coadjutors, have all served to render my task arduous, and to multiply its imperfections."[50] Without this support, even the most gifted individuals could not pursue scientific investigation full time.[51]

At a more fundamental level, Americans sorely lacked the material objects needed for experimentation, such as scientific instruments and reference libraries. Seven years after the war had ended, Samuel Stanhope Smith, the seventh president of the College of New Jersey, was still struggling to overcome the damages it had wrought: most of the scientific instruments that had "formerly belonged to this Seminary" were either destroyed or carried off during the war." The colonists had possessed few precious pieces of scientific equipment to begin with, and the destructive wartime battles fought on American soil did not help their situation. The same piece of scientific glassware so easily procured in Great Britain was extremely rare in the United States, and thus it took transatlantic social connections to obtain replacements. With the "funds of the institution" being "so inconsiderable," President Smith planned a series of campaigns to raise money.[52] After all, the scientific instruments made in Europe were needed to produce enlightened scholars made in America.[53]

Desperate to "supply the deficiency" of money to accomplish what was described as the "necessary object" of acquiring the scientific equipment, Smith targeted his fund-raising efforts on the patriotic egos and consciences of the homegrown sons of Princeton. An official resolution of the board of trustees ordered that a circular letter be printed soliciting donations from scattered alumni and "Friends" of the college in towns across the country and abroad. It attested to the fact that the "reputation of the institution" hinged on possession of these imported goods from Europe. As the minutes of the board of trustees stated, "a proper Apparatus is absolutely necessary for the successful cultivation of, and instruction in, several parts of natural philosophy." Through their determined effort, Smith, the board of trustees, and the friends of the struggling college in New Jersey were somehow able to raise enough private funds to purchase "a tolerable apparatus for chemical experiments."[54] They would need to import more than scientific instruments, however, if they were to one day compete with the mother country.

Shortly after his campaign to purchase new scientific equipment, President Smith was again busy acquiring rare scientific objects from Great Britain. This time, his efforts were more complicated and much more exciting in that he was attempting to import British scholars to his institution. Smith was ultimately successful; he managed to convince an "excellent professor in chemistry from Scotland" to teach at Princeton.[55] When John Maclean arrived from Scotland in 1795, his American friends, including Dr. Benjamin Rush, advised him to go to Princeton, where his European credentials would be highly desired.[56]

As expected, Maclean was welcomed with open arms because he provided Princetonians with the Old World culture and knowledge they desired. The young Glaswegian was the ideal candidate, for he had the very things that were lacking in America. The members of the faculty were quick to boast of their new acquisition. Several periodicals published a glowing letter written by President Smith just days after Maclean's formal appointment. According to Smith, Maclean brought "the highest recommendations from Europe," "personal acquaintance" with important figures there, and knowledge of the "latest scientific information from Great Britain and the Continent."[57]

The importation of this Scottish intellectual, who was bestowed with the distinction of holding America's first professorship in chemistry, contributed to the rising glory of the college and of the nation itself. Maclean was described by scientist Benjamin Silliman as "a man of brilliant mind, with all the acumen of his native Scotland." College leaders chose to make Maclean's newly imported expertise in natural history the key to the development of their curriculum. Before his arrival, the institution had exerted a great deal of effort and money to buy scientific equipment from Britain, and Maclean was desperately needed to instruct students on how to use it. Without the one, the other would be worthless—after all, mountains of rare imported glassware would have been of little help to students without someone to instruct them on their use.

John Maclean was a repository of knowledge, including the latest facts and theories gathered from the centers of learning in the Old World. The son of a surgeon, he was born five years before America went to war with Scotland and the rest of the empire.[58] When the young man arrived in the United States, he had already studied his craft in London, Edinburgh, Glasgow, and Paris. His knowledge of chemistry had been formed in these places between the years 1787 and 1790, during what has subsequently been deemed a definitive phase in the revolution of chemical science in Europe.[59] At this juncture in American history, John Maclean's Europe-based scientific knowledge was a scarce and highly desired commodity. Like an imported medical book published in Scotland, Maclean's mind might be considered a package for transporting vital information from one part of the world to another.

The leaders of the university were conscious of Maclean's importance. As President Smith explained, he was valuable to the fledgling nation because he had transformed chemical knowledge into "an object of cultivation" applicable not only to medicine, but also to agriculture and manufactures, which was "so useful in every country, but especially in a new one." Better yet, the new hire offered an expertise in surgery and anatomy, which were by all accounts the weakest areas in American medical training. By acquiring the European doctor, Princeton, New Jersey, immediately became a center of scientific knowledge in the United States. Smith concluded by noting that he was "well assured" that Americans could not obtain this type of knowledge "at present with more advantage at any place in America than the College of New Jersey."[60]

Maclean significantly increased his personal value by exporting himself from Scotland, the land of his birth, to a distant location in New Jersey. He increased his status and employment opportunities by moving to a distant location. Recruits were often enticed with promises of elevated esteem, financial gain, and sometimes escape from various troubles in their home country. Scots had been coming voluntarily and involuntarily to North America since the seventeenth century, when convicts and political dissenters were forcibly sent to the New World. These so-called undesirables were gratefully received by the Englishmen in America, to whom they were being sent. Scots had a reputation for being good soldiers, and the hope was that they would protect settlers from the "savage" heathen populations.[61] Such was the relative nature of identity in the transatlantic world that English settlers in the New World, when faced with Indians and a colonial existence thousands of miles away from the mother country, actively recruited even Scottish criminals, who would have been shunned "back home."

The Americans who put so much effort into luring Maclean across the Atlantic coveted his presence at their college in the same way that they cherished the fine imported goods that embellished their bodies and dwellings. Whether filling professional posts or their provincial homes, Americans invested a great deal of time and money to acquire some refinement in their small corner of the world. In a way similar to collectors of fine porcelain, the college's trustees found a suitably grand way to best showcase their acquisition: they erected a new building on their grounds to house Dr. Maclean and his family. As Benjamin Silliman suggested, the Scottish doctor represented to aspiring American intellectuals the brilliance of European science, and the possession of his shining light would help illuminate America. If the United States was going to establish itself as a civilized nation, it would need more men like Maclean. The importation of their bodies across the Atlantic formed the links in a chain of migration between Scotland and America that marked the United States as a materially and intellectually dependent nation.

Like glassware, knowledge was an object, and when such knowledge was embodied in human form, then particular human bodies became valued objects. Bodies, like books, could provide a vessel in which one could transport knowledge. Seen in this way, the story of Maclean, like that of the imported glassware, can be described as a tale about increasing the value of an object as you move it from one location, where the object is abundant, to another location where it is scarce.

"THE RAW AND THE COOKED": THE UNITED STATES AND SCOTLAND REDUX

The transatlantic paths of exchange were crowded, and they flowed in both directions during the post-Revolutionary period, just as they had done throughout the colonial era. Mapping the geography of value during that era, and describing the economy of relative location which drove the movements of goods, highlights the changing values of objects as they moved from one site in the Anglo-American transatlantic world to another, and the ways these disparities in value functioned as the basis of a post-colonial relationship between the United States and Britain.

Embedded in this notion of a geography of value was a series of networks of exchange between specific places such as Philadelphia and Edinburgh, Philadelphia and London, and London and Edinburgh. Scots were particularly adept at reading and profiting from this economy of relative location, as evidenced by their success in dominating the tobacco market.[62] Another example of their prowess in profiting from this system was the upward mobility and success of Scottish elites, who, in comparison with their English counterparts, were more willing to export themselves and their knowledge of medicine, science, religion, governance, warfare, and trade to far-flung corners of the British Empire. For instance, a surplus of Scottish graduates at one node of the transatlantic world and a lack of formally educated men at another node in America created a viable network of exchange. Relative Scottish abundance and American need explains both the importation of intellectuals into the former colonies and the enticement of Scots to export their own bodies to the outer reaches of the Anglo-American transatlantic network. The significance of Scottish influence on American culture that intellectual historians, immigration historians, and economic historians have traced can be attributed to the fact that Scottish immigrants fulfilled America's needs in the years after independence. As mentioned previously, Americans' "respect and admiration for Scotland's cultural achievements clearly continued to grow in Philadelphia" over the course of the eighteenth century.[63] Members of the new nation looked across the Atlantic Ocean to Scottish universities to provide them with the expertise needed to establish domestic institutions. For their part, those who decided to come to the United States enjoyed more professional and social success than they could have hoped to attain back in Europe. The willingness of Scots to leave home reflected Scotland's relative lack of power and cultural status vis-à-vis England within the Union.

What unites the objects imported by Americans from Britain is that in one way or another they represented refinement to the Americans who purchased them. Goods made in Scotland, England, and China—books, journals, porcelain tea sets, intricate telescopes, taper-necked glass beakers, and Scottish graduates of the Edinburgh school of medicine—all represented civility in one form or another. On the other hand, the American products that were used to trade for these civilized goods were seen as products of unrefined nature—seeds, dried plant specimen, tobacco, and cotton. Once arriving in Britain, these products would be reworked and refined, and often sold back at a profit to the Americans who originally procured them. As David Hosack's rising trajectory from American provincial to a member of the international scientific community illustrates, of course, there was an alternate way for Americans to profit from this system. In the doctor's case, he increased his personal value by crossing the Atlantic to obtain the polish of the Old World, with the plan to return home triumphantly after refining himself.

The biographies of Hosack and Maclean illustrate the way in which agents could profit from moving between Scotland and America. What also needs to be emphasized, however, is the subjective side of this geography of exchange and the way in which the asymmetry of power between these two locations influenced the lives of its participants during the post-Revolutionary period. In that regard, a final example in the form of the unorthodox career trajectory of Benjamin Smith Barton complicates the rules of exchange as previously outlined.[64] Its beginning is similar to the others: after training for a time in Philadelphia, Barton went to the University of Edinburgh to obtain a more prestigious medical diploma. He returned to the United States three years later in 1789 to a take up a position on the faculty of the University of Pennsylvania. So far, Barton had done everything according plan; he was now a respected doctor whose foreign credentials marked him as having a superior education. Unknown to the public, however, Barton had failed to earn his degree while abroad.[65] Fearing that his success in the United States was dependent on him holding a Scottish degree, Barton did nothing to disabuse anyone of this misapprehension.[66]

Nearly seven years later, Barton's correspondence with individuals at various European institutions records his increasingly desperate efforts to secretly arrange for an honorary degree. Although he managed to serve successfully for almost a decade as a faculty member at the University of Pennsylvania, Barton's lack of credentials obviously haunted him. In a letter to a foreign correspondent, he explained his desire for a European degree by denigrating the value of an American degree. He falsely claimed that it had been "several years since I received the degree of *Medical Doctor* from an university [the University of Pennsylvania] which, I confess, I do not much respect."[67] Although he was denied by several places, to Barton's great relief he finally obtained an honorary degree from the University of Kiel in 1796.[68]

The fact that Benjamin Smith Barton, a man without a degree, was a well-respected professor of medicine at the most prestigious medical school in the United States sheds light on the nation's status as a developing nation. Despite his shortcomings, his career flourished according to the logic of exchange described in this essay. Barton's success was a result of his ability to maximize the benefits of his European experience, and he never missed a chance to maximize the benefits of his European contacts. Although his lack of formal credentials seemed inconsequential to his career, it held a tremendous amount of symbolic significance as reflected in his attempts to obtain a degree from abroad by any means necessary. Despite his numerous publications, and his position in America, Barton still considered himself a fraud without approval from Europe.

The life stories of the individuals discussed here represent the effects of colonial and postcolonial subjecthood on the newly established United States through the lens of the transnational exchange of intellectuals and refined knowledge. The Revolution did not stop the flow of civilized, polished objects from Old World to New. Reflecting this structure of intellectual inequality, Americans continued to look to Britain for training in the sciences, arts, and technology. In this sense, independence was an important legal and political break, but much less drastically a material and cultural one.

LOST IN TRANSLATION? POSTCOLONIAL QUESTIONS

The asymmetrical relationship that remained between the United States as a newly independent nation and Great Britain, its mother country, is characteristic of the postcolonial condition in general. From the perspective of the early twenty-first century, with full knowledge of the eventual emergence of the United States as a world power, it is easy to believe that the nation was destined for greatness. When America split from British rule there was profound uncertainty about the present and future status of the nation, mingled with a sense of inferiority. One of the benefits of studying the history of other emerging nations is that we can see parallels between them and the early American republic that might otherwise be overlooked.[69]

To the disappointment of many new citizens, various inequities inherent in the colonial relationship remained, and in this sense the Revolutionary victory was the first rather than the last step in gaining independence.[70] As Ashis Nandy has aptly observed, "colonialism never seems to end with formal political freedom."[71] Postcolonial scholars have developed nuanced ways to analyze the cultural inferiority that remains after a society gains political independence.[72] They have shown how a "country may be both postcolonial (in the sense of being formally independent) and neo-colonial (in the sense of remaining economically and/or culturally dependent)," although one cannot "dismiss the importance of either formal decolonisation, or the fact that unequal power relations of colonial rule are reinscribed in the contemporary imbalances between 'first' and 'third' world nations."[73]

Before advancing further, the question must be asked: can the United States of America be included under the rubric of postcolonial studies? While acknowledging that this approach has the potential to "redefine central topics in early American history" and "bring it into renewed and deeper dialogue" with more traditional analyses, American historians such as Joyce Chaplin have expressed doubts.[74] These are understandable, considering that postcolonial theory is most often applied to societies in which "native" or "indigenous" peoples regained control of their land and its governance from European imperial rule. Although we must be vigilant about recognizing the ways in which the United States differs significantly from this definition, there are useful comparisons to be made.[75] After all, even those sites usually placed under the rubric of postcolonial scholarship vary greatly from one another, given their social, cultural, and geographical particularities. In light of these differences, shared characteristics can be attributed to their shared colonial experiences.

In the case of America, settlers were simultaneously colonials under the British Empire and colonizers who exploited and controlled the land and labor of Native Americans and African Americans. After shedding their colonial status, they maintained control of the territory that became known as the United States of America.[76] One of the strongest reserva-

tions expressed about applying postcolonial theory to the American context is the danger of "valorizing of accomplishments linked with one racial group that, if anything, continued the colonial legacy of the imperial
era." I agree that it would be wrongheaded to invoke postcolonial theory
in order to "assert the myth of American exceptionalism: the triumphal
view of American history" by portraying "white settlers as heroes who
overcame the British Empire,"[77] and I hope this essay has suggested the
opposite. Historians of early America can benefit from the insights of postcolonial studies to better understand the mechanism powering oppression
in early America. From this view, racism was a function of perceived and
real weakness within a transnational context, rather than solely a function
of power within the domestic sphere.

As for reservations regarding the valorization of those white postcolonial settlers otherwise known as "founding fathers," it is not my intention to demonize or heroicize. Rather, I wish to apply the same standards
of analysis to them as scholars have done for members of later postcolonial societies in Asia and Africa. To assume that the founding generation
felt *no* anxieties regarding their colonial status—if only because of their
whiteness—is equally misguided. As freeborn whites, Anglo-American
settlers certainly enjoyed rights denied to racial minorities living under
British rule, but excluding them entirely from a postcolonial framework
mirrors the same exceptionalist thinking historians have been urged to
avoid.

Although, as mentioned, postcolonial theory has tended to focus on
what has been called "exploitation" colonies in densely populated societies in Africa, Asia, and the Middle East, a subfield focuses specifically on
settler colonies.[78] One of the unique challenges that postcolonial settler
populations faced was the dual task of constructing a sense of belonging, indeed of indigeneity, while at the same time maintaining the power
and privilege granted them by their European inheritance.[79] This duality,
and the tensions it created, has been noted in a variety of temporal and
geographic locations, including postcolonial America. Although they may
have "unsettled" the British Empire with their successful revolutionary
bid for independence, the newly empowered settler population, when
dealing with people of color, did not set about "dismantling" the recently
evacuated structures of power and exploitation they helped build under
the aegis of the British Empire. On the contrary, they were ready, willing,
and able to move in and inhabit them. As Chaplin notes, the Revolution
"removed British *imperialism* only, not white *colonization* in America."[80]

The recognition of the continuity across the political divide between
colony and nation is a vital commonality shared by a strand of postcolo-

nial scholarship that focuses on lingering forms of colonial dependence postdating independence.[81] In early America, the ability to replicate the civilizing and controlling force of the British state, even if exerted unevenly and with limited success, was crucial to the settlers' break from the empire.[82] Postcolonial scholarship draws attention to the importance of the cultural aspects of the colonial experience and their political, social, and economic implications for the nation.[83] Certainly if one's main intellectual project is to study the organization of formal political institutions, the Revolutionary break represents a seismic shift in the terrain. For cultural historians, however, the tremors are less earthshaking, that is, the hierarchical cultural and social relationships between the mother country and her provincial elite offspring were shaken, not severed.

Although some things may be lost in translation, postcolonial scholars pose vital and unavoidable questions about the legacies of the colonial experience that can enrich the study of American history.[84] Their insights help historians understand the legacy of oppression of minority groups in the United States as well as illuminate the experience of the European American settlers. Long before postcolonial theory gained widespread attention, historians of the most dispossessed groups in American society—be they racial, class, or gender—noted that the Revolution was not as "revolutionary" as one would hope and that the founding generation did not go far enough in their historic bid for freedom. In particular, historians of the African American experience compellingly made the case for the failure of American leaders to apply their democratic principles to every member of society.

When examining early American culture from a postcolonial perspective, acts of violence and oppression enacted by the settler community can be viewed as both expressions of power and symptoms of powerlessness vis-à-vis larger economic and cultural systems. In areas of culture and commerce such as science, medicine, cartography, and manufacturing, the United States remained dominated by Europe, and in particular by the "mother country."[85] Thus, early Americans' celebration of their exceptionalism can also be seen as an embrace of weakness or, to put it more positively, making the most of what they had. Americans in the post-Revolutionary period spent a great deal of energy trying to justify their distinctiveness as both insiders and outsiders of the powerful empire to which they had once belonged. They vacillated between defensiveness and celebration of their cultural hybridity. To critical European observers and surely to African Americans and Native Americans who were subject to their actions, white Americans increasingly evinced a volatile mixture of arrogance and ignorance.[86]

Despite the arrival (and as the editors of this collection note, the departure) of the American Century and the economic and military dominance of the United States, there is still a popular belief that the United States lacks cultural refinement and an accurate understanding of the world around it. Contemporary Americans who are aware of the nation's increasingly shaky position as a global power may benefit from studying this tenuous period when the nation faced similar problems of legitimacy. Critics have pointed to the leaders' disregard for international affairs as one of the contributing factors of the nation's downfall. Perhaps this unbecoming tendency did not originate from the United States' dominance in world affairs but rather from the legacy of the founding generation's failure to measure up to international standards in the nation's nascent years.

Notes

I thank Brian Edwards and Dilip Gaonkar for including me in this volume and for their editorial comments and useful suggestions. It has been a pleasure to work with them and the other scholars who have been a part of this project. Thanks also to my research assistant Bobby Smiley.

The epigraphs are from the following publications: [Timothy Dwight], "An Essay on American Genius," *New Haven Gazette and Connecticut Magazine*, February 1, 1787; and Noah Webster, "On the Education of Youth in America" (1788), reprinted in *Essays on Education in the Early Republic,* ed. Frederick Rudolph (Cambridge: Harvard University Press, 1965), 64–65.

1. David Hosack was born on August 31, 1769, in New York City. He was the first son of Alexander and Jane Hosack of Elgin, Scotland. His paternal grandfather was born at Cromarty, and his grandmother Isabel Dunn had come from Eligin, Morayshire, where Alexander was born. Alexander joined the British army in 1755 at nineteen and was stationed in Ireland and then Halifax. Hosack's father had come to America from Elgin, Scotland, via a tour in the British army.

2. Hosack married Catharine "Kitty" Warner on April 14, 1791, in Princeton, New Jersey. The Rev. Samuel Stanhope Smith officiated. Christine Robbins, *David Hosack: Citizen of New York* (Philadelphia: American Philosophical Society, 1964), 22. Hosack's teachers had studied in Edinburgh as well. Most of the leading physicians and men of science in the preceding generation were graduates of Edinburgh. They include Adam Kuhn, who received his degree in 1767; Benjamin Rush (1768); Samuel Bard (1765); and Samuel Latham Mitchill (1786). See Deborah Brunton, "Edinburgh and Philadelphia: The Scottish Model of Medical Education," in *Scottish Universities: Distinctiveness and Diversity*, ed. Jennifer Carter and Donald Withrington (Edinburgh: John Donald Publishers, 1992), 80–85.

3. Letter of introduction written for Benjamin Smith Barton by Benjamin Rush to William Cullen, June 17, 1786, Miscellaneous Manuscripts Collection, American Philosophical Society.

4. Alexander E. Hosack, "Memoir of the Late David Hosack by His Son," in *Lives of Eminent American Physicians and Surgeons of the 19th Century*, ed. S. D. Gross, 289–337 (Philadelphia, 1861). American physicians in the post-Revolutionary period observed that their American patients showed "superior deference" to "European-trained" physicians and scien-

tists. See William Smallwood and Mabel Smallwood, *Natural History and the American Mind* (New York: Columbia University Press, 1941), 151–52.

5. Robbins, *David Hosack*, 294.

6. American artists in the colonial and post-Revolutionary period experienced the same. The most successful American-born painters such as Benjamin West went to England to study. West ended up staying and becoming historical painter to King George III. He mentored many American artists who, like the physicians discussed here, went to Europe for training, such as Gilbert Stuart, John Trumbull, Thomas Sully, Charles Willson Peale, and Rembrandt Peale.

7. American post-Revolutionary dependence on Britain was not limited to knowledge production; it extended to material and economic exchange. At the end of the eighteenth century, the United States was the largest consumer of British exports in the world. Americans not only imported goods, but they also continued to emulate the manner in which the goods were displayed and consumed in Great Britain. See P. J. Marshall, "Britain without America?—A Second Empire?" in *The Eighteenth Century*, vol. 2 of *The Oxford History of the British Empire*, ed. P. J. Marshall (New York: Oxford University Press, 1998), 576–95.

8. Marcel Mauss, *The Gift: Forms and Functions of Exchange in Archaic Societies* (1923–24; reprint, London: Routledge, 1990), 1.

9. Andrew Hook, "Philadelphia, Edinburgh and the Scottish Enlightenment," in *Scotland and America in the Age of Enlightenment*, ed. Richard B. Sher and Jeffrey R. Smitten (Edinburgh: Edinburgh University Press, 1990), 232–33.

10. F. A. Wendeborn, *A View of England towards the Close of The Eighteenth Century*, 2 vols., trans. from the German by the author (London: Printed for G. G. J. and J. Robinson, Paternoster-Row, 1791), quotation at 1:374. For a Scottish response to Samuel Johnson's description of Scotland, see Donald MacNicol, *Remarks on Dr. Samuel Johnson's Journey to the Hebrides; in Which Are Contained Observations on the Antiquities, Language, Genius, and Manners of the Highlanders of Scotland* (London: Printed for T. Cadell, 1779).

11. See Michael Duffy, *The English Satirical Print, 1600–1832: Englishman and the Foreigner* (Cambridge: Chadwyck-Healey, 1986), 18–19.

12. See Andrew Mackillop, *More Fruitful Than the Soil: Army, Empire and the Scottish Highlands, 1715–1815* (East Linton: Tuckwell Press, 2000); Andrew Mackillop and Steve Murdoch, eds., *Military Governors and Imperial Frontiers, 1600–1800* (Leiden: Brill, 2003); Douglas Hamilton, *Scotland, the Caribbean and the Atlantic World, 1750–1820* (Manchester: Manchester University Press, 2005); Angela McCarthy, ed., *A Global Clan: Scottish Migrant Networks and Identities since the Eighteenth Century* (London: Tauris Academic Studies, 2006). For the earlier period, see Alexia Grosjean and Steve Murdoch, eds., *Scottish Communities Abroad in the Early Modern Period* (Leiden: Brill, 2005). For material culture perspectives on the far-flung Scottish population, see Maggie Keswick, ed., *The Thistle and the Jade* (London: Octopus Books, 1982), which covers the China trade; and Ann Buddle, ed., *The Tiger and the Thistle* (Edinburgh: National Galleries of Scotland, 1999).

13. This argument was outlined in the influential article by John Clive and Bernard Bailyn and later developed and refined by scholars such as Ned Landsman, *Scotland and Its First American Colony, 1683–1765* (Princeton: Princeton University Press, 1985); Landsman, "Scotland, the American Colonies and the Development of British Provincial Identity," in *An Imperial State at War: Britain from 1689 to 1815*, ed. Lawrence Stone (New York: Routledge Press, 1994); Landsman, "The Legacy of British Union for the North American Colonies: Provincial Elites and the Problem of Imperial Union," in *A Union for Empire: Political Thought and the British Union of 1707*, ed. John Robertson (Cambridge: Cambridge University Press, 1995), 297–317.

14. Finlay notes this "tendency amongst some scholars to argue that certain dimen-

sions of Scottish society—Church, law, education et al. acted to somehow preserve a pristine, untainted Scottishness underneath the essentially 'political' umbrella of Britishness. These distinctive civic forums undoubtedly preserved a sense of Scottishness, but they were also vital in determining the nature, methods, effectiveness and pattern of Scotland's integration within the domestic Union and, crucially, the empire at large." See R. J. Finlay, "Caledonia or North Britain? Scottish Identity in the Nineteenth Century," in *Image and Identity: The Making and Re-Making of Scotland through the Ages*, ed. Dauvit Broun, R. J. Finlay, and Michael Lynch (Edinburgh: John Donald Publishers, 1998).

15. This pattern was common among elite Americans during this period. For a full discussion of the phenomenon, see Kariann Akemi Yokota, *Unbecoming British: How Revolutionary America Became a Post-Colonial Nation* (New York: Oxford University Press, forthcoming), esp. chap. 4.

16. I discuss James Rush's experience in greater detail in Kariann Akemi Yokota, "'To Pursue the Stream to Its Fountain': Race, Inequality, and the Post-Colonial Exchange of Knowledge across the Atlantic," *Explorations in Early American Culture: A Journal of Mid-Atlantic Studies* 5 (2001): 173–229.

17. James Rush, "Journal of a Voyage across the Atlantic in the Year 1809," Benjamin Rush Papers, box 13, Library Company of Philadelphia (LCP).

18. Benjamin Rush to James Rush, June 8 and February 7, 1810, Benjamin Rush Papers, box 11, LCP.

19. As Gordon Wood described it, "no metropolitan Englishman could have matched the awe felt by the Pennsylvanian. . . . It was as if he were 'on sacred ground' and he 'gazed for some time at the throne with emotions that I cannot describe.'" Rush pleaded with his "reluctant guide to let him sit upon it 'for a considerable time,' even though the guide said that visitors rarely did so. The experience was unsettling, to say the least: 'I was seized with a kind of horror . . . and a crowd of ideas poured in upon my mind.' This was all a man could want in this world; 'his passions conceive, his hopes aspire after nothing beyond this throne.'" As quoted in Gordon S. Wood, *The Radicalism of the American Revolution* (New York: Knopf, 1992), 15.

20. James Rush to Benjamin Rush, September 28, 1809, Edinburgh, Benjamin Rush Papers, box 11, LCP. There are several studies of the intense antagonism between the Federalist and Republican parties, which James Rush refers to in this quote. For examples of recent studies, see Stanley Elkins and Eric McKitrick, *The Age of Federalism: The Early American Republic, 1788-1800* (New York: Oxford University Press, 1993); William Dowling, *Literary Federalism in the Age of Jefferson: Joseph Dennie and The "Port Folio," 1801-1812* (Columbia: University of South Carolina Press, 1999); and Doron Ben-Atar and Barbara Oberg, eds., *Federalists Reconsidered* (Charlottesville: University Press of Virginia, 1998).

21. James Rush to Julia Rush, October 25, 1809, Rush Correspondence, box 11, LCP.

22. James Rush to Benjamin Rush, March 29, 1810, Rush Correspondence, box 11, LCP.

23. Christine Chapman Robbins, "David Hosack's Herbarium and Its Linnaean Specimens," *Proceedings of the American Philosophical Society* 104, no. 3 (June 1960): 294.

24. Julie Flavell observes this phenomenon of the colonial period in Flavell, "'The School for Modesty and Humility': Colonial American Youth in London and Their Parents, 1755-1775," *Historical Journal* 42, no. 2 (1999): 377–403; see also William Sache, *The Colonial American in Britain* (Madison: University of Wisconsin Press, 1956).

25. Robbins, *David Hosack*, 26.

26. After Elgin Gardens was donated to Columbia University, it fell into disrepair. Eventually, the university leased the neglected land, which in the 1930s became the site of Rockefeller Center.

27. Robbins, *David Hosack*, 26.

28. For example, Nuttall's *The Genera of North American Plants* (1818) and *An Introduction to Systematic and Physiological Botany* (1827) gained widespread attention in Europe and renewed interest in the United States. Thomas Nuttall, *The Genera of North American Plants* (Philadelphia: Printed for the author by D. Heartt, 1818); Thomas Nuttall, *An Introduction to Systematic and Physiological Botany* (Boston: Hilliard, Gray, Little, and Wilkins, and Richardson and Lord, 1827).

29. Alexander Wilson, the son of a humble distiller, was born in 1766 in Paisley, Scotland. Although he apprenticed as a weaver, his first love was poetry. Wilson's faced political trouble over his satirical verses, which criticized the inequalities between workers and local manufacturers. He was forced to burn his writings publicly and serve time in jail. These events compelled him to come to America in 1794. For a nineteenth-century biography of Wilson, see George Ord, *Sketch of the Life of Alexander Wilson, Author of the American Ornithology* (Philadelphia: H. Hall, 1828), 16. His biography mirrors that of many Britons who escaped difficulties and increased their social standing by importing themselves to the United States. The first volume of *American Ornithology* was published in 1808; the last one came out in 1814.

30. William Guthrie's *Geographical Grammar: A New Geographical, Historical, and Commercial Grammar* was first published in London in 1770 and later went through several editions, including three in Edinburgh in the years 1790 and 1799, and three editions in Montrose, Scotland, in 1807, 1808, and 1810. By 1827 twenty-four editions had been published, and in 1842 new editions were still being issued. John Rennie Short, "A New Mode of Thinking," in *Surveying the Record: North American Scientific Exploration to 1930*, Memoirs of the American Philosophical Society, vol. 231 (Philadelphia: American Philosophical Society, 1999), 23.

31. Short, "New Mode of Thinking," 26.

32. William Sprague, *The Life of Jedidiah Morse, D.D.* (New York: Anson D. F. Randolph, 1874), 192. Sprague's book is the classic biography of Morse.

33. Ibid., 15.

34. Jedidiah Morse, *American Universal Geography* (Boston: Thomas and Andrews, 1793), 1:vi–vii.

35. Sprague, *Life of Jedidiah Morse*, 192. Sprague's biography was published for Morse's sons, who did not live to see it in print. Although lacking in critical scholarly analysis, it includes numerous important letters, many of which have not survived. Judging from letters that did survive, the author seems to have made faithful copies. For Morse's religious views, see especially Joseph Phillips, *Jedidiah Morse and New England Congregationalism* (New Brunswick, NJ: Rutgers University Press, 1983), but also James King, *Jedidiah Morse, a Champion of New England Orthodoxy* (New York: Columbia University Press, 1939).

36. Jedidiah Morse, *Geography Made Easy: Being a Short, but Comprehensive System of That Very Useful and Agreeable Science*, 1st ed. (New Haven: Meigs, Bowen and Dana, 1784). Undertaken shortly after Morse's graduation from Yale, the book was drawn from his lectures on the subject at a school for young women in New Haven. While pursuing his studies in theology at Yale College, the Federalist and Congregationalist Jedidiah Morse ran a school for young women in New Haven. For a biography that attempts to use psychological evidence to understand the life of Morse, see Richard Moss, *The Life of Jedidiah Morse: A Station of Peculiar Exposure* (Knoxville: University of Tennessee Press, 1995). See also Ralph Brown, "The American Geographies of Jedidiah Morse," *Annals of the Association of American Geographers* 31 (1941): 145–217.

37. Morse, *Geography Made Easy*. Richard Turner, born in 1753, was a 1733 graduate of Oxford. His *New and Easy Introduction to Universal Geography* (London, 1780) was of "an elementary character" and written as a series of letters. It reached its thirteenth edition in 1808. Bolstered by his success with that book, he wrote *An Easy Introduction to the Arts and*

Sciences (London, 1783). It also was very popular and used as a standard schoolbook for several years. Over time Turner made additions and corrections to the book, and by 1811 it had reached its fourteenth edition. *Dictionary of National Biography*, s. v. "Turner, Richard." Martin Bruckner makes the connection between the two works in *The Geographic Revolution in Early America: Maps, Literacy, and National Identity* (Chapel Hill: University of North Carolina Press, 2006), 115.

38. Jedidiah Morse to Christoph Ebeling, May 27, 1794, Manuscripts and Archives, Yale University Library.

39. Short, "New Mode of Thinking," 29.

40. Morse, *American Universal Geography*, 1:v–vi.

41. William Guthrie, *Geographical Grammar: A New Geographical, Historical, and Commercial Grammar; And Present State of the Several Kingdoms of the World . . . With a Table of the Coins of All Nations, and Their Value in English Money* (London: J. Knox, 1771), 502. See Robert Mayhew, "William Guthrie's *Geographical Grammar*, the Scottish Enlightenment and the Politics of British Geography," *Scottish Geographical Journal* 115 (1999): 1, 29.

42. Mayhew, "William Guthrie's *Geographical Grammar*," 29.

43. Morse, *American Universal Geography*, 1:vi–vii.

44. The first volume of the second edition of Morse's *Geography* concentrated on the "Western Continent," with the vast majority of it devoted to the United States. It can properly be considered a second edition of his 1789 work. In the four years that had passed since the publication of the first edition, many changes had taken place in the new nation. Morse found that many additions and corrections were needed. See Sprague, *Life of Jedidiah Morse*, 207.

45. Ibid., 206, 207. Considered an American patriotic gesture of independence, the content was strikingly similar both in its adoption of the genre of geographic writing and in the literal copying of British content.

46. Morse, *American Universal Geography*, 1:vi–vii.

47. John Stockdale to Jedidiah Morse, March 16, 1793, Manuscripts and Archives Division, New York Public Library, New York.

48. See the pamphlet by James Freeman, *Remarks on the American Universal Geography* (Boston: Belknap and Hall, 1793).

49. Mayhew, "William Guthrie's *Geographical Grammar*."

50. Stephen Elliott, *American Journal of Science and Arts* 9 (1825): 276.

51. Instructors who taught natural history and natural philosophy in universities engaged in other activities in order to make a living. For example, Benjamin Smith Barton, Samuel Latham Mitchill, and Benjamin Waterhouse were physicians, served on the medical faculty, and taught natural history as a secondary commitment. Mitchill was also a local politician. Astronomers David Rittenhouse and Andrew Ellicott worked as surveyors and clock makers, and held other jobs to support their families. Henry Ernest Muhlenberg, James Madison, and Manasseh Cutler were clergymen.

52. Samuel Stanhope Smith, circular letter, 1790, box 1, C0028, Princeton Library Collections, Firestone Library.

53. Alice Walters, "Conversation Pieces: Science and Politeness in Eighteenth-Century England," *History of Science* 35 (1997): 121–54.

54. Smith, circular letter, 1790, Firestone Library.

55. Samuel Stanhope Smith, circular letter, January 19, 1796; and Smith to Sam[ue]l Bayard, December 26, 1796; both in box 1, C0028, Princeton Library Collections, Firestone Library.

56. Rush, a 1760 graduate of the College of New Jersey, was a booster of the college and talked Maclean into going to Princeton, knowing it would be beneficial to his alma mater. He

was instrumental in convincing many Scottish intellectuals to join the faculties of American institutions of higher education. The most famous of his "recruits" was the illustrious Scottish minister John Witherspoon. While studying medicine at the University of Edinburgh, the "ingratiating" young Rush, as he is referred to by L. H. Butterfield, was summoned by Witherspoon to convince his wife to move to America. It was said that she became physically ill at the thought of it. Butterfield notes that Rush's tactics mirrored those of the Americans sent to Britain to raise funds for the church. The stance Rush took was that America was like a child in the woods in need of Scottish guidance. "The young daughter of the Church of Scotland, helpless and exposed in this foreign land, cries to her tender and powerful parent for relief." L. H. Butterfield, *John Witherspoon Comes to America* (Princeton: Princeton University Library, 1953), xii.

57. John Maclean, Jr. (tenth president of the college), *Memoir of John Maclean, M.D. The First Professor of Chemistry in the College of New Jersey* (Princeton: Princeton Press, 1885), 21.

58. His father, John Maclean, Sr., was the son of the Rev. Archibald Maclean, minister of the parish of Kilfinichen, Scotland. His mother was Agnes Lang of Glasgow. Shortly after his parents were married, his father went to Canada as a surgeon in the British army and was serving General Wolfe in 1759 when Quebec was won from the French. There is a story, perhaps apocryphal, that he was the third man to scale the Heights of Abraham in the attack of Quebec. After ending his service to the army, Maclean, Sr., returned to Glasgow and practiced surgery there until his death. Both of Maclean's parents died relatively young. John, the youngest of their children, and born in 1771, was raised by a guardian.

59. Maclean studied in Paris during the height of the careers of famous men such as Lavoisier, Berthollet, and Fourcroy. While in Paris he embraced the new system of chemistry that was developing there.

60. Maclean, *Memoir,* 21.

61. See the introduction to Grosjean and Murdoch, *Scottish Communities Abroad in the Early Modern Period,* 13. In his essay in that collection, David Dobson shows how, in the seventeenth century, leaders of the Virginia colony recruited Scottish criminals who, they assumed, would protect them from the native population. Dobson, "Seventeenth-Century Scottish Communities in the Americas," in Grosjean and Murdoch, *Scottish Communities Abroad in the Early Modern Period,* 105-34.

62. T. M. Devine, *The Tobacco Lords: A Study of Tobacco Merchants of Glasgow and Their Trading Activities, 1740-90* (Edinburgh: Donald, 1975).

63. Hook, "Philadelphia, Edinburgh and the Scottish Enlightenment," 232-33.

64. For a longer discussion of Benjamin Smith Barton, see Yokota, "To Pursue the Stream to Its Fountain."

65. The sudden departure of a successful student from the institution he had traveled across the Atlantic to attend, and right before he was to graduate, raises many questions. It seems Barton left Edinburgh late in winter 1788 with money belonging to several prominent societies and physicians, including the Royal Medical Society, the Speculative Society, and a prominent Edinburgh physician known for his patronage of overseas Americans. For investigations into this scandal, see Whitfield Bell, Jr., "Benjamin Smith Barton, M.D. (Kiel)," *Journal of the History of Medicine and Allied Sciences* 26, no. 2 (1971): 197-203; Theodore Jeffries, "A Biographical Note on Benjamin Smith Barton (1766-1815)," *Isis* 60, no. 2 (Summer 1969): 231; D. B. Shumway, "Benjamin Smith Barton," address at the University of Pennsylvania, delivered in 1916, and published in *Papers of the Lancaster County Historical Society* 28 (1924): 59-66; Francis W. Pennell, "Benjamin Smith Barton as Naturalist," *Proceedings of the American Philosophical Society* 86 (1943): 108-22, esp. 110. I found evidence of this incident in various manuscript collections, including the Benjamin Smith Barton Papers, Historical Society of Pennsylvania; the Violetta W. Delafield Collection of the Benjamin Smith Barton Papers,

American Philosophical Society; and the Benjamin Rush Papers, especially Rush Correspondence, bound letterbook, vol. 27, "Drs. Barton, Coxe, Hosack & Miller," LCP.

66. Indeed, some of Barton's family knew he had not finished his degree. While in Europe, he wrote to his elder brother William that upon his return he planned to reenroll at his old school and finally earn his medical credentials. At the moment of his return, however, the twenty-three-year-old Barton was welcomed to the faculty instead. Some scholars posit that because he was gone for the appropriate amount of time, the medical faculty had simply assumed that Barton had received a degree. Bell, "Benjamin Smith Barton," 197–203.

67. Ibid.

68. Benjamin Smith Barton to Scheling, May 11, 1796, Barton Papers, Historical Society of Pennsylvania. When signing his name to the bottom of this letter, the title "M.D." is inserted by Barton above the signature as an afterthought.

69. For discussions on the exclusion of whites from postcolonial theory, see Steve Slemon, "Unsettling the Empire: Resistance Theory for the Second World," in *The Post-Colonial Studies Reader*, ed. Bill Ashcroft, Gareth Griffiths, and Helen Tiffin (New York: Routledge, 1995), 104–10. See also Peter Hulme, "Including America," in *Ariel: A Review of International English Literatures* 26, no. 1 (January 1995): 117–23.

70. In his recent essay, Jack Greene has called for a "a recognition of the profound continuities between the colonial and national segments of the American past." Greene, "Colonial History and National History: Reflections on a Continuing Problem," *William and Mary Quarterly* 64, no. 2 (April 2007): 235–50.

71. Ashis Nandy, *The Intimate Enemy: Loss and Recovery of Self under Colonialism* (Delhi: Oxford University Press, 1983), 3.

72. See, for instance, Bill Ashcroft, Gareth Griffiths, and Helen Tiffin, eds., *The Post-Colonial Studies Reader* (London: Routledge, 1995); Homi Bhabha, *Nation and Narration* (New York: Routledge, 1990); Homi Bhabha, *The Location of Culture* (New York: Routledge, 1994); Patrick Williams and Laura Chrisman, eds., *Colonial Discourse and Post-Colonial Theory* (Hemel Hempstead: Harvester Wheatsheaf, 1993); Ranajit Guha and Gayatri Chakravorty Spivak, eds., *Selected Subaltern Studies* (New York: Oxford University Press, 1988); Gyan Prakash, "Subaltern Studies as Post-Colonial Criticism," *American Historical Review* 99, no. 5 (December 1994): 1475–90. Classic studies include Frantz Fanon, *The Wretched of the Earth*, trans. Constance Farrington (New York: Grove Press, 1963); C. L.R. James, *The Black Jacobins* (New York: Vintage Books, 1963); and Albert Memmi, *The Colonizer and the Colonized* (Boston: Beacon Press, 1965).

73. Ania Loomba, *Colonialism/Post-Colonialism* (New York: Routledge, 2000), 7.

74. For a useful exposition on these issues, see Joyce E. Chaplin, "Expansion and Exceptionalism in Early American History," *Journal of American History*, March 2003, http://www.historycooperative.org/journals/jah/89.4/chaplin.html (accessed October 8, 2009). As Chaplin notes in her review essay, other scholars have expressed skepticism regarding the use of the term "postcolonial"; see, for instance, Hulme, "Including America." See also the roundtable, published in the *William and Mary Quarterly*, discussing Jack Greene's "Colonial History and National History." Responses include my own, which elaborates on the ideas presented here: Kariann Akemi Yokota, "Post-Colonialism and Material Culture in the Early United States," *William and Mary Quarterly* 64, no. 2 (2007): 263–70.

75. Some scholars who have examined the United States take into account issues of the postcolonial condition and imperialism. Most useful is Robert Blair St. George, introduction to *Possible Pasts: Becoming Colonial in Early America*, ed. Robert Blair St. George (Ithaca, NY: Cornell University Press, 2000); and Michael Warner, "What's Colonial about Colonial America?" in Blair St. George, *Possible Pasts*, 50. See also Amy Kaplan and Donald Pease, eds., *Cultures of United States Imperialism* (Durham, NC: Duke University Press, 1993); and esp.

Amy Kaplan, "'Left Alone with America': The Absence of Empire in the Study of American Culture," in Kaplan and Pease, *Cultures of United States Imperialism*, 3–21; Amritjit Singh and Peter Schmidt, eds., *Post-Colonial Theory and the United States: Race, Ethnicity, and Literature* (Jackson: University Press of Mississippi, 2000). See also Malini Johar Schueller and Edward Watts, eds., *Messy Beginnings: Post-Coloniality and Early American Studies* (New Brunswick, NJ: Rutgers University Press, 2003). For studies that examine literature in the early republic, while taking postcolonial perspectives and issues into account, see Leonard Tennenhouse, *The Importance of Feeling English: American Literature and the British Diaspora, 1750–1850* (Princeton: Princeton University Press, 2007); Edward Watts, *Writing and Post-Colonialism in the Early Republic* (Charlottesville: University Press of Virginia, 1998); Lawrence Buell, "Melville and the Question of American Decolonization," *American Literature* 64, no. 2. (June 1992): 215–37; Leonard Tennenhouse, "The Americanization of Clarissa," *Yale Journal of Criticism* 11, no. 1 (1998): 177–96; and Richard Helgerson, "Language Lessons: Linguistic Colonialism, Linguistic Post-Colonialism, and the Early Modern English Nation," *Yale Journal of Criticism* 11, no. 1 (1998): 289–300. As a whole, scholarship that has considered the United States from a postcolonial perspective has come out of the fields of literary theory and literature, rather than history. For recent historical studies that engage in the importance of empire in the development of the American nation, see Peter Onuf, *Jefferson's Empire: The Language of American Nationhood* (Charlottesville: University Press of Virginia, 2000); and Francis Jennings, *The Creation of America: Through Revolution to Empire* (New York: Cambridge University Press, 2000).

76. Scholars have discussed the particularities of "settler colonies" such as New Zealand, Canada, Australia, and the United States, and debated their place in the field of postcolonial studies. See, for instance, the influential volume, Bill Ashcroft, Gareth Griffiths, and Helen Tiffen, eds., *The Empire Writes Back: Theory and Practice in Post-Colonial Literature* (New York: Routledge, 1989); Steven Slemon, "The Scramble for Post-Colonialism," in *De-Scribing the Empire: Post-Colonialism and Textuality*, ed. Chris Tiffin and Alan Lawson (New York: Routledge, 1994), 15–32; Chris Prentice, "Some Problems of Response to Empire in Settler Post-Colonial Societies," in Tiffin and Lawson, *De-Scribing the Empire*, 45–60; and Alan Lawson, "A Cultural Paradigm for the Second World," *Australian and Canadian Studies* 9, no. 1 (1991): 67–78.

77. Chaplin, "Expansion and Exceptionalism in Early American History," 56.

78. The legacies of settler societies are being fought actively in the courts in New Zealand, Australia, and Canada, where First Peoples have begun to challenge the historical outcomes of land clearances and genocidal colonial policies, and to demand the restitution of cultural property.

79. Ashcroft, Griffiths, and Tiffen, *Empire Writes Back*, 134.

80. Chaplin observes that several non-Americanists have made this point previously. She writes: "Independent Americans were postimperial, not post-colonial." Chaplin, "Expansion and Exceptionalism in Early American History," 56. In light of this point, she believes that the label "postcolonial" no longer make sense. Although I agree with this differentiation in spirit, I am not similarly inclined to drop the use of the term because I adhere to a definition that is at the same time more literal and less literal. It is more literal in terms of its temporal definition, meaning after the colonial period. I argue that the term "postcolonial" invokes applicable notions of cultural inferiority inherent in the colonial relationship.

81. Works such as Partha Chatterjee's *Nationalist Thought and the Colonial World: A Derivative Discourse* (London: Zed Books for the United Nations University, 1986) argue that the discourse of independence in decolonizing movements is in fact derivative of what it seeks to repudiate, depending as they did on reproducing forms of nationalism for their success.

82. In his essay in the *William and Mary Quarterly*, Jack Greene points out that the adoption of the British systems of jurisprudence and racial subordination provided "protections" for the rebelling settlers' self-interest. Although useful, this emphasis on formal centralizing forces and on "governance and law" can mask other equally important aspects of historical analysis.

83. Scholars such as Homi Bhabha and Gayatri Spivak have used a range of theories— including deconstructionist literary criticism and psychoanalytic theory—to attack the model of center and periphery and the vesting of power only in the hands of the colonizer. They have emphasized instead the various forms of ambivalence that occur at the cultural level in colonial and postcolonial encounters. Although both of these authors focus mainly on India, which offers an inexact parallel with the United States, and focus mainly on literary texts, much of their work can help us understand the United States in its early years from a new perspective.

84. David Waldstreicher, *In the Midst of Perpetual Fetes: The Making of American Nationalism, 1776-1820* (Chapel Hill: Published for the Omohundro Institute of Early American History and Culture, Williamsburg, VA, by the University of North Carolina Press, 1997), richly illustrates the ambivalences of early national culture and politics, and has raised important questions about national identity for a new generation of scholars. Sean X. Goudie, *Creole America: The West Indies and the Formation of Literature and Culture in the New Republic* (Philadelphia: University of Pennsylvania Press, 2006), suggests the use of the term "paracolonialism" to analyze the unique relationship between the emerging American nation and the West Indies. By making this distinction, he makes the point that one cannot simply import and apply postcolonial theory to the U.S. context. Andy Doolen, *Fugitive Empire: Locating Early American Imperialism* (Minneapolis: University of Minnesota Press, 2005), argues that in the eighteenth century, slavery, war, and territorial expansion were integral components of a continuing imperial context in America. The chronology of his study spans from the late colonial to the early national period. Ed White, *The Backcountry and the City: Colonization and Conflict in Early America* (Minneapolis: University of Minnesota Press, 2005), argues for the importance of the racialized backcountry, developed in the colonial period, in creating the nation. David Kazanjian, *The Colonizing Trick: National Culture and Imperial Citizenship in Early America* (Baltimore: Johns Hopkins University Press 2004), looks at cultural and political process through which America went from settler colony to neocolonial power. The work of earlier historians such as Richard van Alstyne, and the work of William Appleman Williams, for instance, *Contours of American History* (Cleveland: World Publishing Company, 1961), have obvious purchase here as well insofar as they defined the new nation as imperial in its origins. See also Marc Egnal, *A Mighty Empire* (Ithaca, NY: Cornell University Press, 1988); Francis Jennings, *The Creation of America: Through Revolution to Empire* (Cambridge: Cambridge University Press, 2000). I am grateful to David Waldstreicher for suggesting these works.

85. To suggest some specific ways that postcolonial theory can enrich the study of the history of early America, I point out two iterations of the postcolonial project that may prove useful. The first, akin to what has become known as subaltern studies, focuses on social movements that seek emancipation *from* the state rather than through the replication and appropriation of the same centralizing formations that revolutionaries fight to topple. Historians Peter Linebaugh and Marcus Rediker, authors of *The Many Headed Hydra: Sailors, Slaves, Commoners, and the Hidden History of the Revolutionary Atlantic* (Boston: Beacon Press, 2000), provide a recent example of this. The authors present a sweeping transnational history tracing subversive forces that resisted and challenged state control. Consisting of various dispossessed groups, social movements, through their activities, have crossed the temporal

and geographical boundaries that have commonly served as the frameworks of historical narratives, transcending the disruptions of nations and emancipations and continuing across political revolution.

86. Jeremy Tambling writes: "The fate of being an American meeting Dickens is to be a post-colonial subject meeting someone from the center of English culture" and hence to provide fodder for his next social satire. Jeremy Tambling, *Lost in the American City: Dickens, James and Kafka* (London: Palgrave Macmillan, 2001), 26.

[THREE]

Ralph Ellison and the Grain of Internationalism

Brent Hayes Edwards

Thinking about Ralph Ellison as an internationalist requires tinkering with some of our most closely guarded assumptions about his work.[1] Above all, it means sounding his sense of the nation, of the contours and limits of the "America" invoked so often in his writing. In Ellison's essays, as well as in the fiction, "America" is what a linguist would call an unmarked term: whereas most of the other key notions invoked in the Ellison corpus ("Negro," of course, but also "vernacular" and the notion of "culture" itself) are fingered and pressed into rich, changing threads of significance, "America" sometimes seems to remain untroubled, conjured unquestioningly as the self-evident boundary of inquiry.[2] Rather than reject Ellison's seemingly easy use of the term, though, here I push at its edges, to look for its outside or underside—or as Ellison himself might have put it, to "dirty" the tone of that too-clear, too-clarion trumpet.

Tinkering is detail work, meddling at the margins, and one might start with one of the most famous passages in *Invisible Man,* the dream sequence in the prologue that revolves around an antiphonal rendition of a sermon on the "Blackness of Blackness," a sort of dream or vision that the protagonist hears (under the influence of marijuana) in the interstices of Louis Armstrong's music. Many have noted the synesthetic topography of the scene (*"beneath the swiftness of the hot tempo there was a slower tempo and a cave and I entered it and looked around . . . and beneath that lay a still lower level . . . and below that I found a lower level and a more rapid tempo"* [9]), its playful allusion to Melville, and its virtuosic unraveling of any essentialist notion of racial identity. I quote only the end of the sermon, just before the Invisible Man confronts an old woman singing spirituals:

> *"Black will git you . . ."*
>> *"Yes, it will . . ."*
>> *"Yes, it will . . ."*
>> *". . . an' black won't . . ."*
>> *"Naw, it won't!"*

"It do . . ."
"It do, Lawd . . ."
". . . an' it don't."
"Hallelujah . . ."
[. . .]
"Black will make you . . ."
"Black . . ."
". . . or black will un-make you."
"Ain't it the truth, Lawd?"
And at that point a voice of trombone timbre screamed at me, "Git out of here, you fool! Is you ready to commit treason?"
And I tore myself away, hearing the old singer of spirituals moaning, "Go curse your God, boy, and die." (9–10)

The word I want to highlight is the word that doesn't seem to fit here: *treason*. Why, at this level of the dream, is the risk or the accusation signaled with that word—particularly if we hear in it something beyond betrayal in the general sense and instead hear a more pointed suggestion of a violation of one's allegiance to a sovereign or nation-state? Would the implication be that too deep a descent into blackness threatens to undermine or undo the bonds of nation? Or is the voice warning, on a "trombone" frequency below that of Armstrong's horn, of a treachery to blackness itself, to the tautology of congregation? This allusion to disloyalty in seemingly national terms is echoed a few pages later, when the protagonist recalls the dying words of his grandfather: "On his death-bed he called my father to him and said, 'Son, after I'm gone I want you to keep up the good fight. I never told you, but our life is a war and I have been a traitor all my born days, a spy in the enemy's country ever since I give up my gun back in the Reconstruction'" (16). These seem particularly freighted words to use in a book that, as Ellison put it, "erupted out of what had been conceived as a war novel" during the 1940s.[3]

It might seem something close to perverse to seek an internationalist discourse in the work of a writer who titled one 1967 essay "The Novel as a Function of American Democracy," and who time and time again penned pronouncements about the bond between nation and narration, as when he claimed that "the novel's medium consists in a familiar experience occurring among a particular people, within a particular society or nation."[4] Yet the terms *treason* and *traitor* in the passages above (particularly given that the grandfather's words are posed as framing a central task or puzzle for the narrator, one that he must write the novel itself to figure out) point to a tension within Ellison's discourse of Americanness, even a sort of requisite friction, a necessary undertone of threat and dissension.

Coming to terms with what Ellison called the Negro's "special perspective on the national ideals and the national conduct," in other words, might mean coming to terms with a constitutive discomfort with the confines of "America" itself.[5] This edge or irritation is discernible in Ellison's essays and interviews as well; at one point, accused of being a "patriotic" writer, he demurs that "it ain't the theory which bothers me, it's the practice. My problem is to affirm while resisting."[6] In considering the position of black intellectuals, he keeps coming back to this "problem," what he elsewhere terms the "continuing process of antagonistic cooperation," as a way of troubling the very status of "America," when he senses that the national context is becoming too static, too homogenous. "Deep down," he insists, "the American condition is a state of unease."[7]

In part, Ellison undoes the term by conceptualizing "America" in terms of process rather than product, discordance and diversity rather than unity. At such moments, he describes it as a "futuristic concept" and emphasizes the "composite nature of the ideal character called 'the American.'"[8] In this formulation, the experience of the American present can only seem "alarmingly off-key," improvised chord changes that move jarringly toward some cadence, always yet to come—and the nation swings together in dissonance. The African American "special perspective," then, is a clear vision of this unease, gained paradoxically through historical alienation and disenfranchisement. But the term marks an aesthetic stance as well: if the novel is a "function of American democracy," then the black writer's position with regard to genre and history is equally "special." Thus Ellison, writing about *Invisible Man* in the early 1980s, recalled the "inner-outer, subjective-objective process of the developing fiction, its pied rind and surreal heart."[9] "Inner-outer": this paratactic two-step is not just the language of writerly hindsight but also the language of the novel's own self-reflexivity about the insight it achieves: in the scene where a crowd gathers to protest the eviction of an elderly Harlem couple in the middle of the winter, the protagonist stands at one point over a spilled drawer of their possessions in the street, "star[ing] again at the jumble, no longer looking at what was before my eyes, but inwardly-outwardly, around a corner into the dark, far-away-and-long-ago, not so much of my own memory as of remembered words, of linked verbal echoes, images, heard even when not listening at home" (273).

Still, to locate the roots of an Ellisonian rhetoric of *treason*, it is necessary to look past *Invisible Man* and Ellison's masterly essays of the 1950s and 1960s in order to contend with the essays that Ellison was writing during World War II. I am thinking both of his writings for the *New Masses* and, perhaps more provocatively, his pieces for the short-lived journal he edited with Angelo Herndon, *Negro Quarterly*, which strove to position itself as an "independent publication providing political and cultural reviews far more sophisticated than journalism and focusing on issues facing American Negroes and colonial nations."[10] For example, the unsigned "Editorial Comment" in the fourth issue of the journal enumerates the "attitudes held by Negroes toward their war-time experiences."[11] The editorial opens by contrasting two responses it finds to be unsatisfactory and self-defeating: on the one hand, an attitude of "unqualified acceptance" of segregation in the armed forces, and on the other, a "cynical" attitude of "unqualified rejection" of the war as a white man's struggle by definition (296). The latter attitude, though "in a sense" an "admirable" nationalism, is finally futile: it is "the attitude of one who, driven into a corner, sees no way of asserting his manhood except to choose his own manner of dying" (296). "Fortunately," the editorial continues, "there is a third attitude," which is "also a manifestation of Negro nationalism," but neither one of "blind acceptance" nor of total rejection:

> This is an attitude of critical participation, based upon a sharp sense of the Negro people's group personality. Which is the basis of its self-confidence and morale in this period of confusion. Thus, while affirming the justice of the Allies' cause, it never loses sight of the Negro peoples' stake in the struggle. This for them is the point of departure, a basic guide to theory and action which allows for objectivity and guards against both the fearful acceptance of the first and the sullen rejection of the second. . . . This attitude holds that any action which is advantageous to the United Nations must also be advantageous for the Negro and colonial peoples. Programs which would sacrifice the Negro or any other people are considered dangerous for the United Nations; and the only honorable course for Negroes to take is first to protest and then to fight against them. And while willing to give and take in the interest of national unity, it rejects that old pattern of American thought that regards any Negro demand for justice as treasonable, or any Negro act of self-defense as an assault against the state. (298–99)

In the phrase "critical participation," Ellison anticipates his later formulation, "antagonistic cooperation." And, in a manner that resonates with the passage in *Invisible Man*, part of the critique is aimed at the "old" American attitude that would pose any civil rights agenda as a form of "treason." That critique, of course, aims simultaneously "inwardly" and "outwardly": it is oriented toward "national unity," but it also is explicitly aligned with all peoples under imperial domination. Justice is a demand both at the core of the nation form and always exceeding it. That is, the editorial calls for a "Negro nationalism" that is also and at the same time an anticolonial internationalism.

Indeed, there is a surprising wealth of material on internationalism in Ellison's extensive drafts for the editorials in *Negro Quarterly* between 1942 and 1944. Interestingly, in one fragment he calls the prevailing "Negro sense of internationalism" a "myth" arising out of the slave trade and capitalist exploitation of peoples of African descent. The "common brutalization" that blacks suffered, "even more than their common African racial origin gave them a sense of kinship." Ellison singles out black literature as the main culprit in the elaboration of this "myth": "Negro literature has made of Africa a mythical Sangrila since Philis Weatley [*sic*]. And this mythical internationalism has been a factor in hindering the development of a national consciousness among American Negroes."[12] For the young aspiring writer, this passage implies an intellectual commitment and even a literary aesthetics: a mode of writing that may ground a Negro nationalism in the current conditions of capitalism in the United States so that it can expand toward a "real" or efficacious internationalism. As he puts it, "what is needed is a consciousness which can invent instrumentalities through which the real equivalent of the myth might be brought into being."

This orientation, if by no means the most explicit in Ellison's work, is nonetheless one of the main forces shaping it over the next decades, even long after the end of his flirtation with the organized left. In the drafts for the 1965 essay "Tell It Like It Is, Baby," one finds a similar stance in an extended passage in which Ellison offers a close reading and amplification of Henry James's essay "The Art of Fiction." Responding to the U.S. congressional defiance of the Supreme Court's call for school desegregation, Ellison argues that U.S. history since Reconstruction has been marked by a series of "damaging" moral evasions with regard to the country's history of racial oppression. For him, it is the "function of art to reduce to aesthetic and ethical form" what he calls "that element of chaos lurking about the edges of social nationality."[13] This unusual phrasing gives a different charge to the well-known passage from the conclusion of *Invisible Man*, in which the narrator says that "the mind that has conceived a plan of living must never lose sight of the chaos against which that pattern was conceived." We are forced to notice that the next sentence in the novel extends the point: "That goes for societies as well as for individuals" (580). Of course, the valences of internationalism shift in the wake of anticolonial struggles, but throughout, for Ellison it is this expanded sense of "chaos" that defines the literary enterprise.

One might have expected that if it were possible to trace the influence of internationalism in *Invisible Man*, the route would involve looking for the ways the book records a certain kind of *departure* from internationalism: a rebuttal of the worst pretenses of proletarian radicalism, or of the ugliest excesses of revanchist black nationalism. That is, one would look to Brother Jack's proclamations about being situated at "a terminal point in history, at a moment of supreme world crisis" (307); or one would notice that the activist Ras the Exhorter, the first time the Invisible Man sees him, is giving a "violent" speech about "the government"—crying, "We gine chase 'em out"—standing on a ladder decorated with small American flags (159). Later, when Ras battles the protagonist and Tod Clifton in hand-to-hand combat, he berates them with a different accusation of betrayal, now grounded in a world-girdling racial essentialism: "Where you think *you* from, going with the white folks? I know, godahm; don't I know it! You from down South! You from Trinidad! You from Barbados! Jamaica, South Africa, and the white mahn's foot in your ass all the way to the hip. What you trying to deny by betraying the black people?" (371). Looking at such passages, one might say that when, during the riot, the protagonist throws a spear that passes through Ras's cheeks, locking his jaws shut, it is precisely a sort of black internationalism that is being shut up (560).

I have approached the topic from another angle in order to avoid the temptation to offer yet another postdiluvian narrative (or to put it more bluntly, a tale of "treason") about Ellison's political commitment and its supposed "decline."[14] I will not participate here in the critical exercise of charting the process of what Barbara Foley terms Ellison's "anticommunistization," nor will I second her diagnosis that, by making his portrait of the Brotherhood more negative as he revised *Invisible Man*, Ellison "engaged in an act of purposive self-disappearing"—a sorry conclusion that turns invisibility from a resonant metaphor of race into a heavy-handed figure of false consciousness.[15] What is intriguing about internationalism as an "attitude" in Ellison's work is precisely that it is never reducible to the Communist International. Internationalism is not a discourse Ellison swallows whole-cloth one decade and voids or renounces the next; instead, it is part of the fabric of his work, one among what he termed the "things going on in its depths."[16] That it may be found in the details, even buried underground, does not necessarily mean that it is unimportant, much less that it is denied. Internationalism may be less institution than intuition, but it still must frame our reading and above all force us to ask questions rather than to impose conclusions. When the protagonist of *Invisible Man* comes upon the elderly couple being evicted that winter day in Harlem and finds himself mesmerized by a "drawer that spilled its contents in the snow" at his feet, what is the relation between his nausea and the items he picks up from the ground: "three lapsed life insurance policies with perforated seals stamped 'Void'; a yellowing newspaper of a huge black man with the caption: MARCUS GARVEY DEPORTED" (272)?

It is well documented that Ellison was drawn to a rich repertory of formalist metaphors to describe his fiction, mainly choosing words that pointed to a sort of spatiotemporal or sonic proliferation ("levels," "depths," "frequencies"). The word "grain" is drawn from this vocabulary, and it is an especially useful term because it indicates at once a temporized stratification (wood given layers by the passing of time), a mode of formal organization that one might term institutional, predicated on a certain founding interpretive violence (one can't see the grain without a crosscut), and even a quality of consciousness (recall that in Ellison's essay "Richard Wright's Blues," that music is described as an "impulse" to "finger the jagged grain" of a "brutal experience" in one's "aching consciousness").[17] To speak of a grain of internationalism running through his work, then, is to reference these various levels of implication and to draw our attention to a structural force that may be indispensable to the elaboration of a writerly discourse, even if not apparent on its surface.

I now turn briefly to another of Ellison's early works, this time a short story in the *New Masses* titled "Mister Toussan," one of the tales constructed around the adventures of two preadolescent African American boys, Buster and Riley.[18] In "Mister Toussan," the boys are sitting on Riley's front porch, fuming that the old white man across the street, Rogan, has refused to let them eat any of the ripe fruit in his cherry tree. The grumbling boys are surrounded by examples of flight, things breaking free of limitation: there are birds flocking to Rogan's tree, feasting on the cherries; and inside, Riley's mother is singing about deliverance ("I got wings, you got wings, / All God's chillun got a wings / When I git to heaven gonna put on my wings") in a beautiful voice as she irons clothes (24). The story is no more or less than a staging of the imaginative transport of the two boys as they improvise verbally with each other. "What would you do if you had wings?" Riley asks, and Buster responds: "Shucks, I'd outfly an eagle," which kicks off a round of jive and banter:

> "Hecks, with wings you could go anywhere, even up to the sun if it wasn't too hot . . ."
> "I'd go to New York . . ."
> "Even around the stars . . ."
> "Or Dee-troit, Michigan . . ."
> "Hell, you could git some cheese off the moon and some milk from the Milky Way . . ."
> "Or anywhere else colored is free . . ."
> "I bet I'd loop-the-loop . . ."
> "And parachute . . ."
> "I'd land in Africa and git me some diamonds . . ."
> "Yeah, and them cannibals would eat the hell outa you, too," said Riley.
> (24–25)

If "anywhere ... colored is free" is one of the wished-for destinations, still there is no sense of internationalism here, no sense of equivalent, other spaces of blackness, no hint of solidarity. On the contrary, stereotypes of Africa are simply fodder for their wordplay. But the dynamic shifts when Buster responds that the African cannibals wouldn't eat him because "them suckers is too lazy" (25). Still playful, the boys debate whether all Africans are lazy, and at the core of the argument is a negotiation of the degree of trust they put in the educational institutions around them: the "geography book" (which claims Africans are slothful), on one side, and Riley's father (who has told him otherwise), on the other. Buster remembers that his schoolteacher told the class about "one of the African guys named Toussan what she said whipped Napoleon!" (26). Riley is skeptical, but Buster persists, inflating an exuberant if somewhat confused tale of the "African" Toussan into a parable of resistance:

> "Really, man, she said that Toussan and his men got up on one of them African mountains and shot down them peckerwood soldiers fass as they'd try to come up ... "
>
> > "Why good-God-a-mighty!" yelled Riley.
> > "Oh boy, they shot 'em down!" chanted Buster.
> > "Tell me about it, man!"
> > "And they throwed 'em off the mountain ..."
> > "... Goool-leee! ..."
> > "... And Toussan drove 'em cross the sand ..."
> > "... Yeah! And what was they wearing, Buster? ..."
> > "Man, they had on red uniforms and blue hats all trimmed with gold and they had some swords all shining, what they called sweet blades of Damascus..."
> > "Sweet blades of Damascus! ..."
> > "... They really had 'em," chanted Buster.
> > [...]
> > "... Go on, Buster!"
> > "An' Toussan shot into them boats ..."
> > "... He shot into 'em ..."
> > "... shot into them boats ..."
> > "Jesus!"
> > "... with his great big cannons ..."
> > "... Yeah! ..."
> > "... made a-brass ..."
> > "... Brass ..."
> > "... an' his big black cannonballs started killin' them peckerwoods ..."
> > "... Lawd, Lawd ..."
> > "... Boy, till them peckerwoods hollowed, *Please, Please, Mister Toussan, we'll be good!*"

[. . .]

"And what'd ole Toussan say then?"

"He said in his big deep voice: *you all peckerwoods better be good, 'cause this is sweet Papa Toussan talking and my nigguhs is crazy 'bout white meat!*" (26–28)

Riley eventually gets so carried away by the rhythmic antiphony that, although he knows nothing about the history being alluded to, he insists on participating in the recitation himself: "Come on, watch me do it now, Buster. Now I bet ole Toussan looked down at them white folks standing just about like this and said in a soft easy voice: '*Ain't I done begged you white folks to quit messin' with me?*'" (29).

As Robert O'Meally has commented, "Buster and Riley are—to say the least—dubious historians of the Haitian revolt, but they are excellent storytellers." As he points out, they may not catch the facts of the revolution, but they certainly get the heroic "spirit and essence of the *tale*."[19] Buster and Riley are the primary fictional exponents of what Ellison in his essays calls "Negro American style," and as characters they jibe with Ellison's vivid descriptions of his own boyhood wordplay and imaginative games with buddies in Oklahoma, who played by "projecting archetypes, re-creating folk figures, legendary heroes, monsters even, most of which violated all ideas of social hierarchy and order and all accepted conceptions of the hero handed down by cultural, religious and racist tradition." Certainly Ellison is correct to view this activity as intensively language-bound, an improvisational "mode of humanizing reality and of evoking a feeling of being at home in the world" which "expressed a yearning to make any- and everything of quality *Negro American*; to appropriate it, possess it, re-create it in our own group and individual images."[20] Here the Haitian revolutionary Toussaint L'Ouverture is emphatically, from the title on, "Mister Toussan," "Sweet Papa Toussan," the down-home hero who "don't take no foolishness," who calls Napoleon himself out as a "peckerwood."

At the same time, however, we should notice that the raw material Buster and Riley are working off is not at all "American" (at least not in the way that Ellison normally relegates that adjective to a synonym for the United States). The boys' fascination with the story is related in particular to their sense (mistaken as it is) that Toussan is "African," that he's hero material because he confounds common racist stereotypes of the African savage or cannibal. Thus Toussan is important to the boys' own improvised identity, as a buttress against their perceptions of even such distant racist attacks as attacks on *them*. In an interview in 1960, Ellison recalled his childhood "geography class, the usual crap, Africans as lazy people, living in the sun. I always knew we were partially descended from African slave stock. I knew that Negroes were black and that blacks came from Africa."[21] In a sense Buster and Riley riff off Toussan precisely to respond to such pseudo-educational "foolishness"; it may not be properly historical, but the riff is crucial to the ways they are able to invent themselves. In one unpublished interview, Ellison reflected that he didn't "know how conscious I was of all the implications of the story. I wanted to get down some of the style of little kids of that nature. In fact the story is almost agit-prop, as I think back, because it's an assertion of a story of a Black leader as against the geography book description of African leadership."[22]

The story seems to involve more agitation than propaganda, though, given that it depends so much on *mis*hearing, on a *deflected* and appropriated (even caricatured) tale of black male heroism. It might be more useful to consider the tale in light of Ellison's related fascination with what he called the pressing need for a "sociology of ideas in the United States"—a better understanding of the complex and always unpredictable ways that *"ideas* move from one level of society to another."[23] Ellison always emphasized the ways that intellectual discourse, and art in particular, refused to be limited or constrained by the hierarchy of a given social formation: so the shoe-shine boy might know more Freud than the businessman whose shoes he's shining, or the janitor might be the quintessential opera buff.[24] But the story "Mister Toussan"—as well as the work of historians like James Sidbury, Jeffrey Bolster and Robin D. G. Kelley,[25] who have demonstrated complex networks of communication among black workers, sailors, and slaves over far-flung distances—makes the point that this movement of ideas is not just vertical, defying class and status, but also horizontal, defying language and the very borders of the nation-state itself. It should be no surprise then that Ellison turns to Haiti again for an example in discussing these unexpected routes—or what he prefers to speak of in paradoxical terms as the "mysterious possibilities generated by our unity within diversity and our freedom within unfreedom."[26] In one lecture, he comments that

> You cannot tell who is thinking what or where he gets the ideas. This was vaguely understood back during the Haitian Revolution early in the nineteenth century, when Southern governors and politicians became distraught because the ideas of the French Revolution had surfaced among the slaves. This tells you something about the availability of ideas beyond the levels of literacy. In our society, modes of conduct, styles, ideas, and even the most esoteric intellectual concepts find their ways into strange places, and even the most unfree or illiterate American is aware of ideas and will act on them.[27]

Although Buster and Riley mangle and abuse the facts of Haitian history, even the slip from Toussaint to "Mister Toussan" should not be understood simply as "mistaken," a lack of historical accuracy. It also represents a certain kind of work, a certain performance of *abstraction*, that Ellison considers to be the ground of creative expression in general, and the great historical advantage (rather than disadvantage or lack) of New World black communities. "When we began to build up a sense of ourselves," he suggests,

> we did it by abstracting from the Bible, abstracting the myths of the ancient Jews, the early Christians, modifying them as we identified with these people and projecting ourselves. This was an abstract process. . . . This was a creative process, one of the most wonderful things which ever happened on the face of the earth. This is one of the great strengths which now people seem to want to deny. But this was the *reunification* of a shattered group of people.[28]

This creative response to dispossession is not diasporic in the sense of being rooted in some primordial "African" identity (a notion which is itself an abstraction, albeit of a different sort, as Ellison points out). If it is diasporic, that term must be taken to allude to a persistent dialogism that willfully launches the imagination beyond the forces that contain it. Its performativity is agonistic, not only due to the tension, the goading, the escalation of invention between the boys, but also because its mode is insatiably heuristic. Most adults "caint tell a story right" because "they don't know how to put the right stuff to it" (29), Riley asserts, with a curious phrasing that might be taken to suggest both a requisite lyricism (in the sense that one puts something to music) and an unrelenting trial (in the sense that one puts something to the test). If this practice "reunifies" a "shattered group," that reunification seems to happen only across and through difference; it is predicated on perpetual "modifying," on the radical fungibility of "myths" and origins, on the creative misuse of a "blackness" wrenched into another space: on translation, in other words.

One way to pose the question of internationalism with regard to Ellison's work is to ask how this insistence on creative abstraction—on what one might term a diasporic poetics, understood as a "process" of appropriation and modification—is related to political solidarity.[29] Provocatively, in another editorial in *Negro Quarterly* published in the summer of 1942, Ellison finds political implications in this African American legacy of "creative" response. The editorial opens by arguing that one of the secret weapons of the Axis in World War II is the unfulfilled contract between the West and its "darker peoples." The strength of African American culture in particular, for Ellison, is that "the Negro people seek to define the world in their own terms." As he puts it, "they have created a culture and the basic outlines of a truly democratic vision of life. Indeed, when one looks around the globe for the truly human motivation behind this potentially peoples' war, one finds it expressed most intensely among the darker peoples." In this light, it is not surprising that the editorial, in concluding with a list of topics to be examined in future issues, specifies a needed focus on African Americans' "unity of interest with India, China, Africa, the Philippines, Latin America, and all other darker peoples of the world."[30] For Ellison, such an interest must not be rooted in "mythic internationalism" but instead involves a political consciousness that must be nurtured and "translated" from the African American affective response to "five hundred years of oppression and cultural devastation."[31] As he phrases it in one of the drafts of the editorial, the "darker peoples" of the world "supply the emotional basis for world unity. All of this, however, impinges upon the translation of their emotion into consciousness, their bitterness into the understanding which arises out of a wholesome tragic sense of their distrust into a will toward cooperation."[32]

What is particularly striking in the early Ellison is a corollary argument that such an emotional, responsive "sense of the whole world" among African Americans implies what he terms "potential creative possibilities"—that is, possibilities for literature.[33] I have suggested that "Mister Toussan" may be read as an attempt by Ellison to explore such possibilities; it would be possible extend such a reading to other examples in the early fiction, such as the 1944 short story "In a Strange Country."[34] Nor is this grain of internationalism entirely absent from *Invisible Man*, a few years later, even if Ellison's revisions to the novel (above all his late excision of Leroy, a drowned merchant marine whose journal becomes a sort of guidebook for the narrator, providing him a model of what Lawrence Jackson calls "an international political consciousness") tend to downplay these possibilities in the interest of a specifically national allegory—or, as he puts it in one of the best-known passages in the novel: "America is woven of many strands. . . . Our fate is to become one, and yet many—This is not prophecy, but description" (577).[35] Even after *Invisible Man*, Ellison was voicing similar themes, as in his 1955 "Art of Fiction" interview with the *Paris Review*:

> One function of serious literature is to deal with the moral core of a given society. Well, in the United States the Negro and his status have always stood for that moral concern. . . . There is a magic here worth conjuring, and that reaches to the very nerve of the American consciousness—so why should I abandon it? Our so-called race problem has now lined up with the world problems of colonialism and the struggle of the West to gain the allegiance of the

remaining non-white people who have thus far remained outside the Communist sphere; thus its possibilities for art have increased rather than lessened.[36]

The issue, then, revolves around the mutation, under the pressures of the cold war in the 1950s, of Ellison's previous concern with the development of international political consciousness among African Americans—a "unity of interest," to use the phrase from the 1942 editorial in *Negro Quarterly*—and its "possibilities for art."

One of the often-noted characteristics of Ellison's career is that despite two years in Rome at the American Academy (1956–57), he had little interest in expatriation,[37] and did not participate in any of the key Pan-African intellectual projects of his time, such as the Council on African Affairs, or the International Congresses of Black Artists and Intellectuals organized by *Présence Africaine* in Paris in 1956 and Rome in 1959. In the late 1950s, though, he participated in one literary endeavor that placed him among the "princes and powers" of négritude and black expatriate writers.[38] The interview, titled "Some Questions and Some Answers" in *Shadow and Act* (1964), in fact originated as a questionnaire from the French journal *Preuves* (an organ of the anticommunist left, linked to the Congress for Cultural Freedom), which was sent to a number of prominent black intellectuals from Africa, the Caribbean, and the United States.[39] In 1958, Jean-José Marchard organized a two-part feature for the journal, titled "Enquête sur la culture noire" (Inquiry on black culture), which asked eight broadly formulated questions to an impressive constellation of intellectuals, including Ellison, but also the Martinican poets Gilbert Gratiant and Emmanuel-Flavia Léopold, the *Crisis* editor James Ivy, the Senegalese poet and politician Léopold Sédar Senghor, the expatriate American novelists Richard Gibson and Richard Wright, and the painter Beauford Delany.[40] There is not space here to give a detailed comparison of their responses to the questions, although some of the divergences are fascinating; instead, I highlight a few points in Ellison's contribution because they give clues regarding the shifts in his formulation of a "unity of interest" among the "darker peoples" of the world.

The first question posed seems simple: "What do you understand today by 'Negro culture'"? Unlike the majority of the other respondents, Ellison resists at length the notion of a unique, global "Negro culture." He restricts the adjective "Negro" to the situation of peoples of African descent in the United States and then contends that "the existence of a specifically 'Negro' idiom" in "American culture" as a whole does not imply the existence of anything like a "black culture" more broadly. As he puts it, echoing the passage from *Invisible Man* quoted earlier, "rather it is a matter of diversity within unity."[41] He continues with a complex effort to extricate the notion of culture from any contamination by issues of "race":

> One could indeed go further and say that, in this sense, there is no other "Negro" culture. Haitians, for instance, are an "American" people and predominantly dark but their culture is an expression of Haitian conditions: it reflects the influence of French culture and the fusion of Catholic and native Haitian religious outlooks. Thus, since most so-called "Negro cultures" outside Africa are necessarily amalgams, it would seem more profitable to stress the term "culture" and leave the term "Negro" out of the discussion. It is not culture which binds the peoples who are of partially African origin now scattered throughout the world, but an identity of passions. (263)

Ellison seems to argue that there is no "profit" in considering possible "Negro" (African derived) characteristics that link or cut across the different "amalgams" of cultures in the New World. The only ground of inquiry, apparently, is that syncretic ground of "culture" itself, and cultures are inherently divided by nation and language. In the next sentence, however, he does not go on to "stress the term 'culture,'" evaluating the complexity of new world "amalgams"; instead, Ellison draws our attention to what he considers the true link among peoples of African descent around the globe. Rather than by culture, Ellison claims that those populations are bound by what he terms "an identity of passions."

The phrase is at once seductive and treacherous. Many commentators—without reading further—have read "an identity of passions" as the Ellisonian model of diaspora, an affective paradigm designed to evade or transcend the never-ending arguments about acculturation and African "survivals." But the "passions" evoked here cannot be cultural, in Ellison's definition, nor indeed can they be primarily a question of "race." Thus Ellison goes on, in the next sentence, to relegate these "passions" to a "hatred," a rejection of European colonialism shared by the "darker peoples" of the world. He writes, "we share a hatred for the alienation forced upon us by Europeans during the process of colonization and empire and we are bound by our common suffering more than by our pigmentation. But even this identification is shared by most non-white peoples, and while it has political value of great potency, its cultural value is almost nil" (263–64). In other words, the "identity of passions" is purely reactive, and purely political. Here, "culture" is the term that goes unmarked and undefined. One might question Ellison's radical extraction of this term from the political: wouldn't an anticolonial "identity of passions" have to be articulated first and foremost in a broad ensemble of social signifying practices that are nothing if not "cultural"—nothing if not a form of creative abstraction? In Ellison's distinction, however, if culture and politics are inherently separate, then an anti-imperialist internationalism can only have "value" in the political arena.

Although it has gone unnoticed by commentators, this shift from a "unity of interest" to an "identity of passions" is one of the most important transformations in Ellison's work in the 1950s. One might say that as Ellison's writing changes in this decade, there is an abdication of the "possibilities for art" he once had considered to be provided by the discourse of anticolonial internationalism. Put differently, the shift indicates an attempt to transmute political stakes into affective investments, and solidarity into homology. Yet, as I have already indicated, I am not convinced that this shift can simply be termed a "depoliticization," as some critics would have it. Reading the published sections of Ellison's unfinished second novel, it is clear that internationalism (that is, the potential for a politics of common "interest" among the darker peoples of the world) is one of the fiction's key, albeit unintegrated, themes. In the first published version of what was apparently intended to be the opening scene of the novel, Reverend Hickman is sitting in the gallery of the U.S. Senate with one of his congregation members, Sister Neal, listening to Senator Sunraider's speech. Interestingly, the subject of his speech (in the moments before his attempted assassination, the event which triggers the interwoven reminiscences of the novel) is foreign aid to newly independent nations in Asia and Africa. The senator "plans to use those Asian folks," Hickman explains to Sister Neal, "to divide the men down there who don't like some of the things he's trying to do over here. This way he can even put those Asian leaders in his hip pocket. They need they money he's trying to get for foreign aid so bad that naturally they will have to shut up and stop criticizing the way things go over here. Like the way we're treated, for instance."[42] Elsewhere, during a discussion among a group of newspapermen of a jazz musician's absurdist protest against the senator's racist policies (he sets his Cadillac on fire on the senator's front lawn), one Southern journalist avers that "if you allow the Nigra to see Indians killing white folks week after week—which is another Yankee mistake—he's apt to go bad and then next thing you know he's learning about that Nehru, Nasser, and those Mau-Maus and that's most politically unwise."[43]

The point is that the politics of radical internationalism *remains* a problem in Ellison's fictional architecture—a "grain" both in the sense of a structuring feature and in the sense of a concern continually being put to the test. This is to say that it is, as one might expect, one of the "forces which are implicit" in a novel set (as Ellison told one interviewer) in a time span from "1954 to 1956 or 1957," at the height of the anticolonial independence moment.[44] In the recently published manuscript drafts of the unfinished novel, whether in passages like the ones quoted above or in the other moments such as the reporter McIntyre's memory of a mysterious nighttime encounter with a resistance fighter in a French cathedral during World War II, internationalism is one of the many elements that outraced Ellison, that defied his attempts to integrate his numerous narrative strands into a coherent book.[45] In other words, one might call the failure of Ellison's second novel a particularly *postcolonial* failure, in that Ellison was unable to adjust his vision from the "possibilities for art" inherent in the politics of anticolonial internationalism in the 1940s and 1950s, on the one hand, to the rather different "possibilities" arising out of the politics of decolonization, nonalignment, and incipient globalization in the 1960s and 1970s, on the other. History left his fiction behind.[46] At the same time, this persistent problem deposited a "a built-in feed-back" in the drafts of the second novel: a concern with antiracist internationalist solidarity that is never entirely transcended or muted.[47] It is one of the "disturbing overtones" in the later fiction, as Ellison phrases it in one of the published sections of the unfinished novel, in a particularly resonant reformulation of the famous last line of *Invisible Man*. Even in writing that increasingly declares itself to be limited to an "American" sphere, internationalism keeps coming back, "like the brief interruption one sometimes hears while listening to an F.M. broadcast of the musical *Oklahoma!*, say, with original cast, when the signal fades and a program of quite different mood from a different wavelength breaks through."[48]

Notes

1. It is worth recalling that "tinkering" is not only one of the key metaphors of *Invisible Man*, in which the unnamed protagonist says "Call me, since I have a theory and a concept, a 'thinker-tinker.'" Ellison, *Invisible Man* (1952; reprint, New York: Vintage, 1989), 7. Subsequent page references are indicated parenthetically in the text. One may also hear in "tinkering" one of its possible (if uncertain) etymological roots as the transcription of a sound; the "concept" would then metaphorically be linked to a certain sort of musical practice, a certain improvisatory or errant approach to aesthetics (given that a tinker is an itinerant craftsman who repairs or bangs an object or utensil into shape in a makeshift way). We may hear a suggestion of the word, then, when Ellison describes himself as a "compulsive experimenter" with the latest high fidelity stereo equipment; see Ellison, "Living with Music" (1955), in *The Collected Essays of Ralph Ellison*, ed. John F. Callahan (New York: Modern Library, 1995), 234. In a biographical sketch for the *Saturday Review of Literature*, Ellison is described suggestively as someone who had "tinkered with audio electronics." Eloise Perry Hazard, "The Author," *Saturday Review of Literature* 36 (April 12, 1952): 22, as quoted in Barbara Foley, "From Communism to Brotherhood: The Drafts of Invisible Man," in *Left of the Color Line: Race,*

Radicalism and Twentieth-Century Literature of the United States, ed. Bill V. Mullen and James Smethurst (Chapel Hill: University of North Carolina Press, 2003), 163.

2. Ellison liked to recount an anecdote of one white professor friend, who, upon hearing him rhapsodize one more time about the national "concord of sensibilities," grumbled half jokingly: "Ah, here's Ralph again, talking about America. There's no goddamn America out there." Ellison and James Alan McPherson, "Indivisible Man," *The Atlantic* (December 1970), as published in *Collected Essays*, 360.

3. Ellison, introduction to *Invisible Man*, vii. See John S. Wright, "The Conscious Hero and the Rites of Man: Ellison's War," in *New Essays on "Invisible Man,"* ed. Robert O'Meally (New York: Cambridge University Press, 1988), 157–86.

4. Ellison, "The Novel as a Function of American Democracy," *Wilson Library Bulletin* 41, no. 10 (June 1967): 1022–27, as published in *Collected Essays*, 755–765; Ellison, "Society, Morality and the Novel," in *Collected Essays*, 696.

5. Ellison, "The World and the Jug," in *Shadow and Act* (New York: Vintage, 1964), 131.

6. As quoted in John Callahan, introduction to *Collected Essays*, xxii.

7. Ellison, "The Little Man at Chehaw Station," in *Going to the Territory* (New York: Vintage, 1986), 26, 20–21.

8. We may speak of a national culture, he argues, but "the whole is always in cacophonic motion. Constantly changing its mode, it appears as a vortex of discordant ways of living and tastes, values and traditions; a whirlpool of odds and ends in which the past courses in uneasy juxtaposition with those bright, futuristic principles and promises to which we, as a nation, are politically committed." Ellison, "Hidden Name and Complex Fate," in *Shadow and Act*, 164–65.

9. Ellison, introduction to the thirtieth anniversary edition of *Invisible Man* (1982), as published in *Collected Essays*, 480. He used the same language to describe the general task of the black fiction writer, charged with cultivating just this kind of "inward-outwardness." See Ellison and McPherson, "Indivisible Man," 364.

10. Lawrence Jackson, *Ralph Ellison: Emergence of Genius* (New York: John Wiley, 2002), 264.

11. "Editorial Comment," *Negro Quarterly* 1, no. 4 (Winter–Spring 1943): 295. This editorial was almost certainly written solely by Ellison; extensive drafts in his hand are in the collection at the Library of Congress. Subsequent page references are indicated parenthetically in the text.

12. In another draft, he wrote of the Garvey movement as representing "an international consciousness, a regard for Africa that is mythological." Undated handwritten drafts, "Editorial Comments in *The Negro Quarterly* (1942–44)," box 96, folder 1, Ralph Ellison Papers, Manuscript Division, Library of Congress, Washington, DC.

13. Ellison, "Tell It Like It Is, Baby," typed draft p. 21, box 107, folder 3, Ralph Ellison Papers. The finished essay was published in *The Nation* (September 20, 1965) and is also available in Ellison's *Collected Essays*, 27–46.

14. A great deal of Ellison criticism evidences such a predilection. The recent work of Barbara Foley counters the anticommunist bias of much of the scholarship by making the story *only* about Ellison's relation to the Communist Party, as though his historically mediated relationship with that institution is the sole lens through which one is able to gauge his radicalism and commitment to a liberatory politics. See Barbara Foley, "Ralph Ellison as Proletarian Journalist," *Science and Society* 62, no. 4 (Winter 1998–99): 537–56; Foley, "Reading Redness: Politics and Audience in Ralph Ellison's Early Short Fiction," *JNT: Journal of Narrative Theory* 29, no. 3 (Fall 1999): 323–39; Foley, "Roads Taken and Not Taken: Post-Marxism, Antiracism, and Anticommunism," *Cultural Logic: An Electronic Journal of Marxist Theory and Practice* 1, no. 2 (Spring 1998); Foley, "The Rhetoric of Anticommunism in *Invisible Man*," *Col-*

lege English 59, no. 5 (September 1997): 530–47; Foley, "From Communism to Brotherhood," 163–82.

15. Foley, "From Communism to Brotherhood," 164, 179.

16. Ellison, "The Art of Fiction: An Interview," *Paris Review* (Spring 1955), as published in Ellison, *Shadow and Act*, 211.

17. Ellison, "Richard Wright's Blues," in *Shadow and Act*, 78–79. I have discussed this figure in relation to music in Brent Hayes Edwards, "The Seemingly Eclipsed Window of Form: James Weldon Johnson's Prefaces," in *The Jazz Cadence of American Culture*, ed. Robert G. O'Meally (New York: Columbia University Press, 1998), 580–601.

18. Ellison, "Mister Toussan," *New Masses* (November 4, 1941), as published in *Flying Home and Other Stories*, ed. John F. Callahan (New York: Vintage, 1996), 22–32. Subsequent page references are indicated parenthetically in the text.

19. Robert G. O'Meally, *The Craft of Ralph Ellison* (Cambridge: Harvard University Press, 1980), 65.

20. Ellison, introduction to *Shadow and Act*, xvi, xvii.

21. Harold Isaacs, "Five Writers and the African Ancestors," *Phylon* (Winter 1960): 317–36, as collected in *Conversations with Ralph Ellison*, ed. Maryemma Graham and Amritjit Singh (Jackson: University Press of Mississippi, 1995), 66.

22. David L. Carson, "Ralph Ellison, 20 Years After," transcript of an interview conducted September 30, 1971, box 177, folder 5, typescript pp. 10–11, Ralph Ellison Papers. A portion of this interview (not including this exchange) was published in *Studies in American Fiction* 1 (1973); see David L. Carson, "Ralph Ellison: Twenty Years After," in Graham and Singh, *Conversations with Ralph Ellison*, 192–214.

23. Ellison, "On Initiation Rites and Power," in *Going to the Territory*, 51.

24. I am thinking of the closing pages of "The Little Man at Chehaw Station," 32–38.

25. W. Jeffrey Bolster, *Black Jacks: African American Seamen in the Age of Sail* (Cambridge: Harvard University Press, 1997); James Sidbury, *Ploughshares into Swords: Race, Rebellion, and Identity in Gabriel's Virginia, 1730–1810* (New York: Cambridge University Press, 1997); Sidbury, "Saint Domingue in Virginia: Ideology, Local Meanings, and Resistance to Slavery, 1790–1800," *Journal of Southern History* 63, no. 3 (August 1997): 531–52; Robin D. G. Kelley, "'This Ain't Ethiopia, but It'll Do': African Americans and the Spanish Civil War," in *Race Rebels: Culture, Politics, and the Black Working Class* (New York: Free Press, 1994), 103–22.

26. Ellison, "On Initiation Rites and Power," 52.

27. Ellison, "Roscoe Runjee and the American Language" (Black Perspective Conference, May 14, 1972), as published in *Collected Essays*, 458.

28. Ellison and McPherson, "Indivisible Man," 368.

29. I have considered the complexity of "influence" and appropriation in African diasporic literature at greater length in Brent Hayes Edwards, "Aimé Césaire and the Syntax of Influence," *Research in African Literatures* 36, no. 2 (Summer 2005): 1–18.

30. "Editorial Comment," *Negro Quarterly* 1, no. 2 (Summer 1942), iii, v.

31. "Editorial Comments in *The Negro Quarterly* (1942–44)"; "Editorial Comment," *Negro Quarterly* 1, no. 2 (Summer 1942), iii.

32. Undated handwritten draft, box 96, folder 1, Ralph Ellison Papers.

33. In another version of this passage, he writes: "Suffering on the ostensible grounds of color has made Negroes sensitive to the problems of colored peoples throughout the world, and in a time when the cracking up of the West makes possible the rebirth of a sense of the whole world, and when historical development points to the establishment of an international world order this has potential creative possibilities. For by starting at the opposite pole of the political, technological, and cultural developments that has brought about the present crisis in world history, it supplies the trully [*sic*] human, emotional basis for world unity." Undated handwritten draft, box 96, folder 1, Ralph Ellison Papers.

34. Ellison, "In a Strange Country," *Tomorrow* (July 1944), as published in *Flying Home and Other Stories*, 137–46.

35. See Jackson, *Ralph Ellison: Emergence of Genius*, 427. Jackson calls Leroy's text a "journal of philosophical guerrilla warfare" (415) and writes that "the decision to eliminate Leroy's journal removed chunks of the novel that would have reflected the international scope of Ellison's earliest intentions" (426). As he comments elsewhere, in drafts of the novel throughout 1951, "Ellison used Leroy's journal to suggest the difficult dialectical interaction between the poles of a familiar opposition: (1) international humanism, unrestricted by racial logic and profoundly reluctant to pursue a liberation agenda by any other means than Western-based reason, justice, ethics, and morality; and (2) violent rebellion that justifies the cruelty of its resistance due to the confluence of interests between racist imperialism and civilizing enlightenment rationalism." Lawrence Jackson, "Ellison, Fanon and Guerrilla War," *Cahiers Charles V* 40 (2006): 240–41. Although Ellison removed this strand of the novel at the recommendation of his editor, both Jackson and Adam Bradley point out that the political perspective it articulates is not entirely quashed: Ellison carefully wove key passages from Leroy's journal into the epilogue of the published novel, and so Leroy's voice to some degree was merged into the narrator's. See especially Adam Bradley, *Ralph Ellison in Progress: From "Invisible Man" to "Three Days before the Shooting"* (New Haven: Yale University Press, 2010), 181–208.

36. Ellison, "Art of Fiction," 182.

37. See, for instance, Ellison's letters to the editor of *Time* magazine (dated November 27, 1958) and to Bela Zempleny, an official in the Division for Americans Abroad in the U.S. State Department (dated May 18, 1964). He writes that "I feel that my proper place is here on the scene," and that "personally I am too vindictively American, too full of hate for the hateful aspects of this country, and too possessed by the things I love here to be too long away." Ellison, "'American Culture Is of a Whole': From the Letters of Ralph Ellison," ed. John F. Callahan, *New Republic* (March 1, 1999): 40, 39.

38. I am alluding, of course, to the title of James Baldwin's report for *Encounter* magazine on the 1956 Paris *Présence Africaine* Congress, "Princes and Powers," reprinted in *Nobody Knows My Name* (New York: Dial, 1961), and in *James Baldwin: Collected Essays*, ed. Toni Morrison (New York: Library of America, 1998), 143–69.

39. On *Preuves* in particular and the Congress for Cultural Freedom more generally, see Giles Scott-Smith, *The Politics of Apolitical Culture: The Congress for Cultural Freedom, the CIA, and Post-War American Hegemony* (New York: Routledge, 2001); Frances Stoner Saunders, *The Cultural Cold War: The CIA and the World of Arts and Letters* (New York: New Press, 2000); Pierre Grémion, *Intelligence de l'anticommunisme: Le congrès pour la liberté de la culture à Paris, 1950–1975* (Paris: Fayard, 1995); Peter Coleman, *The Liberal Conspiracy: The Congress for Cultural Freedom and the Struggle for the Mind of Postwar Europe* (New York: Free Press, 1989); Irene L. Gendzier, *Managing Political Change: Social Scientists and the Third World* (Boulder, CO: Westview, 1985), 87–97.

40. "Enquête sur la culture noire (I)," *Preuves* 86 (April 1958): 32–38; "Enquête sur la culture noire (II)," *Preuves* 87 (May 1958): 33–44. See also the original questionnaire, and the manuscripts of Ellison's response, collected in "Ralph Ellison: 'Notre lutte nous proclame à la fois "nègres" et américains,' *Preuves*, 1958," box 104, folder 9, Ralph Ellison Papers.

41. Ellison, "Some Questions and Some Answers," in *Shadow and Act*, 261. Subsequent page references are indicated parenthetically in the text.

42. Ellison, "And Hickman Arrives," *Noble Savage* 1 (1960): 14–15, as published in Ellison, *Three Days before the Shooting . . .*, ed. John F. Callahan and Adam Bradley (New York: Modern Library, 2010), 1010. This lengthy exchange does not appear in the version of this scene included in *Juneteenth*, the book that Ellison's executor, John H. Callahan, complied in 1999. See Ellison, *Juneteenth: A Novel*, ed. John F. Callahan (New York: Vintage, 1999), 35. Interest-

ingly, this exchange appears in a "specially written transitional scene" that Ellison composed for the 1960 publication of this excerpt of the novel-in-progress. See the editorial note "Eight Excerpts Published by Ellison," in *Three Days before the Shooting*, 1003.

43. Ellison, "It Always Breaks Out," *Partisan Review* 30, no. 1 (Spring 1963): 20, as published in *Three Days before the Shooting*, 1049.

44. John Hersey, "'A Completion of Personality': A Talk with Ralph Ellison" (1974), in Graham and Singh, *Conversations with Ralph Ellison*, 300.

45. Ellison, *Three Days before the Shooting*, 80–84.

46. On more than one occasion Ellison himself voiced this sense of being outraced by history. In the 1980s, he told a journalist that "part of what's taken so long is that so many things have changed so fast in our culture that as soon as I thought I had a draft that brought all of these things together, there would be another shift and I'd have to go back and revise all over again." Walter Lowe, "Book Essay," *Playboy* (October 1982): 42, as quoted in Arnold Rampersad, *Ralph Ellison: A Biography* (New York: Knopf, 2007), 533. In one of the few essays on the unfinished second novel, Kenneth Warren makes a similar point about Ellison's grappling with history, but poses it in the familiar realm of domestic racial politics without considering the international sphere of decolonization: "the incomplete transit from *Invisible Man* to the second novel," Warren suggests, should be "understood as Ellison's unsuccessful attempt to negotiate the difference between writing about segregation and writing about desegregation." Kenneth W. Warren, "Chaos Not Quite Controlled: Ellison's Uncompleted Transit to *Juneteenth*," in *The Cambridge Companion to Ralph Ellison*, ed. Ross Posnock (New York: Cambridge University Press, 2005), 189.

47. Ellison, "A Song of Innocence," *Iowa Review* 1 (Spring 1970): 35.

48. The next sentence wrenches us back to the normative orientation, in a manner that might be taken to suggest the degree to which humor (as a sort of national mood: one character calls the country "the United States of Jokeocracy") is not always necessarily a progressive force in Ellison's work: "It had happened but then a blast of laughter had restored us automatically to our chosen frequency." Ellison, "Cadillac Flambé," *American Review* 16 (February 1963): 269, as published in *Three Days before the Shooting*, 1096–97. (The phrase "the United States of Jokeocracy" is found in Ellison, "It Always Breaks Out," 16.) Of course, the last line of *Invisible Man* is "Who knows but that, on the lower frequencies, I speak for you?" (581).

FOUR

Cold War, Hot Kitchen

*Alice Childress, Natalya Baranskaya, and
the Speakin' Place of Cold War Womanhood*

Kate Baldwin

The 1950s American housewife. Who cannot claim to have some sense of the image this phrase conjures? June Cleaver, picket fence, pot roast, Jell-O molds, domestic incandescence—whatever your association, there is undoubtedly an image attached to it. Call it iconic—icons are, after all, known for being known—your image participates in a logic of public persuasion. Following Robert Hariman and John Lucaites and their work on iconic photojournalism, I suggest that the iconic housewife's "combination of mainstream recognition, wide circulation, and textural impact" positions her as a site for ideological relay and as a site of ideological excess. In this sense, the iconic housewife follows the four vectors of influence that Hariman and Lucaites identify as important for an iconic image: it communicates social knowledge, reproduces attendant ideology, shapes collective memory, and provides figural resources for communicative action.[1] Yet although we may call this housewife image iconic, it is not an iconic image per se. In fact, there is a range of images summoned by the ideas of female domesticity in the 1950s. There is no iconic image of the housewife commensurable with, say, Dorothea Lange's "Migrant Mother" of the 1930s, or even with Marilyn Monroe's billowing skirt in *The Seven Year Itch*. So although we all lay claim to a commonsense understanding of what this female looks like, we may wonder why this is the case. What are the conditions of intelligibility for this iconic image that lacks both an icon and a singular image?

We may wonder, in fact, if what our communally summoned images have in common is less about the specific picture than about the sensibility or emotional register brought to the fore by the image—the affective component of female domesticity. In this sense the housewife image we have all just conjured bears witness to something that exceeds words at the same time that it presents a visual commonplace. Captured in or by the ordinary are relations of power that seem natural, articulated as they are through seemingly banal signs of housewifery. But why do we see what we see? How can we think about this ordinary image as perception? Again, what are the conditions of intelligibility that make this so? And what are some alternative registers of intelligence put under erasure so that these conditions might emerge?

To underscore the rhetorical ambivalence in which the American housewife is enshrined, I turn to a site in which her uncertainty was captured with unparalleled aplomb, the 1959 Moscow debate between U.S. vice president Richard Nixon and Soviet premier Nikita Khrushchev. Famously held in the kitchen of a one-track modular house that had been split in half and thus dubbed "splitnik" by the Soviets—a pun on the Soviet satellite *Sputnik*—the exchange between Nixon and Khrushchev was quickly dubbed by U.S. journalists the "kitchen debate."[2]

The setting is important, for although the debate appeared to be impromptu, it was strategically chosen by the Americans in an effort to showcase the advances made by the United States in domestic technologies, and thus to bring the battle for technological superiority down to earth. So key was the staging for the ideological showdown between Nixon and Khrushchev that the previous evening, photographers and journalists were summoned to the site to line up their cameras for their best angle.

As other scholars have observed, the use of the kitchen to advertise the bounty of American consumerism quickly dispensed with the notion that the home was anything but political. As the *New York Times* put it, "the purpose was to show the American economy as it is broadly shared by all the people, the immense variety and great freedom of choice."[3] Responding in part to *Sputnik*—the Soviet's unmanned space satellite launched in 1957—the American exhibition countered Soviet technological sophistication with national ideologies splayed out in an abundance of consumer choices and the productive capacity of the economy to please the buyer. Described by the U.S. press as a "little America in the heart of Moscow," the kitchen encapsulated freedom American-style.[4] What could be more exemplary of an emancipated populace than their easy access to the appliances of the free market?

In fact, Nixon's correlation between good citizenship and good domesticity could not have been made clearer. As Nixon declared, "Americans were interested in making life easier for their women." When Khrushchev replied that the Soviet Union "did not have the capitalist attitude towards women," Nixon retorted, "I think that this attitude toward women is *universal*. . . . What we want to do is make easier the lives of our housewives."[5] Nixon's collapsing of woman into housewife provides the ammunition for his pride in U.S. superiority as exemplary of universal attitudes toward housewives. In this universalist account of democratic liberties, consumer choice begets human rights in the interest of female autonomy and an exceptional idealization of American domesticity as sacred.

Before taking Nixon at his word, however, we must unpack the confluence of images and their connective networks here. To be sure, Nixon deployed the image of the housewife as a powerful ideological weapon. But in so doing he relied on associations among domesticity, female sentiment, and American Empire, for which a path had been laid in the previous century. As numerous other scholars have observed, at least as early as the nineteenth century the term "domestic" had two simultaneous registers: it gestured at once to the home and to the homeland. These spheres were conventionally split through a division of labor: women occupied the home; men occupied the land. As Amy Kaplan has pointed out, however, if women and men were divided into private and public spheres during this period, they were at the same time aligned nationally against the foreign. Slippages among these various intonations of the domestic enabled domesticity to do the work of establishing the racial boundaries of the foreign, because woman's sphere of sentiment was set up as the morally privileged site (however unstable) that condoned and authorized the expansion of American Empire. Thus the image of social unity, of universal attitudes and emotions generated from the home kitchen, actually depends on and sustains visions of domestic expansion. At the same time, these universal attitudes parse who and what can be accepted into the national space. What is so interesting, then, about Nixon's posturing in Moscow is the way in which he usurps the moral authority of female influence at the heart of sentimental ethos not only by making it his own, but by proclaiming it universal, thereby abetting and underwriting the imperial expansion of the United States *and* implicitly proclaiming its internal limits.

To articulate this sentimental ethos, however, Nixon must erase the actual woman from the house. Although Nixon and Khrushchev debated the relative merits of appliances and household gadgets in the borrowed kitchen of a one-tract house shipped in from New York, there was no American housewife anywhere to be seen. Khrushchev noted the housewife's absence when he asked the American guide to "Thank the housewife for letting us use her kitchen for our argument."[6] Khrushchev's address of thanks to the absent housewife underscores not only the tired trafficking in women as a mode of commerce between men, but a constitutive ambivalence between presence and absence when it comes to discussions of the American housewife.

Here I briefly detour from Moscow and direct your attention to an advertisement published in a 1956 issue of *Time* magazine. The ad is for a Kitchen Aid dishwasher, and the heading reads, "How to bring a Ghostess

How to bring a Ghostess back to life

by KitchenAid

You know what a "ghostess" is: that's a hostess who disappears right after the meal. And leaves her guests with that awkward choice—pitch in to help with the dishes, or try to ignore those stacks of soiled tableware.

But change the scene just slightly ...add a KitchenAid automatic dishwasher...and see the hostess be a part of the party! Now she has *time*. Time for gracious entertaining and living. Time to really enjoy her family. Time for so many of the better things.

Why a KitchenAid? Because a KitchenAid *belongs* in this scene. Because the product itself is unequaled.

Ask a dealer! He'll explain that a dishwasher has three important actions. *Washing* and *rinsing* (it must remove every trace of food). *Drying* (it must leave no spots). He'll show you why a KitchenAid, by Hobart, does *both* jobs better—the exclusive Hobart revolving power wash system, the separate electric blower-dryer unit—no other make has either one! Compare these superior features with ordinary "splasher" type or "needle-spray" washers...see the *big* difference for yourself!

How will it go in your kitchen? The answer—beautifully! Your dealer can provide the model, style and fin-

ish you prefer, the color you wish... place in your kitchen as naturally as it fits your way of life.

For information, write Dept. KT, KitchenAid Home Dishwasher Division, The Hobart Manufacturing Co., Troy, Ohio. Canada: 175 George St., Toronto 2.

KitchenAid
The Finest Made...by Hobart

World's Largest Manufacturer of Food, Kitchen and Dishwashing Machines

Figure 4.1. Kitchen Aid advertisement, *Time* magazine, September 24, 1956.

back to life." This advertisement helps explain the ambivalence housed in this promise of consumer choice by the assertion of domesticity's liberating vectors. In effect this ad introduces the same housewife we collectively conjured a moment ago: absent and present at the same time. "You know what a 'ghostess' is," the advertisement reads, "that's a hostess who disappears right after the meal." The ghostess is the figure that haunts the hostess, the apparitional *G* that adheres to her figure, even when she is present. The duty of the dishwasher is to scrub away that *G* and return her to her rightful place as autonomous hostess. The acts of purification, cleansing, and mechanization rehearse the emotional affectlessness of the kitchen— devoid of emotional engagement. Yet, as that pesky "ghostess" may remind us, the kitchen is also the space of overwrought frustration, rage, girl talk, female sociality, and the like. Proper domesticity, through acquiescence to the manicuring tendencies of the modern appliance, exhibits itself as the device for the organization of the emotions.

Thus this ad documents the ways that norms of domesticity sought to strip women of the emotional equivalents of freedom, autonomy, and sociality and to replace these emotional valences with appliances. In this advertisement, and across the spectrum of middle-class, consumerist domesticity more broadly, appliances became prosthetic devices for the emotions. In the Kitchen Aid ad, the appliance brings her "back to life," becomes the site of her emotionality, which is paradoxically automatized, like a dishwasher. This rerouting of affect through appliance is an eerie reminder of the housewife's de rigueur emotional absence or the dedication of her emotional life to the labors of home maintenance. In the Kitchen Aid version and elsewhere, emotion itself becomes a domestic chore. Thus technological progress recreates the material practice of domesticity, but in so doing it also creates more work. Simultaneous to an erasure of women's labor in the home is the advent of a new consumerist model in which consumption itself becomes women's labor. This notion is nowhere better illuminated than in the planned obsolescence of appliances, such as the Kitchen Aid dishwasher. Its proverbial demise in three to five years promises to bring about the burden of more consumer choices, the perpetual resurrection of the ghostess.

Back in Moscow, we hear Nixon's declarations about housewifery in the context of other timely pronouncements by Eisenhower's administration, namely, the declaration of Captive Nations Week just as Nixon was departing for Moscow. Captive Nations Week was a measure approved by Congress that called for, among other things, a week of prayer for peoples enslaved by the Soviet Union. Nixon, in his use of doublespeak in the kitchen, thus declares, on the one hand, support for diversity in the marketplace in the name of liberating women. On the other hand, by claiming that this attitude is universal, he also compulsorily puts women in a position of captivity. (He isn't in Moscow promoting a wealth of new job opportunities for women, after all.) The universalizing tendency of Nixon's global democracy encourages ease for its women, so long as they stay within the domestic sphere.[7] Thus women are, ironically, the "captive nation" brought to attention by Nixon's presence in his Moscow kitchen; yet female domesticity is not simply the incarceration of unwilling subjects. Housewives are not simply captives but also positioned within that space as part of an ideology that lays claim to the universal, as I mentioned earlier—what Amy Kaplan has called, regarding another era, manifest domesticity.[8] Bolstering confidence in consumer choice and abundance may have provided a partial means of defraying the psychological and ideological costs of *Sputnik*. It also, however, displaced questions of diversity from the social to the supermarket and dismissed actual economic diversity—the systems and structures of which had enslaved millions of working-class blacks, whites, Latinos, Asians, and American Indians in the United States.

In the 1950s, moreover, the term "domestic" was not limited to the bipolarity that Kaplan suggests. Indeed, "domestic" meant more than private home or national home front: it also outlined a subjectivity, that of *the* domestic, frequently African American, who labored in the American kitchen. Indeed kitchens in America have been segregated spaces at least as far back as the plantation kitchen, which was literally separate from the rest of the house. This physical and structural separation reenacts segregation, and as Trudier Harris has argued, a symbolic chasm between white and black spaces exists even after the kitchen becomes part of the house. The American kitchen retains the remnants of this association— the kitchen as the space where black labor provides white nourishment that is then consumed in the dining room. So the constitutive ambivalence between presence and absence is already caught, captivated as it were, by the larger vectors of domesticity, diversity, and captivity within which the kitchen debate was staged. How might these vectors relate back to our earlier inability to come up with the housewife's iconic image and the conditions of intelligibility that, at the same time, render her familiar?

Offering the kitchen as a space in which forms of cold war sociality were both articulated and silenced, I turn to the work of two writers, one Soviet, one American, both of whom redress Nixon and Khrushchev's terms of domesticity and captivity. Alice Childress and Natalya Baranskaya wrote at a great distance from one another. Childress wrote *Like One of the Family: Conversations from a Domestic's Life* in Harlem; Baranskaya wrote *A Week Like Any Other* in Moscow. My somewhat jarring juxtaposition of geography and literary location is intentional in that bringing these novels into conversation enables us to see a deep correspondence between the two. Baranskaya's and Childress's texts register Nixon's misplacement of the housewife and redress it by constructing visions of diversity that belie an easy association between choice and the market. Both texts present a heterogeneity not reliant on the captivity of women and minorities (or the erasure of their histories of inequity). Both put women back, as it were, into the kitchen. But rather than a transparent position of captivity, the position of housewife in both Childress and Baranskaya announces itself and the labor of the kitchen as material, not ephemeral. Theirs is a dissident feminist poetics of the kitchen. Unlike the ghostess showcased in

Moscow, whose emotional life is rerouted and mechanized with the advent of technological progress, the women in these novels proclaim an emotional presence, thereby challenging Nixon's sphere of sentiment meant to ensure social unity and universal emotions.

In fact, as these novels teach us, the American housewife is central to the emotive realm of the African American domestic and the Russian working woman—she is an image around which their emotional life is constellated. At once attached to the idea of a conversation among women, and defiant of the conversation relegated to them, both writers demand a revision of the terms of address of the sphere from which they are writing. In this sense, both writers recognize and demand revision of the terms of recognition accorded to them, and both texts articulate alternative intelligences about the relationships between diversity and captivity.

The correspondence between these novels is not only thematic, however; it is also formal. Both novels use an experimental form to inscribe their meditations. In Childress's case the shape began before the novel was published: written originally as columns for Paul Robeson's *Freedom* magazine, *Like One of the Family: Conversations from a Domestic's Life* relies on a kind of vernacular intellectualism indebted to its periodical origins. Alongside articles by Eslanda Robeson, Lorraine Hansberry, Shirley Graham, and Claudia Jones, Childress's columns helped to shape *Freedom* as an experimental magazine that realigned terms of the familial, the racial, and the national through a dynamic mix of social democracy, antiracism, and anticolonialism. As fictional pieces, Childress's contributions offset the news-oriented shape of the magazine, shifting attention to the powerful imaginary of a black female domestic worker. Her pieces also undercut the predominance of news about men that the publication showcased and thus offset, in key ways, its focus on a representative black masculinity as the face of blackness. The novel appropriates its own contribution to *Freedom*, and its chapters are best described as nonnarrative installments.[9] Written as conversations between women, the chapters are elocutionary missives, each of which begins with a salutation in which Mildred, a black domestic, greets her friend Marge and then chafes conversationally against her white employers. To read Mildred's addresses to Marge is to engage in their conversation. Yet we may ask, what is the horizon of exchange here? Can there be new modes of sociality imagined within the space of this conversation in which the kitchen is the central conceit? And how may these communicative modes reconfigure the relationship between diversity and captivity? How may they challenge the mechanized affect of female domesticity in Nixon's kitchen?

Originally published in the prized literary journal *Novyi Mir*,[10] Baranskaya's *A Week Like Any Other* takes up the diary, playing on the association of this form with personal record. Indeed, it is in response to state mandate that the protagonist, Olya, keeps a diary. For any Russian reader, *A Week Like Any Other* thus immediately summons images of nineteenth-century Russian scribe Nikolai Gogol's civil servant in "Diary of a Madman," whose record of his own descent into madness is also a thinly veiled record of petty bureaucracy in St. Petersburg. Moving between the personal and the official, Baranskaya's novel records a week, but it covers much more than a week: the diary is neither spatially nor temporally accurate. In this sense, the diary both attends to the assignment of journal keeping and moves beyond it. *A Week Like Any Other* rehearses Olya's movement between the unstable poles of attention and distraction. How might Olya's ensuing madness, as her husband calls it, reveal an affective layer of Soviet female consciousness that chafes against the confines of the American kitchen?

"HI MARGE!"

Alice Childress is best known for her work with the American Negro Theater. She was the first woman to win an Obie Award (for her 1955 *Trouble in Mind*) and the first black woman to have a play produced professionally on Broadway. In addition to *Like One of the Family*, her other works include *Florence, Wedding Band, A Hero Ain't Nothin' but a Sandwich*, and *Moms: A Praise Play for a Black Comedienne*.

In *Like One of the Family* the heroine, Mildred, recounts for her friend Marge the daily battles she has with her white employers, who, as Elizabeth Brown-Guillory astutely remarks, either "treat her like she is invisible or . . . try to overwork and underpay her for her services as a maid. Unlike the docile, self-effacing, one-dimensional domestics often found in American literature, Mildred is assertive, intellectually superior, quick-witted and dignified. She questions authority, attacks stereotypes, and challenges white bias."[11] From her very inception, Mildred generates friction.

Like One of the Family takes its name from the opening conversation in which Mildred debunks the myth that black domestics are like one of the family. Mildred hears her employer, Mrs. C, say to a guest, "'She's like one of the family. We don't know what we'd do without her! We don't even think of her as a servant.'" According to Mildred's account of the incident to Marge, Mildred confronts Mrs. C after the guest leaves: "I am not just like one of the family at all! The family eats in the dining room and I eat in the kitchen. . . . You think it is a compliment when you say, 'we don't think of her as a servant,' but after I have worked myself into a sweat cleaning the bathroom and the kitchen, making the beds, cooking the lunch, washing the dishes and ironing, I do not feel like no weekend house guest. I feel like a servant" (1–3).[12] Proclaiming the work she does as work that changes the nature of the family into which her employer would interpolate her, Mildred not only makes material the labor she provides for the housewife, but she blocks the fantasy of the family as a space of sociability that flow, intimacy, and identification across difference can bridge. Her material labor creates a feeling state of difference that exhibits this grammatical alterity—of being alike and apart simultaneously.

Like the resonance of the ghostess, Mildred's intrusion into the white familial fantasy requires a vacillation between female subjectivities, between presence and absence. The novel opens with the words "Hi Marge!" Commencing as it does with the summoning into being of an imagined other, Childress's novel insists that we ask and re-ask, as Mildred does, "Where is the Speakin' Place?" The implied repetition of this question throughout the book gives shape to black woman's location in the matrix of American selfhood and black radicalism, offering this complex site as a model for a dissident sensibility. Although the novel's opening line brings the character Marge into being, we never learn much about her. Marge is Mildred's interlocutor, the subject with whom Mildred engages in conversation. Indeed Mildred comments at one point that she would "lose her mind if she had to come home after a hard day of work, rasslin' around in other folks' kitchens" (34) and not have Marge to confide in. Marge's agency, however, is usurped by Mildred's recapitulation of Marge's words into her own. All we ever know about Marge are the ellipses that represent what she would have said or what she probably said. In fact the novel doesn't present conversations at all—it presents erased conversation, setting up a female intimacy into which the reader is put in the position of the silent and yet necessary Marge.

So, as the novel is consumed with trying to broach the question of enunciation and its location—Where is the speaking place for the domestic?—this multiple Mildred/Marge asks: From what position *can* a domestic speak? From what position can a "like" but not an "of" articulate selfhood—is black female selfhood in this era suggestive of an "as if"? This posing of a hypothetical subjective space recalls the Kitchen Aid ghostess, but with a twist. In fact, the black female servant may have been the presence more fully evacuated by the arrival of the dishwasher and the postwar boom in household appliances. Their creation of the kitchen as a reworked space of emotionality in which surfaces gleamed like the blade of a stainless steel knife is undercut by Mildred's staunch insistence on standing her ground in the kitchen and proclaiming her difference from the housewife. In the chapter titled "All about My Job," Mildred is asked by a wealthy, white matron about her occupation. Mildred replies, "I do housework." "Oh," says the matron, "you are a housewife." "Oh no," says Mildred, "I do housework" (35). Although three years later Betty Friedan would claim that American housewives suffered from a problem that had no name, Mildred is way ahead of her and ready to name it. For Mildred the material practice of domesticity is not only about home maintenance based on a consumerist model; it is about the hands-on labor that creates social difference and that would remain transparent if we believed in an undifferentiated continuum of female bonds created in the American kitchen. As the ad so pointedly reminds us, the ghostess poses on the threshold of kitchen and proper dining room—a permeability of boundaries never afforded Mildred.

Finally, by reminding us that the kitchen is the space in the white home most frequently occupied by people of color, the novel foregrounds the idea that the authority of who speaks is bound up in the space of the telling. One scene in particular elaborates the distinctive demarcations of space within U.S. domesticity. In a conversation titled "The Health Card," Mildred recounts to Marge the story of Mrs. Jones, whose hovering between the kitchen and living room causes Mildred concern: "I looks up and there she was in the doorway, lookin' kind of strained around the gills. First she stuttered and then she stammered and after beatin' all around the bush she comes out with, 'Do you have a health card, Mildred?'" (42–43). Not one to be caught off guard, Mildred responds by asking to see not only Mrs. Jones's health card but also that of her husband and each of her three children. As Mildred explains, "since I have to handle laundry and make beds, you know." Mrs. Jones pointedly backs out of the kitchen and scurries to the library, where her husband lays in wait; then she returns with the news that Mildred need not bring a health card after all. Mildred's response: "I looked up real casual kind-of and said, 'on second thought, you folks look real clean too, so . . .'" (43). The kitchen vacillates here between Mildred's authority and the authority of her employer, which resides, along with Mr. Jones, in the living room. Rather than submit to humiliation, erasure, a life without value to which the kitchen proper would assign her, Mildred claims that space as her own. Partly undermining Mrs. Jones's authority to segregate and discriminate against her as apart from the family, Mildred assumes equal human standing with her employer. The chapter, however, ends in the kitchen with a ricocheting of smiles between Mrs. Jones and Mildred. Although they are smiling, this is, to be sure, not a moment of interracial solidarity. Rather, the unevenness of the exchange and the multiple levels of incommensurability, of communication and miscommunication, are emphasized.

Childress's text challenges Nixon's stance in the kitchen. The American kitchen's history of segregation—and the affective states associated with this history—are ignored by him as much as they are called attention to by Childress.[13] She achieves this attention through the space of Mildred's "as if." Formally and thematically the text provides an improper repetition of American housewifery, a feminist theorization of affect that opens up the differential space between women in the kitchen.

"PLASTICS, MY BOY, PLASTICS"

In Natalya Baranskaya's best-known novel, *Nedelia kak nedelia* (A week like any other), we hear an echo of Childress's reworking of female domesticity, but through a very different set of associations. The conceit behind Baranskaya's novel is a survey that some of the women who work in a plastics lab, as Olya does, are asked to fill out; the questionnaire requests that they record "hour by hour, in the given period of time, a week" how much time they spend on housework, child care, and leisure. The object of the questionnaire is to provide the authorities with a statistical understanding of the declining Soviet birthrate. Most of its questions presuppose what Soviet women workers do when they are not at work: they work. As Maria Mies points out in her study *Patriarchy and Accumulation on a World Scale*, "the high rate of employment of women in [Soviet world], the limited availability of public services and communal facilities ... and the refusal of men to share housework means that women have much less leisure time than men and are constantly overburdened."[14] Baranskaya renders the poignancy of the very term "leisure," *dosug*, formally, by having Olya linger over it longingly: "Ekh, dosug, dosug. . . . Slovo kokoe-to neukliuzhee 'do-sug'" (28) (Ha, leisure, leisure. . . . The very word presupposes an awkwardness: "lei-sure"). Russian women's resentment of what Mies calls "the persistent and reinforced patriarchal attitudes of men, who fill their leisure time with drinking and watching TV without bothering in the least how the housework is done," provokes Olya's ire, but it also provokes her guilt.[15] Indeed as a woman fully identified with the emotional labors of family life, Olya doubly feels the pressures of motherhood, which throughout the Soviet era was extolled as a patriotic duty. Olya's story becomes one of feminine anxiety to achieve the impossible: good Soviet/good mother. This failure is captured in the stark and staccato-like beat of the text, which opens, only briefly, to romantic interludes of lush prose when Olya daydreams about her honeymoon with her beloved. This shifting between anxiety and distraction enables her to remain close to the idea of love and the promise of reciprocity she anticipated in that love. Through her prose Baranskaya renders the undoing of this promise of exchange, which then becomes the potential undoing of Olya's site of enunciation.

Preoccupied as the novel is with the place of enunciation for Soviet women who are burdened with the task of achieving the impossible integration of "good Soviet/good mother," Baranskaya's text recalls a question I asked of Childress: From what position can a "like" but not an "of" articulate selfhood—is Soviet female selfhood representative of a particular kind of correspondence, partiality, an "as if"?

The story opens on Monday: "begu, begu" (I'm running, I'm running.) Although Olya is running, it is clear that she will never catch up. Temporality is structured in the text so that Olya is always behind; she is never coincident with the present. Rather, Olya runs through the frantic pace of the story beneath the mandate that she "couldn't possibly forget": "you won't be late with the testing," her boss asks her, "will you?" (657). But Olya, as we know, has already forgotten; she is already late. Instead of assuring her boss "no of course not," she "keeps silent: how can I be sure?" she asks herself. Olya negotiates these conflicting roles with an active, vernacular silence, not unlike that of the character Marge. For example, her encounters with her male superiors at work lead her to repeatedly remain silent when confronted with the impossible necessities demanded of her. As readers, however, we are privy to the workings of her active mind.

Baranskaya's point is to show how Olya maintains her sense of self despite an anxiety that charges through the text like a ticking time bomb. In her day-to-day activities Olya keeps from losing her mind by shifting between hypervigilance and inattention. She is emotionally present for her husband and family, then loses track of time at work and misses her train home. Rather than suggesting integration of the selves put forth here— Soviet worker/Soviet mother—however, Baranskaya's form suggests that this kind of erraticism is actually an ordinary form of Soviet feminine consciousness. In the end Olya does not come apart, although one may argue (as her husband does) that she is unraveling. Rather, her undoing is her mode of competence. This conclusion puts the reader in the position of trying to make sense of Olya's world and her modes of perception.

Like Mildred's, Olya's consciousness is shaped by the overarching binarism between East and West. Olya is a valued scientist, working to develop a new plastic to help fulfill the Five-Year Plan, one of a string of state plans intended to launch the Soviets ahead of the West in industrialization. Plastics, and Olya's involvement with them are not incidental to the era. The role of plastics in the utopian visions of a modern Soviet society was central. As one East German scientist put it, plastics "represent a revolution in technology that contradicts in every way the conservative capitalistic relations of production" because they enable "a dialectical unity between utility and economy."[16] Thus, Olya's occupation bespeaks her embeddedness in a cultural logic in which the West plays a starring role. Perhaps even more suggestive than plastics are the particular ways in which the United States is named, located, and signified in the text. The presence of Americanness speaks less to a globalizing momentum of the market than it does to an unexpected mobilization of that impulse. When Olya and her husband Dima try to have a conversation, Olya moves from the kitchen to the common room, suggesting that they talk about Jim Garrison (an American who put forward conspiracy theories about JFK's assassination).[17] And when Dima, again poised on the threshold of the kitchen, suggests that she quit her job so that he can have a more relaxed life, she calls him a "capitalist!" (701). To not talk about the family—to escape the everyday occupations of the household or what is called *byt* in Russia—Olya exhibits her worldliness by choosing Kennedy's death as a topic. Olya is aware of the competing claims on women that each nation makes, and she sees a capitalist or American attitude toward women and work as one that collapses women into housewives and makes presidential discussion superfluous, the everyday/*byt* inescapable. Olya staunchly refuses to disengage her emotions, to accommodate her husband's appeal for a life of felt simplicity.

As Nixon was perhaps not aware, by the time he arrived in Moscow, the Soviet Union was submerged in antithetical ideologies of domesticity. On the one hand there was an influx of modernist, streamlined asceticism, and on the other hand there was a cozy, comfy, and lumpy aesthetic that dominated the earlier Stalinist period of the 1930s and 1940s. In Olya's era the new standard of beauty prescribed by Soviet taste "was an austere, simple, 'contemporary style' that bore a close affinity to international Modernism, both in its visual characteristics and in such imperatives as 'form follows function' and 'less is more.'"[18] Khrushchev's third-party program encouraged self-regulation, spontaneous action, and voluntary appropriation rather than outright coercion. Instead of focusing on the containment of "women's needs" within the home, the Soviet project increased mechanization in the collective world by building laundries, communal dining facilities, child care facilities, and the like. As the saying went, "*byt ne chastnoe delo*"—the everyday is not a personal affair. It is significant, therefore, that although she is a respected scientist at work, Olya is a failure at the scientific management of her home. It is her failure to blend these two worlds, to make her home run like clockwork and her office personable and connected, that creates her arc of anxiety.[19] Women were to be the chief protectors of the state against the potential corruption of consumption, acquisitiveness, and the complacency of irrational consumption—precisely the feeling states of domesticity on display at the American exhibition. Nonetheless, as Baranskaya describes for us, modernization, rationalization, and standardization—the prescribed "feeling states" of domesticity during the Soviet period—are completely at odds with the ways in which Olya experiences her domestic life.

Thus, negotiating female selfhood in *A Week Like Any Other* requires negotiating not so much identity as the false emotional iconography of Soviet womanhood, as Olya's co-worker puts it, of integrated "good mother/good worker" (659).[20] As the conceptual artist Martha Rosler has pointed out, female emotionality in Russia "was expelled except in representations of leaders' public appearances, where woman could be permissibly depicted as overcome with justified emotion.... Women were shown in a state of emotional uncertainty only in those instances where they were waiting the return of husbands who were fighting for their country."[21] Although Baranskaya's women are ensnared in the uncertainty of opting to be both, they are also enmeshed in the racial coding of the Russian nationalist project. Baranskaya's women are constituted in part by a presumption of whiteness or universal womanhood demanded by the doubling rhetoric of the state: one that produced multiracial iconography but operated within largely sedimented presumptions of (white) Russian superiority. As Svetlana Boym has pointed out, Russian national identity refers "to all ethnic groups which for better or for worse happened to share Russian and Soviet Russian history."[22] Thus Soviet women's place is assigned a hierarchical function of superiority in which whiteness operates through its own privilege of not knowing and diversity is made to feel like a kind of Western exploitation. Olya's story, however, also opens to the impossibility of that kind of racial foreclosure; if diversity feels like a kind of Western exploitation, it is, as the story reveals to us, already part of the Soviet configuration—what the story opens to is that difference. Diversity does not have to mean captivity. *A Week Like Any Other* seeks to move the horizon of exchange beyond the wavering terms of selfhood to a larger collective.

Let me be more specific by addressing the function of "hully gully" in the story. "Hully Gully" was a dance song written in 1960 by the black rock band the Olympics and rerecorded by the Beach Boys in 1965. The hully-gully was an unstructured line dance in which an endless stream of steps was called out by an alternating leader and enacted by everyone at the same time. Olya and Dima call the "hully gully" their "signal," their wake-up call. Once it is announced they begin their day. Dismissing the compelling cultural routing of this reveille, the notes to the Russian text explain that "hully gully" are "nonsense words from a popular song."

If we dig deeper than the Russian editor, we find that although it may have been the Beach Boys who made the hully-gully popular, they were simply following a trend—fusing (or some may say appropriating) an African dance into their own idiom. Scholars have traced the hully-gully as far back as 1894, to U.S. slave culture, when "hully-gully" or "hull da gull" referred to a phrase in a children's game.[23] So although Baranskaya's femininity may be contained within the problematical "white" contours of Russian national identity, which would dismiss the hully gully as nonsense, her story also breaks with the racializing confines of that model. Baranskaya's story makes use of silence to foreground how evasion, in fact, may serve as a strategic dissension from and point of intervention into the cultural norm. Anticipating the articulation of an already present heterogeneity, Olya uses silence as her speakin' place.

Squeezed between the two impossibilities of good worker and good mother, Olya finds herself waking up in the middle of the night. She says, "What is disturbing me? I don't know. I lie and listen to the silence." Silence, it turns out, isn't silence at all, but the steady pace of a clock ticking "like a drum roll" (703). We are left waiting for the "hully gully," the "wake up call" or a signal. This call signifies not so much the intrusion of the United States into Soviet daily lives but rather women's negotiation of this intrusion, a negotiation of the burdens of multiple demands or a female "as if" yet to be elaborated: a little America, quite different from the one Nixon advertised, in the heart of Moscow.

To return to my opening question—What are the conditions of intelligibility for the iconic image of the American housewife? —I venture to say that to answer this question we need to return to the photo op: Nixon and Khrushchev are poised at the threshold of the splitnik kitchen, just as the ghostess is poised at the threshold of the Kitchen Aid kitchen, and Mrs. Jones is hovering at Mildred's kitchen door. These threshold spaces speak to the constitutive and yet unstable presence and absence of women and the many millions of figures who are absent from these pictures and yet implied in their context. Not too many cooks in the kitchen, but too few. Thinking comparatively about Russian and American work in this way enables us to attend to the silenced figures of otherness that undergird cold war narratives such as those surrounding the "kitchen debate." Through such seemingly unlikely juxtapositions, we may better comprehend the lesser-known narratives, the silenced linguistic and affective registers, that continue to adhere to the figures, images, and emotions through which we commonly identify a period.

If the Nixon–Khrushchev kitchen debate announced once and for all the highly politicized interior of the kitchen, it also revealed the mutually constitutive relationship between Russianness and Americanness during the cold war era. The exclusion of women and minorities—the material bodies who do the kitchen's work—from the kitchen intensifies the affective confusion between inside and outside, state and self, public and private on display in Moscow. The conditions of intelligibility thus point to (1) the ambivalence between maternal plentitude and female absence, or the diversity of market choice held out as interpersonal intimacy, and (2) the erasure of alternative feeling states of domesticity through which we might transform the "as if" into a speaking place of broader sociality that might be heard.

Notes

1. Robert Hariman and John Lucaites, *No Caption Needed: Iconic Photographs, Public Culture and Liberal Democracy* (Chicago: University of Chicago Press, 2007).

2. See "Ivan Takes a Look at American Life: Photo Report from Moscow," *U.S. News and World Report*, August 10, 1959, 40–50. For a detailed description of the event from a contemporary perspective, see Walter L. Hixson, *Parting the Curtain: Propaganda, Culture and the Cold War, 1945–1961* (New York: St. Martin's Press, 1996).

3. As quoted in Eric Sandeen, *Picturing an Exhibition: The Family of Man and 1950s America* (Albuquerque: University of New Mexico Press, 1995), 128.

4. "Better to See Once," *Time*, August 3, 1959, 16.

5. "The Two Worlds: A Day-Long Debate," *New York Times*, July 25, 1959, 1.

6. "Better to See Once," 15.

7. Indeed, since John Steinbeck toured a war-ravaged Russia in 1947 with the photographer Robert Capa in search of what he termed the "great other side of politics"—"There must," he wrote, "be a private life of the Russian people"—the sense that a capitalist attitude toward women was universal provided an enduring model. Steinbeck's search detailed an inability of postwar America to fathom Russia without invoking femininity as a battle ground. Like other texts by equally left-leaning authors such as Marguerite Higgins, Margaret Bourke White, and Ella Winter, Steinbeck's *A Russian Journal* is actively engaged in teaching a new postwar Americanness in which "the Russian woman" as determined by a compulsory relationship to capitalist femininity (or "the private") figures as key in determining a binary relationship between the United States and the USSR. As early as 1943, a focus on the shortcomings and limitations of women abroad (particularly in the USSR) became a way of reiterating American national superiority, even during wartime. The fascination with Soviet femininity became especially fashionable in the late 1950s, when numerous articles in the *New York Times*, *Life*, *Newsweek*, and elsewhere showcased the dreary attempts of Russians to be real, which is to say consumer-oriented, women. See John Steinbeck, *A Russian Journal* (New York: Viking, 1948).

8. Kaplan explains: "If domesticity plays a key role in imagining the nation as home, then women, positioned at the center of the home, play a major role in defining the contours of the nation and its shifting borders with the foreign." Amy Kaplan, "Manifest Domesticity," *American Literature* 70, no. 3 (1998): 582.

9. These installments are not presented chronologically, however, and in many ways they leave the form of the monthly behind them. For example, absent is the polyphonic discursive space of the magazine in which articles are juxtaposed with advertisements, photographs, op-eds, and letters.

10. Natalya Baranskaya, *Nedelia kak nedelia* [A week like any other], *Novyi Mir* 11 (1969): 23-55. *Novyi Mir* has been described as "the most prestigious and politically independent journal of its day." One indicator of U.S. lack of perception (and questionable translation) of Baranskaya's novel emerges when one considers the place of its first translation into English: in *Redbook* magazine, as "The Alarm Clock in the Cupboard," trans. Beatrice Stillman (March 1971): 179-201. Throughout this chapter I quote from the standard English translation, "A Week Like Any Other Week," trans. Emily Lehrman, *Massachusetts Review* (Autumn 1974): 657-703, or use my own translation of the 1969 *Novyi Mir* text. Page citations are in parentheses in the text. Unless otherwise noted, translations from the Russian are my own.

11. Elizabeth Brown-Guillory, "Like One of the Family," in *The Concise Oxford Companion to African American Literature*, ed. William L. Andrews, Frances Smith Foster, and Trudier Harrissuperior (New York: Oxford University Press, 2001), 258. Quotations from the novel are from Alice Childress, *Like One of the Family: Conversations from a Domestic's Life* (Boston: Beacon Press, 1986). The page citations are in parentheses in the text.

12. Mildred's selfhood thus speaks not so much beyond as alongside prevailing notions of double consciousness as articulated in Du Bois's famous description of black American selfhood. Mildred offers us a means of investigating how black women may be made to experience differently the constraints of this cultural nationalism. For a different take on Mildred's location in the kitchen, see Sonya Lancaster, "Too Many Cooks: Contested Authority in the Kitchen," *Southern Literary Journal* 38, no. 2 (Spring 2006): 113-30.

13. With its title and its intimate coupling of Mildred and Marge, the novel sets itself up in a sphere of female fiction: Pauline Hopkins, Jessie Fauset, Fannie Hurst, and Olive Higgins Prouty come to mind. Yet the novel teaches us that femininity, as it is conceived in terms of the "family," is typically a concept or metaphor for not changing—for remaining in an emotional register that can be adapted as it props up the play of surface relations such as those on display in Moscow. See Lauren Berlant, *The Female Complaint* (Chicago: University of Chicago Press, 2008).

14. Maria Mies, *Patriarchy and Accumulation on a World Scale* (New York: Third World Books, 1998), 181.

15. Ibid.

16. Ray Stokes, "Plastics and the New Society: The German Democratic Republic in the 1950s and 60s," in *Style and Socialism: Modernity and Material Culture in Post-War Eastern Europe*, ed. Susan E. Reid and David Crowley (Oxford: Berg Publishers, 2000), 75.

17. In the standard English version, this phrase is incorrectly translated as "the American Presidency" (699). The Russian text reads, "Razve my ne govorili o prokurore Garrisone?" (52). The difference is key as it indicates the specificity of the (rejected) topic of conversation.

18. Susan Reid, "Women in the Home," in *Women in the Khrushchev Era*, ed. Melanie Ilic, Susan Reid, and Lynne Atwood (New York: Palgrave Macmillan, 2004), 157. See also Susan Reid, "Cold War in the Kitchen: Gender and the De-Stalinization of Consumer Taste in the Soviet Union under Khrushchev," *Slavic Review* 61, no. 2 (Summer 2002): 211-52.

19. As one Soviet critic has commented, "Excessive, useless, decorative objects were among the chains that bound [women] into domestic slavery, since it fell to them to dust and polish them. . . . Zealous converts, liberated from the tyranny of trash, women were to lead the crusade for taste." As quoted in Reid, "Women in the Home," 167.

20. As others have noted, there is no word in Russian for "privacy." *Lichnoe* (personal) or *chastnoe* (separate) are the closest the Russian lexicon comes to "private." Even outside the communal kitchen, domestic space is marked as not private: housing is state owned, furni-

ture is government issued, and so forth. Emotion, however, is of complex and messy sociality. The longing for a "private" in Baranskaya is thus also about a negotiation in the market. Her private is available to her to the extent that its violations reinvent the search. Interestingly, Olya finds more freedom on the street with her co-workers than she does in the seclusion of her home.

21. Martha Rosler, "Some Observations on Women as Subjects in Russia," in *After Perestroika: Kitchenmaids or Stateswomen?* (New York: Independent Curators International, 1994).

22. Svetlana Boym, *Common Places: Mythologies of Everyday Life in Russia* (Cambridge: Harvard University Press, 1994), 253.

23. See Lynn Abbot and Doug Seroff, eds., *Out of Sight: The Rise of African American Popular Music, 1889–1895* (Jackson: University of Mississippi Press, 2003), 308–9, for the fascinating history of the Hampton Institute Folk-Lore Society's pathbreaking "Folk-Lore and Ethnology" column in which this early report of the hully-gully was cited.

PART II

FIVE

Circulating Empires

Colonial Authority and the Immoral, Subversive Problem of American Film

Brian Larkin

Empire, the projection of political power across space, is a function of circulation. Imperial control organizes diverse territories into a hierarchical system that "resonates together" by placing into motion a ceaseless movement of persons, laws, administrative practices, commodities, texts, images, and religious orders.[1] Lines of transportation and communication—the media system of Empire—regulate this mobility, giving empires their sense of space and time, organizing relations with an imperial center and other nodes in the system. As technologies of communication change over time, so too do the structure and character of Empire itself and the forms of sociality and subjectivity that result from it. This sheer diversity and unpredictability mean that an entity like the British Empire was a system regulating other systems. It was a network of networks comprising missionaries, administrators, traders, and soldiers, themselves interacting with preexisting trade, religious and ethnic orders existing all over the world, each with their own organizational structure, their own media of communication. Understanding Empire depends on comprehending the diversity of these nodes of operation, while keeping in mind the system as a totality.

The rise of American film in the first two decades of the twentieth century represented a new kind of communication infrastructure for an emerging economy and a different kind of empire that came to pose a major challenge to the British imperial hegemon. Victoria's empire was organized through control of seas, postal systems, telegraphic networks, and chains of wireless stations through which a command and control structure existed, tying far-flung nodes into a single territorial system. The push here was toward tighter integration, faster linkages, greater centralized control, less autonomy for outlying areas. American Empire, by contrast, was a system ruled not by settlers and the annexation of territory but organized around the faster movement of goods and a preference for proxy political regimes as long as they guaranteed that speed of movement.[2] Cinema was an infrastructure that embodied this new decentralized mode of control. It was a communications system based on the elicitation of desire and the seduction of affect, suffusing lifestyles and commodities with glamour and prestige in ways that were to have enormous consequences for the future expansion of U.S. trade. The emergence of cinema represented the first great transnational communications structure dominated by the United States, and the anxious reaction it generated in the British Empire tells us much about shifts in imperial power and the nature of empires as circulatory systems.

When cinema-going became a popular form of recreation in the colonial world in the early years of the twentieth century, it generated what can only be described as a moral panic among expatriate whites, from businessmen to colonial officials to travelers to the military. This panic began in the 1910s, reached its height in the 1920s, and had largely subsided by the late 1930s—although the tropes it established continued to be mobilized for decades. The panic centered on fears that the circulation of American cinema, with its images of crime, violence, and sexuality, were providing negative images of white culture to native audiences and eroding the prestige of the white man and woman upon which colonial authority rested. On July 10, 1930, Sir Henry Hesketh Bell (G.C.M.G.), former governor of Northern Nigeria, Uganda, and Mauritius, wrote a letter to the *Times* on the subject. I quote it at length because it provides a succinct summary of the anxieties driving this fear:

> Sir—Up to a few years ago the people of Tropical Africa, India, Malaya and the Far East had only the vaguest notions of the home life of the Europeans to whose authority they had submitted. In most cases they accepted their rulers as belonging to a race superior to them in culture, morals and enlightenment and in India especially the prestige of the white man has rested largely on the respect and consideration in which he has been held.
>
> But about fifteen years ago a new and most mischievous influence made its appearance in the tropical world. Almost suddenly and without warning, cinema films, usually of a deplorable type, placed before the eyes of hundreds of thousands of unsophisticated natives travesties of the lives and habits of white people. Pictures representing white people indulging in every form of criminal act—robbery, rape, arson and murder—were displayed to the gaze of any native. . . . Worse than this, the exhibition of white women in a state of almost complete nudity and behaving in a shameless manner dealt a formidable blow at the respect in which the womenfolk of the ruling races had previously been held. It is hardly too much to say that nothing has done more to destroy the prestige of the white man and to conduce the general revolt of the colored races against the government of the European, which we are seeing everywhere today, than the spread of these deplorable pictures.[3]

Prestige is a mode of representation, a signifying apparatus, and when Bell writes he conceives of this representation as a display of hierarchy, a force central to the authority of European rule. By the time of his letter, Bell was already identified as one of the most outspoken experts on the subject of films in the colonies, a subject he had dealt with in some detail in his *Foreign Colonial Administration in the Far East.*[4] In this study, drawing on his extensive experience, he worried over the pressure Hollywood films exerted on imperial social and political relations. Bell outlined major themes that recur throughout the panic over commercial film: the immorality of Hollywood films; the sexual threat of the "native" gaze at European women; the objectification of "whiteness" for native viewing; and the causal link between prestige and colonial power. This fear of the demoralizing effects of film was a major scandal in late imperial Britain. It generated a stream of newspaper articles, outraged letters to editors, questions to Parliament, government reports, and articles in learned magazines and colonial memoirs that form the literate shallows of a much deeper oral reservoir of rumor, anxiety, and fear. It may seem surprising today that a cultural form such as film could be so anxiety provoking to political and military authority, but this is because film was an engine for a very different form of prestige, one that circulated all over the world and created an alternative representational practice to British colonial ritual. Both cinematic images and the circulatory system they relied on were maddeningly outside of British control. Bell's concern for the moral and political effects of cinema thus articulated with a related yet wider anxiety about economic power and the fact that the global ubiquity of Hollywood was driving an enormous boom in the U.S. economy. Hollywood was a visible symbol of a far-reaching transfer of economic and political dominance from Europe to the United States and was a central infrastructural mechanism of twentieth-century commodity culture. Bell was a political administrator. His main concern was the effect of Hollywood on political authority, yet his agitation was matched by British industry, whose leaders were motivated by quite different economic interests but who were just as fearful about the increasing power of Hollywood cinema. The global spread of American film forced a clash of imperial cultures between the waning political dominance of the British Empire and the rise of an expansionist, aggressive, American mass culture in the early years of the twentieth century.

These two anxieties brought about by the circulation of Hollywood rest on overlapping theories of the power of film.[5] Bell believes that screening degrading images has the mimetic power to debase and undermine the objects represented in those images. It is as if, like magic, cinema has a contagious power whereby the representation can physically affect and harm that which it represents. Not only does this power degrade through representation, but audiences are also transformed through the act of witnessing. Cinema for Bell, in a peculiar foreshadow of Siegfried Kracauer,[6] has political significance because its seemingly shallow emptiness actually exposes the fabricated nature of social power, potentially awakening audiences to challenge that power and thus threaten colonial rule. For British and American industrial and trade representatives, by contrast, cinema's importance lay not in debasing objects it represented but in glamorizing them and investing them with signification. Here too there is a belief that the representation can magically feed back into the object it represents, only this time the object is valorized and made desirable rather than degraded. These related theories of film have strikingly different consequences and generate radically different views of film-watching colonial subjects. Bell sought to limit what he saw as the corrupting nature of film, conceiving of audiences as ignorant, vulnerable natives requiring supervision and control. British (and American) industry conceived of audiences as consumers, of film as advertising, and wished to harness its power, not limit it. The only desire of British industry was to wrest control of image production away from Hollywood and place it in their own hands so the stimulation of desire could be directed toward British products. It is this interesting opposition and conflation between repulsion and desire, corruption and spectacle, that underlay competing ideas of the power and influence of film.

Colonial rule rested, in part, on the symbolic constitution of boundaries placing ruler and ruled, white and nonwhite, in carefully demarcated positions. "Whiteness" was not just the color of one's skin but a complex of attributes that included wealth, education, class status, manners, and deportment. The circulation of American film appeared to threaten those boundaries by undermining the carefully constructed performance of whiteness as an imperial category. By showing "backstage" images of white culture and morality, cinema undercut the dichotomy separating "depraved" natives from "civilized" rulers. Much of the anxiety over Hollywood, therefore, lay in its ostensible reversal of the hierarchy of colonial signification: Europeans were objectified and displayed for consumption of native viewers; European sexual excess was contrasted to Asian modesty; Europeans were dissolute criminals; and the European gaze was restricted while the colonial subjects' gaze was left free. This was an anxiety brought about by the process of circulation that took images formed in accord with the set of norms of one public and promiscuously disseminated them across cultural and religious boundaries, where they began to accrue new meanings. They seemed to objectify whiteness in the colonial arena in ways wholly unforeseen by their makers in America.

Film exhibition was a performative social event in which the semantic relay of meaning between film and audience was shaped by the precise conjuncture of racial, sexual, and political relations that preconstituted the citizens and subjects who encountered each other in colonial cinemas. In this sense it was intimate and tied to the particular relations of cinema-going in Mombasa, Penang, or Bombay. Films that seemed unremarkable in Europe or the United States became charged with undercurrents of sexual and racial tension, pregnant with political sedition, as they circulated in and out of different publics. Colonial cinemas were some of the few spaces in which rulers and ruled were brought into physical proximity. Nonwhite subjects gazing at images of white actresses generated an unnerving threat to expatriates sharing that same uncomfortable social space—part of what Fanon later called the "the drama of sexual preoccupation" in Empire.[7] By watching films in the presence of colonial subjects, expatriate whites became highly attuned to the reactions of those subjects and began to imagine what those reactions might be. The affectual flush of shame, outrage, and anger felt by expatriate Europeans emerged from these interactions, which were highly specific to the racial and social dynamics of particular colonial societies.

Imperial anxieties forged in intimate and specific encounters located in particular imperial nodes were then swept up in the information system of Empire. These anxieties, relayed in letters to the *Times* and the *Manchester Guardian*, in lectures to learned societies, through chapters in memoirs, and in books on political administration, circulated from colony to metropole and back again, transforming the specificity of those encounters into a patterned narrative. Outraged viewers in places as diverse as Uganda, Malaya, and India could articulate their fears in almost exactly the same language. These stories about cinema relied on the embodied experience of the teller for their legitimacy and authenticity, but through the act of circulation they lost their specificity and became part of a generalized pattern that had the power to terrify and fascinate. This transformation reveals ways in which Empire operated as a circulatory system, moving ideas, goods, and peoples, subjecting them to forces of standardization, abstraction, and genericization. It points to the information order of Empire, which moved around colonial officials, architectural design, troops, languages, legal regulations, cuisine, aesthetic forms, and economic goods between center and periphery and between colonies themselves. Indians are taken to East Africa to staff a new bureaucracy; British colonial civil servants move from Nigeria to Malaysia and on to the Caribbean, taking with them ideologies of rule worked out in one colony and applying them in another; laws designed for Indian hill tribes are used in the building of Iraq; films censored in India are banned in Nigeria and so on. It also points to the difficulty of analyzing Empire. One has to approach Empire through the historical specificities of actual encounters in diverse peripheries, while recognizing how Empire operated as a self-regulating circulatory system.

AMERICAN EMPIRE

The rise of Hollywood made clear that the communicative architecture of the British Empire, based on the control of trade routes and military command, sea lanes and railway systems, telegraphs and submarine cables, was now bumping into a new circulatory system of American economic, cultural, and political power that was dependent on very different forms of publicity and spectacle, and in which cinema, because of its supreme symbolic and economic position, occupied a privileged place. The issue lay in the fact that not only was American film seen as an industrial good in and of itself, but, because of the peculiar representational nature of this commodity, it invested other objects with its glamour, operating as an extended advertising system for American products and the American way of life. Will Hays, president of the Motion Pictures Producers and representative of Hollywood to industry, argued famously that "every foot of American film sells $1.00 worth of manufactured products some place in the world." The tenet that "trade follows the film" became widely used in discussions about the rise of American industry at the expense of Britain,[8] so much so that it became a truism referred to by British and Americans alike. Julius Klein, director of the Bureau of Foreign and Domestic Commerce, described cinema as a "silent salesman"; in the 1930s the producer Walter Wanger wrote that the circulation of film prints represented the equivalent of "120,000 ambassadors" for American economic and political interests.[9] In 1926, at the behest of the Federation of British Industry, these issues were made a central focus of the Imperial Conference that brought together Britain, the dominions, and colonies to try to create a system of protection for imperially produced goods within the British Empire as a means of combating the rise of American industrial power. Cinema was seen as central to this project because of its ability to shape the buying habits of audiences. "It requires little imagination," argued Sir Phillip Cunliffe-Lister, president of the U.K. Board of Trade and the conference host, "to picture the effect on tens of millions of people seeing American films, staged in American settings, American clothes, American furniture, American motor cars, American goods of every kind." The conference proposed the creation of an Empire Marketing Board designed to increase publicity for empire goods and famously led the call for a quota system intended to encourage British cinemas to show more British-made films. Civil servants and industrialists alike accepted the signifying power of film as a key element of industrial growth, and the *Report of the Imperial Conference* is a fascinating document for its recognition that in a commodity culture, control of signification is as necessary a part of the economy as the production of goods. "The constant showing of foreign scenes or settings ... powerfully advertises (the more effectively because indirectly) foreign countries and their products,"[10] the report concluded, cementing the sense that cinema had ramifications for manufacturing that went beyond the film industry itself.

Cinema occupied a privileged role in the transformation of capital in the twentieth century and of the place of the United States in this new economy. This transformation was part of the emergence of a commodity culture in which forms of spectacle and representation took on economic as well as cultural significance. Walter Benjamin describes the changes in the presentation of goods in new arcades and department stores of the nineteenth century as comprising a "great poem of display" chanting "stanzas of color."[11] He argues that new visual technologies such as photography and film had the ability to alienate objects that were previously inalienable or at best available only to single customers (such as landscapes or buildings) and to discharge them onto the market in unlimited quantities. This process generated a series of transformations. Objects are abstracted as images and circulated on film and as photographs. The urban leisure class attracted to the arcades and great exhibitions are "elevated" from the status of consumer to that of commodity. This transformation is achieved through the solicitation of attention and the regulation of desire enacted through new spectacles of display. Jonathan Crary pushes this argument farther, arguing that the regulation of attention and the creation of a properly "attentive" workforce became a key activity of the new systemic organization of labor, production, and consumption in early twentieth-century modernity.[12] Cinema, in this analysis, is only one of a series of new perceptual technologies, but one that comes to occupy an important symbolic and economic position. To create value, film must secure one's attention. It does so by stimulating the senses, promising excitement, laughter, or desire in order to draw in viewers, and as it does so it transforms attention into a form of value.[13] "Rather than requiring a State to build the roads that enable the circulation of commodities, as did Ford," argues the film theorist Jonathan Beller, "the cinema builds its pathways of circulation directly into the eyes and sensoriums of its viewers."[14] Beller sees cinema as a dematerialized commodity that generates value not from its thingness but from its ability to elicit desire and affect—a very modern form of value creation. But he sees cinema as distinct (and radically different) from older forms of industry that preceded it, whereas in the 1920s the two were seen as symbiotic. Hollywood films were commodities—exchanged and sold as objects—and signifying forms that represented other commodities, stimulating their sales. U.S. government and industry quickly realized that the trade power of film lay in the publicity it provided for American industrial products. As early as 1926 the U.S. Department of Commerce created a Motion Picture Section to track the link between Hollywood and the sale of U.S. consumer goods. The emergence of Hollywood cinema as a global commodity was part of this wider emergence of the United States as a dominant economic power, largely at the expense of Britain's leadership in trade and industry—a fact of pressing economic, political, and popular concern in Britain.

In 1932, Sir Stephen Tallents, secretary of the Empire Marketing Board and one of the founders of public relations in Britain, published the widely influential pamphlet *The Projection of Britain* in which he laid out the connection between the decline of the empire and the emergence of new communications infrastructures. He began by lamenting the fact Hollywood had "turned every cinema in the world into the equivalent of an American consulate" and argued that diplomacy was now a matter of controlling the "projection" of a national culture through mass media as much as it was about control of territory. Before, Tallents argued, nations were largely self-contained, but in an increasingly globalized world "a people is known to its fellows by the impression it makes upon them through the cable and the printing press, on the air and upon the screen." Tallents recognized the shift toward a world in which the circulation of images "less tangible but not less significant" has replaced the control of the seas as a means of wielding economic and political power. This "supremacy can only be secured through the exercise of . . . the art of national projection." Political and economic conflict would thereafter be fought over controlling the means of representation of national cultures. This represented a new order of information, and countries that failed to stabilize the meaning of their national identity or failed to invest in new infrastructures of meaning would be left behind. "No civilized country can to-day afford either to neglect the projection of its national identity or to resign its projection to others."[15] Here Tallents was summarizing widely held fears on behalf of British industry and government about the inseparability of new technologies of representations from economic and political power. Cinema was the infrastructure and signifying machine par excellence that dominated this new information order and lay almost entirely in the hands of the United States. Tallents's position as head of the Empire Marketing Board was to generate publicity for empire products and promote interimperial trade as a means of limiting American influence and creating a communicative system for a new sort of empire.[16] It is fascinating to read the report of Imperial Conferences in which the discussion of film in terms of American economic hegemony and the need to support British industry slips continually into a symbolic discussion of British and imperial identity and back again. Film was, for businessmen like Cunliffe-Lister, "this new and all-pervading influence," one that affected feelings, desires, and fantasies as well as commodities and industries.[17] The emergence of figures such as Tallents, the rise of the Empire Marketing Board, and the imposition of a quota system all indicate the innovations with which British government and industry were experimenting to try to deal with a phenomenon they saw as radically new and that demanded an entirely new approach to industry and economy. Anxieties over "white prestige" came to stand for a series of distinct yet related fears in British modernity. One emerged from the weakening authority of imperial rule and was located within the symbolic and social structures of colonial societies. The other concerned the transformation of twentieth-century capital and the emergence of American economic dominance, yet both anxieties crystallized around debates about the circulation of Hollywood film. It is no wonder cinema proved to be such an explosive, contradictory cocktail.

WHITE PRESTIGE: GOODBYE TO ALL THAT

In the first two decades of its existence, cinema in Britain was evolving as a social, economic, and artistic institution whose effects on the British public were imperfectly understood and subject to constant change. Controversy over the effects of film in the empire was part of a wider moment in which cinema was constituted as a public sphere of regulation, with intense efforts made by governmental and private bodies to control and limit its exhibition.[18] By 1914, domestic debates in England about the demoralizing effects of film on "immature minds" (most especially children) were being transferred into concerns about the influence of films in colonial territories. The concern for the influence of film in Empire was in part an outgrowth of debates about the moral effects of film within Britain itself. Colonial subjects, like children and women, were supposed to possess "less mature minds" and were thus more vulnerable to the negative effects of films.[19] But the dynamics of colonial rule created a potential for fear and anxiety that was distinct from the debates in Britain. From 1921 on, travelers, military and colonial officers, and missionaries began to report back about the perils of commercial film exhibition in the colonies. These diverse expatriates represented an authoritative group whose concern for the negative effects of film on white prestige was buttressed by considerable knowledge of colonial life. Their firsthand experience transformed the debate over the influence of films in the colonies by addressing issues that were unique to the colonial context itself.

"It is probable," wrote the *Times* in 1926, "that more has been said and written during the past year about the connexion between British films and British Empire than ever before. It is certain that less has been done. . . . Countless people write and talk about it, but no-one does anything."[20] By the mid-1920s British newspapers were publishing articles and letters on the subject of "white prestige" on a regular basis. The issue was taken up by Constance Bromley, former manager of the Opera House in Calcutta, who wrote to the *Leeds Mercury* about films "imperilling the prestige of the white woman" and leading to "an attitude of increasing disrespect on the part of the native."[21] Earlier, in the *Times*, Bromley wrote passionately about the need for strict censorship in the colonies, arguing that commercial film "has proved the worst possible 'dope' on which to feed 300,000,000 natives . . . to whom 'pictures' are as a universal tongue."[22] She cited the abduction of a European officer's wife at Rawalpindi to prove her point. Rear Admiral Smith-Dorrien concurred: "Can nothing be done," he complained in a letter to the *Times*, "to prevent undesirable films being sent to India?"[23] These writers, including many colonial officers, could rest on their expertise of colonial social and political relations and their claim to familiarity with the "mind" of the native. A Malay censor concluded his interview with the *Manchester Guardian* by warning that "the control of the cinema business is one of the most important decisions to be made in Eastern politics today."[24] A. J. W. Harloff, an officer from Netherlands Indies, agreed: "*The pernicious influence of picture shows*" is "an evil," a "colonial social danger" that has "undermined the prestige of the western leader on whom, to a considerable extent, the structure of colonial civilization work has been based."[25] Hesketh Bell stated the matter even more baldly: "The success of our government of subject races depends almost entirely on the degree of respect which we can inspire."[26]

The anxiety exhibited here is both political and sexual and speaks to a powerful instability that threatened colonial ideas of racial superiority and political legitimacy. George Bilainkin, editor of the Malay *Straits Echo* and part of the Malay expatriate elite, argued in his memoirs that Hollywood had plastered the screen with the weakness and hypocrisy of white men

and women. "The Asiatics conclude that the whites, who were always proclaimed to be superior and thus able to govern and rule subject races must
be, below the surface, a vile crowd of women snatchers."[27] These fears suggest that many Europeans conceived their political legitimacy to rest on
standards of behavior, modes of dress, and codes of morality as well as
legal regimes, conquest, and the plebiscite. To European eyes the legitimacy of rule rested on a representational complex, carefully cultivated and
performed, and the circulation of unauthorized images of white society
threatened both the complex and the claim to authority it sustained. This
perception is why Hollywood films were so quickly linked to claims of nationalism and revolt and appeared to expatriates to be a political as well
as a cultural threat.

Shrill warnings had their impact back in London. Stephenson states
that after the publication of Bell's first letter to the *Times* in 1926, His Majesty King George V instructed his private secretary to write the following to Leo Amery, the secretary of state for the colonies: "The King much
regrets ... the deplorable effect of cinema pictures on the prestige of the
Europeans in the Far East.... The King asks whether anything can be
done ... to put a stop to these deplorable pictures." Amery was well aware
of the growing chorus of complaints about cinema. He responded to the
king's letter by stressing the importance of the situation, but then argued
that the rising moral outrage was "exaggerated" and that "the influence of
the films is not one of the principle factors affecting the decline of European prestige which is undoubtedly taking place in the Far East."[28] Despite
these reassurances, Amery took the issue seriously. In 1927 he sent a confidential circular from Downing Street to all British colonies on the "undesirable effects produced by the exhibition of certain types of cinematograph films in the colonies." Amery's intervention signified that concern
about the influence of films was no longer just a local matter to be decided
by individual censorship boards but was also an issue of empire-wide
regulation: "each Administration shall without fail exercise its powers
by preventing the exhibition of any film ... which is open to objection
whether on general grounds or in view of the special character and sus-
ceptibilities of the native people before whom the film would be exhibited,
or which is calculated to arouse undesirable racial feeling by portraying
aspects of the life of any section of His Majesty's subjects which, however
innocent in themselves, are liable to be misunderstood by communities
with other customs and traditions."[29]

Government response to the anxiety over film was established through
a series of committees and official reports. Cinema was a key issue in the
1926 Imperial Conference established to regulate imperial trade, and

mounting pressure by expatriates led the Indian government to propose a committee to examine the matter in depth.[30] The *Indian Cinematograph Committee Report* summarized a massive collection of information about the state of film production, exhibition, and reception on the Subcontinent.[31] The committee explicitly addressed the concern that "letters and articles that have appeared from time to time in the British Press asseverating that much harm was being done in India by the widespread exhibition of Western films" and promised to institute strict censorship.[32] The proposal by the committee met with warm response in Britain.[33] One ex-MP wrote to the *Times* that "all old Indians like myself will welcome the fact the Indian government is taking censorship seriously."[34] Official attention culminated with the report of the Colonial Films Committee, which was convened in 1930 to examine the political, moral, educational, and economic aspects of film in the empire. The constitution of committees such as these tended to be unholy alliances of interest blocs with widely differing investments in the regulation of American film. Those worried about political sedition wished to censor negative images of white people, the British film industry and trade representatives sought restriction of American films but the wide availability of British cinema, whereas missionaries and intellectuals worried about the negative effect of mass culture on native sensibilities. The Colonial Films Committee's recommendations represented an amalgam of these interests: an increase in censorship; the production of British-made educational films that would properly "uplift" native audiences; and the wide distribution of British commercial films.[35] None of this debate, interestingly enough, took into account the dynamic emergence of domestic film industries in colonies such as India. As a leading colonial officer, Hesketh Bell sat on the committee but dissented vigorously from its conclusion, feeling that it promoted economic interests over political ones. He wrote a long minority report castigating his colleagues for not being concerned with addressing the central question (for him) of the political order. "Incalculable damage [was being] done to the prestige of Europeans in India and the Far East" he argued, warning that "it behooves us . . . *while there is yet time,* to see that the same harm shall not be repeated in our Tropical African Empire."[36]

Reports in the *Times* made it clear that agitation for greater censorship of films came mainly from white expatriates rather than from Indians themselves. "It may be said that while the Government [of India] are taking the initiative [to set up a committee] they are only doing so at the express instigation of unofficial opinion. Every Englishman acquainted with the films which are shown in India has long been apprehensive of the mischief which they must be doing." The *Times* acknowledged that

"Indian voices" were being added to the calls for censorship, but they "were not stirred by the same considerations" about the representations of European behavior; instead they lamented the erosion of Indian religious and cultural values.[37] Indeed it is unclear whether white prestige was ever as fragile as colonialists feared. Indian film scholarship on this period argues that audiences were far more engaged with the rise of a domestic film industry and unconcerned with debates about white prestige, which seemed largely irrelevant to an emerging film public.[38] Many expatriate contemporaries also challenged the claims of Bell and others as exaggerated. The concern about the effect of cinema on white prestige was quieted by the report of the Indian Cinematograph Committee (ICC), based on extensive investigation that resulted in five volumes of interviews and evidence. Seven years later when the British government's report *The Film in National Life* was issued, it relied heavily on the ICC to downplay allegations about the negative effects of cinema.[39] Although arguments about the effects of film in the colonies continued until the era of decolonization, the moral panic over commercial cinema's erosion of white prestige was largely over; it had lasted little more than twenty years before burning itself out and becoming largely forgotten.

EUROPEANS BACKSTAGE

Underneath assertions that American film presented "travesties" of Western life was the fear that film merely provided access to those sides of Western life that expatriates did not want colonial audiences to see. By projecting images of white people ten or twenty feet high, cinema placed whiteness and Europeanness on exhibition for the gaze of colonial audiences. The large body of scholarship on the visual culture of Empire has concentrated on the forms of colonial objectification of native peoples in world's fairs and exhibitions, early cinema and travel photographs, censuses and cadastral surveys.[40] Its main emphasis, following Said and Foucault, has been on the forms of classification and racial typing by which collectivities of people were arranged into groups of tribes, cultures, nations, and civilizations. But the encounter of colonialists and subjects in imperial cinemas also created an ethnographic cinema that, for colonialists, gave native subjects representational access to European lives that were otherwise unknown to them.

Cinema collapsed the distance between the metropolitan world and the colonial. The richness of the cinema provided a visceral and profuse presentation of metropolitan Western life that bore a homology to the exhibition of colonial cultures in world's fairs. Imagine the effect of melodramas and crime films on "the Oriental mind," a journalist commanded his readers in 1921: "Like us, the Indian goes to see the 'movies,' but is not only impressed by the story of the film, but by the difference in dress, in customs, and in morals."[41] The fear that native fascination for films was the result of their ethnographic content was frequently commented on by expatriates. René Onraet, commissioner of police in 1920s Malaya wrote in his memoirs that the danger of cinema was that it presented images of whiteness to audiences who "had no real contact with Europeans. . . . To these people, cinema not only gave amusement, *it taught*. In Malaya it represented the life of the European or American at home—his manners, his customs, his ethics."[42] Onraet captures this ability of film to provide indexical information far in excess of the narrative focus, as indeed all films are ethnographic in some respect, but for him and other expatriates this access to "backstage" European life was deeply unsettling. Aldous Huxley, writing of his travels around Asia, reiterates the sense that European life in the colonies was a performance created and shaped in and for the colonial arena. "It was better surely," he wrote, "in the old days before the cinema was invented when the white man's subjects were totally ignorant of the world in which their masters lived. It was possible for them, then, to believe that white men's civilization was something great and marvelous— something even greater and more extraordinary than it really was."[43] But if this civilization was a performance, the anxiety remained that something may disrupt it, revealing its illusionary effect. Hesketh Bell wrote eloquently about this anxiety: "Until the cinemas laid bare the worst sides of the life of the white man most of the natives were ignorant of the depths of vice which afflict certain sections of white society. It is true that no man is a hero to his valet, and it is probably true that the Sahib's 'boy' has few illusions as to the vaunted moral superiority of the European. But to the vast mass of black, brown and yellow people the inner life of the European, especially that side of it which flourishes in centers of crime and infamy, was unknown until the spread of American films showed them a travesty of it."[44]

Huxley and Bell point to the ways in which racial hierarchy in Empire was premised on a complex of cultural attributes, including, education, wealth, and religious practice.[45] Frantz Fanon argues that black colonial subjects, for instance, became white in direct proportion to their mastery of the French language, acknowledging that "whiteness" emerged from the mastery of a range of cultural competencies, of which language (for Fanon) was most important. As a form of status, then, "whiteness" is something that was publicly performed in Empire, demonstrated through the cultivation of social manners and rituals. Ann Stoler has written at length about the problems for a binary racial hierarchy brought about by the emergence of categories of people—illiterates, poor whites, wealthy, educated natives—that contravene the performative attributes associated with their status. Stoler's argument highlights the concept of prestige as a performative practice produced through the particular representational complexes by which colonial authority was signified in imperial Britain. It was that representational complex that Hollywood dislodged through its own very different practices of illusion, glamour, and prestige.[46]

THE SOCIAL SPACE OF CINEMA AND "LOOKING" LIKE A NATIVE

The arrival of cinema created a physical space of racial and sexual interaction that was crucial to the production of the "experience" of watching films for colonial expatriates. Although films exhibited images of white dissolution and criminality, these images were experienced as objectifying particularly because whites watched these images in the copresence of nonwhite viewers. Cinema was a physical space of social interaction in which the sights and sounds of audience reaction forcibly impressed themselves on expatriate viewers, creating an intimate setting that radically transformed viewing experience.

This shift is why films and scenes from films that were never seen as offensive in London or Manchester became deeply subversive to the white sense of self when exhibited in the colonial context. It comes across strongly in an extraordinary account by George Bilainkin, editor of the Malay *Straits Echo,* who wrote about attending cinema as part of his wider memoirs of society and sociability in the Federated Malay States. "The entrance to the various picture palaces is [a] magnificent panorama of color as of dress and skin. Men in white or cream silk, and women in all the creations imagination can invent stand about." Bilainkin described going to the cinema in Malaya as though it were opening night on Shaftesbury Avenue. "A crowd of onlookers fought to get nearer, all the while commenting on the dress of the European men and women as well as of the Asiatics." Bilainkin's extended description of attending the cinema provides an almost tactile sense of what the weekly ritual was like as spectacle and event. More than most, his description marks an ambivalence about his attitude toward cinema. Ostensibly, the chapter "Damaging European Prestige, " in his volume *Hail Penang,* is designed to warn of the dangers of exhibiting commercial films (which he does), but his duty as a citizen of Empire is offset by his fascination with the excitement of cinema as a social event: "Inside . . . was reminiscent of a dream rather than of reality.

Far away from the main balcony, where the Europeans sat shepherded with the wealthier Orientals, were two side galleries. In these only women were allowed, most of them Chinese and Indian. Now and then I saw a single face turning around curiously to admire the galaxy of white beauty and charm.... Shawls in the gallery were popular, perhaps even obligatory. And so from the balcony we could only see heads swathed in colourful silk."[47]

Bilainkin is entranced by cinema as a physical space of social display, irrelevant of whatever film may be playing that evening. He moves from the scenes of "rickshas" pulling up and disgorging the Penang elite, through the panoply of ethnic and social finery inside the theater, to his journey back to his hotel, passing the late-night groups of Chinese and Indians sitting in the dark. For Bilainkin, cinema was a place to see and be seen. The spectacle lay as much in the display of fellow audience members as it did in images on the screen. Bilainkin laments that native audiences are given access to "half-naked" images of white women on the screen but also dwells at length on the audience's gaze at the "galaxy of white beauty and charm" within the theater itself. He comments on those natives who turn to look at white people and elite Malaysians but does not discuss his own wandering gaze, which passes over, ranks, and assesses the complicated movements of vision in this arena.

Cinema created a new social space where colonial audiences of rulers and subjects confronted images of Western life in the presence of each other. This copresence was integral to the colonialist appreciation of the objectification of their own images both on screen and in the immediate physical space of the cinema. Film generated the ideological and emotional backlash that it did precisely because of the interaction of this new signifying technology with the emerging public space of the cinema theater. One must read Bilainkin's loving description of the races coming together at the cinema hall in conjunction with a later chapter in his memoirs, titled "White Outcasts," in which he writes of racial intermarriage producing "despised" outcasts and reveals the emotional depth of racial segregation in Malaya at that time.[48]

Bilainkin's intense emotional rejection of interracial relationships and his stigmatizing as pariahs those who would commit "the sin of intermarriage" place his loving statements about the cinema being the place "where the coloured and the white people literally rub together" into a starkly different context.[49] Cinema theaters are arenas of potential transgression, one of the few places where white and nonwhites might meet, where the excesses displayed in Hollywood films are matched by the excesses in the cinema theater itself, and for Bilainkin it is clearly a site of attraction and repulsion, a social space particular to the field of Malayan colonial society. Cinema is a social site where that transgression is most threatening especially because it raised so forcibly the colonialist fantasies about the threat of black sexuality. Cinema halls created new means of association that proved to be sexually disturbing for both male and female expatriates, making the hall itself a discomforting place to be. Consider Hesketh Bell's experience: "The act of kissing, save among the natives who have had the 'benefits' of education, is never practiced among peoples of the Far East, and the prolonged and often erotic exhibitions of osculation frequently shown on the screen cannot but arouse in the minds of unsophisticated natives feelings that can best be imagined than described. To hear, indeed, the remarks and cat-calls which often proceed from the cheap seats occupied by young coolies during those 'love passages' is sometimes enough to make one's blood boil."[50]

Bell's outraged racial and sexual pride gives a particularly graphic indication of the experience of sharing social space. One woman quoted in the *Times* echoed Bell's unease in recounting her visceral experience of going to the cinema in Uganda: "The truly horrible part is that ... lovemaking is all that seems to amuse them ["the natives"], and that from the point of view of the white woman is degrading herself. It's horrible. We came out very quickly. I think the whole thing ought to be stopped.... I have never felt so uncomfortable. It's like having white women degraded in public."[51] This woman's identification with the image of white women projected on the screen is so strong that when African audience members began to laugh at the representations, she felt implicated and personally affronted. Her alarmed reaction indicates how images on cinema screens could have direct significance for the wider constitution of gender relations in colonial society.

The film scholar Poonam Arora supports this significance in her analysis of the spectatorial relations of colonial screens in India. Before the advent of cinema, Arora argues, urban racial segregation in the colonial arena combined with local cultural codes of modesty restricting eye contact to create a form of visual unavailability of the memsahib. After the introduction of cinema, "the memsahib became available to the native gaze not only on the screen but in the racially integrated public sphere of the cinema house."[52] In cinema theaters, moreover, Indian women entered through a separate entrance and sat apart from both white and Indian men in specially reserved boxes that were covered by a thin mosquito-type net. Arora points out that while white women were made available for display, their Indian counterparts were concealed from view—a reality that Bilainkin also noted: "The Asiatic ... sees white women in a state bordering on nudity ... [while] his own women are dressed to the neck. The Indian, Chinese and Malay women are as carefully guarded from strangers' gaze as if they were unused photographic paper."[53]

The copresence of rulers and ruled in cinema halls was integral to the colonialist appreciation of the objectification of their own images exhibited on screen. Mixed-race viewing distanced expatriates from images of themselves and made them watch as if through the eyes of their subjects. This experience was partly the result of the physical relations of viewing, but another factor was the colonial expertise of expatriates. Most had enough knowledge of local values and customs to know what the reaction might be to certain sorts of images and narratives. George Bilainkin indicates this anticipation in his account of attending cinema in Penang. He writes, "Many dancing girls shown on the screens in Penang had so little clothing as to excite the audible surprise not only of white people but of the usually silent Asiatics. Again and again I have looked from my seat to see people turning their heads to one another in astonishment.... What is the average Asiatic ... to think of the white people in his home town?" Bilainkin realizes how these images must appear to a conservative Malay, Indian, and Chinese audience, and he reacts by turning around to gauge their response, but more than this, however, he attempts to project what they might be thinking. This visual ventriloquism, the attempt to view films as if from the native point of view, emerged from expatriates' fear and their desire to know what colonial audiences were thinking. When Bilainkin asks, "What is the average Asiatic ... to think?" he signifies that the crux of the moment is not his opinion of the images but his interpretation of the opinion of the native audience. The mixed-race context of colonial reception forces Bilainkin to take up what he considers to be the native point of view, to see his image as "Others" do. It enforces on him a constant vigilance as he surveys the audience ("It was interesting to watch the reaction of the mixed audience") so that his experience is mediated by his assessment of the reactions of others.[54]

Colonialism was, in part, a clash of information orders. Gyan Prakash has written of the stubborn problem of the "unknowable native" that emerged despite the increasing powers of legibility and information collecting imposed by the colonial state: cadastral surveys, ethological reports, and censuses.[55] The more the British surveyed, the more they realized there was a world outside of their control. Christopher Bayly has referred to these spaces as zones of ignorance—information gaps or information panics—in which fantasy flourished and ignorance was overcome by identification with, or rather projection onto, "looking" like a native.[56]

Huxley, in his visit to an open-air cinema in Java, reveals this sort of colonial move. As he watches what he sees as a depressing, generic Hollywood movie, he wonders:

> The violent imbecilities of the story flickered in silence against the background of the equatorial night. In silence the Javanese looked on. What were they thinking? What were their private comments on this exhibition of Western civilization. I wondered. In North Africa, in India, I have also wondered. [The "untutored mind" of the poor Indian] sees the films, he thinks they represent Western reality, he cannot see why he should be ruled by criminal imbeciles. As we turned out disgusted from the idiotic spectacle and threaded our way out of the crowd, that strange aquarium silence of the Javanese was broken by a languid snigger of derision. Nothing more. Just a little laugh. A word or two of mocking comment in Malay, and then, once more, the silence as of fish. A few years more of Hollywood's propaganda and perhaps we shall not get out of an Oriental crowd quite so easily.[57]

Like the white woman in Uganda, Huxley's anxiety is provoked by laughter, a sound whose stubborn nonreferential meaning makes palpable the ignorance of colonialists who do not understand the cultural wellspring from which the joke emerges.[58] Huxley and the British more generally are haunted by their lack of knowledge, the difficulty in understanding a laugh, a giggle, a phrase or two spoken in a language one doesn't understand. Into this gap Huxley projects an entire theory of political revolt based not on his knowledge of the Javanese but generated from his own fears of American mass culture.

The colonial context is crucial to this white imagining of black subjectivity because the same films would not be contentious in London or New York. The social space of cinema viewing in the particular racial and gender relations of the colonial arena was integral in forming the experience of cinema for white expatriates. It was not a question of the images themselves, no matter how "naked" or criminal the representations might seem, but a question of how this symbolic flow was reconstituted within colonial power relations. René Onraet, writing about the same audiences in Penang that Bilainkin describes, argues that "from a European or an educated point of view the films were not offensive," but that in the colonial context they were. L. S. Amery, secretary of state for the colonies, recognized as much when he sent a circular to all colonial governments warning of the increasing problem of cinema exhibition. "You are well aware," he wrote, "that films prepared in this country or in America are liable to be misunderstood when exhibited out of Europe and that it must not be assumed that a film which has passed for exhibition to a general audience here is necessarily suitable for public exhibition in the colonies."[59] This disparity is why women appropriately dressed in evening clothes pass unremarked on in the imperial metropole but become "half-naked," and "immodest" in the colonial arena. The morals of the viewing white subject have changed because he or she is forced to see the same image anew, through the imagined fears of the native gaze. It is this curious tension—between the intimate specificity of the cinemas where anxiety is recorded and the generic narratives in which those experiences are entextualized—that reveals the difficulty in analyzing the standardizing nature of Hollywood and Empire itself.

CIRCULATORY CINEMA AND THE COLONIAL CONTEXT

One of the central features of the moral panic over cinema in Empire was the diversity of situations in which cinema found itself, and the regularity of the stories narrated about those films. This move from particularity to standardization is part of the work of circulation itself, the reach of the information system of Empire, which places into motion the government reports, memoirs, travel writings, newspaper articles, and letters that comprise the literary infrastructure of colonial experience. It is because of the ubiquity of this circulation that the reports of expatriate British women in Uganda can be read as uncannily similar to those in Malay or Singapore, despite the difference in depth of colonial administration, in economies, in religious adherence, and in racial dynamics that marked these territories. Part of the similarity can be accounted for by the Colonial Office's issuance of circulars designed to coordinate and unify the attitudes toward film and censorship all over the empire.[60] But this office is only one part of the broader colonial network whose standardizing power was located in the diffuse accumulated movement of texts, people, images, laws, and mission societies that created the circulatory system of the colonial information order.

This system entailed a particular organization of space and time that was subverted by the emergence of Hollywood. The stereotypical assumption that the journey by ship from England to Africa was at the same time a journey back in time was disrupted by this new global distribution of film. American cinematic dominance placed the United States and Hollywood at the center of a worldwide network that transformed both imperial metropole and colony into equal nodes in a new world circuit of film distribution. If audiences in London and Manchester were watching the same films as audiences in Penang or Calcutta, the fiction that colonized peoples inhabited a space somewhere in the evolutionary past of the colonizer became harder to maintain—especially when colonial audiences began to receive popular films before they opened in London. "It is worthy of note," wrote the editor of the Malay *Straits Echo* in the 1920s, "that many of the productions from Hollywood attacked Malaya before being seen in London. Sometimes a month before."[61] His observation was confirmed by the British government's report *The Film in National Life*, commissioned in 1931: "An Englishman returning from Hong-Kong, for example, may see in a large provincial town in England big American films released a week or two before, which were already out of date in the Colony before he sailed."[62]

American dominance of film distribution altered the hierarchy of cultural flows under imperialism. In terms of geography, at least, London could now be considered as much of a periphery as Bombay. Hollywood replaced the standardizing techniques of British imperial order with its mass culture by operating a different logic of repetition. Huxley is acutely aware of the homogenizing political consequences of this replacement:

> There are many races, skins of many shades; there are colonies and protectorates and mandated territories; ... a great variety of political institutions and subject people. But there is only one Hollywood. Arabs and Melanesians, negroes and Indians, Malays and Chinamen—all see the same films. The crook drama in Tunis is the same as the crook drama at Madras. On the same evening, it may be, in Korea, in Sumatra, in the Sudan, they are looking at the same seven soulful reels of motherlove and adultery. The same millionaires are swindling for the diversion of a Burmese audience in Mandalay, a Maori audience in New Zealand.[63]

Huxley describes how Hollywood integrates different localities into its new circuits of distribution by linking racially and geographically disparate peoples. In the nineteenth century, the only institutions pulling such wildly diverse places into a coherent network would have been imperial, but in the twentieth century Hollywood has created a new unity based on a homogenizing mass culture, reconfiguring imperial networks and providing the cultural base for a new collective experience. Hollywood marginalized imperial hierarchies of space and introduced new economic and technological motors of modernity.

In defending their own culture and customs, European expatriates repeatedly stressed the American origins of commercial films. They lamented the clumsy stereotypes Hollywood used to depict "European" culture. In 1934, A. J. W. Harloff, a member of the Council of Netherlands India, wrote a strongly worded article about white prestige in the journal *British Malaya*: "In the unsophisticated minds of the uneducated rural population, the belief is established that the most deplorable and repulsive abnormalities and sporadic extravagances of American society represent the ordinary conditions obtaining among Westerners."[64] In his scholarly study *The Modern Malay*, drawing on his seven years' experience as an expatriate, L. Richmond Wheeler wrote a chapter on the cinematograph in which he concluded that "it is little short of a tragedy that the production of films should be mainly in the hands of a nation which has none of the difficulties and dangers of contact with vast populations of alien standards and beliefs."[65] These critiques encode a larger fear that Europe was losing control of the means of communication to represent itself. Britain, France, Germany, and Italy all went through public panics about growing "Americanization" and becoming "temporary American citizens."[66] Richmond Wheeler concluded his analysis of cinema by observing that "the continuance of this huge Yankee monopoly is a scandal from every point of view: educational, financial, patriotic, imperial, moral"[67] and demanding in its stead more British films and applauding the decision to impose quotas on U.S. exhibitions. Behind the fear about the effect of cinema on colonial morality and white prestige lies larger political and economic fears about the end of the British Empire.

Huxley, in his account of his travels around Asia during this period, discussed this issue at length but from a different point of view, arguing that the negative influence of Hollywood was a harbinger of a mass culture that had already corrupted England and was making its influence felt in the colonial arena. "What is this famous civilization of the white men that Hollywood reveals?" he asked. In his answer he betrays his gloomy prognosis for the future of European civilization:

> The world into which the cinema introduces the subject peoples is a world of silliness and criminality. When its inhabitants are not stealing, murdering, swindling or attempting to commit rape they are dashing about the earth's surface in fast-moving vehicles. Their politics are matters exclusively of personal (generally amorous) intrigue. Their science is an affair of secret recipes for making money. . . .
>
> Such is the white man's world as revealed by the films. . . . A world without subtlety, without the smallest intellectual interests, innocent of art, letters, philosophy, science. A world where there are plenty of motors, telephones and automatic pistols, but in which there is no trace of a modern idea. . . . A world, in brief, from which all that gives the modern West its power and I like to think, its spiritual superiority to the East . . . has been left out.[68]

Huxley's critique of cinema is a lament for the passing of a way of life. The coming American world is one in which modernity is reduced to technology, preferably technological commodities that can be sold, while the way of life that produced an elite British sensibility will vanish. In his writings, Huxley was fiercely critical of colonialism but not from a point of egalitarianism. He was convinced of the superiority of cultured individuals such as himself, but it was just his sort of humane cultured life that was in retreat in the face of an emerging American materialism. Huxley fully adopted the argument that cinema eroded white prestige, but he reasoned from the opposite point of view of old colonial blowhards like Hesketh Bell. The British were increasingly infected by mass culture, he argued, and bereft of the ideologies of service and intellectual introspection, so how could they claim any right to rule anyone? This reality, he believed, was being discovered by educated Indians and was being revealed to the masses through cinema.

CONCLUSION

The first decades of the twentieth century saw the control of world communications shift from the old world to the new. The epic laying of submarine cables that allowed instantaneous telegraphic communications across continents represents the last moment of British control of international communications, a control that had dominated the nineteenth century. The rise of radio, cinema, and airplanes took place decisively in the United States. These new infrastructures of circulation were at once technical and bureaucratic, creating new laws to facilitate and control them, new personnel to administer them, and new forms of temporal and spatial standardization. Cinema was a dominant part of this transformation. It exemplified in spectacular form the dual nature of the commodity rooted in the materiality of objects under a regime of use value and their dematerialization once they entered into relations of exchange. Cinema was not just a commodity but represented the unmooring of relations of representation and an increase in the speed and range of their circulation by drawing more and more widely disparate places into a single regime of distribution. Because of cinema, Javanese sweatshops were purchasing American sewing machines, Brazilians were building California bungalows, and French secretaries were demanding American typewriters. Cinema represented a new economic regime where value was to be found not in production but in the regulation of vision and affect. Yet cinema also created value through its infrastructural role in generating publicity and meaning for consumer goods, which fed back into production itself. Looking at film within Empire means moving beyond the study of national cinemas to assess larger networks, and thus the subject raises questions about the nature of circulation and how in the process of exchange and mobility objects are shaped and refashioned by the circulatory matrix itself. The rise of cinema was part of the expansion of American capitalism in the twentieth century that provided a fundamental challenge for the British Empire and the forms of circulation and infrastructure it relied on.

Anxiety about the unstable meanings of film in Empire came from the assemblage of two forces of abstract circulation and specific locality. When colonialists told each other stories about the negative role of cinema, when they wrote angry letters to the *Times* or devoted chapters of their memoirs to this pressing social problem, they were encoding these fantasies and anxieties into a material form that was mediated by newspapers, journals, and publishing houses of the empire. These forms created a set of standardized narratives that circulated over the imperial realm and fed back into the ethnographic experience of everyday life. It is why the stories of women in Uganda and Calcutta and officers in Penang and Singapore could all inhabit the same narrative form. These stories, however, had to draw on the extensive firsthand knowledge of expatriate Europeans in order to gain their authority and force. It means we have to understand the tension between the ethnographic encounters between colonizer and colonized. The cinematic experience is never simply an abstract exchange of meaning between a technology and its addressee; rather, audiences come preconstituted by sharply demarcated categories of race, of colonial citizenship, and of religious and cultural identities. One cannot privilege locality over circulation or vice versa but must instead see the mutual imbrication of the two and their recursive and ambivalent interrelations.

The long-term outcome of the moral panic over white prestige was the institution of strict censorship laws, which, as some scholars argue, still influence postcolonial nations.[69] It also resulted in agitation for more educational films that would not repress images (through censorship) but provide a productive means of regulating behavior and offsetting the negative impact of film. After 1930, a series of experiments was conducted in making films in and for the colonies. Initiated primarily by missionaries and then taken up by the British government with the formation of the Colonial Film Unit in 1939, these experiments resulted in a series of films on health, imperial culture, farming, and education.[70] The final story of the panic over commercial film is told by these mobile film units, which provided another attempt by colonial governments to exert control over the potentially subversive effects of cinema. This time, however, instead of censorship and repression, the aim was governmental cultivation of a modern colonial subject.

Notes

I have accrued many debts in the process of writing this article. I am grateful for feedback received during presentations at the University of Michigan and Syracuse University, and especially for detailed comments at the Globalizing American Studies conference at Northwestern University. Stefan Andriopoulos, T. O. Beidelman, Faye Ginsburg, Alison Griffiths, and Fred Myers all read and gave valuable comments. Brian Edwards and Dilip Gaonkar have been especially helpful with encouragement and critical insight.

1. Gilles Deleuze and Felix Guattari, *A Thousand Plateaus: Capitalism and Schizophrenia* (Minneapolis: University of Minnesota Press, 1987).

2. The anthropologist and historian Eng Seng Ho refers to this as an "invisible" empire, one that eschewed the elaborate durbars and rituals of royal and imperial spectacle by which the British staged their authority in favor of a dematerialized "remote control" authority. Eng Seng Ho, "Empire through Diasporic Eyes: A View from the Other Boat," *Comparative Studies in Society and History* 46, no. 2 (2004). See also Eng Seng Ho, *Graves of Tarim: Genealogy and Mobility across the Indian Ocean* (Berkeley: University of California Press, 2006). On imperial spectacle, see Bernard S. Cohn's famous essay "Representing India in Victorian Britain," in *The Invention of Tradition*, ed. Eric Hobsbawm and Terence Ranger (Cambridge: Cambridge University Press, 1992).

3. Letter to the editor, *Times* (London), July 10, 1930, 15.

4. Sir Henry (Joujou) Hesketh Bell, *Foreign Colonial Administration in the Far East* (London: Edward Arnold and Co., 1928).

5. I thank Stefan Andriopoulos for drawing out these implications.

6. At the cinema, Kracauer argues, "the audience encounters itself; its own reality is revealed in the fragmented sequence of splendid sense impressions. Were this reality to remain hidden from the viewers, they could neither attack nor change it; its disclosure in distraction is therefore of moral significance." Siegfried Kracauer, *The Mass Ornament: Weimar Essays*, ed. Thomas Y. Levin (Cambridge: Harvard University Press, 1995), 326. Cinema "conveys precisely and openly to the thousands of eyes and ears the disorder of society" (327). For Kracauer, cinema revealed to audiences the commodity logic of contemporary urban society and was positive in bringing mass audiences to a greater critical awareness of contemporary capitalism. For Hesketh Bell, cinema exposed the constructed nature of white "civilization" and was negative in undermining the authority of imperial power. Their different interpretations, however, share commonalities in understanding the political import of mass cinema.

7. Frantz Fanon, *Black Skin, White Masks* (New York: Grove Press, 1967), 72.

8. See Margaret Dickinson and Sarah Street, *Cinema and State: The Film Industry and the Government* (London: BFI, 1985); Ian Jarvie, *Hollywood's Overseas Campaign: The North Atlantic Movie Trade, 1920-1950* (Cambridge: Cambridge University Press, 1992); Toby Miller, Nitin Govil, John McMurria, and Ting Wang, *Global Hollywood 2* (London: British Film Institute, 2005); John Trumpbour, *Selling Hollywood to the World: U.S. and European Struggles for Mastery of the Global Film Industry, 1920-50* (Cambridge: Cambridge University Press, 2002).

9. Julius Klein, "What Are Motion Pictures Doing for Industry?" *Annals of the American Academy of Political and Social Science* 128, no. 1 (November 1926): 79-83; Walter Wanger, "120,000 American Ambassadors," *Foreign Affairs* 18, no. 1 (October 1939): 45-59. Wanger, in fact, was eloquent in drawing a picture of Hollywood as a circulatory system. In his *Foreign Affairs* article he wrote, "Long before an American motion picture finishes its exhibition life at home it begins voyaging among the 50,025 cinemas wired for sound outside the United States. . . . An average of 200 prints each makes a vast circular tour from Vladivostock to Patagonia, from Land's End to Yokohama." A decade later he repeated the same theme in an article describing the feedback loop of this system: "we maintain a huge distributing organiza-

tion throughout the world manned by experts who watch the reactions to our films daily. . . . We have a greater check on the latest reactions throughout the world, I venture to say, than does the State Department. Every important distributor receives a constant flow of reports which reflect current attitudes in dozens of countries." Walter Wanger, "Donald Duck and Diplomacy," *Public Opinion Quarterly* 14 (1950): 443–52, quotation at 445.Wanger tended to write his articles about the great influence of American film during periods when Congress was thinking of stepping in to regulate the film industry. His published articles in prominent journals lent a scholarly gloss to what is clearly a self-interested argument about the importance of Hollywood and therefore the need for freedom from regulation.

10. H. M. Government, *Report of the Imperial Conference, 1926*, Cmd. 2768 (London: HMSO, 1926), 41, 404. Cunliffe-Lister cited approvingly American arguments about the necessity of recognizing the link between cinema and trade. He continued: "This is not theory. It is borne out in practice. This year Dr. Klein of the U.S. Bureau of Commerce, giving evidence before a Committee of Congress, emphasised the value of American films as an advertisement for American goods." He then cited at length several examples of the boost for consumer products after their appearance in Hollywood films.

11. Walter Benjamin, *The Arcades Project* (Cambridge: Harvard University Press, 2002).

12. Jonathan Crary, *Suspensions of Perception: Attention, Spectacle and Modern Culture* (Cambridge: MIT Press, 2000).

13. Ibid. See also Jonathan Beller, *The Cinematic Mode of Production: Attention Economy and the Society of the Spectacle* (Lebanon, NH: Dartmouth University Press, 2006).

14. Beller, *Cinematic Mode of Production*, 209.

15. Sir Stephen Tallents, *The Projection of Britain* (London: Faber and Faber, 1932), 29–30, 11–13, 12.

16. One result of this effort was the creation of the influential Empire Marketing Board film unit under the direction of John Grierson.

17. H. M. Government, *Report of the Imperial Conference*, 42.

18. See Annette Kuhn, *Cinema, Sexuality and Censorship, 1909–1925* (London: Routledge, 1988); Jeffrey Richards, *The Age of the Dream Palace: Cinema and Society in Britain, 1930–39* (London: Routledge, 1984); James C. Robertson, *The British Board of Film Censors: Film Censorship in Britain, 1896–1950* (London: Croom Helm, 1985); James C. Robertson, *The Hidden Cinema: British Film Censorship in Action 1913–1972* (London: Routledge, 1989).

19. L'Estrange Fawcett, *Films, Facts and Forecasts* (London: Geoffrey Bles, 1927). "The difference between the European and the Asiatic is fundamental and irreconcilable. The Asiatic matures early, and the development of his mentality does not keep pace with his physical growth. . . . At maturity he is still like a child." Thus wrote Constance Bromley, a resident of Calcutta and, like Hesketh Bell, one of the most outspoken critics of commercial film in the empire. Bromley's article "Censorship and India—Influence of Foreign Films" was written for a special February 21, 1922, supplement of the *Times* on cinema. The supplement is fascinating as a contemporary collection of articles addressing the range of social and economic issues facing the developing British film industry. Economic and aesthetic reports on the status of British film are set next to Bromley's polemic on the subversive effects of film on Empire and the bishop of Birmingham's (a leading member of the National Council for Public Morals) arguments on the proper modes of censorship. On Bromley, see also Poonam Arora, "Imperilling the Prestige of the White Woman: Colonial Anxiety and Film Censorship in British India," *Visual Anthropology Review* 11, no. 2 (1995): 36–50.

20. "Films and the Empire—Lack of British Production—Proposed Joint Action," supplement on Empire, *Times*, April 24, 1926, xiv.

21. Constance Bromley, letter to the editor, *Leeds Mercury*, August 26, 1926, 5–6. Arora, "Imperilling the Prestige of the White Woman," provides a fuller discussion of the Bromley letter.

22. Bromley, "Censorship and India," xiv.

23. Rear Admiral Smith-Dorrien, letter to the editor, *Times*, July 27, 1926, 17.

24. As cited in L. Richmond Wheeler, *The Modern Malay* (London: George Allen and Unwin, 1928), 175

25. A. J. W. Harloff, "The Influence of the Cinema on Oriental Peoples," *British Malaya*, February 1934, 213. In the special supplement of the *Times* on cinema and censorship in India, Constance Bromley declared that films provide "a first class handbook to the teachings of Mr Gandhi" ("Censorship and India," xiv).

26. Sir Henry Hesketh Bell, minority report of H. M. Government's *Report of the Colonial Films Committee*, Cmd. 3630 (London: HMSO, 1930).

27. George Bilainkin, *Hail Penang! Being the Narrative of Comedies and Tragedies in a Tropical Outpost among Europeans, Chinese, Malays and Indians* (London: Sampson and Low, 1932), 61.

28. Rex Stephenson, "Cinema and Censorship in Colonial Malaya," *Journal of Southeast Asian Studies* 5, no. 2 (1974): 209–24, quotations at 212.

29. "Simple List of Files Removed from Cabinet," R918: Films and Film Censorship, Kano State History and Culture Bureau (HCB), Nigeria.

30. H. M. Government, *Report of the Imperial Conference.*

31. Government of India, *Indian Cinematograph Committee Report* (Madras: Government of India Press, 1928).

32. As cited in Erik Barnouw and S. Krishnaswamy, *Indian Film* (New York: Columbia University Press, 1963), 40. See also Priya Jaikumar, "More Than Morality: The Indian Cinematograph Committee Interviews, 1927," *Moving Image* 3, no. 1 (2003): 83–109.

33. In *Indian Film*, Barnouw and Krishnaswamy point out that there was a great deal of conflict among committee members in India. The concern over the image of the white man was largely a white issue (unsurprisingly). The argument that it would be better if American films were replaced by "less offensive" British films was derided by Indian members of the committee, who argued that for Indian audiences both American and British films represented equally foreign values. They were more interested in promoting the production of Indian films and saw the argument about white prestige as an irrelevancy. Jaikumar, in "More Than Morality," pushes this argument farther, saying that the rhetoric surrounding the moral effects of films was of much less interest to the subjects interviewed by the ICC, who saw the matter primarily as an issue of trade and an attempt by Britain to replace the dominance of the United States with that of Britain.

34. "The Cinema in India—Need for Thorough Control," letter to the editor, *Times*, September 13, 1927, 13.

35. Priya Jaikumar makes a compelling argument that scholars of India have tended to accept colonial arguments that the debate around cinema was an issue of morality and racial hierarchy when in fact it is better appreciated as economic. "British policy makers well understood the ways in which direct state intervention into the Indian film market through the creation of preferential economic policies were politically inadmissible by the 1920s and 1930s," she argues. "While imperial economic policies were unacceptable, intra-imperial reciprocity and censorship on moral grounds were defensible ways of influencing the Indian film industry," and thus the debate about white prestige is an acceptable way to address a restructuring of economic relations within Empire (Jaikumar, "More than Morality," 91–92). While I agree with Jaikumar's argument about the importance of the economic question, I see the debate about white prestige as driven by an amalgam of differing interests within the imperial project itself. Recognizing the economic interests at stake does not necessitate rejecting the powerful emotive way that issues of racial hierarchy played into cinema policy but suggests how the anxiety about American mass culture played out over a number of different registers.

36. Hesketh Bell, minority report of the *Colonial Films Committee Report*, 24 (emphasis added).

37. "The Cinema in India—Need of Control—Attitude of the Government," *Times*, September 8, 1927, 13–14.

38. Parag Amladi, "New Apprehensions: The Ambivalence of Modernity in Early Indian Cinema, 1913–1939," Ph.D. diss., New York University, 1997; Kaushik Bhaumik, "The Emergence of the Bombay Film Industry: 1913–1936," D.Phil. diss., St. Anthony's College, Oxford University, 2001; Stephen P. Hughes, "The Pre-Phalke Era in South India: Reflections on the Formation of Film Audiences in Madras," *South Indian Studies* 2 (1996): 161–204; Stephen P. Hughes, "House Full: Silent Film Exhibition and Audiences in South India," *Indian Economic and Social History Review* 43, no. 1 (2006): 31–62; Priya Jaikumar, *Cinema at the End of Empire: A Politics of Transition for Britain and India* (Durham, NC: Duke University Press, 2006).

39. When the governor of the Straits Settlements wrote to the British Colonial Office about the state of films in Malaya, he dismissed Hesketh Bell's writings as based on "a superficial and inaccurate knowledge of conditions and tendencies in the East" (as cited in Stephenson, "Cinema and Censorship in Colonial Malaya," 216). This point of view was supported conclusively by the authoritative report of the Indian Cinematograph Committee: "The great potentialities of the cinematograph for good or for evil are generally recognized. In the forefront of our report we desire to place on record our unanimous conviction that the general effect of Western films in India is not evil, but on the whole good. . . . A careful study of the facts will show that much of the criticism of the cinema in India had its origin outside India, and sprang from persons . . . not conversant with Indian conditions." As cited in Commission on Educational and Cultural Films, *The Film in National Life: Being a Report of an Enquiry Conducted by the Commission on Educational and Cultural Films into the Service Which the Cinematograph May Render to Education and Social Progress* (London: George Allen and Unwin, 1932), 130.

40. Nicholas Dirks, ed., *Colonialism and Culture* (Ann Arbor: University of Michigan Press, 1992); Timothy Mitchell, *Colonising Egypt* (Berkeley: University of California Press, 1991); Robert W. Rydell, *All the World's a Fair: Visions of Empire at American International Expositions, 1876–1916* (Chicago: University of Chicago Press, 1984).

41. *Westminster Gazette*, November 17, 1921, 13; as cited in Aruna Vasudev, *Liberty and Licence in the Indian Cinema* (New Delhi: Vikas Publishing House, 1978), 21.

42. René Onraet, *Singapore: A Police Background* (London: Dorothy Crisp and Co., 1947), 16 (emphasis added).

43. Aldous Huxley, *Jesting Pilate: An Intellectual Holiday* (New York: George H. Dorian and Co., 1926), 226–27.

44. Hesketh Bell, *Foreign Colonial Administration*, 121. Both Stoler and McClintock have extended discussions about domesticity and its subversive relations in Empire. See Ann Laura Stoler, "Carnal Knowledge and Imperial Power: Gender, Race and Morality in Colonial Asia," in *Gender at the Crossroads of Knowledge: Feminist Anthropology in the Postmodern Era*, ed. Micaela di Leonardo (Berkeley: University of California Press, 1991), 51–101; Anne McClintock, *Imperial Leather: Race, Gender and Sexuality in the Colonial Contest* (New York: Routledge, 1995).

45. Ann Laura Stoler, *Race and the Education of Desire: Foucault's History of Sexuality and the Colonial Order of Things* (Durham, NC: Duke University Press, 1995).

46. Aldous Huxley was especially articulate about the illusory nature of the colonialist image. He saw Empire as populated with Europeans of little status back home but for whom racial hierarchies in Empire gave them a "sense of power" and a "feeling of grandeur and importance" that was "purely illusory." For Huxley the rise of mass culture was exposing this illusory nature. "We are accepted much as paper money is accepted, because there is a general belief that we are worth something. Our value is not intrinsic, but borrowed from the opinion of the world. . . . Our paper currency has begun to lose its value in Europe. We still

continue to offer ourselves ... as five pound notes; but the more skeptical of our 'inferiors' refuse to regard us as anything more precious than waste paper." Huxley, *Jesting Pilate*, 11.

47. Bilainkin, *Hail Penang!* 58, 59.

48. In an eerie echo of Homi Bhabha's discussion of colonial mimic men, Bilainkin describes whites who marry outside the race as "pariahs": "you may see them in dress that is European, but not quite; and you will see their white faces that suggests they are European but not quite; and you will listen to their conversation and know at once they are products of some first class school and college but not quite." Ibid., 100.

49. Ibid., 101, 58.

50. Hesketh Bell, minority report of the *Colonial Films Committee Report*, 121-22.

51. "Films for Natives," *Times*, August 27, 1923, 6.

52. Arora, "Imperilling the Prestige of the White Woman," 38.

53. Bilainkin, *Hail Penang!* 61-62.

54. Ibid.

55. Gyan Prakash, *Another Reason: Science and the Imagination of Modern India* (Princeton: Princeton University Press, 1999).

56. C. A. Bayly, *Empire and Information: Intelligence Gathering and Social Information in India, 1780-1870* (Cambridge: Cambridge University Press, 1996).

57. Huxley, *Jesting Pilate*, 203.

58. George Bilainkin also notes that natives "laugh loudest at the kissing scenes" (*Hail Penang!* 61).

59. L. S. Amery, Secretary of State for the Colonies, to the Officer Administering the Government of Nigeria, January 8, 1927, HCB/R918/Films and Film Censorship.

60. For instance in 1928, a confidential circular was sent from Downing Street to colonies warning of the film *After the Storm*, "a sensational description of the worst kind" in which "white women appear in a drunken orgy" in a low-class cabaret in Singapore. Later a white woman is depicted drinking with "Asiatics" in an Asiatic saloon. The governments are warned to notify their censorship boards. This centralized censorship was, in fact, relatively rare in the British Empire precisely because different colonial governments wished to preserve the prerogative of administering their own territories. Yet the fact that a film censored in one place could lead to censorship all across the empire and that the Colonial Office was involved in regulating this activity shows the attempt to create and administer a centralized system. "Simple List of Files Removed from Cabinet," R918: Films and Film Censorship, HCB.

61. Bilainkin, *Hail Penang!* 60.

62. Commission on Educational and Cultural Films, *Film in National Life*, 134. K. R. Blackwell of the Malay civil service wrote in his memoirs that the best cinemas in the territory were air-conditioned and that "films shown were often the latest American productions which had not yet been generally-released in Britain." K. R. Blackwell, Malay Curry (n.d.) Rhodes House, Papers of K. R. Blackwell, MSS Ind. Ocn. S90.

63. Huxley, *Jesting Pilate*, 224-25.

64. Harloff, Influence of the Cinema on Oriental Peoples," 215.

65. Wheeler, *Modern Malay*, 175.

66. See Mark Glancy, "Temporary American Citizens: British Audiences, American Films and the Threat of Americanization in the 1920s," *Historical Journal of Film, Radio and Television* 26, no. 4 (2006): 461-84; Thomas Saunders, *Hollywood in Berlin: American Cinema and Weimar Germany* (Berkeley: University of California Press, 1994).

67. Wheeler, *Modern Malay*, 175.

68. Huxley, *Jesting Pilate*, 199-200.

69. See Arora, "Imperilling the Prestige of the White Woman."

70. See Brian Larkin, *Signal and Noise: Media Infrastructure and Urban Culture in Northern Nigeria* (Durham, NC: Duke University Press, 2008), chap. 3.

SIX

Scarlett O'Hara in Damascus

Hollywood, Colonial Politics, and Arab Spectatorship during World War II

Elizabeth F. Thompson

On a Friday afternoon in the spring of 1942, a crowd of women, children, and their household servants gathered in a cinema in Damascus, Syria. As they did nearly every week, they settled down with their picnic lunches, cushions, and water pipes to watch a new movie. That week's feature was *Gone with the Wind*. The lively crowd cheered and wept for Scarlett O'Hara as she married her various husbands and struggled to survive the American Civil War. The women cursed Rhett for leaving his wife and adored Mammy so much that they asked the projectionist to repeat her scenes.[1] Previously, at premieres in Beirut and Cairo, audiences dressed in gems and tuxedos had joined British, French, and American officials to greet this marvel of movie history. Like audiences around the world, Arabs flocked to *Gone with the Wind* in the early years of World War II.

Gone with the Wind enjoyed a spectacular career abroad, as it had in the United States. That career has been strangely neglected in the reams of scholarship on the film, despite our understanding that foreign markets were crucial to Hollywood's decisions about producing big-budget movies.[2] Recapturing *Gone with the Wind*'s foreign reception enriches our understanding of the film and illuminates how cinema had become, by 1940, a powerful nexus of cultural exchange between Americans and foreign audiences around the globe.[3]

This essay inaugurates a recuperation of the film's foreign career by examining its first run in the Arab world, during the early years of World War II. Historians have generally assumed that Arabs held a high opinion of American culture until the Arab-Israeli war of 1948. They base their views on a perceived preference for American schools and businesses in the Middle East.[4] Some historians, however, have emphasized the continuity of centuries-old Muslim hostility toward the West; Islam, they argue, made Arabs reluctant to absorb American culture and modernity well into the twentieth century. They base their views mainly on the writings of elites.[5] Both sides of the debate suffer from reliance on a paucity of sources. The case of *Gone with the Wind*—and the exhibition of Hollywood movies in general—can bring needed nuance to the poorly documented history of American–Arab cultural relations. Because movies appealed to a diverse audience of Arabic-speaking peoples, they can offer a glimpse into the views of common people, not just political, business, and religious elites.

As film scholars everywhere know, evidence of moviegoers' responses is rare. Fortunately, *Gone with the Wind*'s extraordinary popularity has left behind valuable clues in the press, in memoirs, and in industrial and government archives. These sources suggest that while some religious and nationalist elites in the Middle East deployed a politics of cultural difference critical of Hollywood, mass audiences continued to consume American movies eagerly. And contrary to those who have argued that cultural differences impeded communication, these Arabic-speaking audiences watched and understood the pictures as the studios intended—as texts written in what Miriam Hansen has called a "global vernacular," a flexible narrative code open to multiple interpretations.[6] Moviegoers in Arab societies were as familiar with Hollywood's global vernacular as were other audiences around the world. Such familiarity equipped them to understand producer David O. Selznick's themes of struggle for survival in war and love for one's homeland.

The evidence presented here on how *Gone with the Wind* was received suggests that well into the early 1940s, American culture was not yet fully regarded as part of the hegemonic engine of French and European colonialism. It also suggests the ways in which historical context shaped reception of Hollywood's universal vernacular: war conditions, movie advertising, and the particular conditions of urban public spheres appear to have variously altered responses to the film in Cairo, Beirut, and Damascus. This essay considers what admittedly remains a limited body of evidence as a first step toward a history of Middle Eastern movie spectatorship. Such a history enriches our understanding of how Arabs' attitudes toward American culture have changed over time. It also throws light on popular values in Arab politics at a specific moment, near the close of the colonial era. Arab responses to the film reveal profound tensions between universal humanism and particularist religious and national identity.

SELZNICK, THE WAR, AND OVERSEAS MARKETS

David O. Selznick wanted everyone in the free world to buy a ticket to his picture. He was nearly bankrupt on December 15, 1939, when he arrived in Atlanta for the world premiere of *Gone with the Wind* (hereafter *GWTW*). To cover his debts, Selznick negotiated with the distributor,

MGM/Loew's, to promote the film as an epic like the 1915 blockbuster *Birth of a Nation*. *GWTW* was to be a memorable—and costly—night out. Selznick sent a stream of memos urging movie theaters to charge higher ticket prices and hold a ten-minute intermission. The marketing hype and high production values worked: critics immediately hailed *GWTW* as the "mightiest achievement in the history of the motion picture."[7] It earned an unprecedented $20 million in its first six months of exhibition in the United States and soon set records for foreign earnings.[8]

For three years, Selznick fired off telegrams urging foreign distributors to increase their box office receipts. A liberal and a capitalist, he was absolutely convinced of the movie's universal appeal. When *GWTW* in English became a huge hit in Bombay, he immediately negotiated its rerelease across India with Hindi subtitles.[9] When Quebecois attended the film at a lower rate than Americans, he fumed: "There is no reason on earth why interest among the French Canadians should be any less than interest in London or in Singapore."[10] By 1943, *GWTW* had earned $43 million worldwide, as prints circulated the globe with subtitles in Spanish, French, Portuguese, Hindi, and potentially "the native language of all non–English speaking countries."[11]

The global appeal of *GWTW* was built into the studio system. In the 1920s Hollywood moguls had pioneered international marketing strategies, such as charging foreign distributors lower rents than European producers did.[12] They also discovered that they could use foreign profits to finance big productions like *GWTW*, which could recover only basic costs in the U.S. market. They built foreign markets by choosing popular genres, like the costume drama of *GWTW*, that always earned good returns on repeat runs overseas. In the 1930s the studios embraced the Hays Production Code not just in reaction to pressures from domestic religious groups, but also to appease foreign governments that threatened to censor immoral pictures. By 1941, when *GWTW* premiered in the Middle East, foreign markets supplied nearly 40 percent of Hollywood's annual box office receipts.[13] Film scholars now regard the classic Hollywood movie as a transnational cultural product that homogenized, bridged, or embraced cultural differences in the pursuit of profit.[14]

The outbreak of world war in September 1939 alarmed studio moguls who had built their empires on this global appeal. "The intensification of difficulties abroad has resulted in a falling off, from 70 percent to 65 percent, in America's domination of the world's motion-picture screens," warned Nathan Golden of the U.S. Commerce Department in early 1939.[15] Russia and Japan had already closed their markets. Within two years, the Nazis would ban all American movies from their occupied territories.

MGM, like other distributors, intensified marketing in Latin America and Asia to compensate for the loss of European ticket sales.[16]

Selznick had reason to worry: he had justified *GWTW*'s record-breaking $4 million production budget with the promise of foreign sales. In the summer of 1940, the Nazis occupied France, preempting *GWTW*'s Paris premiere, and Hitler banned all MGM movies from occupied Europe. Although Selznick's share of the $20 million box-office receipts already accrued in the American market covered his production costs, he still struggled to pay for new film prints and advertising.[17]

Selznick had not, however, anticipated that the war would whet home-front appetites for war movies. *GWTW* had not been produced primarily as a war picture, but when it opened at London's Ritz Cinema on April 17, 1940—a week after the Nazis occupied Norway and Denmark—it struck a chord with besieged Brits, who had just been issued ration cards. *GWTW* played to sellout crowds at the Ritz for more than a year and across England for the duration of the war.[18] In September 1940, "Elsie Kingdom, struck by the film's burning of Atlanta scenes, emerged from the cinema to see the City of London and docks on fire; the Blitz had begun," reports Helen Taylor, author of a book on women's memories of the film.[19] The movie grossed more than $4 million in the United Kingdom and Ireland in the next three years; in 1943–44, it still earned more than $500,000 in England alone.[20]

GWTW filled a gap left by the Hollywood studios, which in 1939 still preferred to produce inoffensive musicals, comedies, and romances that would pass censors in hostile countries. Consequently, few war movies were available on the market when the London Blitz hit.[21] Spectators in markets yet untouched by the war hungered for war themes. *GWTW* was not only a spectacular war picture, but it was also a movie about the hardships of life on the home front, where many of the world's remaining spectators lived and struggled. The home fronts nearest to the carnage in Europe were the Arab countries on the southern and eastern shores of the Mediterranean.

GONE WITH THE WIND'S CAIRO PREMIERE: HOLLYWOOD MARKETING AND COLONIAL SOCIETY

Arabic-speaking countries in the Middle East were a vital, early front in World War II. By the time *GWTW* made its Middle Eastern premiere—in May 1941 in Cairo—Vichy France ruled much of North Africa and Syria and Lebanon. Germany's famed Gen. Erwin Rommel threatened the British in Egypt from his base in the Italian colony of Libya. The Germans were also lending support to an anti-British coup in Iraq. The Allies were concerned, most of all, to protect supplies of oil in the Gulf and the passage of ships through the Suez Canal.

Arab peoples were concerned about surviving wartime food shortages and ousting European armies from their soil. Since 1920, they had been divided into discrete nation-states created by French, British, and Italian colonizers; only Saudi Arabia was not occupied by foreign troops. Nationalists from Casablanca to Baghdad were just beginning to imagine and advocate a greater sense of cultural and political unity. Cultural unity, since the advent of education, a press, and radio, had proceeded farthest in the Arab societies of the eastern Mediterranean by the time of the Second World War.

This Arabic-speaking world had also become important to Hollywood as another substitute for lost European markets. The market was small, with only 500 movie theaters in the region stretching from Morocco to Iraq—a figure that equaled the number of theaters in Mexico alone, and only one-tenth of England's 5,300 theaters (the United States had 16,228). More than half of the 500 cinemas were in North Africa, where European colonial elites dominated the urban audiences. The core of indigenous moviegoing lay in the 221 cinemas of the Arab East: in Syria, Lebanon, Palestine, Transjordan, Iraq, and Egypt. Egypt was by far the biggest of these markets, with 118 theaters.[22] A mix of Arabic-speaking elites and Levantines (of Italian, Greek, and Jewish descent) dominated the best theaters, which showed first-run Hollywood movies, while a broader Arab audience watched reruns of Egyptian and "B" Hollywood movies at neighborhood and village cinemas.[23] Side screens with text in French, Greek, Italian, and Arabic provided translation of Hollywood films, which were only rarely dubbed into Arabic before 1945.

MGM had recently built the first studio-owned theater in the region. The Metro Cinema opened in 1940 as an Art Deco palace, with 1,500 leather seats and air conditioning, in the heart of Cairo's theater district. Swanky, modern offices on an upper floor housed MGM's Middle East distribution headquarters.[24] "You entered the Metro as if it were a temple," recalled the eminent Egyptian movie director Youssef Chahine.[25] Warner Brothers, Paramount, Columbia, and RKO also opened offices in Cairo; in Beirut, MGM, Twentieth-Century Fox, and Columbia opened branches.[26]

These studios cashed in on Middle Eastern audiences' thirst for entertainment: the war had disrupted both the circuit of live shows and the importation of movies from France, Hollywood's primary rival.[27] The nascent Egyptian movie industry mushroomed in markets protected by wartime disruptions; it would become a serious competitor to Hollywood after 1945.[28] During the war, Egyptian moviegoing more than tripled, from 12 million tickets sold in 1938 to 42 million in 1946.[29] "The cinemas were always full," recalled a wartime resident of Cairo. "We had here, a few weeks after they had been shown in America and England, the finest films in the world."[30] Movies were also popular in wartime Syria and Lebanon, where cinemas sold about 20 million tickets a year. By the early 1950s Lebanon attained the highest rate of moviegoing in all of Asia.[31]

GWTW premiered at the Cairo Metro on May 14, 1941, following a blitz of publicity in Cairo's top daily paper, *Al-Ahram*. Two days later, photos of the premiere were splashed across *Al-Ahram*, displaying an elegant audience dressed in tuxedos and evening gowns. Selznick must have been delighted to receive this cable from Cairo:

> Never before has any picture had such terrific advance booking as *GWTW*. Afternoon and evening performances first four days ninety-percent already sold out, while hundreds still queueing daily for seats. . . . Audience dazzled by splendor scenes and moved by story. Reaction unequalled by any picture. Galaxy [of] social and political celebrities headed by his Excellency Hussein Sirry Pacha, prime minister; British Ambassador and Lady Lampson; British minister [Terence] Shone and Embassy staff; American minister Alexander Kirk and legation staff; General Sir Archibald and Lady Wavell and daughters; General Catroux, Free French troops; General Atalla Pacha, Chief of Egyptian General Staff.[32]

Selznick surely appreciated the social buzz created by the distinguished guest list of top Egyptian, British, French, and American officials. Because Egypt was Britain's headquarters for the war effort in the Middle East, Cairo had become a crossroads of eminent royalty and heads of state, who inflated the occasion with celebrity. The son of an MGM employee claimed that people talked about *GWTW*'s premiere in Cairo for years afterward.[33]

RECEPTION OF *GONE WITH THE WIND* IN CAIRO'S PRESS

We cannot, of course, enter the minds of *GWTW*'s spectators to divine their personal reactions, but we can study how press publicity framed the expectations of the thousands of moviegoers who filled the seats of the Metro for weeks in the summer of 1941. Egyptian journalists' articles about the premiere, often based on MGM's press releases, framed the expectations of Egyptian audiences and so influenced the ways they interpreted the movie's global vernacular.[34]

Cairo's major daily paper, *Al-Ahram*, cooperated eagerly with MGM in implementing Selznick's strategy to market *GWTW* as a rare jewel and a milestone in movie history. For two weeks before the premiere, *Al-Ahram* published oversized ads and press releases translated into Arabic. On

April 29, under a photo of Scarlett dancing with Rhett Butler, a headline read: "The Longest Film Ever Made in Hollywood: Preparations for Its Arrival in Cairo." A May 1 article reprinted Hollywood boilerplate about 1,400 "girls" screened for the role of Scarlett, the record price paid for rights to the story ($50,000), and the full year it took to write the script.[35] On May 4, MGM ran the first ad for the movie itself, in the form of an elegant invitation to the premiere.[36] Later in May the paper ran a pseudo-review that praised the actors' talent but mainly advertised the continuing enthusiasm of Cairo's public for the picture.[37]

Paid advertising overwhelmed these stories with eye-catching images. The report on the May 14 premiere was surrounded by a full page of advertisements linking *GWTW* to the consumption of luxuries like beauty soap (with a movie still of Scarlett's face gazing up at Rhett's) and wedding dresses (with a photo of Scarlett wearing one). Another full-page spread of advertisements linked *GWTW* to the consumption of foreign imports like French sweets for "the refined classes" (with a photo of Rhett and Scarlett being served by a butler), Brazilian coffee (with a photo of Scarlett holding an elegant tea cup), and "modern beds of Paris" (with a photo of Scarlett waking up in her famous big bed).[38]

MGM's publicity campaign appealed directly to Egypt's landowning arabophone elites, and especially to the wealthy women who ran vast households that matched Tara in size and luxury. It is unclear whether this focus was intentional. The press releases and advertisements appeared to replicate Selznick's American marketing strategy to inflate expectations and charge higher prices. They also reproduced themes of the Old South deployed in the Depression-era United States as an escapist fantasy for the poor. In Egypt, however, these images appeared in newspapers read by the tiny minority of literate Egyptians, who by definition constituted the wealthiest 5 percent of the country. The indigenous landowning class had prospered under the British suzerainty since 1882: about 12,000 families owned large estates comprising more than one-third of all farmland in Egypt. At the very apex of Egyptian society were perhaps 2,000 families, whose estates exceeded 200 acres, and the royal family, with more than 100,000 acres.[39] Their plantations employed sharecropping peasants, not African slaves, but like the nineteenth-century Southerners they produced cash crops for export—mostly cotton. Export profits enabled Egypt's wealthiest families to maintain rural villas and urban palaces, where they entertained on a scale comparable to the great barbecue at Twelve Oaks in the opening scenes of *GWTW.*

Elite Egyptian women watching the social rituals at Twelve Oaks would have found familiar the segregation of the sexes, the ranking of families around ideals of honor, the family politics of matchmaking, and the presence of Africans as household slaves. Advertisements for the luxuries sup-posedly enjoyed by Scarlett—imported dresses, bedding, tea services, and chocolates—directly linked the lifestyles of the Old South's upper crust and Egypt's colonial aristocracy. It is no surprise that *Al-Ahram* uncritically played to MGM's script: the paper evaded censorship by avoiding contro-versy, playing to royal interests, and maintaining a mildly pro-British line.[40]

Most of *GWTW*'s Egyptian spectators, however, were urban and middle class. Some may have sought escapist fantasy in watching South-ern belles prance at balls, but movie criticism in other Arabic periodicals suggests that many others did not welcome *GWTW* as a public celebration of the colonial elite's luxury. Consumption was an especially controversial issue at a time when Egyptians faced shortages of basic necessities like wheat and clothing. Under the circumstances of heavy censorship imposed on Egypt's press, the omission of *GWTW*'s publicity in these other peri-odicals might be interpreted as negative criticism. "Editors found ways to bypass or penetrate the walls of censorship," writes Ami Ayalon, a leading historian of the Egyptian press, "by insinuating when unable to speak ex-plicitly and by delivering their messages between the lines."[41]

It is striking, for example, that *Al-Mokattam*, a leading evening paper, ran just three short press releases about *GWTW* sandwiched among other stories about Egyptian movies. It published nothing about the premiere.[42] *Al-Musawwar*, the Egyptian equivalent of *Paris Match*, omitted all mention of *GWTW*. The exclusion is remarkable for a magazine that fed on celeb-rity, royalty, and elite social affairs. Like *Al-Mokattam*, it devoted its movie coverage exclusively to the Egyptian cinema.[43] Another highbrow maga-zine, *Al-Sabah*, likewise published no stories about *GWTW*, limiting cover-age to three small photo stills. Both *Al-Sabah* and *Al-Musawwar* catered to the nationalist intelligentsia and youth movement; they regularly published articles that promoted Egyptian movies and condemned competition from foreign imports. They also voiced Muslim resentment of Levantines who socialized with colonial elites.[44] These tepid responses to *GWTW* were not likely accidental. They coincide with a split in Cairo's elite between An-glophile collaborationists and Islamic-leaning nationalists. That split grew wider as the war raised hopes for full independence from Britain.

SCARLETT O'HARA A LA FRANÇAISE: *GWTW*'S PREMIERE IN BEIRUT

Differences in Lebanon's public sphere altered *GWTW*'s reception there: wartime conditions delayed the premiere, and market conditions de-flated the film's publicity. The weeks-long advertising campaign of Cairo was trimmed in Beirut to a few days, and it was the French government that issued the elegant invitation, not MGM. The French delegate and his wife, Gen. and Mme Catroux, published their invitation to the premiere, "to benefit Allied military charities in the Levant," on the front page of a French-language daily.[45] They thereby inscribed *GWTW* directly into colonial politics and elite social rituals, which revolved around charity balls and relief works. On the night of February 22, 1942, the Roxy theater was decked with Allied flags and the "Marseillaise" played as Gen. Catroux entered.[46] In a speech, Mme Catroux thanked MGM and the Roxy cinema owners, and applauded charities that aided wounded soldiers and relieved wartime hunger.[47]

Beirut's public sphere was truncated not just by social class but also by language: francophone Lebanese Arabs read periodicals that inhabited a different social world from Arab ones. Like *Al-Ahram*, Beirut's foreign-language press framed *GWTW* as an elitist social event. The *Eastern Times* hailed the premiere as "the opening of the social season in Beirut."[48] *La Syrie et le Proche-Orient* proclaimed it "le clou de la saison."[49] The latter paper ran a series of front-page articles that profiled lead characters and their actors with gushing praise: Vivien Leigh's "Scarlett O'Hara was at once violent and gentle, selfish and charitable, tender and authoritarian," and Clark Gable's Rhett was a "solid male, merry, bold, a swashbuckler . . . but also how tender and good and noble."[50] The Lebanese who read these papers apparently saw themselves as participants in a transnational, cosmopolitan culture. Editors assumed that their readers were familiar with Margaret Mitchell's 1936 novel, which was available in French translation (but not Arabic). Unlike the editors of *Al-Ahram*, however, the francophone editors in Beirut openly challenged the colonial terms of participation in modern civilization. *La Syrie et le Proche-Orient* went so far as to assert social parity between Beirut elites and Hollywood stars: it reported that the prominent Arab nationalist George Antonius had met Vivien Leigh onboard the transatlantic ship she took to her Hollywood audition and that he had correctly predicted she would win the part of Scarlett.[51]

In contrast, Beirut's Arabic-language papers presented *GWTW* to their reading public in small items that abutted stories about the siege of Leningrad, a Japanese attack in Bali, Rommel's advance on Egypt, and local stories on rising food prices and workers' protests for higher pay.[52] Beirut suffered from a paper shortage that shrank newspapers to two or four pages, and its Arabic papers appear to have been less willing to sacrifice space to a social event organized by France. *An-Nahar*, Beirut's most prestigious Arabic daily, omitted all mention of the premiere; *Bayrut*, the city's leading nationalist paper, published only one advance notice, a two-inch story that neglected French sponsorship to emphasize that the party's cohosts were the Lebanese and Syrian presidents.[53] Insofar as press coverage laid a framework for how audiences approached *GWTW*, we may infer that in early 1942 the majority of Beirut's arabophone residents were predisposed to view it as a war movie, not the glamorous romp that francophone audiences were led to expect.

In Beirut and Cairo, the global publicity campaign for *GWTW* exacerbated not only divisions among colonial elites but also between elites and other social groups. Movie ads unwittingly—or not—played into crosscutting social tensions between foreign wealth and indigenous deprivation by linking the film to the consumption of luxuries. Premieres that featured British and French officials reinforced the movie's elitist allure. Egyptian and Lebanese elites performed their privileged status by attending *GWTW* at their cities' most expensive and swankiest cinemas, the Metro and the Roxy, where lower-class spectators, and especially Arabic speakers, felt unwelcome. Distributors compounded this message of exclusivity by not dubbing or subtitling the film. In spite of Selznick's promise of subtitles for "all non-English speaking countries," there is no evidence that Arabic subtitles were prepared for prints that circulated in the Middle East or North Africa.[54] The movie that played in Beirut likely had only the French subtitles required by law (and prepared for the aborted Paris premiere). Egyptians, better equipped to handle multilingual audiences, may have used side screens to project summaries in Arabic, Greek, and other languages.[55]

The physical dimensions of the public sphere also determined the dynamics of inclusion and exclusion in the two cities. In Beirut, conflict was mitigated because the Bourj movie district had historically been a mixed and inclusive public space.[56] Christians and Muslims, arabophones and francophones, likely joined each other at the Roxy theater, which would nonetheless have excluded lower classes. In Cairo, the movie district had become by 1941 an open battleground. Nationalists had joined with Egyptian moviemakers to challenge Hollywood's dominance by building the Studio Misr theater to showcase Egyptian movies. Religious conservatives, led by the Muslim Brotherhood, played on class exclusion to incite popular opposition to foreign cinema as a moral corruption opposed to Islamic values. Hasan al-Banna, the Muslim Brothers' leader, urged King Farouk in an open letter to impose strict censorship on cinema—along with dance halls, theaters, radio, and cafes.[57]

TARA: LOVE OF THE HOMELAND
AS A UNIVERSAL VERNACULAR

Between the Allied push and the anticolonial pull, *GWTW* might have fallen between the cracks of colonial and class politics. It did not. *GWTW*'s three-week run at Beirut's Roxy was extraordinary; no other film that season ran more than a week.[58] Its nine-week run in Cairo also beat local records.[59] Across the region, *GWTW* grossed nearly twice as much as previous MGM films.[60] In its second release, in 1943–44, *GWTW* earned nearly $33,000 in Egypt alone, matching Mexico's box office and surpassing India's for the same period.[61] These figures suggest that many middle-class moviegoers defied nationalist and leftist political leaders who had discouraged them from seeing the picture. No doubt many of these spectators flocked to *GWTW* for the same reasons that Americans and British did, to escape wartime deprivations by buying a seat in an air-conditioned theater and indulging in fantasies of abundance.[62]

GWTW also likely appealed to mass audiences as a war movie. During its first run in Egypt, in June 1941, the Germans bombed Alexandria. More than 3,000 people were killed, and half of the city's panicked population fled by foot, bus, or train—much as Scarlett escaped the burning of Atlanta.[63] Earlier in 1941 *Al-Sabah* had published an article criticizing Egyptian moviemakers for ignoring the war: "We don't necessarily want artists to portray combat scenes . . . but we want them to paint a humanistic picture of what's happening in the world because of the war."[64] *Al-Ahram* also hailed Charlie Chaplin's *The Great Dictator* that spring as a film that "treats the most important issue facing people today . . . big crowds await the film eagerly." The review condemned Hitler's tyranny and fascist racism.[65]

Some spectators identified with Scarlett O'Hara not just as a fellow war victim but also as a nationalist who drew strength from her homeland. *Bayrut* published a preview of the film the day before the Lebanese premiere. The article was no translation of MGM boilerplate but a uniquely personal piece of criticism. The writer began by summarizing the novel's plot for Arabic readers who had not read it (an Arabic translation appeared after the war). He called it a page-turner that followed "Vivien Leigh, during an eventful life, full of misery and conspiracy and lost love, bewildered motherhood and failed marriage and astounding selfishness." He alerted his readers to the movie's core theme: "Truly, the story that the Roxy theater has rented for next week is worthy in every aspect of viewing," he said. The title of the movie "ought to have been *Handful of Earth*, the earth that we entrust with the buried remains of generations, the earth that we serve, that we till, that we invest in with our money, with our effort and with our spirit . . . because it is our nation."[66] This devotion to the land was a core theme of nationalists opposed to Free French rule. It also inspired the Muslim-Arab scouting movement led by *Bayrut*'s publisher, Muhi al-Din al-Nasuli.

The *Bayrut* preview is remarkable because it defiantly crossed the battle lines of colonial politics: it neither dismissed *GWTW* as foreign contagion nor embraced it as a totem of higher civilization. The preview was nationalist without being anti-American, and it sympathized with Scarlett even though she broke social and sexual taboos of Arab (and American) culture. It appreciated her character as a struggling and patriotic survivor, in contrast to the French newspaper's portrayal of Scarlett as a femme fatale. Indeed, *Bayrut* captured the very theme that Selznick had personally grafted onto Mitchell's novel—the theme of love of the land. Selznick had personally intervened in the movie's production to emphasize this theme first at the intermission, when Scarlett grabs a carrot from the earth and vows never to go hungry again, and then at the conclusion, when Scarlett returns to Tara after Rhett leaves. Selznick's ending, not drawn from the book, shows Scarlett recalling her father's voice, reminding her that the land of Tara is all that matters.[67]

Bayrut and its nationalist readers absolutely understood Selznick's message. They appropriated his universal theme to their own experience and so read *GWTW* as a lesson for their own struggle and survival. Beirut's nationalist spectators would have sympathized with Scarlett's travails because their homeland was also under occupation—by the French. The Free French had invaded the previous summer of 1941 to oust Vichy from Lebanon and Syria. And like Southerners after the 1864 burning of Atlanta, the Lebanese faced dire shortages of clothing and food as the war cut supply lines and as the Allies requisitioned all surpluses for their military needs. Arab nationalist readers of *Bayrut* looked on the Free French as illegal occupiers who no longer enjoyed a mandate from the defunct League of Nations.

The Beirut paper's nationalist reading of the film also contrasts with the nationalism of the Cairo press. While the Egyptian opposition viewed Americans as British collaborators and Hollywood as an unfair competitor, *Bayrut* lauded the film with little reference to its origin. It did not frame the American picture as a vehicle of European dominance or Christian contagion, nor did it embrace the film as a totem of cosmopolitan elitism. Perhaps because Americans were not seen as close allies of the Free French, there was still room in the pages of Arabic papers in Beirut to regard Hollywood pictures as a popular and universal cultural form.

"I'LL NEVER BE HUNGRY AGAIN": WOMEN'S RESPONSE TO *GWTW* IN DAMASCUS

A second piece of evidence also suggests that the general popularity of *GWTW* sprang from counterhegemonic readings that resisted the colonial/nationalist rhetoric of cultural difference. In the spring of 1942, the wife of a French officer, Anne Collet, attended a women's Friday afternoon matinee of *GWTW* at the Roxy cinema in Damascus, Syria. After the war, she published a uniquely detailed description of the screening in a memoir.[68] The Roxy was situated on a quiet boulevard linking new wealthy suburbs to the old city. Far from the hype of the Cairo and Beirut premieres, Damascene audiences encountered *GWTW* without political framing by the press. Local papers had given the movie almost no notice. On that Friday afternoon, as on most others, Collet joined her Damascene friends at the Roxy matinee. They were avid movie fans, and they used the matinees as a social occasion to visit friends. The women were immediately attracted to the new brunette star, Vivien Leigh. Their interest in Scarlett O'Hara grew with each new husband she married, Collet wrote, but it peaked just before the intermission, when Scarlett returned home after the burning of Atlanta:

> The heroine of *Gone with the Wind*, standing on her native soil of Tara, a carrot in her hand, cried: "I will steal, I will lie, I will deceive and I will kill, but never will I be hungry. God is my witness!" The emotion stirred in the audience by these words deserves to be recorded. These Muslim women ... living in security inside the walls of a harem, some of them not knowing how to write, knowing less than that of life, who never knew hunger, who would never kill, dupe, lie or steal for a meal, these women stood up and applauded furiously. Some sobbed loudly. Others yelled "Bravo!" until they were out of breath.[69]

In Collet's account, this scene drew far more emotion from the Damascene women than did any of Scarlett's romantic encounters with Rhett Butler.

Collet takes pains to explain this moment of enthusiasm to her postwar French readers. She assures them that the Syrian women must have reacted from irrational pathos, not from any true feeling of identification with Scarlett's feelings of desperation. Collet deploys a language of cultural difference that emphasizes the distance between the culture of hardworking Western women and the stereotype of the lazy harem princess. In so doing, Collet reflects the colonial rhetoric of the French regime, to which her husband belonged, which asserted the superiority of European culture and so justified their duty to rule Arabs.

The historical context of the *GWTW* screening in Damascus, however, suggests a compelling alternative interpretation of the Muslim women's emotional response to Scarlett O'Hara's soliloquy. Scarlett's struggle on the home front likely resonated as deeply with this crowd as it did with audiences who watched *GWTW* during the London Blitz. During the previous world war, only twenty-two years before, one-sixth of the Syrian and Lebanese population had died in a famine. As in the American Civil War, women had been left alone on the home front to protect their families. The *safar barlik* (wartime privation) was a deep trauma, a shame that was never spoken about in public.[70] When Lebanese and Syrians heard that Hitler had invaded Poland in 1939, they reacted with fear that famine might return. Now in 1942, elite Syrian women again organized soup kitchens, while their poorer sisters led hunger marches that ominously disintegrated into bread riots.[71] Collet's friends at the Roxy likely cheered because they, or their loved ones, had shared Scarlett's experience of hunger and destitution. And like the writer of the *Bayrut* preview, they shared Scarlett's determination to struggle for survival, and for her land.

Both the Damascus audience and the *Bayrut* movie critic responded most forcefully to the very theme that had made the movie popular in the United States. Audiences across the American South, and also in the North, cheered and cried at screenings in response to the picture's "message that a society strong enough in its beliefs could survive almost anything."[72] *GWTW* appealed to audiences in Depression-era America because it displaced their suffering onto another time and place. In the 1930s, as in the 1860s, an agrarian way of life was destroyed. Families starved during the Depression just as the O'Haras had, and like Scarlett, many were forced to adapt to the new capitalist, industrial world wrought by war.[73]

So, too, were wartime conditions in Damascus, Beirut, and Cairo similar to those in 1864 Atlanta. Audiences in these cities might also have found in *GWTW* a satisfying site of displacement for their anxieties. In the Levant and in Egypt, the reign of the old landowning elite was crumbling under the wartime pressure of labor, nationalist, and Islamic movements that gave voice to popular grievances.[74] These movements aimed to overturn the patriarchal world of privilege ruled by landed elites and to capture the state at independence for the benefit of middle or working classes. Elite spectators may have also found resonance in *GWTW*'s story of how a new middle class, personified by Rhett Butler, supplanted the weakened aristocracy of the Old South. In the Middle East, too, a new industrial bourgeoisie contested the colonial regimes' agrarian policies and promoted state-led industrialization. The war brought visions of independence, and a new social life, closer.

In other words, Anne Collet's wealthy women friends at the Roxy and the critic at *Bayrut* likely read *GWTW* in a global vernacular, that is, as a text legible across cultures and open to their full comprehension. They seized on key narrative elements and themes, and adapted them to their own, local circumstances. Selznick had carefully developed Scarlett's story around universal themes of woman's endurance and the conflict between love of home and love of adventure.[75] The story left space for Damascene viewers to adapt key narrative elements to their local circumstances. An incident following the women's matinee suggests how complicated a process that adaptation was.

When the show finally ended, and the women filed out of the Roxy cinema, Collet recalled, they felt angry at Rhett for leaving Scarlett. They vented their anger at the theater owner by demanding refunds for their tickets. "Why do we have to pay to see an American abandon his wife, when in Syria we can see that every day for nothing?" they asked him. Despite their disappointment, the women continued to discuss the movie for days afterward, and their criticism moved from Rhett's behavior to that of Scarlett. When Collet offered to arrange a meeting with Vivien Leigh during her Middle East tour, her friends had no interest.

Collet does not explain how or why the women's response to Scarlett/Leigh changed from empathy at the time they left their seats to disdain days later. Ambivalence toward the character of Scarlett O'Hara was not unusual. American spectators also engaged in debate about her transgressions, as did Collet's British friends and her French readers. In her memoir, however, Collet frames the women's disenchantment with Scarlett in the language of colonial difference: the women were ignorant snobs with no appreciation of Western art forms, and they were vindictive nationalists who resented Western women. On other Friday afternoons, Collet remarked, her friends cheered loudly at Egyptian movies, especially when European dancers who had seduced the Egyptian male star were murdered by their jealous fiancées.

Collet excludes from her intimate tale of harem life in Syria all reference to outside influences. We may interrogate this elision and query whether something in the women's social milieu, outside of the cinema, intervened to encourage the shift in their views. The women had attended the matinee without exposure to MGM publicity or to criticism in the press. Did conversations with husbands, relatives, and friends introduce doubt about Scarlett's heroism? Did the light of day and the women's return to wartime life transform their intimate memories of Scarlett as fellow woman in struggle into a symbol of the West that had brought war to Syria?

Collet's account of the women's matinee raises other questions about the nature of female spectatorship in the Middle East. Middle-class Lebanese and Egyptian women had during that period begun attending movies in large numbers.[76] In Beirut and Cairo, they attended the same shows as men, although sometimes seated in separate balconies. Photos of the

Cairo premiere as published in *Al-Ahram* showed women sitting in seats next to men.

Such photos of gender mixing in cinemas aroused controversy among the general populations of Egypt and Lebanon, where Muslim women who attended movies downtown donned veils before returning to their more conservative neighborhoods. Women often attended these movies in defiance of conservatives and religious activists, who feared the films' immoral influence. And women often viewed movies with other women, separate from the gaze and comment of men.

Collet's Damascene friends, whom she depicted as sheltered and passive, were actually quite daring. In the capital and much of Syria, segregated women's matinees continued into the 1950s, out of preference and fear.[77] Islamic populists had shut down women's matinees, had stoned women who entered movie theaters, and would, two years after the *GWTW* premiere, lead a group in attacking a cinema near the Roxy, where a women's matinee was in progress. They feared and condemned what they believed women would think and see behind those closed doors, apart from men's supervision. At the time of the *GWTW* premiere in 1942, French authorities banned an Egyptian movie with a female Syrian star, Asmahan, because her elite family deemed public performance an embarrassment. Asmahan (whom one Egyptian critic compared to Vivien Leigh in looks and manner) was portrayed in the press as a rebel against patriarchal norms.[78] The Moroccan feminist Fatima Mernissi recalls that watching Asmahan movies was a subversive female pleasure in Fez, Morocco, in the 1940s and 1950s.[79]

Asmahan was just one of many female stars in classic Egyptian cinema. Collet's friends watched their movies avidly, as did their sisters in Cairo. Fully one-half of Egyptian movies produced from 1936 to 1942 starred a woman; some were made by female producers and directors.[80] For women in Arab capitals in 1941–42, going to the movies was a daring act of defiance and liberation. Scarlett O'Hara, in this cinematic context, would have appeared to them as just one among many women of the screen who dared to cross boundaries. This context makes Collet's description of sheltered women who ignorantly dismiss Vivien Leigh seem implausible. Preliminary research on the linkages of theme and style in women's pictures made in Hollywood and women's melodramas of the classic Egyptian cinema suggests that a real exchange occurred between the rival industries, to the delight of their fans.[81]

Although Selznick likely did not anticipate the ways in which his story of the Old South would intersect with colonial politics in the Middle East, he would have nodded in approval if he had read Collet's account. Hollywood's global vernacular was in full operation that Friday in 1942 Damascus. Less a universal language than a universally accessible code, the studio formula had ensured the women's enthusiastic engagement with the movie, even on the remote boulevards of Damascus.

"TOMORROW IS ANOTHER DAY": ADAPTATIONS OF GONE WITH THE WIND IN THE ARABIC CINEMA

These small traces of *GWTW*'s reception in the Middle East cannot and should not support generalizations about how Arabs viewed American culture. The press coverage and memoir presented here do, however, challenge historians' debates about general affection or disdain. The historical contexts of Cairo, Beirut, and Damascus created movie publics with differing interests and approaches to the same cinematic text, and responses were not overdetermined by prejudices opposed or favorable to American culture.

Evidence presented here also challenges the story told by colonial elites in the Middle East, who framed Hollywood within discourses about Americanization as salvation—the route to modern prosperity—or as a contagion that would weaken Muslim, Arab, or Eastern society. Anecdotal evidence and the number of ticket sales suggest that many, if not most, Middle Eastern moviegoers paid little heed to polarizing ideologies of colonizers, Islamists, fascists, and the Allies. The texts examined here also challenge Anne Collet's views that Eastern peoples could not understand Western culture. Moviegoers in Damascus, Beirut, and Cairo responded to common human themes in Hollywood movies and adapted them to their own experience.

Perhaps the most compelling evidence of mutual comprehension and appreciation lies in the adaptation of the *GWTW* story into popular Egyptian movies. Gamal Abdel Nasser—leader of the 1952 Egyptian revolution that would sweep aside the monarchy and plantation-owning elite—was widely known to be a fan of American movies. In the 1940s he visited Cairo's theaters; after becoming president of the republic, he had movies projected in his home. Despite his regime's socialist aims, he permitted Egypt's vibrant, commercial movie industry—nicknamed Hollywood on the Nile—to thrive. Egyptian producers competed with Hollywood rivals by imitating the moguls' methods. After 1952, they tweaked plot formulas of their own cinematic vernacular to tell the stories not of aristocrats but of working-class heroes and peasants who defied their landowners. Although some revolutionaries experimented with grim social realism, entertainment remained the dominant narrative motive in Egyptian cinema.[82]

In the quarter century after *GWTW*'s premiere, no less than three Egyptian and Lebanese movies were inspired by *GWTW*'s story. Much as *GWTW* was linked with *Birth of a Nation* (1915) as an epic of a nation sundered and reconciled in war, so these movies located national origins in Middle Eastern wars. *Return My Heart* (1957), an epic shot in Cinemascope, took place during the period from the 1948 Arab-Israeli war to the 1952 revolution that saw the birth of modern Egypt. Based on a popular Egyptian novel, it tells the story of a love affair between an estate gardener and a pasha's daughter who overcome class differences after the revolution—in contrast to the final incompatibility of the middle-class opportunist Rhett Butler and plantation aristocrat Scarlett O'Hara.[83] A second movie, *Whom Do I Love* (1966), replayed the plot of *GWTW* as a love triangle during the 1948 war. Produced by an Egyptian actress, it was the least successful of the three adaptations.[84]

The third film, *Safar Barlik* (1967), was a milestone Lebanese-Egyptian collaboration starring one of the most famous of Arab singing stars, Feyrouz.[85] It tells the story of Lebanon's birth as a nation during the years of famine and Ottoman military oppression in World War I. Feyrouz's role of Adla directly recapitulates that of Vivien Leigh as a fearless woman who braves the danger of enemy soldiers to rescue her fiancé from a forced labor camp and to help smuggle food to starving villagers. She is more heroic and less selfish than Scarlett, but, like the rebellious Southern belle, she is willing to violate social convention to save her land and her village. Direct comparisons with *GWTW* may have occurred to *Safar Barlik*'s audiences. At the time of *Safar Barlik*'s release, Lebanese women were still flocking to theatrical projections of *GWTW*. In the recollection of a child spectator dragged to a Beirut cinema by his mother around 1970, the theater was filled with women who cheered loudly and wept profusely at Scarlett's travails, much as female audiences had done in 1942.[86]

Also noteworthy is that *Safar Barlik* applied the cinematic vernacular of universal humanism to a theme of national unity. The story unfolds on Mount Lebanon, the scene of terrible sectarian violence in 1860. In the movie's setting of 1914, however, there is no distinction among Lebanese by sect: modern Lebanon was created by the social unity and common effort of Arabs against the oppressive Turks. This theme mirrors Selznick's depiction of the Old South as a society in which the races remained united in their struggle for survival.[87] Like the Southern myth, this legend of Lebanese solidarity challenged a counternarrative that emphasized conflict. Many Lebanese had viewed their state as a sectarian and colonial creation of the French in 1920, for the benefit of Maronite Catholics. Just eight years after *Safar Barlik*'s successful release in Beirut (at the same Roxy theater where *GWTW* had premiered), Lebanon crumbled into sectarian civil war.[88]

The homage to *GWTW* in three films says something about the power of the story and its special appeal to women and men in societies undergoing violent national transitions. The bits of evidence assembled here about the first encounter with *GWTW* by spectators in Damascus, Beirut, and Cairo also elucidate how specific historical contexts shape reception of broad themes. In each city the dynamics of spectatorship differed. In all three places, however, evidence of resistance to dominant framings of the film appeared.

Cinema constituted, for moviegoing audiences of the war years, a vital and separate public sphere created within the new moviegoing culture of the Arabic-speaking world. It created a space for counterhegemonic imaginings of class, gender, and national identities at a moment when political venues were closed by wartime censors and when Arab societies were nonetheless motivated to debate the terms of their imminent decolonization. *GWTW*, and perhaps other Hollywood movies, became a nexus of cultural exchange that was far more fluid and contested than dominant nationalist, religious, and colonialist ideologues constructed it to be. The global vernacular invented by Hollywood opened *GWTW* to contested local readings and so shaped debates among Lebanese, Syrians, Egyptians, and likely others in the Arabic-speaking world not only about their relationship to American culture, but also about the possibility of a universal civilization and their membership in it.

Notes

This chapter represents the start of a larger study of *Gone with the Wind*, movie spectatorship, and decolonization in my forthcoming book, *Cinema and the Politics of Late Colonialism.* I thank the American Council of Learned Societies, the Library of Congress Kluge Center, and Chuck McCurdy of the University of Virginia history department for supporting research for this chapter. I also thank audiences at annual conferences of the Middle East Studies Association and American Historical Association, Princeton University, University of North Carolina-Chapel Hill, University of California-Davis, Northwestern University, and the École des Hautes Études in Paris for comments on earlier versions. I thank Mary Beltran for research assistance at the Selznick archive.

1. Anne Collet, *Collet des Tcherkesses*, trans. Suzanne Valliene (Paris: Corrêa, 1949), 125–33. I thank Pierre Fournié, formerly of the Quai d'Orsay archives in Paris, for mentioning this memoir to me.

2. The authoritative *American Film Institute Catalog*'s lengthy entry on the film omits any mention of its marketing overseas: *The American Film Institute Catalog of Motion Pictures Produced in the United States: Feature Films, 1931–1940, Film Entries A–L* (Berkeley: University

of California Press, 1971), 801–6. See also Ronald Haver, *David O. Selznick's "Gone with the Wind"* (New York: Bonanza Books, 1986); Richard Harwell, ed., *"Gone with the Wind" as Book and Film* (Columbia: University of South Carolina Press, 1992). Brief mentions of the film's wartime popularity in Europe are made in Edward D. C. Campbell, Jr., *The Celluloid South: Hollywood and the Southern Myth* (Knoxville: University of Tennessee Press, 1981), 119; Herb Bridges and Terry C. Boodman, *Gone with the Wind: The Definitive Illustrated History of the Book, the Movie, and the Legend* (New York: Simon and Shuster, 1989), 240. An exception is Helen Taylor's inclusion of British women in *Scarlett's Women: "Gone with the Wind" and Its Female Fans* (New Brunswick, NJ: Rutgers University Press, 1989). On the influence of foreign markets, see Ruth Vasey, *The World according to Hollywood, 1919–1939* (Madison: University of Wisconsin Press, 1997); Kristin Thompson, *Exporting Entertainment: America in the World Film Market, 1907–34* (London: BFI Publishing, 1985); John Trumpbour, *Selling Hollywood to the World* (New York: Cambridge University Press, 2002); and Ian Jarvie, *Hollywood's Overseas Campaign: The North Atlantic Movie Trade, 1920–1950* (New York: Cambridge University Press, 1992).

3. This essay contributes to an emergent literature on movie spectatorship in colonial contexts: Brian Larkin, "Theaters of the Profane: Cinema and Colonial Urbanism," *Visual Anthropology Review* 14, no. 2 (Fall–Winter 1998): 46–62; Prem Chowdhry, *Colonial India and the Making of Empire Cinema* (New Delhi: Vistaar Publications, 2001); Charles Ambler, "Popular Films and Colonial Audiences: The Movies in Northern Rhodesia," *American Historical Review* (February 2001): 81–105; Brian T. Edwards, "Preposterous Encounters: Interrupting American Studies with the (Post)Colonial, or *Casablanca* in the American Century," *Comparative Studies of South Asia, Africa and the Middle East* 23, nos. 1 and 2 (2003): 70–86.

4. Rashid Khalidi, *Resurrecting Empire: Western Footprints and America's Perilous Path in the Middle East* (Boston: Beacon Press, 2004), 30–36; Ussama Makdisi, "'Anti-Americanism' in the Arab World: An Interpretation of a Brief History," *Journal of American History* 89, no. 2 (September 2002): 14–25, http://historycooperative.org/cgi-bin/printpage.cgi. Erez Manela is among the few international historians to challenge this sanguine view, in Manela, "Goodwill and Bad: Rethinking U.S.-Egyptian Contacts in the Interwar Years," *Middle Eastern Studies* 38, no.1 (January 2002): 71–88.

5. Preeminent among this school is Bernard Lewis, *What Went Wrong? The Clash between Modernity and Islam in the Middle East* (New York: Oxford University Press, 2001), 133–60.

6. Miriam Bratu Hansen, "Fallen Women, Rising Stars, New Horizons: Shanghai Silent Film as Vernacular Modernism," *Film Quarterly* 54, no.1 (Fall 2000): 10–22.

7. *Hollywood Spectator*, December 23, 1939, reprinted in Harwell, *"Gone With the Wind" as Book and Film*, 151. Selznick's memos are preserved at the David O. Selznick Collection, Harry Ransom Humanities Research Center, University of Texas at Austin (hereafter Selznick Collection); see also Haver, *David O. Selznick's GWTW*, 68, 72, 75.

8. *American Film Institute Catalog*, 805; and Jay Robert Nash and Stanley Ralph Ross, *The Motion Picture Guide*, vol. E–G, 1927–83 (Chicago: Cinebooks, 1986), 1067. The highest grossing film to date had been *Snow White and the Seven Dwarfs*, which earned $8 million in 1938. See Haver, *David O. Selznick's GWTW*, 75.

9. D. O. Selznick to J. H. Whitney, memo, May 7, 1940; and memo, July 9, 1941; both in Selznick Collection, Administrative/Production Files, 1936–42/*Gone with the Wind*, BK 359 foreign distribution.

10. Selznick to L. Calvert, memo, April 16, 1942, Selznick Collection, BK 359.

11. Quotation from Morty Spring, in Calvert to Selznick, April 28, 1942; see also July 9, 1941, memo on Hindustani titles; Calvert to Selznick, February 6, 1942; Selznick to Calvert, April 16, 1942; all in Selznick Collection, BK 359. Arabic subtitles were not specifically mentioned.

12. Thompson, *Exporting Entertainment*; and Jarvie, *Hollywood's Overseas Campaign*.

13. Kerry Segrave, *American Films Abroad* (Jefferson, NC: McFarland, 1997), 287. Hollywood box office receipts for 1941 totaled $252 million from U.S. distribution and $140 million to $160 million from foreign distribution.

14. Vasey, *World according to Hollywood*, 158–228; Hansen, "Fallen Women, Rising Stars, New Horizons." Vasey argues that Warner Brothers was able to make edgier movies because its smaller budgets did not require foreign profits.

15. Nathan D. Golden, *Review of Foreign Film Markets during 1938* (Washington, DC: U.S. Department of Commerce, 1939), i; at the time, Golden was chief of the Motion Picture Division. See also David Thomson, *Showman: The Life of David O. Selznick* (New York: Knopf, 1992), 253.

16. Golden, *Review of Foreign Film Markets*, iii–iv. Latin America had more than 5,000 theaters.

17. "Producers Gird for War," *New York Times*, September 10, 1939; and "War's Double-Entry," *New York Times*, September 17, 1939; both reprinted in vol. 3 of *The New York Times Encyclopedia of Film*, ed. Gene Brown (New York: Times Books, 1984); Haver, *David O. Selznick's GWTW*, 65, 75; Thomson, *Showman*, 348. Selznick underestimated *GWTW*'s future appeal and sold his rights to the film before the war's end in order to avoid taxes.

18. Selznick to Calvert, August 16, 1939; MGM press release on London opening, April 19, 1940; Selznick to Altstock, July 7, 1941; Geddes to McDonnell, November 7, 1942; all in Selznick Collection, BK 359; and Legal Files 1936–54, BK 1106, Selznick to Alstock, etc., July 7, 1941.

19. Taylor, *Scarlett's Women*, 214.

20. "Loew's Incorporated: Gone with the Wind: Showing Gross Income and Charges from All Countries Which had Income and Charges on August 31, 1944," enclosure in Mills to Bardt, October 20, 1944, Ron Haver Collection, Academy of Motion Picture Arts and Sciences Library (hereafter AMPAS). I thank Barbara Hall of AMPAS for her research assistance. The figure for the UK and Ireland was £1 million: Loews report, "Gone with the Wind (in local currency)," July 5, 1942, BK 359, Selznick Collection.

21. See list of MGM productions by year in John Douglas Eames, *The MGM Story* (New York: Crown Publishers, 1975), 145–64. Movies about the war were often censored in the United States and Europe. The few released before 1941 included *Blockade* (1938), about the Spanish Civil War; *Idiot's Delight* (1939), an antifascist film starring Clark Gable that was cut to please Mussolini; *Confessions of a Nazi Spy* (1940), about an actual trial in New York; Chaplin's *The Great Dictator* (1940); *Pastor Hall* (1940), about a pacifist former U-boat captain who opposed the Nazis; and *Foreign Correspondent*, whose original treatment of Spanish fascists and German Jews was cut. See Clayton R. Koppes and Gregory D. Black, *Hollywood Goes to War* (New York: Free Press, 1987), 1–47.

22. Golden, *Review of Foreign Film Markets*, 337–49 and charts after 378. Some theaters in Beirut, Cairo, and Alexandria cultivated a wartime clientele of Allied soldiers, but Egypt's overall moviegoing rate remained inflated after their departure. No theaters were listed in Libya, Saudi Arabia, or other Gulf countries; Transjordan had just one theater. Lebanon was counted within Syria.

23. Survey of movie listings in Beirut and Cairo papers, and Robert Vitalis, "American Ambassador in Technicolor and Cinemascope: Hollywood and Revolution on the Nile," in *Mass Mediations: New Approaches to Popular Culture in the Middle East and Beyond*, ed. Walter Armbrust (Berkeley: University of California Press, 2000), 280–82.

24. "MGM Builds Cinema in Cairo," *Al-Ahram*, June 26, 1939, 14; Midhat Mahfouz, "Les salles de projection dans l'industrie cinématographique," in *Egypte: 100 ans de cinéma*, ed. Magda Wassef (Paris: Institut du Monde Arabe, 1995), 126.

25. Marie-Claude Bénard, "Palaces et ciné-jardins: Les cinémas au Caire, hier et aujourd'hui," *Monde Arabe: Maghreb-Machrek*, no. 1 (1994): 105.

26. Cairo Consulate General Records, box 35, file 850.31, "American Interests—Cairo Consulate," April 10, 1941, RG 84; Beirut 1940-44, box 5802, James T. Scott, "Motion Pictures," March 9, 1943, 4, RG 59; both at the National Archives and Records Administration (NARA).

27. Jean Lugol, *Egypt and World War II*, trans. A. G. Mitchell (Cairo: Société Orientale de Publicité, 1945), 77, 143.

28. Golden, *Review of Foreign Film Markets*, 333, 342, 345, 348, 360, on Egypt, Iraq, Palestine, Syria/Lebanon, and Morocco, respectively; Vitalis, "American Ambassador in Technicolor," 281.

29. Jacob M. Landau, *Studies in Arab Theater and Cinema* (Philadelphia: University of Pennsylvania Press, 1958), 160. Attendance continued to rise after 1945, to 92 million in 1951, confirming that Egyptians represented the major portion of the movie audience throughout the 1940s.

30. Lugol, *Egypt and World War II*, 265.

31. Scott, "Motion Pictures," RG 59; Samir Khalaf, *The Heart of Beirut: Reclaiming the Bourj* (London: Saqi, 2006), 210-11. The number of cinemas in Lebanon alone rose from 48 to 170 between 1940 and 1960.

32. Robert Vogel to D. Dern, cable, May 16, 1941, BK 1106, Selznick Collection. Robert Vogel was MGM's chief of foreign distribution in New York. The cable was edited for punctuation and length by the author. Other officials named in the cable included Egyptian military and cabinet officials, members of the royal family, the leader of the main opposition (Wafd) party, and a director of Egypt's foremost investment firm, Bank Misr.

33. An MGM employee's son recalled family conversations about the film while growing up in 1950s Cairo: "I remember my mom and dad saying how big an event it was." Telephone interview with Clément Dassa, November 20, 2007; see also Lugol, *Egypt and World War II*, 262-66.

34. I follow film theorists who propose that all audiences are historically constructed and so bound to read films through their particular social context. See Miriam Hansen, *Babel and Babylon: Spectatorship in American Silent Film* (Cambridge: Harvard University Press, 1991); Jackie Stacey, *Star Gazing: Hollywood Cinema and Female Spectatorship* (New York: Routledge, 1994); Judith Mayne, *Cinema and Spectatorship* (New York: Routledge, 1993); and Richard Maltby, "The Americanisation of the World," in *Hollywood Abroad* (London: BFI, 2004), 1-20.

35. *Al-Ahram*, April 29, 1941, 7; and "Latest News on the Film *Gone with the Wind*," *Al-Ahram*, May 1, 1941, 7.

36. *Al-Ahram*, April 29, 1941, 7; May 1, 1941, 7; and May 4, 1941, 2. The ad was repeated May 12 and 14.

37. "Thahaba maʿ al-rih," *Al-Ahram*, May 31, 1941, 3.

38. *Al-Ahram*, May 16, 1941, 3, and May 31, 1941, 3.

39. Robert L. Tignor, *State, Private Enterprise, and Economic Change in Egypt, 1918-1952* (Princeton: Princeton University Press, 1984), 10; Jacques Berque, *Egypt: Imperialism and Revolution*, trans. Jean Stewart (New York: Praeger, 1972), 618-19; and Doreen Warriner, *Land Reform and Development in the Middle East*, 2nd ed. (New York: Oxford University Press, 1962), 24-27.

40. Ami Ayalon, "Journalists and the Press: The Vicissitudes of Licensed Pluralism," in *Egypt from Monarchy to Republic*, ed. Shimon Shamir (Boulder, CO: Westview Press, 1995), 267-71.

41. Ibid., 270.

42. "Thahaba maʿ al-rih," *Al-Mokattam*, April 30, 1941, 5; *Al-Mokattam*, May 6, 1941, 6;

"Rhett Butler," *Al-Mokattam*, May 8, 1942, 5; "Thahaba maʿ al-rih," *Al-Mokattam*, May 27, 1942, 5.

43. Author's survey of *Al-Musawwar* for September–December 1940 and January–May 1941. The exception was a story on Chaplin's *The Great Dictator* in April 1941.

44. "Challenge of Foreign Cinema and the Lack of Shows for Egyptian Films," *Al-Sabah*, February 14, 1941, 40. The article reports that Egyptian movie producers had petitioned the prime minister for taxes to support local production and for a requirement that all cinemas show a minimum of local films. See February 28 and March 4 for articles on a similar theme. The photos stills of *GWTW*, with captions, appeared after the premiere, on May 16, 23, and 30. See also Vitalis, "American Ambassador in Technicolor," 277–78.

45. A copy was also sent to the American consul: Beirut Legation General Records, box 77, 1942, no. 814/840.6/123, Forces Françaises Libres, Bureau Central d'Assistance aux Soldats, to M. le Consul Général des États-Unis, February 3, 1942, RG 84, NARA.

46. *La Syrie et le Proche-Orient*, February 24, 1942, 1.

47. *La Syrie et le Proche-Orient*, February 26, 1942, 2; *Eastern Times* (Beirut), February 24, 1942, 2; *Bayrut*, February 24, 1942, 2.

48. *Eastern Times* (Beirut), February 24, 1942, 2.

49. *La Syrie et le Proche-Orient*, February 24, 1942, 1.

50. *La Syrie et le Proche-Orient*, February 17–18, 1942, 1.

51. *La Syrie et le Proche-Orient*, February 7, 1942, 1; and "A propos d'un Gala," *La Syrie et le Proche-Orient*, February 26, 1942, 2. George Antonius, born of Lebanese parents, had spent most of his life in Egypt and Palestine but settled in Beirut in 1940. He left Lebanon around the time of the premiere and died in Jerusalem a few months later. He had traveled to the United States in 1938 on a lecture tour, after publishing *The Arab Awakening*, so the story about meeting Vivien Leigh may have basis in fact. See Susan Silsby Boyle, *Betrayal of Palestine: The Story of George Antonius* (Boulder, CO: Westview Press, 2001).

52. Author's survey of *Bayrut* and *An-Nahar* for the period mentioned.

53. "First Official Party for the film *Gone with the Wind*," *Bayrut*, February 24, 1942, 2.

54. Dubbing in Arabic was costly and rare before 1945; movie ads of 1941–42 would therefore have alerted readers if *GWTW* were shown in Arabic.

55. Golden, *Review of Foreign Film Markets*, 333–49; Muhammad Soueid, *Ya Fu'adi: Sirah sinima'ihab ʿan salat Bayrut al-rahilah* (Beirut: Dar al-Nahar, 1996), 59–65; Vitalis, "American Ambassador in Technicolor," 280–81; Bénard, "Palaces et ciné-jardins," 100–103. As Golden, Vitalis, and my own survey of movie listings in newspapers suggest, popular theaters in Arab neighborhoods played the few Egyptian movies available repeatedly, as well as American "B" action pictures.

56. As Samir Khalaf remarked, "Unlike in other cities in the Levant, cinemas were not socially and politically contested forms of entertainment." Khalaf, *Heart of Beirut*, 215–16.

57. "Nahwa al-Nur," in *Majmuat risa'il al-Imam al-Shahid Hasan al-Banna* (Beirut: Dar al-Andalus, 1965), 195.

58. Survey of weekly film listings in *Eastern Times*, October 7, 1941, to May 4, 1942. Weekly runs were the norm at Beirut's other five cinemas, except for two-week runs of four Egyptian films at the Empire. *GWTW* played two weeks in Aleppo and Damascus, which was also unusual.

59. The Egyptian film *Intisar al-Shabab* (Victory of youth) had just set a record of eight weeks in March–April 1941.

60. "*Gone with the Wind* (in local currency)," table dated July 5, 1942, BK 359, Selznick Collection. *GWTW* earned 26,611 Egyptian pounds (£E) in Syria, Egypt, and Palestine to July 1942. MGM's previous top earners were *Marie Antoinette* (£E18,500) and *The Devil's Brother* (£E15,000). See MGM foreign distribution ledgers for 1933 to 1945, boxes 1:1–5, Cinematic Arts Library, University of Southern California.

61. "Loew's Incorporated: *Gone with the Wind*: Showing Gross Income and Charges from All Countries, 1944," total gross income, August 1943–July 1944, AMPAS.

62. Stacey, *Star Gazing*, 80–125; Taylor, *Scarlett's Women*, 91–108.

63. Cairo General Records 1941, box 60, file 711, "Bombing of Alexandria," January 1–September 9, 1941, RG 84, NARA; Lugol, *Egypt and World War II*, 110.

64. "Theater, Cinema, and the War," *Al-Sabah*, March 21, 1941, 19.

65. "Charlie Chaplin's *Dictator*: All the World's Movie Fans Laugh," *Al-Ahram*, April 10, 1941, 7; also "*The Dictator*: The Glory of Twentieth-Century," *Al-Musawwar*, no. 860 (April 1941): 15.

66. "Maʿ al-rih" [With the wind], *Bayrut*, February 21, 1942, 2. The proposed title, in Arabic, was *Hafna min turab*.

67. David O. Selznick, *Memo from David O. Selznick*, ed. Rudy Behlmer (New York: Viking, 1972), 212–13, quoting an unsent memo to Kay Brown, September 20, 1939. See also Thomas H. Pauly, "*Gone with the Wind* and *The Grapes of Wrath* as Hollywood Histories of the Depression," in Harwell, "*Gone with the Wind*" as Book and Film, 223–27.

68. Collet, *Collet des Tcherkesses*, 128–33; the discussion of Collet and her memoir throughout the rest of the chapter reference these pages. Collet's husband was Catroux's primary ally within the Vichy regime and was appointed delegate of Damascus for the Free French.

69. Collet, *Collet des Tcherkesses*, 130–31. Collet does not give the date of the show: it was either Friday, March 27, or Friday, April 3, 1942. The film was likely shown in English with French subtitles. Collet was British, and her English text was translated into French for publication; I have translated the French back into English. The original soliloquy in the movie is slightly different: "As God is my witness. As God is my witness, they're not going to lick me. I'm going to live through this and when it's all over, I'll never be hungry again. No, nor any of my folk. If I have to lie, steal, cheat or kill. As God is my witness, I'll never be hungry again."

70. The term *safar barlik* refers literally to the Ottomans' military craft. Lebanese expand the meaning of the term to include the suffering and hunger caused by wartime requisitions.

71. Elizabeth Thompson, *Colonial Citizens: Republican Rights, Paternal Privilege, and Gender in French Syria and Lebanon* (New York: Columbia University Press, 2000), 19–27, 231–37.

72. Edward D. C. Campbell, "*Gone with the Wind*: The Old South as National Epic," in Harwell, "*Gone with the Wind*" as Book and Film, 134.

73. Pauly, "*Gone with the Wind* and *The Grapes of Wrath*," 218–28, 223, 226.

74. Brian Larkin has studied the displacement of taboo topics in Nigeria, where sexual norms are debated in response to Indian movies; see Larkin, "Theaters of the Profane."

75. Thomson, *Showman*, 319, 398.

76. Ruth Frances Woodsmall, *Moslem Women Enter a New World* (New York: Round Table Press, 1936), 82–83; Edwin Terry Prothro and Lutfy Najib Diab, *Changing Family Patterns in the Arab East* (Beirut: American University of Beirut Press, 1974), tables 6.15, 6.16.

77. Hassan Abu Ghunaymah, *Sirat al-naqid al-sinima'i: Ayyam sabah, 1952–1965* (Cinema Club of Jordan, 1994). This memoir by a Syrian film critic describes women's matinees in terms remarkably similar to Collet's.

78. Thompson, *Colonial Citizens*, 197–210.

79. Fatima Mernissi, *Dreams of Trespass* (New York: Addison-Wesley, 1994), 105.

80. These figures are my count of Egyptian movies listed and summarized in Mahmud Qasim, *Dalil al-aflam fi al-qarn al-ʿishrin fi Misr was al-ʿalam al-ʿarabi* (Cairo: Madbuli, 2002), 28–58. Analysis of the prevalence of women's movies is developed in my forthcoming book, *Cinema and the Politics of Late Colonialism*.

81. Thompson, *Cinema and the Politics of Late Colonialism*.

82. Sayed Said, "Politique et cinéma," 106–7; and Samir Farid, "La censure, mode d'emploi," 198; both in Wassef, *Egypte: 100 ans de cinéma*.

83. *Return of My Heart/Rudda Qalbi* (1957), produced by Assia, directed by Izz al-Din Zul-

ficar. Joel Gordon called the film Egypt's *GWTW* in Gordon, *Revolutionary Melodrama: Popular Film and Civic Identity in Nasser's Egypt* (Chicago: Middle East Documentation Center, 2002), 115–16. I have relied on his plot summary and that of Viola Shafik, *Popular Egyptian Cinema: Gender, Class, and Nation* (New York: American University in Cairo Press, 2007), 266–69.

84. *Whom Do I Love?/Man Ubibb?* (1966), produced by Magda al-Sabbahi, starring Ahmed Mazhar and Ihab Nafei. See Mahmoud Kassem, "Adaptation, egyptianisation et 'remake,'" in Wassef, *Egypte: 100 ans de cinéma*, 242. The film was poorly received, according to Shafik, *Popular Egyptian Cinema*, 190.

85. *Safar Barlik*, produced by Assi and Mansour Rahbani, directed by Henri Barakat, starring Feyrouz and Nasri Shams al-Din; viewed on DVD produced by Prime Pictures, 2004.

86. Memory of Akram Khater, historian at North Carolina State University, who saw *GWTW* at a cinema in the Hamra section of Ras Beirut. His mother took him with her as a male "escort," when he was about seven years old. He recalls much Kleenex thrown on the floor during the show, and much shouting too: "My mother screamed at Rhett for being a jerk." Personal communication, January 11, 2004, and October 20, 2009.

87. Response to the depiction of slavery and race relations in *GWTW* is treated in a forthcoming article and in my forthcoming book, *Cinema and the Politics of Late Colonialism*.

88. My ideas about the film were shaped by a draft of David Lawrence Livingston's dissertation, "Sect and Cinema in Lebanon," for Columbia University, and through discussion with him in September 2007.

SEVEN

Chronotopes of a Dystopic Nation

Cultures of Dependency and Border Crossings in Late Porfirian Mexico

Claudio Lomnitz

In this chapter I examine the early formation of the culture of dependent nationalism, a form of historical consciousness that fosters a pragmatic and immoral realism (often with a gesture of melancholic remorse) and justifies private benefits gained from the regretful present with a language of evolutionary transition. I conceive of dependency as a specific condition that emerged in Latin America when the national economies of those countries were reoriented to the United States and the United States became the guardian of their national credit, a process that began to take shape in the 1870s but that only became a palpable reality by the late 1890s. I explore the culture of dependency by way of its "chronotopes," that is, through the ways in which the nation was figured in space and time. Specifically, I describe two competing figures that emerged in this period. One of these took shape in a new field of international relations, whereas the other was a product of emerging grassroots transnational organization. I argue that these two competing spatiotemporal frameworks (or chronotopes) are a defining characteristic of dependency as a form of historical consciousness.

CHRONOTOPES AND INDEPENDENCE

The concept of the chronotope was first formulated by Mikhail Bakhtin to refer to the spatiotemporal matrices that are the base condition of all narratives and linguistic acts.[1] These spatiotemporal matrices are key elements of ideology, and in them a single image can stand iconically for a set of posited connections between time and place. Movement in space can be figured as movement in time, and vice versa, which is why a chronotope is conceived as a matrix.

Major political transformations involve changes in orientation. They require changing the situation, and the horizon of expectations, of collective actors. For this reason, political change is either guided by or leads to the invention of new chronotopes. So, for instance, conservative leaders of Spanish American independence movements, such as Agustín Iturbide of Mexico, used the image of a tree, or of a family, to represent the connection between Spain and New Spain and to justify independence: New Spain was a branch of the Spanish tree, but it had grown so robust that it sprouted its own trunk, and a new tree took form naturally in its own soil. The Mexican nation was thus an offshoot of the Spanish nation, and its independence was the natural development of the growth cycle. Just as children become independent of their parents, so must Mexico be independent of Spain.

The implication of this chronotope, captured in the spatiotemporal development of life forms such as trees or families, was both revolutionary and conservative, since it justified national independence while framing it as a natural reassertion of the parental model. Mexico may therefore aspire to its own imperium, and its regions, its peoples, its sacred sites and city squares might each be used as a metonymic sign of the new Mexican Empire.

This conservative chronotope was not the only available orientation for the Spanish American republics on the world stage. A second formulation rejected the idea that the republics were like the grown children of loving parents, or the proud offshoots of a grand old oak. Spain was no loving parent: American lands and peoples had been pillaged by ruthless conquistadors, kept willfully in abject ignorance by a scheming and retrograde clergy, and then mercilessly exploited by penny-pinching "foreign" (Spanish) merchants who wanted nothing better than to keep the American people in their degraded state. In this formulation, the American peoples existed as nations before Spain's despoliation. Independence was a rejection of colonial exspoliation, by a people who had found hope in the new age of reason. Rather than standing before Spain as a youth stands before his parents, the people were simultaneously proof of the enlightened potential of the new republics as well as degraded, deformed, and despoiled victims of Spanish usurpation. This second chronotope of national liberation, which eventually found its symbols in pyramids and virginal landscapes, framed independence as the grand beginning of a process of emancipation that would last until the final vestige of the colonial presence had been extirpated.

WHY DEPENDENCY?

"Dependency" is a concept first put forward by Latin American sociologists Fernando Henrique Cardoso and Enzo Faletto as a new theory of imperialism that underscored a long history of unequal exchanges between manufacturing centers and the extractive economies that they imposed on their colonies. Dependency theory's key idea was that underdevelopment, rather than lack of development, was a special kind of capitalist development.[2] As economic theory, "dependency" was disproved in several key aspects.

I do not intend to revive dependency theory as such but rather invoke "dependency" because the term usefully names a historical era within the broad arc of postcolonial history. The term "postcolonial" is too broad for an analysis of Latin America's almost two-hundred-year history of independent existence. Dependency, in my usage here, refers to an era in postcolonial history that can be dated roughly from the 1890s to the recent disarticulation of the Washington Consensus, when independent nations were reoriented to a new (noncolonial) imperial power whose capital generated rapid intensive development and new modalities of "underdevelopment." Mexico was perhaps the first nation to undergo this transition.

NEW CHRONOTOPES OF DEPENDENCY

Seen from a broad historical lens, Mexico's modes of narrating the nation into historical time during the early postcolonial period can be described as an arc that moved from a horizon of utopian expectation during the early days of the nationalist movement, to a feeling of despair around civil strife and the various "sins of the nation," a sentiment that reached its nadir in the years immediately following the war with the United States (1848), to a sentiment of tentative new national aspirations after the triumph over the French in 1867, and finally to a formula of development that involved a progressive, and often self-serving, "realism" that formulated the present as a perpetual state of becoming, as a kind of prelude to true national history, to true national sovereignty.

The latter of these transitions, from the sense of possibility that followed the French Intervention (1867) to the legitimation of a progressive dictatorship under Porfirio Díaz (ca. 1888), can be summarized in the guiding chronotopes of presidents Sebastián Lerdo de Tejada and Porfirio Díaz, respectively. Lerdo, who was ousted in a coup by Díaz in 1876, opposed a rail linkup with the United States, coining his famous motto *Entre la debilidad y la fuerza, el desierto*—"Between weakness and strength, the desert." The utopia of national sovereignty and self-determination that had been reopened with the triumph over the French was understood by Lerdo to be quite fragile. Mexico was too weak to withstand a rush of U.S. investors, colonists, fortune hunters, speculators, and dollars. Yankee involvement should be kept to a minimum, and direct lines of mass transport should not be built.

Díaz's famous counterformulation was "Poor Mexico, so far from God and so close to the United States." At the time, this chronotope had a different nuance than it does today. The reference to Mexico's "distance from God" neatly synthesized a critique of earlier liberal utopianism: Mexico was far from God because Mexicans were far from being virtuous citizens. By 1876, this was obvious enough, because after the defeat of the French and of the Mexican Conservative Party in 1867, the triumphant liberals had not ceased to fight among themselves. The new consensus was that Mexicans still lacked the qualities necessary to attain the high ideals of liberal democracy. For this reason, Díaz contended, the United States' power was the unsavory reality that Mexico had to wrestle with. Rather than insist on an unattainable republican utopia whose only guarantor was the Mexican desert, true patriotism called for a pragmatic manipulation of international relations: opening up Mexico to U.S. capital investment but using peace and progress to transform the citizenry; and balancing concessions to the United States with concessions to European powers in order to avoid the nation's subsumption into a new colonial relationship. That is the logic of dependency; and indeed the Porfiriato was the time when the chronotopia of dependency came into being.[3]

The Díaz dictatorship marked a sea change in the relationship between Mexico and the United States. U.S. investments in mining, railroads, and agriculture skyrocketed.[4] Alongside these investments came broad publicity campaigns for Mexico in the United States. These campaigns usually involved recasting the history of Mexico, and of its relationship with the United States. On the U.S. side, they were orchestrated in the early days by Mexican diplomat Matías Romero, who, together with major investors in New York, Philadelphia, and elsewhere, offered countless banquets that served as useful occasions for publicizing Mexico's new image, and for doing business.

On these occasions, Romero and the great investors of the period worked together to cast the history of Mexico in a new light. So, for instance, at an 1891 investors' banquet in New York City titled "A Mexican Night," Walter Logan gave a long speech in which he praised both Díaz and Mexico: "Will [Díaz] in fact be like our Washington, immensely great in wartime, but even greater in peace? Will he, like Washington, be as apt for building as he was for destroying? The destiny of Mexico hangs on the solution to this question. . . . More than any living being, it can be said of this man that he is the Creator of a Nation."[5]

Why was Díaz, a man who first took office fully fifty-five years after independence and nine years after the defeat of the French, being called the father of the nation? By 1891, the Díaz government had laid conditions for a deep reorientation of the Mexican economy and society. Under Díaz the nation moved from being a highly unstable, economically stagnant, and internationally isolated democracy, to a country at peace, the recipient of international credit, and the beneficiary of economic growth under a progressive dictatorship.

Matías Romero wrote up, circulated, and refined the new versions of national history in which he defended Mexico against its detractors and provided statistical, historic, economic, legal, and political information on Mexico for the American public. For example, he helped explain how Mexico's low wages were offset by low productivity and high transportation costs, so they did not represent a threat to U.S. labor, or why peonage in southern Mexico was not the same as slavery.[6]

Mexico itself became an arena of display for American capitalists, diplomats, intellectuals, and journalists, with choreographed demonstrations of public order, hospitality, financial potential, and human enjoyment. In addition, Mexico invested in its international image through participation in world's fairs, international scientific congresses, and publications. In sum, an elaborate system of communication with and through the U.S. public, and its economic counterpart, Wall Street, was well established by the time of the late Porfiriato.[7]

THE TALES OF FOUR BORDER CROSSINGS

Despite all of this burnishing, Mexico's carefully managed international image faced a tenacious, although at first seemingly inoffensive, challenge from its border with the United States, a space of intensifying and often unsettling traffic. Beginning in the late 1880s, and prompted by the end of the Apache Wars and by the construction of the rail line linking Mexico to the United States at El Paso/Ciudad Juárez, a much wilder and less easily managed set of representations flourished. These were the early years of intensified immigration by laborers to the United States.[8] In the fields of Texas and the mines of Arizona, Mexicans became "a race" rather than a nationality. In the New Mexico territory, where the Mexican population had been largest at the time of the U.S.-Mexican War (1848), Mexicans were racialized in order to guarantee their political disenfranchisement and retard the transformation of the territory into a state.[9] The racialization of Mexicans in the United States was itself a disturbing development for the Mexican national image, even if it touched only a minority of Mexicans directly. Moreover, border cities became relevant cultural sites for Mexico: Díaz's political opponents could publish their views there, while maintaining political connections on both sides of the border.[10] By the 1890s there was a thriving newspaper business in both Spanish and English on the border, and a dynamic political scene, as people moved between Mexico and the United States, and utilized the conditions in one country to intervene in the other.

This new modality of transnationalism had productive, but also destabilizing, effects. Each nation had its own "regimes of value"—instantiated not only by different currencies (backed by gold and silver standards), but also by the contrasting relative value of such things as labor, consumer items, and mechanical tools. As a result of these differences, traffic across the border could have almost magical effects: common American folk, for instance, were turned into members of a quasi-aristocratic caste, attended by servants, and received by the local elite.

Border movement also had the effect of turning Mexican immigrants into members of a segregated and discriminated "race," and as such they could become true champions of their nationality. So, for instance, Catarino Garza, a journalist who had migrated to South Texas in 1877, defended the Mexican race against slander in the Texan press in the following terms: "We Mexicans consider ourselves to have purer blood than the Americans, given that in our country there is only a mixture of Spanish and Indian, and they [the Americans] are generally descendants of Irish adventurers, Polish beggars, Swiss, Prussians, Russians, and more than anything else filthy Africans." Mexicans, Garza argued, also had nobler traditions and better manners than Americans, yet they were treated as an unthinking mass and used as electoral cannon fodder when, in exchange for alcohol, they were carted across the border to Texas to vote in fraudulent elections. "Mexico is badly judged because of the immigrants to this country," he stated. Garza's self-image as defender of the race was exercised regularly through his journalistic practice, by his challenging of insulting Anglos to duels, and in his alleged gallantry toward American women, who, he claimed, "love for convenience, they are as easy to love, as they are easy to forget and to abandon."[11] For Garza, the growing pressures to "defend the race" only made the temptation to change things back in Mexico greater. Eventually these pressures led Garza to desperate (or megalomaniacal) extremes, such as insulting the honor of Mexican army general Bernardo Reyes and leading a rebellion from South Texas intended to topple President Díaz. It was their movement across the border that emboldened these Mexican immigrants, these *libres fronterizos*; they had demystified the falsely superior Anglos and made themselves into representatives of the manliest qualities of their race.

During the years when Mexico was merely "far from God" and not yet very conscious of being "so close to the United States," the ideal of national unity was a political obsession. Although a few ideologues imagined the possibility of achieving national unity in a racial key (by way of *mestizaje*), this ideal was unattainable, expressed in utopian terms. Racial divisions in Mexico ran too deep and were too combustible for the idea of a "Mexican race" to gain traction. When Mexico began managing its proximity to the United States under Porfirio Díaz, however—when, as Friedrich Katz put it, the frontier became a border—Mexicans became a race in the United States. Thus, the racialization of the Mexican in the United States gave experiential reality to what had been merely an ideal: in the United States, the "Mexican race" became a (grim) reality. Although in Mexico the ideal of national unity had at times been expressed in a racial key or idiom before the racialization of Mexicans in the United States, the experience of racialization in the United States was a key factor in rendering the Mexican race (the *mestizo*) credible as a national idea.

Another example of the cultural dissonance and productive instability produced by the new transnationalism is the case of Teresa Urrea, the so-called Santa de Cabora, a virgin folk-healer turned messianic religious leader, who was raised as an icon of revolt during a set of uprisings in Sonora, among the Mayo and Yaqui, and in Chihuahua, most famously at Tomochic, in 1893. The Santa de Cabora has been compared to other millenarian leaders of Latin America during this period, and especially to Antonio Conselheiro at Canudos, in Brazil's northeast, who was martyred by the Brazilian army. The U.S.-Mexican border situation, however, takes the story of Teresa Urrea in an entirely different direction.

In the face of Santa de Cabora's astounding popularity, and her proximity to the border, the Díaz government decided it was better to exile Teresa than to make a martyr of her. So Teresa went to the American side of Nogales, where she was received by the local business community as "a Mexican Joan of Arc." Contrary to her experience in Mexico, where she had been hunted by the law, Nogales offered Teresa every facility to settle there, knowing there was money to be made from the mobs she attracted and healed. From Nogales, the Santa de Cabora moved to Tucson, Douglas, and eventually to California. From those places, Teresa occasionally directed her attention back to Mexican affairs, decrying Porfirio Díaz's policies against the Yaqui, for example, but her life was completely transformed. In Cabora, Urrea had received pilgrimages of Mayo and Yaqui Indians, and of Mexicans from the outback, and her image had been printed on scapulars and raised on banners in village rebellions. In the United States, however, she had an agent who paid her $10,000 to go on a national tour, during which she exhibited her "miracle cures."[12] Border crossing had transformed a millenarian religious charismatic into a freak show attraction. The case of Teresa Urrea suggests that a racialized identity could be as easily harnessed for exoticized commercial purposes as for nationalist ends.

Both the Garza and Urrea cases are, in different ways, examples of the cultural transformations occurring on the U.S.-Mexico border during the 1890s. While the Mexican government and American business interests worked to stabilize the image of Mexico as a peculiar kind of "sister republic," the new borderlands were generating new social movements and cultural forms.

Mexico had found a new formula for being in the world that was brokered internationally at the highest levels of government, science, and business. Stimulated by massive capital imports and booming export markets for Mexican commodities, the new development strategy also generated a less controlled grassroots version of internationalism, which we have been calling transnationalism, that involved movement of people between the two countries. These two modalities of internationalism—government-brokered international relations and grassroots transnationalism—generated contrasting chronotopes for Mexico.

To understand why these two modalities generated such different chronotopes, it is useful to look to the different kinds of border-crossing experiences that went with these contrasting modalities and then to inspect the sort of knowledge products that emanated from them. I illustrate these contrasting forms by offering two further images of border crossings as ideal-typical (rather than as statistically representative) cases.

In 1891, the Norwegian anthropologist Carl Lumholtz crossed the U.S.-Mexico border near Bisbee, Arizona, on his way to the Sierra Madre as head of a geographical expedition. Before starting off on the expedition, however, Lumholtz went to Washington, D.C., where "the late Mr. James G. Blaine, then Secretary of State, did everything in his power to pave my way in Mexico, even evincing a very strong personal interest in my plans." Armed with the political support of the U.S. secretary of state, and with the financial support of the American Museum of Natural History and some of New York's most prominent captains of finance and of industry—including Andrew Carnegie, Pierpont Morgan, Augustus Schermerhorn, and George Vanderbilt, among others—Lumholtz traveled to Mexico City, where "I was received with the utmost courtesy by the President, General Porfirio Díaz, who gave me an hour's audience at the Palacio Nacional, and also by several members of his cabinet, whose appreciation of the importance and the scientific value of my proposition was truly gratifying."[13]

Figure 7.1. Tarahumara, 1890s. Lumholtz was attracted to the Sierra by reports that cave dwellers similar to the extinct Anasazi of New Mexico still inhabited this remote area of Mexico. Photo by Carl Lumholtz. Courtesy of the American Museum of Natural History Library.

Boosted by letters of introduction from the president, various ministers, and state governors, Lumholtz returned to the States, finished preparing his expedition, and set off, crossing into Mexico at the Arizona-Sonora border.

His aims combined recording the ways of life of a primitive people and opening up a region that had been out of reach of Mexican and U.S. investors as a result of the Apache Wars, which had only concluded a few years before. Thus Lumholtz stated that "primitive people are becoming scarce on the globe. On the American continents there are still some left in their original state. If they are studied before they, too, have lost their individuality or been crushed under the heels of civilization, much light may be thrown not only upon the early people of this country but upon the first chapters of the history of mankind."[14]

Lumholtz was attracted particularly by the Tarahumara because they were reported to be cave dwellers, like the extinct and mysterious Anasazi of New Mexico. Yet Lumholtz's research was designed to be both a monument and an epitaph for these primitive peoples, since the expedition, with its team of scientists—including a botanist, a geologist, and a cartographer—was intended to open up the Sierra Madre for economic exploitation. Thus, "the vast and magnificent virgin forests and the mineral wealth of the mountains will not much longer remain the exclusive property of my dusky friends; but I hope that I shall have rendered them a service by setting them this modest monument, and that civilized man will be the better for knowing of them."[15] Lumholtz's project was a distinctly international production, characteristic of the new conditions of dependency. It rested simultaneously on the interests of New York investors, and U.S. and Mexican authorities. It is true that his "orientalist" sensibilities led to forms of exoticization and unacknowledged appropriation that are generally associated with colonialism. These representations and practices, however, were also embraced by Mexican authorities and by Mexico's educated public. Lumholtz's work is, in other words, a kind of "orientalist" science that is attuned to a postcolonial form of dependency, rather than to colonialism per se.

The Sierra Tarahumara had only recently been opened to Mexican or foreign ventures; it had been a favorite hideout of Apache warriors until their final defeat in the mid-1880s. The fierce traits of the Apache were symbolically appropriated by the Mexican *colonos* who had "pacified" this frontier. "In the colonists' eyes," writes Ana Alonso, "the Apache became the epitome of an untamed masculinity construed as the 'natural' basis of power and authority."[16] Lumholtz, however, partook of this appropriation of the extinguished Apache in his own, and very different, way.

When he first set out on his expedition, Lumholtz had thirty men with him, including rowdy and racist Americans, Mexicans, and Indians. After some months, he decided to shed the entourage and keep only his dog, Apache, to whom he later dedicated some touching lines: "Apache hailed from San Francisco. He was presented to me by a young friend, and while yet in his infancy had ventured out alone, in an express box, to join my expedition at Bisbee, six summers ago. On his mother's side he came from one of the best canine families in the United States, and throughout my travels in Mexico had been my constant and efficient aide-de-camp. . . . We buried him, like an Indian brave, with his belongings, his collar and chain, his trays and bedding."[17] Rather than employing the Apache people as representative of his own masculinity, Lumholtz harnessed them, the very people who had kept travelers like him out of the Sierra Madre until 1890, into the spirit of the thoroughbred canine that was Lumholtz's most loyal companion and servant. The Apache and the Tarahumara both represented the past in the present—the first as indomitable spirit, the second as the living confirmation of the truth of a past that was taking shape in museum and textbook, thanks to the efforts of those like Lumholtz and his faithful dog Apache.

A different border crossing occurred at the end of the period we are examining, in 1914, on the Texas-Chihuahua border. Greenwich Village bohemian, journalist, Harvard graduate, and socialist John Reed arrived at the dusty town of Presidio, Texas, to cross into Ojinaga and cover the revolution in the south. His socialist newspaper afforded him no letter of introduction to President Huerta, who in any case was being ousted from power at that very moment. Nor did his trip involve long conversations with New York investors or with the State Department. Instead, Reed made his contacts in a bar in Presidio, Texas, in a scene he ably recounted in a memorable thumbnail sketch: "At all times of the day and night, throngs of unarmed [Mexican] Federal soldiers from across the river swarmed in the store and the pool hall. Among them circulated dark, ominous persons with an important air, secret agents of the Rebels and the Federals. Around in the brush camped hundreds of destitute refugees, and you could not walk around a corner at night without stumbling over a plot or a counterplot. There were Texas rangers, and United States troopers, and agents of American corporations trying to get secret instructions to their employees in the interior." Reed sought to get to General Salvador Mercado, who was being routed by Pancho Villa's forces. "I wanted to interview General Mercado; but one of the newspapers had printed something displeasing to General Salazar, and he had forbidden the reporters in the town. I sent a polite request to General Mercado. The note was intercepted by General Orozco, who sent back the following reply: Esteemed and honored sir: if you set foot inside of Ojinaga, I will stand you sideways against a wall, and with my own hand take great pleasure in shooting furrows on your back."[18]

This reply did not exactly promise the sort of red-carpet treatment Lumholtz had received from the Mexican authorities. Nevertheless, Reed waded across the Rio Grande, interviewed his man, joined up with the rebel army, rode with Pancho Villa, and wrote one of the most compelling portrayals of the revolutionary process. Both Lumholtz and Reed wrote important books, but whereas Lumholtz's work found its way into Spanish immediately and made a deep mark in Mexican ethnology, Reed's went practically unnoticed until the 1960s, despite the fame later garnered by Reed for his coverage of the Russian Revolution. This difference is related to the social factors that made their border crossings so different.

We are now ready for a close inspection of the contrasting chronotopes generated by international and transnational relations. To this end I study two well-known works: the Creelman-Díaz interview (1908) for the new internationalism, and John Kenneth Turner's (1910) *Barbarous Mex-*

ico for the new transnationalism. I have suggested that the border cross-ings brokered by the new international relationship between Mexico and the United States generated representations of the connection between the two countries that were distinct from those that emerged from the new grassroots transnational connections. These representations differed in content, style, and also in the story of their circulation as texts. I now turn to study these differences in detail, with special attention to the problem of coevalness, that is, to the way in which Mexico and the United States were imagined to relate to one another in time and space.

INTERNATIONAL INVESTMENTS IN A CHRONOTOPE OF DEPENDENCY: THE CREELMAN INTERVIEW

In March 1908, *Pearson's Magazine* of New York published a richly illus-trated interview with President Porfirio Díaz. In that interview by James Creelman, the aging dictator announced that Mexico was finally ready for democracy, that he would welcome and even support the formation of an opposition party, and that he was eager to retire to private life at the end of his term. Although during earlier preelectoral periods Díaz had made a practice of denying an interest in prolonging his presidency, he had never before supported the formation of an opposition party, nor cast his presidency so clearly as an already finished bridge to democratic life. An abridged version of the interview was immediately translated into Span-ish and reproduced throughout the country. Afterward, Mexican politics opened up to fierce electoral competition, and Díaz's firm hold on national politics was over. The interview therefore has been referenced by histori-ans as the symbolic conclusion of the dictatorship.

The Creelman interview has generally been studied for its effects on Mexican political life, with special attention to the constant and multiple allusions to the interview as a cover for the new political opposition to Díaz. Beyond analyses of the political effects of Díaz's declaration of tol-erance and support for the opposition, however, the contents of the inter-view have received surprisingly little attention.[19]

What was the implication of giving this key set of pronouncements to an American, rather than to a Mexican, medium? What was the historical and cultural framing device that Creelman used to contextualize Díaz's sensational pronouncements? An analysis of the publication provides in-sight into Mexican public opinion as an internationally shaped artifact. One striking and unexplored feature of the Creelman interview is its dis-crete racism, especially the way in which racism is used to justify the dicta-torship. Creelman opens his piece with a lofty and melancholic image that foreshadows his justification and glorification of Díaz:

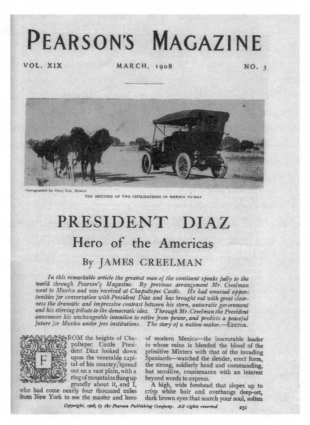

PEARSON'S MAGAZINE

VOL. XIX   MARCH, 1908   NO. 3

Photographed by Percy Cox, Mexico

THE MEETING OF TWO CIVILIZATIONS IN MEXICO TO-DAY

PRESIDENT DIAZ
Hero of the Americas
By JAMES CREELMAN

In this remarkable article the greatest man of the continent speaks fully to the world through Pearson's Magazine. By previous arrangement Mr. Creelman went to Mexico and was received at Chapultepec Castle. He had unusual opportunities for conversation with President Diaz and has brought out with great clearness the dramatic and impressive contrast between his stern, autocratic government and his stirring tribute to the democratic idea. Through Mr. Creelman the President announces his unchangeable intention to retire from power, and predicts a peaceful future for Mexico under free institutions. The story of a nation-maker.—EDITOR.

FROM the heights of Chapultepec Castle President Diaz looked down upon the venerable capital of his country, spread out on a vast plain, with a ring of mountains flung up grandly about it, and I, who had come nearly four thousand miles from New York to see the master and hero of modern Mexico—the inscrutable leader in whose veins is blended the blood of the primitive Mixtecs with that of the invading Spaniards—watched the slender, erect form, the strong, soldierly head and commanding, but sensitive, countenance with an interest beyond words to express.

A high, wide forehead that slopes up to crisp white hair and overhangs deep-set, dark brown eyes that search your soul, soften

 231

Figure 7.2. First page of the Creelman-Díaz interview, "President Díaz, Hero of the Americas." In *Pearson's Magazine* 19, no. 3 (March 1908).

From the heights of Chapultepec Castle President Díaz looked down upon the venerable capital of his country, spread out on a vast plain, with a ring of mountains flung up grandly about it, and I, who had come nearly four thousand miles from New York to see the master and hero of modern Mexico—the inscrutable leader in whose veins is blended the blood of the primitive Mixtecs with that of the invading Spaniards—watched the slender, erect form, the strong, soldierly head and commanding, but sensitive, countenance with an interest beyond words to express.

Creelman turns from this striking chronotope—a new meeting between Mexico and the United States at Chapultepec Castle, a meeting no longer of two nations in war—to do homage to the great leader who singlehandedly delivered his country from the grip of European invaders and from its eternal gravitation toward indolence and revolution. The hero thus demanded a portrait:

A high, wide forehead that slopes up to a crisp white hair and overhangs deep-set, dark brown eyes that search your soul, soften into inexpressible kindli-ness and then dart quick side look—terrible eyes, threatening eyes, loving, confiding, humorous eyes—a straight, powerful, broad and somewhat fleshy nose, whose curved nostrils lift and dilate with every emotion; huge virile jaws that sweep from large, flat, fine ears, set close to the head, to the tremendous, square, fighting chin; a wide, firm mouth shaded by a white mustache; a full, short, muscular neck; wide shoulders, deep chest; a curiously tense and rigid carriage that gives great distinction to a personality suggestive of singular power and dignity—that is Porfirio Díaz in his seventy-eighth year, as I saw him a few weeks ago.[20]

This detailed description is written in the ciphered idiom of physiognomy, a pseudoscience that was popular in France, Germany, England, and the United States, and indeed in Latin America, and widely used by writers and journalists to key readers into the racial characteristics and prepon-derant qualities of a personality. I showed Creelman's description to a historian of physiognomy, Sharrona Pearl, who did not hesitate to offer her interpretation: blood mixing is the key dimension of the description, and it is cast principally as positive. Most of the features that are taken by Creelman as marking power and strength would also be read by his audience as primitive—as both a positive improvement on degenerating Spaniards and potentially a mark of intellectual limitations. The forehead marks intelligence, as do Díaz's eyes; the fact that they are deep set could be a sign of lack of rigidity and perhaps some irresponsibility, as well as some limitations in his ability to read. The nose is a "Greek nose," which is excellent, but it also has features of the "snub nose," which mitigates Díaz's heroic virtue somewhat, as do the shiftiness of the eyes and the flar-ing nostrils that emerge in other sections of the interview. In short, Díaz is brave, refined, rash, intelligent, but somewhat brutal.[21]

All of these qualities, which led Creelman into veritable hero-worship, also mark Díaz as a leader of his people, that is, as the natural leader of an inferior people, a concept developed in American physiognomy during the mid-nineteenth century and not infrequently used by pulp journalists like Creelman, and indeed by novelists of the period on both sides of the bor-der. The deployment of physiognomy by international correspondents of the yellow press deserves some attention, because it provides a clue to the way in which a kind of "ethics of temporality" was being managed and de-veloped by the pro-Díaz publicity machine in the United States.

Physiognomy was popularized mainly to help urbanites navigate in-terpersonal relations in the new environment of the nineteenth-century industrial city.[22] It also served to figure and justify race relations more

Figure 7.3. Portrait of Díaz in the Creelman interview: "President Díaz, the creator and hero of modern Mexico, as he was a few weeks ago at the age of seventy-seven years."

broadly. So, for instance, Samuel Wells, an American physician whose handbook of phrenology and physiognomy was still in circulation during Creelman's day, argued that "the special organs in which the Caucasian brain most excels, and which distinguish it from those of less advanced races, are Mirthfulness, Ideality, and Conscientiousness, the organs of these faculties being almost invariably small in savage and barbarous tribes."[23] More specifically, the European colonization of America was in some way a natural outcome of the European brain's greater development of the "selfish group" of propensities. In their turn, slavery, colonial domination, and class exploitation of the black man also found similar support from this popular "science."

Thus Creelman's painstaking descriptions of Díaz's cranial structure and general demeanor—and the interview is littered with them—are a si-

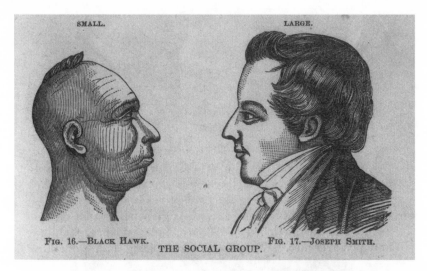

SMALL.   LARGE.

FIG. 16.—BLACK HAWK.   FIG. 17.—JOSEPH SMITH.
                    THE SOCIAL GROUP.

Figure 7.4. Black Hawk versus Joseph Smith. From Samuel Wells, *How to Read Character: A New Illustrated Hand-Book of Phrenology and Physiognomy for Students and Examiners* (1869; reprint, New York: Fowler and Wells, 1894), 31. According to Wells, the organs of the brain are grouped together in regions: the spiritual region, the region of intellect, and the region of propensities. The "propensities" are, in turn, subdivided into two groups, the social group and the selfish group. This figure was to help readers understand why the Native Americans relinquished their property so easily to the acquisitive Britishers.

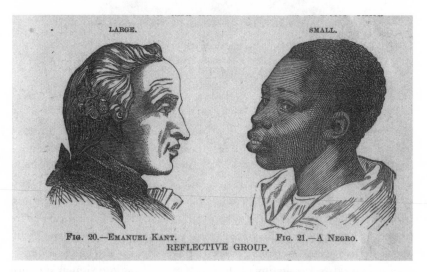

LARGE.   SMALL.

FIG. 20.—EMANUEL KANT.   FIG. 21.—A NEGRO.
                    REFLECTIVE GROUP.

Figure 7.5. Emanuel Kant versus "A Negro." From Samuel Wells, *How to Read Character*, 33. Here Emanuel Kant—apparently in some way a typical specimen of the Caucasian race—is shown to have a cranial structure that fosters much more analytical prowess, inventiveness, and originality than an equally famous representative of another race, "a Negro."

multaneous portrait of the hero and of his race. An uncanny example of
how this approach works can be found in another popular American physiognomy manual. James Redfield's 1852 *Comparative Physiognomy*, which
was still relevant for popular writing, says that the highest kind of leaders
resemble lions—Redfield cites John Jacob Astor and New York governor
and Erie Canal builder DeWitt Clinton as examples. As a people, Germans
are like lions.

Other kinds of leaders, however, are more like cats. Interestingly,
Spanish conqueror Hernán Cortés is among them: "On the following page
is a portrait of Cortez, and it is seen to resemble a puma. A formidable
cat is to pounce down upon the mice whose portraits are sculptured on
the monuments of Central America, and is represented in the 'Aztec children!'"[24] Indeed, in this book, and on the force of numerous international
exhibitions of two malformed children—Máximo and Bartola, who were
alleged to be pure descendants of the Aztecs—Redfield identifies Aztec
physiognomy with that of mice.[25] Moreover, Redfield claimed that there
existed a natural affinity between victims and executioners. Thus, "people
who resemble owls are attracted to the Aztecs, and find in them a gratification of their tastes and an ample field for the exercise of affection and
fondness. The same is true of those who resemble cats. In the cat the qualities of the mouse are assimilated, and she can but love that which gratifies
her, and which corresponds to the playfulness, the refinement, the cunning and so many other things, in her nature."[26]

If we transpose this racial logic forward to Creelman, we discover a
double movement in Creelman's psychophantic portrayal of Díaz. On the
one hand, according to Creelman, Díaz was "the foremost figure of the
American continent," "an astonishing man," and "there is not a more romantic or heroic figure in the world." On the other hand, Creelman suggests that Díaz's grandeur was conjunctural, a fleeting historical artifact,
rather than a harbinger of, say, a new dominant race. Díaz's grandeur was
the product of the meeting of a willful leader and a degraded people. The
successful elevation of that degraded people was a fitting tribute to Díaz
in his twilight years.

This reading is easily extracted from the Creelman interview, but it is
more bluntly laid out in Creelman's biography of Díaz, written two years
later, in 1910, in a much more defensive spirit, in the face of the harsh
criticism that the Díaz government now faced, both in Mexico and the
United States. There Creelman is more forthright about Mexico's racial
problem, and about Díaz's role in it. The country that Díaz inherited had
a serious birth defect: "In the raw attempt to apply the perfected institutions of Anglo-Saxon civilization to the descendants of the dusky races

66   COMPARATIVE PHYSIOGNOMY.

set, has but one pair of cutting-teeth in each jaw. To the exercise of gnawing we should imagine that nothing could be better suited than the cracker which constitutes their principal food. They are wonderfully mischievous but not

wilfully or maliciously so. The boy is fond of teasing his sister, of intermeddling, of having "a finger in the pie," but it is all for the sake of fun and frolic, the gratification of curiosity, the largest liberty, and the indulgence of the senses.

You must not look in their countenances for the expression of delight so much as in their feet: their nether extremities are curiosities equal to those of the mouse, and the appearance and feeling of their hands confirm the resemblance. There is no warmth in them — they are like dead things; and though there is a certain glow in the countenance of the girl, it is too literally ruby to answer the expectation arising from the association of "ruby lips." If you would understand the strange sensation that is produced by contact, you can experience it by kissing the lips of a marble statue. Of this we are assured on good authority, for it is no unusual thing for matronly ladies to manifest the common fondness for children toward the girl Bartola. But the countenance of Maximo is absolutely dead, except a faint attempt at roguishness which may be occasionally discovered in the corners of his mouth. The greater amount of love which falls naturally to the female, gives a lifelike appearance

Figure 7.6. "The Aztec Children are like mice." From James Redfield, *Comparative Physiognomy or Resemblances between Men and Animals* (New York: Redfield, Clinton Hall, 1852), 66. The picture of Máximo (*left*) is a faithful reproduction of the drawing included of him in the *American Journal of Medical Sciences* 20 (1851): 290. Reproduced in Juan Comas, *Dos microcéfalos "aztecas": Leyenda, historia y antropología* (Mexico City: UNAM, 1968), unnumbered appendix.

which inhabited Mexico before the discovery of America by Columbus, the Mexican statesmen of 1824 put the principles of democratic government to a terrible ordeal." Díaz, in this context, "was summoned to power from a youth of poverty and obscurity by the necessities of his divided and demoralized country; and he is as truly a creation of the weakness of his people as the peaceful and progressive Mexico of today is largely the product of his strength and common sense."[27]

Creelman's interview with Díaz, contrary to his later biography of the man, was written at a moment of relative optimism with regard to Mexico, and because it was meant to be translated and published in Spanish, this historical frame was developed more subtly, favoring a melancholic eulogizing over direct criticisms of the Mexican race. Díaz's grandeur, and the

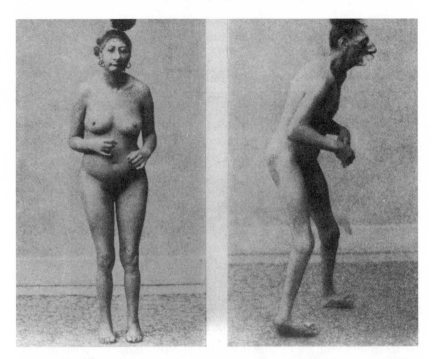

Figure 7.7. Bartola and Máximo, the so-called Aztec Children who allegedly were captured from an untouched Aztec city called "Izamal." This fraudulent story was created from a report by the American traveler John L. Stephens, whose travels in Yucatan were described in a raging best seller. Bartola and Máximo were actually bought and taken from their parents in their native Costa Rica, and toured the United States and Europe from 1851 until their deaths. This 1901 photo is from their inspection by German anthropologist Rudolf Virchow. From *Zeitschrift für Ethnologie* 33 (1901):349–50.

grandeur of the Mexico that he represented had peaked, and the general was now willingly relinquishing power and giving way instead to the new American era: "It is something to come from the money-mad gambling congeries of Wall Street and in the same week to stand on the rock of Chapultepec, in surroundings of almost unreal grandeur and loveliness, beside one who is said to have transformed a republic into an autocracy by the absolute compulsion of courage and character, and to hear him speak of democracy as the hope of mankind."[28] In its melancholic strain, Creelman's portrayal of Díaz is not unlike his earlier published account of an interview he conducted with the great Sioux chief Sitting Bull: "There he stood—the mightiest personality of a dying people whose camp fires were burning in America before Solomon built the temple in Jerusalem—native America incarnate, with knife and tomahawk and pipe, facing a stripling writer from a New York newspaper and telling the simple story of his retreating race."[29] Indeed, as one reads Creelman's interview of Díaz in a racial key, the question of why Díaz chose to give that journalist such an important interview becomes increasingly puzzling, and also quite revealing.

Let me say outright that we are not entirely certain why Díaz decided to make his momentous revelations to Creelman, and to *Pearson's Magazine*. At the time of the interview, and for years thereafter, Díaz's motives were very much the subject of speculation. Few members of Díaz's closest circle seem to have been privy to his decision on the matter. The finance minister José Yves Limantour recalled that "the members of the cabinet— myself included—and all of the people who were close to the president, except his private secretary, were unaware of the interview, and we were all equally surprised when we read it in the papers."[30]

Porfirian economist Toribio Ezequiel Obregón suggested that in the aftermath of the 1907 crisis, the Díaz government wished to calm jittery U.S. investors concerning Mexico's long-term stability, so Díaz gave this interview to a foreign journalist and directed it to a foreign audience, badly miscalculating its effects—both internal and external.[31] Limantour's memoirs suggest otherwise, however, since the former finance minister claims to have had no knowledge of the interview. Indeed, Limantour pondered Díaz's motives for giving this interview and concluded that, although it was likely that the translator or Creelman exaggerated Díaz's responses and caused undue harm, the only explanation for the interview itself was Díaz's weakening mental capabilities, brought on by senility.[32]

Basing his conclusions on material from the U.S. State Department archives, which were not open to Díaz's contemporaries, historian William Schell has determined that the Creelman interview was foisted on Díaz by the highest U.S. functionaries: Ambassador David Thompson, Secretary of State Elihu Root—who had made a visit to Mexico City immediately prior to the interview—and President Roosevelt himself, with the intermediation of their candidate for Mexico's presidential succession, Chihuahua governor Enrique Creel. Roosevelt's aim was to extract a statement against reelection from Díaz, as part of their tough negotiation with the dictator on international policy. Roosevelt wanted Mexico to intervene in—and probably to absorb—Central America, in order to stabilize the region and to make it safe for the Panama Canal project. Díaz, however, had systematically resisted intervention. Yet he had to negotiate with Roosevelt because he needed Roosevelt's support to deal with the Magonista agitation on the border. Roosevelt's "plot" failed in that Díaz was reelected despite the Creelman interview, instability in Mexico was not averted, and neither Díaz nor Mexico served as the United States' proxy in Central America.[33]

Still, we do not know Díaz's calculations in the matter. It is clear he did not entirely disapprove of Creelman's work in the interview, since he subsequently authorized the journalist to become his biographer. Indeed, the questions we ask of this event as cultural historians are a little different from those of the political or diplomatic historian: Why did Díaz give a key interview to, and then authorize the writing of a biography by, a newspaperman who had covered every imperial endeavor of the era with consistently chauvinistic racism? True, Creelman was a renowned journalist who had interviewed European monarchs, but his disdain for the tropical races was as apparent as his interest in Great Men. Creelman had been in Cuba, in Haiti, in the Philippines; he had covered the Japanese invasion of Manchuria; he had interviewed Sitting Bull; he had published an impassioned defense of the role of yellow journalism in the Spanish American War, stating approvingly, with reference to Hearst, Pulitzer, and the rest of them, that "the modern editor is seldom contented unless he feels that he is making history as well as writing it."[34] Why prefer this man, who had a substantial published track record, to any of the Mexican journalists available to Díaz? Why, indeed, did Díaz later entrust Creelman especially with the writing of a full-fledged biography and defense?

There are political reasons that help explain Díaz's choice. A more left-leaning U.S. journalist would certainly have been reticent to produce the sort of psychophantic portrayal that Creelman served up. Still, there is more to it than this: by the early 1900s, the Díaz dictatorship had its own dependence on the racist narrative reproduced by Creelman. The degradation of the Mexican nation, and the foreign recognition and admiration of Díaz as a human specimen and of his historical accomplishments, provided Díaz with the framework he needed to float a scenario of managed democratic transition to the public.

The demeaning representations of the Mexican race such as those offered up by Creelman allowed U.S. and Mexican opinion to join in the chorus of praise for the dictator and to assert that the country as a whole still deserved nothing better, while providing a melancholic language of transition as a legitimating device for the capitalist feeding frenzy that the dictatorship promoted. In this context, the subtleties of American racism could be profitably deployed as an internationally intelligible rationale and used to subdue utopian currents in both American and Mexican opinion. Indeed, the chronotope of dependency proposed by Creelman—a backward race that could be brought to the very brink of democratic life by sheer political will—had gained such currency during the Díaz dictatorship that it was common sense even to the opposition.

Luis Cabrera, despite his proclaimed disdain for Creelman, whose handiwork had left Díaz's cry "disfigured by the presumptuous and vulgar literature of yankee journalism," concurred with Creelman's assessment of the connection between the grandeur of Díaz and the inferiority of the Mexican race, if only to extract a very different conclusion: "Feeling weak and tired, the dictator for the first time saw his work with the perspicacity that proximity to death brings, and with the clearness of vision that one has from great altitudes. And he understood that because it was a work that was founded on the weakness of our race by the will of a single man, it was brittle and unsubstantial [*deleznable*]." The difference between Cabrera and Creelman was not in the guiding chronotope, but rather in its political implications, for whereas Creelman went headlong into hero worship, Cabrera imagined a Díaz who found himself before death, terrified of the degraded state in which he was leaving his people. The interview, according to this revealing interpretation, was a cry for help to the Mexican people: "And the dictator felt a pang of terror, as if he'd slipped at the edge of a deep precipice, and let out that cry for help [the Creelman interview], which was nothing but a desperate call for the Mexican people to save his work in ruins, because the people were the only ones who could save it."[35]

On the eve of the Mexican Revolution, Mexican public opinion was already inflected by U.S. opinion in a deep and subtle way, leading political figures tacitly to rely on the racist chauvinism of the American imperialists of the day as a workable chronotope with which to frame the nation's delicate political process. We saw, by way of Catarino Garza, that the construction of "the Mexican race," which had been a nationalist utopia for some around the time of independence, became a credible (although anti-utopian) reality in the United States. American racial constructions of Mexicans also helped justify the hero worship of dictator Porfirio Díaz, and it was used by Mexican ideologues to frame the dictatorship as a transitional institution, a prerequisite to democracy.

JOHN KENNETH TURNER AND THE RISE AND LIMITS OF TRANSNATIONAL TIME

International relations couched either in the language of scientific racism or in the popular idiom of physiognomy justified the Díaz dictatorship and tempered its harsh realities by framing it within a language of becoming. Progress, for a racially inferior country like Mexico, meant acquiring the necessary accoutrements to sit at the table with the civilized progressive nations. It was, in other words, an evolutionary prerequisite to the true progressivism of the civilized world.

While international relations in politics, in the scientific community, and in the press tended to buttress the Mexican state, a new field of transnational relations undermined Mexico's dominant structure, at the very moment in which the dictator sought support from the prestige of American opinion. If border crossings such as those of Lumholtz and Creelman served to qualify the Mexican dystopia—"far from God and close to the United States"—and to justify the regime as a stern but benign solution to it, the consolidation of the U.S.-Mexico border provided conditions for the formation of an alternative historicity for Mexico.

The best example of this process is probably found in the work of John Kenneth Turner. Not coincidentally, Turner framed his reportage—first printed as a set of blockbuster articles on Mexican slavery for the *American Magazine*, and then compiled and expanded into the book *Barbarous Mexico* (1910)—as a response to Creelman's panegyric, and more generally to the way in which the Díaz machine and its U.S. allies mediated the coverage of Mexican affairs in the United States. If Creelman's interview involved a robust web of connections at the top of the United States' and Mexico's political systems, Turner's reporting relied on an equally impressive set of connections between each nation's dissidents.

John Kenneth Turner decided to go to Mexico thanks to his acquaintance with the radical leaders of Mexico's opposition Partido Liberal Mexicano, including Ricardo Flores Magón, all of whom were imprisoned in the Los Angeles County jail at the time. The meeting was not serendipitous. The consolidation of the U.S.-Mexico border meant that major American capitalists—the Guggenheims, the Rockefellers, Otis, Hearst, Stillman—now operated on both sides of the border. It also meant that Mexican laborers, and American welders, merchants, and engineers, were working on both sides of the border. Mexico's dissidents in the United States met with the same kind of harassment faced by the Wobblies and other American anarchists, particularly during the years following the 1901 assassination of President William McKinley by the young anarchist Leon Gzolgosz; it was compounded by the hardened racism against Mexicans that had developed in the Southwest.[36]

Despite these difficulties, the United States remained a crucial point of reunion for Mexico's opposition groups. Indeed it is possible that the leadership of the Partido Liberal Mexicano, which had been founded in 1902, avoided creating an anarchist party even as they became progressively radicalized, and retained their "liberal" credentials instead, not only because of the popular resonance of liberalism in Mexico but also because anarchism was a crime in the United States, and anarchists were explicitly banned from immigration.[37]

According to his account, Turner felt impelled to go to Mexico because of the dissidents' insistence on the continued existence of chattel slavery there. His reportage was both a remarkable performance of the new possibilities brought forth by the new transnationalism and a radical reframing of Mexican national time. It is also a case study of the limited (though not inconsequential) success of disseminating a new border temporality that involved synchronizing Mexican and American time.

Turner's performance was "transnational" in at least three ways: first, the project was forged out of solidarity within an internationalist union movement, which made sense now that Mexican and American miners and rail workers were employed by the same companies, operating on both sides of the border, and now that they faced the antagonism of the same publicity machine in both countries.[38] Indeed, Turner's effort to reveal Mexican conditions was as much a battle against Díaz as it was against American media moguls, politicians, and capitalists. Second, Turner's reporting relied crucially on the guidance of Mexican socialist Lázaro Gutiérrez de Lara, who accompanied Turner throughout his travels. Third, like the Creelman interview, Turner's journalistic feat would have been impossible for a Mexican newspaperman to achieve: Turner only gained access and the confidence of Mexican slave owners and taskmasters because he was able to pass himself off as an American investor.

This double status as a privileged outsider and collaborator of privileged—because oppositional—insiders allowed Turner to defamiliarize the framework within which Mexico was routinely cast to the American public, turning stock images of travel writing into a denunciation of Mexican slavery and peonage that resonated with the United States' recent and current social struggles. Rather than casting Mexicans as being radically Other, or as backward members of a "dusky" race, Turner emphasized similarities between conditions in Mexico and recent conditions in the United States, particularly the existence of slavery, and peonage in contemporary southern states, like Florida.[39] Within Turner's framework, Díaz, rather than elevating the Mexican people, was the lynchpin in a system designed to keep them down.

One of Turner's most subtle—and radical—moves was his use of stock images from travel writing as pieces of evidence that fit seamlessly in a new narrative, thereby exhibiting their earlier distorted nature. For instance, an image of an Indian woman in front of a cactus—there were at the time dozens of picture postcards like it—is labeled "Slave mother and child; also henequen plant," the cactus being here the cash crop around which Yucatecan slavery was built.[40] Similarly, Indian porters carrying wood or baskets—a typical image in the travel literature of the nineteenth century—were now lined up and exhibited as bonded laborers. Rather than portraying the country as some exotic place, Turner painted Mexico as an extreme case of the familiar horrors of tyranny, of the power of trusts and monopolies, of peonage, of harsh anti-union repression, and, especially, of chattel slavery—all key themes in the history of American freedom. So, for instance, in his moving story on the enslavement, deportation, and extermination of the Yaqui Indians, Turner takes a moment to clarify that "like the Mayas of Yucatan, they are Indians and yet they are not Indians. In the United States we would not call them Indians, for they are workers. As far back as their history can be traced they have never been savages. They have been an agricultural people."[41]

As for the qualities and characteristics of the Mexican race more generally, Turner reflects that "the Yaquis are Indians, they are not white, yet when one converses with them in a language mutually understood one is struck with the likenesses of the mental processes of White and Brown. I was early convinced that the Yaqui and I were more alike in mind than in color. I became convinced, too, that the family attachments of the Yaqui mean quite as much to the Yaqui as the family attachments of the American mean to the American."[42] Through an engagement with the forced separation of husbands and wives and of parents and their children, through detailed and thoroughly documented discussions of bodily punishment and of rape, Turner rehearses for Mexico the key themes of American abolitionism, which is why his pieces—and then his book—which sold over a million copies—were likened in content and impact to *Uncle Tom's Cabin*.[43]

James Creelman had spoken of Porfirio Díaz as "the father of the nation," whose personal defects were in any case a reflection of the failures of his people. Turner turned this kind of argument on its head: "The slavery and peonage of Mexico, the poverty and illiteracy, the general prostration of the people, are due, in my humble judgment, to the financial and political organization that at present rules that country—in a word, to what I shall call the 'system' of General Porfirio Díaz."[44] In their selfserving support for the dictatorship, American interests were supporting abroad a system that had been eradicated at home. In collaborating with the Díaz repressive apparatus, "the United States has been turned into a military dictatorship as sinister and irresponsible as that of Díaz himself."[45] Díaz, the coterie of planters and slave owners of the south, the band of *jefes políticos* and corrupt officials, and the American moguls who supported them, were, all of them, a kind of hellish reincarnation of the slave-owning castes of the American South, hellish because they were fiercer: "Over and over again I have compared in my mind the condition of the slaves of Yucatan with what I have read of the slaves of our southern states before the Civil War. And always the result has been in favor of the black man."[46]

In denouncing the "Díaz system," Turner availed himself of the entire

Figure 7.8. "Slave mother and child; also henequen plant." From John Kenneth Turner, *Barbarous Mexico* (1910; reprint, Chicago: Charles H. Kerr, 1914), 20.

Figure 7.9. "Cargadores with baskets, seen everywhere on the Mexican plateau." From Turner, *Barbarous Mexico,* 110.

arsenal of journalistic techniques that had been deployed in the United States, and so his work resonates not only with that of Harriet Beecher Stowe and other abolitionists, but also, and very strongly, with the work of the muckrakers. Turner is the first—and to my knowledge the only—reporter who ever applied the technique that was developed by Jacob Riis in *How the Other Half Lives* (1890), to expose the living conditions in Mexican

Figure 7.10. "Midnight in a Mexico City 'meson,' cheap lodging house of the poor. One pays three centavos for a grass mat and hunts a place to lie down in the enclosure. From a flashlight by the author." This example of Mexican muckraking, as a strategy of social denunciation, was entirely novel in Mexico. It went and continues to go unheeded in Mexican commentary on Turner's work. From Turner, *Barbarous Mexico*, 116.

lodging houses and tenements (*mesones*) by the use of night photos, taken with the aid of a flashlight.[47] The combined effect of abolitionist-inspired reportage and the most powerful documentary techniques of the muckraker, compounded by Turner's collaboration with Mexican liberals—who were represented in his work as patriotic freedom fighters rather than as anarchists—was powerfully understood by the American public.

The same was not necessarily the case with the Mexican public, however. In 1912, after Porfirio Díaz had been ousted, Turner was honored with an interview with President Francisco I. Madero at Chapultepec Castle, the very site where Creelman had interviewed Díaz four years earlier. Madero told Turner that *Barbarous Mexico* had aided his cause greatly, because it allowed the American people to understand that he was in fact fighting for freedom.[48] It did not, however, aid the Mexican people in conducting an open discussion of Mexican slavery and of its social conditions.

Turner's book would not find its way into print in Spanish until 1955, forty-seven years after the initial publication of Turner's articles. That first Mexican edition, Eugenia Meyer reminds us, was prefaced by Daniel Cosío Villegas, the dean of Mexico's modern historians of the time and still the most widely revered historian of the Porfiriato. Cosío Villegas not only dismissed the value of *Barbarous Mexico* as an accurate portrayal of Mexican conditions but went on to doubt the very existence of John Kenneth Turner himself, speculating that the text had probably been penned by an (anonymous) Mexican liberal. He concluded that *Barbarous Mexico* is "worthless as a scientific document" but that it could be profitably read by his contemporaries, instead, as a particularly effective political pamphlet.[49] Turner's "propaganda," however, was apparently not so effective in Mexico itself.

Although Mexicans had their own critique of peonage, and revolutionaries addressed most of the conditions that Turner discussed, they made few attempts to emphasize similarities and synchronicity between Mexico and the United States. Cosío Villegas's frosty reception of Turner is symptomatic of this—particularly his reticence to embrace the fact that *Barbarous Mexico* had been penned by an American. John Reed's book, too, was left languishing without translation into Spanish for fifty years, and when it was published in Spanish in 1954, it went practically unnoticed until the late 1960s. Thus, writer and former Villista Renato Leduc wrote of his surprise when he discovered, browsing a secondhand bookstore, that "Johnny, Juanito, the smiling pug-nosed gringo of Chihuahua, was none other than the famous John Reed, heroic chronicler of the October Revolution."[50]

The slowness to translate and the reticence to embrace, discuss, and circulate these border products, even when they supported the ideas of the Mexican Revolution, are testament to the fact that the tensions between the two chronotopes we have explored remained in place. After the Revolution, national time was framed in ways that still relied more on Creelman's chronotope than on Turner's. National time was framed in ways that still hesitated to embrace Mexico's contemporaneousness with the United States.

Notes

An early version of this chapter was presented at the Davis Seminar in Princeton and later published in the volume *Clio/Anthropos: Exploring the Boundaries between History and Anthropology*, edited by Eric Tagliacozzo and Andrew Wilford (Stanford University Press, 2009), 102–39 (copyright © 2009 by the Board of Trustees of the Leland Stanford Jr. University). Carlos Bravo, Friedrich Katz, Mauricio Tenorio, and Alan Wells pointed me to useful materials. I owe a special debt of gratitude to Sharrona Pearl for her advice on physiognomy. The usual disclaimers apply.

1. Mikhail Bakhtin, "Forms of Time and the Chronotope in the Novel," in *The Dialogic Imagination: Four Essays by M. M. Bakhtin*, trans. Caryl Emerson and Michael Holquist (Austin: University of Texas Press, 1981).

2. Fernando Henrique Cardoso and Enzo Faletto, *Dependency and Development in Latin America*, trans. Marjory Mattingly Urquidi (Berkeley: University of California Press, 1979).

3. The framework promoted a credible, and yet always challenged, language of perpet-

ual transition, which became the object of criticism and elaboration well into the twentieth century. The paradigmatic example is Samuel Ramos, who introduced a kind of Freudianism to Mexican philosophy in his 1930 work on national character in which he argued that Mexicans suffered from a collective inferiority complex. The implication was that this "complex," which found its ideal-typical subject in the urban lower-class *pelado*, was principally a mentality and therefore curable. A therapeutic horizon to cure Mexicans of their "distance from God" had opened up with the Revolutionary state. Samuel Ramos, *Perfil del hombre y la cultura en México* (1931; reprint, Mexico City: P. Robredo, 1938). For a brilliant critique of Mexican theories of eternal becoming, see Roger Bartra, *La jaula de la melancholia* (Mexico City: Grijalbo, 1987).

4. John Mason Hart, *Revolutionary Mexico: The Coming and Process of the Mexican Revolution* (Berkeley: University of California Press, 1987), 129–62; John Mason Hart, *Empire and Revolution: The Americans in Mexico since the Civil War* (Berkeley: University of California Press, 2002); Daniel Nugent, ed., *Rural Revolt in Mexico: U.S. Intervention and the Domain of Subaltern Politics* (Durham, NC: Duke University Press, 1998); William Schell, *Integral Outsiders: The American Colony in Mexico City, 1876–1911* (Wilmington, DE: SR Books, 2001).

5. Matías Romero, *Artículos sobre México publicados en los Estados Unidos de América* (Mexico City: Oficina Impresora de Estampillas, 1892), 168–70.

6. See, for an impressive compilation, Matías Romero, *Mexico and the United States: A Study of the Subjects Affecting Their Political, Commercial, and Social Relations, Made with a View to Their Promotion* (New York: G. P. Putnam's, 1898).

7. See Mauricio Tenorio-Trillo, *Mexico at the World's Fairs: Crafting a Modern Nation* (Berkeley: University of California Press, 1996); Schell, *Integral Outsiders*; Justo Sierra, *Mexico, Its Social Evolution*, 3 vols. (Barcelona: Ballescá, 1900).

8. For an overview, see John Mason Hart. ed., *Border Crossings: Mexican and Mexican-American Workers* (Wilmington, DE: SR Books, 1998).

9. For the racialization of Mexicans in New Mexico, see Laura E. Gómez, *Manifest Destinies: The Making of the Mexican American Race* (New York: NYU Press, 2007); for Arizona/Sonora, see Miguel Tinker-Salas, *In the Shadow of the Eagles: Sonora and the Transformation of the Border during the Porfiriato* (Berkeley: University of California Press, 1997); for Texas, see Neil Foley, *White Scourge: Mexicans, Blacks and Poor Whites in Texas Cotton Culture* (Berkeley: University of California Press, 1997); and Arnoldo de León, *They Called Them Greasers: Anglo Attitudes toward Mexicans in Texas, 1821–1900* (Austin: University of Texas Press, 1983).

10. See, for example, on San Antonio, Daniel Arreola, "The Mexican American Cultural Capital," *Geographical Review* 77(1): 17–34.

11. As quoted in Elliott Young, *Catarino Garza's Revolution on the Texas–Mexico Border* (Durham, NC: Duke University Press, 2004), 50, 31–33, 46.

12. The most recent and thorough study of the rebellion at Tomochic and Teresa Urrea is Paul Vanderwood, *The Power of God against the Guns of Government: Religious Upheaval in Mexico at the Turn of the Nineteenth Century* (Stanford: Stanford University Press, 1998), 304. The classical work on the Canudos rebellion in Brazil is Euclides da Cunha, *Rebellion in the Backlands*, trans. Samuel Putnam (1901; reprint, Chicago: University of Chicago Press, 1944). The bibliography on both Tomochic and Canudos is relatively abundant.

13. Carl Lumholtz, *Unknown Mexico: Explorations in the Sierra Madre and Other Regions, 1890–1898* (1902; reprint, New York: Dover Publications, 1987), I:viii, viii–ix.

14. Ibid., xvi.

15. Ibid., xvi–xvii.

16. Ana Alonso, *Thread of Blood: Colonialism, Revolution, and Gender on Mexico's Northern Frontier* (Tucson: University of Arizona Press, 1997), 71.

17. Lumholz, 78–81.

18. John Reed, *Insurgent Mexico* (1914; reprint, New York: International Publishers, 1969), 32, 29–30.

19. The principal pieces on the interview are Eduardo Blanquel, "Setenta años de la entrevista Díaz-Creelman," *Vuelta* 2, no. 17 (April 1978): 28–33; and Schell, *Integral Outsiders*, chap. 6.

20. James Creelman, "President Díaz, Hero of the Americas," *Pearson's Magazine* 19, no. 3 (March 1908): 231–32.

21. Sharrona Pearl, written communication, February 4, 2007.

22. Richard Gray, *About Face: German Physiognomic Thought from Lavatier to Auschwitz* (Detroit: Wayne State University Press, 2004); Sharrona Pearl, "As Plain as the Nose on Your Face: Physiognomy in Nineteenth-Century England," Ph.D. diss., History of Science, Harvard University, 2005.

23. Samuel R. Wells, *How to Read Character: A New Illustrated Hand-Book of Phrenology and Physiognomy for Students and Examiners* (1869; reprint, New York: Fowler and Wells, 1894), vii.

24. James Redfield, *Comparative Physiognomy or Resemblances between Men and Animals* (New York: Redfield, Clinton Hall), 31–32.

25. For a detailed account of the dismal story of Máximo and Bartola, see Juan Comas, *Dos microcéfalos "aztecas": Leyenda, historia y antropología* (Mexico City: Universidad Nacional Autónoma de México, 1968); and Nigel Rothfels, "Aztecs, Aborigines, and Ape-People: Science and Freaks in Germany, 1850–1900," in *Freakery: Cultural Spectacles of the Extraordinary Body*, ed. Rosemary Thomson (New York: NYU Press, 1996). Bartola and Máximo were first exhibited at the Barnum Circus, and they were toured continuously, mostly in Europe, until at least 1901. Their death dates are unknown. Although their status as "Aztecs" was quickly disputed by some scientists, the fame of the "Aztec children" and their influence on public opinion was deep, widespread, and long lasting. They were viewed and discussed not only by the public but also by the monarchs of Britain and Prussia, and by leading European and American scientists into 1900. The drawing of Máximo in Redfield's *Comparative Physiognomy* is a copy of a drawing that was published in the *American Journal of Medical Sciences* 25 (1851): 290.

26. Redfield, *Comparative Physiognomy*, 67.

27. James Creelman, *Díaz, Master of Mexico* (New York: D. Appleton and Company, 1911), v.

28. Creelman, "President Díaz," 232–34.

29. James Creelman, *The Wanderings and Adventures of a Special Correspondent* (Boston: Lothrop Publishing, 1901), 295.

30. José Yves Limantour, *Apuntes sobre mi vida pública* (1921; reprint, Mexico City: Editorial Porrúa, 1965), 154.

31. Toribio Ezequiel Obregón, "El epílogo de la conferencia Creelman sera la entrevista Díaz-Taft," *El Antirreeleccionista*, September 23, 1909.

32. Limantour, *Apuntes sobre mi vida pública*, 154–56.

33. Schell, *Integral Outsiders*, chap. 6.

34. Creelman, *Wanderings*, 358.

35. Luis Cabrera, "El grito de Chapultepec" (1909), in *Obras completas*, vol. 2 (Mexico City: Ediciones Oasis, 1974), 28.

36. Dirk Raat, *Revoltosos: Mexico's Rebels in the United States, 1903–1920* (College Station: Texas A & M Press, 1981); James Sandos, *Rebellion in the Borderlands: Anarchism and the Plan de San Diego, 1904–1923* (Norman: University of Oklahoma Press, 1992); Foley, *White Scourge*; Léon, *They Called Them Greasers*.

37. Turner describes U.S. authorities' use of immigration law, including the antianarchist clause, as a ploy to collaborate closely and directly with the Díaz repressive machine; John Kenneth Turner, *Barbarous Mexico* (1910; reprint, Chicago: Charles H. Kerr, 1914), 272–79.

38. The strike at the Cananea copper mine (1906) provided the occasion for a rapprochement between the Díaz and Roosevelt governments; Mexico acquiesced to Roosevelt's Central American policies in exchange for U.S. support in policing the *magonistas* in the United States and sharing intelligence on their border activities. Schell, *Integral Outsiders*, chap. 6.

39. The campaign against peonage in the South was still fresh in American public discussion at the time of Turner's writing. See Pete Daniel, *The Shadow of Slavery: Peonage in the South, 1901–1964* (Urbana: University of Illinois Press, 1972).

40. For general histories of Mexican photography, see Olivier Debroise, *Mexican Suite: A History of Photography in Mexico* (Austin: University of Texas Press, 2001); Estela Treviño, *160 años de fotografía en México* (Mexico City: CONACULTA/CENART/Oceano, 2005); and Emma Cecilia García Krinsky, ed., *Imaginarios y fotografía en México: 1839–1970* (Barcelona: Lunweg, 2005).

41. Turner, *Barbarous Mexico*, 38.

42. Ibid., 61.

43. For a discussion, see Eugenia Meyer, *John Kenneth Turner, periodista de México* (Mexico City: Ediciones Era), 13.

44. Turner, *Barbarous Mexico*, 110.

45. Turner, "Preface to the Third Edition" (1914), in *Barbarous Mexico*.

46. As quoted in Turner, *Barbarous Mexico*, 20.

47. Alberto del Castillo Troncoso, "La historia de la fotografía en México," in *Imaginarios y fotografía en México*, ed. Rosa Casanova, Alberto del Castillo, and Rebeca Monroy (Barcelona: Lunwerg, 2005), 71–72.

48. J. K. Turner correspondence, 1912, as cited in Meyer, *John Kenneth Turner*, 55.

49. As cited ibid., 49–50.

50. John Reed, "Preface to the New Edition," in Reed, *Insurgent Mexico*, 17.

EIGHT

Transpacific Complicity and Comparatist Strategy

Failure in Decolonization and the Rise of Japanese Nationalism

Naoki Sakai

For the last two decades, since the burst of the economic bubble in the early 1990s, Japanese mass media have often broadcast statistics indicating alarming trends in Japanese demographics: a rapidly aging population (20.8 percent of the population were sixty-five years of age or older in 2006, compared with 7 percent in 1970); the highest life expectancy in the world (85.52 years among females and 78.56 among males in 2005); a decline in total population (from 128 million in 2005 to 90 million by 2055); and a very low birth rate (with 1.26 children born to a woman during her lifetime in 2006). These figures indicate that Japanese society does not deviate from the projected patterns of a postindustrial society. Interestingly, these same figures are often used to predict how increasingly hard it will be, in a matter of a decade or two, for the Japanese to reproduce the systems of everyday life that help sustain the stability of their family life, work environment, medical welfare, and social services in general. With a shrinking work population, more persons will be dependent on fewer for the national budget; insurance of many sorts—life insurance, property insurance, and so forth—will become too expensive for an average citizen to afford; social welfare—national health insurance, national pensions, nursing homes, and so forth—will be cut back drastically. In short, it seems that fewer and fewer Japanese will be able to take for granted a middle-class family life—a nuclear family with two children, a house in the suburbs, and an annual income of US$70,000 or more—which, only two decades ago, it was believed that the majority of the nation could achieve. Until the 1980s, according to sociologists, approximately 90 percent of the Japanese regarded themselves as belonging to the middle class, but in the last decade or so we have seen the return of old concerns for class differences and new concerns for the loss of hope. I do not think these demographics need necessarily be read as predicting Japan's doomsday, but what is certain is that these figures have reinforced the prevalent perception that the Japanese as a nation have lost hope for their future. Consequently, one of the most popular research areas in the social sciences in Japan today is "the study of hope," and a new field of academic discipline—*kibô-gaku*—has emerged. One is reminded that it was against the backdrop of demographic decline—low birth rates and shrinking populations—that the political climate of fascism was nurtured in many countries in Europe during the interwar period.[1]

It is important to note that Japanese nationalism has gained its peculiar belligerence against the background of the loss of hope. Without doubt the loss of hope reflects many aspects of Japanese society today, two of which are an increasing income disparity and the loss of upward social mobility.

The Liberal Democratic Party, which has been in power for more than a half century, except for a short period in 1993–94, has been unable to elect a prime minister who could remain in the job for more than a year, and during the three years of 2006–8, prime ministers were replaced one after another. Hence Japan saw three prime ministers, Abe Shinzô, Fukuda Yasuo, and Asô Tarô, in rapid succession, and it was increasingly apparent that Japan's ruling party had exhausted its pool of talent. The overwhelming victory of Japan's Democratic Party in the general election of the House of Representatives on August 30, 2009, was no surprise to many voters in Japan.

Since the end of the Asia Pacific war, which prompted the collapse of Japan's colonial empire in 1945, Japanese nationalism has never manifested its jingoistic tendency so unambiguously as it has in the first decade of the new millennium. During Japan's so-called Lost Decade of dismal economic growth, higher unemployment, and retreat of traditional leftist organizations including the Socialist Party and the General Council of Labor Unions of Japan, not only national television networks and national newspapers but also the publishing industry at large seem to have taken a definitive turn toward the political right. One cannot help but see a certain parallelism between the development of a peculiarly aggressive and xenophobic nationalism in Japan and an increasingly jingoistic voice in the mass media of the United States during the last two decades, until the public's distrust of the Bush administration's policies could no longer be contained in 2006. In both countries, it appeared that mass media succumbed to the systematic information management of government agencies—and also the military, in the case of the United States—and acted as if the media were the government's publicity department. In contrast to the United States, however, whose nationalism serves to justify unilateral diplomatic policies and is grounded in American military domination of the world, Japan occupies an entirely different position in international politics. It is in this context that we can observe an interesting paradox characteristic of postwar Japanese nationalism, a paradox that may illustrate the structural complicity of the United States with nationalism in Japan.

Space restrictions compel me to construe this paradox in a cursory manner. On the one hand, Japanese nationalism manifests itself in the collective disavowal of historical facts and colonial guilt, in relation to countries in Asia, and Northeast Asia in particular. Since the end of the Second World War, the Japanese government has tried to maintain a low profile and appear to play no active or leading diplomatic role in Northeast and Southeast Asia, even though Japanese capital started to invest extensively in the regions under the directive of the Kishi administration from the late 1950s, following the guidelines of the United States' cold war policies. Of course, the exception was China, and Japanese corporations did not have direct access in the People's Republic of China until the 1980s, even though trade between China and Japan has continued since 1963 under the Liao-Takasaki agreement.

One may think of a number of reasons for this situation: Japan's subordinate status as a typical satellite of the United States within the cold war configuration, and the issues of colonial responsibility, which the Japanese state had managed to disavow until the 1990s. At that time, the issue of the wartime Comfort Women—the sex slavery network, established during the Asia Pacific war by the Japanese government, which forced many women from Japan's colonies and occupied territories to work as prostitutes among the soldiers—could no longer be concealed thanks to international women's activism.[2] In this respect, one might find certain similarities among right-wing nationalist tendencies such as historical revisionism, then known as New Racism in western Europe in the late 1970s and 1980s, and the prevailing nationalistic sentiment in today's Japan. In one respect or another, these reactionary movements are all responses to decolonization. As far as it was reported by Japan's mass media, the dominant public opinion insisted that Japanese national pride must be exhibited and that the dignity of the nation must be insulated from possible assaults by both the Asians and "the masochism of the leftists." This sentiment goes hand in hand with a certain anti-Americanism in Japan, an adulterated version of anticolonial nationalism, according to which Japan was unjustifiably violated by the United States and so is still a victim rather than a victimizer.

Inversely, some Japanese nationalists demand a change in the constitution, which was originally introduced by the U.S. Occupation Administration in 1947, so that Japan can have its own national military forces and

become more independent as "a normal nation-state." Since the inauguration of the Koizumi administration—prior to the Abe administration—the
controlling Liberal Democratic Party openly sought a number of pieces
of legislation that would promote the Self-Defense Agency to the status
of Ministry of Defense, and an eventual change in the constitution, even
though the 2009 victory of the Democratic Party seemed to put the brakes
on this hostility toward the constitution. Although the document was
originally prepared and legislated by the U.S. Occupation Administration,
since 1953 or earlier the U.S. government has consistently advocated that it
be changed, particularly article 9, which proscribes Japan's use of military
force to solve international conflicts. Delivering a letter from President
Eisenhower to Prime Minister Yoshida Shigeru and Emperor Hirohito in
November 1953, Richard Nixon, then vice president of the United States,
publicly declared in Tokyo: "Now if disarmament was right in 1946, why
is it wrong in 1953? And if it was right in 1946 and wrong in 1953, why
doesn't the United States admit for once that it made a mistake? And I am
going to do something that I think perhaps ought to be done by people in
public life. I'm going to admit right here that the United States did make
a mistake in 1946."[3]

As these policy statements indicate, there is no reason why Japanese
nationalists' demand for changing the constitution has to be perceived as
anti-American, either by the United States or the Japanese government. It
is no more than an endorsement of U.S. initiative and leadership. I find
it difficult to conceptualize what is meant by "a normal nation-state," but
my guess is that the right-wing nationalists have in mind the nineteenth-
century ideal of national sovereignty, the nation-state with a homogeneous national language and culture, equipped with a regular military and
national conscription. The nationalists, it seems to me, believe that they
would be able to introduce "proper" military forces to Japan by removing
article 9 and some other pacifist terminology from the constitution. Yet
regardless of whether article 9 has been effective in directing the legislation and administration of the Japanese state, military forces have existed in Japan since 1950. Under the current constitution, the Japanese Supreme Court offered a juridical interpretation that the existent Japanese
military forces, although both the most costly in annual expenditure and
the most technologically sophisticated in Asia, are "self-defending" forces
which supposedly are more like a police force. (Within a few years of the
end of World War II, the United States introduced to Japan the idea of a
police force consisting of specialists in military maneuvers. I return to this
point concerning the constitutional difference between military violence
and police violence.) So, the current nationalist sentiment seems to revital-

ize the public's demand for a constitutional change to remove article 9 and for Japan's military forces to be more than self-defensive.

What has been deliberately withdrawn from public debate about constitutional change is the question of national sovereignty with regard to the already existing Self-Defense Forces in Japan. A peculiar and unexamined assumption has prevailed, according to which, in the wake of the implementation of a new constitution without pacifist articles, the Japanese state would automatically regain its sovereignty so that its military forces would be under the command of the Japanese government and its leading officials. It is glaringly obvious, however, that this is a fantastic scenario. Ever since its initial establishment as the Supplementary Police Force (Keisatsu Yobitai) under the U.S. Occupation Administration, Japanese Self-Defense Forces have been designed and organized as subordinate organs within the U.S. global command network in the United States postwar collective security system in the Pacific and East Asia. It is unlikely that this constitutional change will allow for Japan's military independence from the United States, with its extensive network of military bases and intelligence throughout the world. Instead, the change will only deprive the Japanese government of grounds for policy choices, such as refusing to send troops overseas to solve international conflicts, as almost mercenary troops under U.S. command, just like the South Korean troops sent to Southeast Asia under U.S. command during the war in Vietnam.[4] In other words, it seems more probable that a constitutional change will accelerate Japan's military subordination to the global system of U.S. unilateral military control.

Consequently, what I call "the paradox of Japanese nationalism" encourages the Japanese to develop two seemingly contradictory attitudes. While they insist on the separation from and even indifference toward people of neighboring countries in East and Southeast Asia, they perversely welcome United States' domination and tend to find their own desires within the scenario of Pax Americana.

To understand this paradox of Japanese nationalism, we probe the history of postwar Japan and refer to what has been known in East and Southeast Asia as Japan's amnesia toward its colonial and war responsibility. Most importantly, we look at the paradox of Japanese nationalism not within the framework of linear national history but through a comparatist perspective.

A comparatist analysis of transpacific complicity reveals the formation of a new governmentality whose emergence did not necessarily lead to the disappearance of the nation-state. Virtually, the new governmentality reduces humanity to nationality and is most violently effective through national humanism. What I explore in this essay is the historical transition from the U.S. occupation of Japan to the recent violent manifestation of national humanism. My scope, therefore, is not limited to the transpacific complicity of the United States and Japan. The new governmentality attests to the general transformation of state sovereignty in the late twentieth and early twenty-first centuries. It enhances the relationship of complicity with each nation-state and thereby redefines the sovereignty of that nation-state. The fate of the postwar Japanese Constitution is probably the best testimony to the fact that the complicity of the United States and Japan followed the embryonic logic of this emerging governmentality.

Toward the end of the Asia Pacific war, the issue with which Japanese leaders were primarily concerned in their negotiations with the Allied Powers about the conditions of Japan's surrender was neither the welfare of the population of the Japanese Empire nor the integrity of its territories but, instead, the preservation of *kokutai*, that is, "nationality," "national sovereignty," or "the national body." In the language of the prewar Japanese state of the 1920s and 1930s, the national body (*kokutai*) was defined in terms of a combination of private property rights and emperorism. To violate the national body meant either socialist and communist activism that denied the unlimited validity of private property rights, or the critique or refusal of the emperor as the national sovereign. In the late nineteenth century, when the institution of the emperor was first installed[5]—this institution is a most illuminating case of "the invention of tradition"—the national body (*kokutai*) was often referred to as a translation of the *nationality* of British Liberalism. During the early years of the Meiji period (1868–1911), some intellectuals argued that the figure of the emperor was a representation of the sense of nationality.

As the Japanese Empire expanded in the late nineteenth and early twentieth centuries, annexing Hokkaido, Okinawa, Taiwan, Korea, the Pacific Islands, and finally in the late 1930s and early 1940s large parts of Northeast and Southeast Asia under the umbrella of the Greater East Asian Co-Prosperity Sphere, the emperor was increasingly associated with the universalistic principle of the Japanese reign under which people of different ethnic backgrounds, of different languages and mores, and of different residences were entitled to be integrated into the imperial nation and treated as "equal subjects." In this light, Japan being an imperial nation, the prewar emperor was rarely made to represent the unity of a particular ethnicity or national culture. No doubt there were extremists, such as Watsuji Tetsurô,[6] who insisted on the purity of blood, but the intellectuals who participated in the policy making of the Japanese state could not afford to indulge openly in ethnic narcissism. They had to prevent the multiethnic nation from being fragmented into ethnic and class rivalry.

In the years subsequent to Japan's defeat and the loss of the empire, the legal status of the emperor underwent a drastic change. Prewar emperorism was replaced by a juridically different one, which was also called *ten'nôsei* (the emperorism). Under the Meiji Constitution the emperor had been defined as the sovereign of the Japanese state and the commander in chief of all Japanese military forces, but the new constitution implemented by the U.S. Occupation Administration defined the emperor as "the symbol of the unity of the Japanese nation." From our viewpoint in the twenty-first century, it appears that the implementation of the new emperorism coincided with the culturalist discussions of Japanese national unity in Japan as well as in the United States. From the late 1940s onward, well into the 1980s, it gradually became fashionable to explain the historical features of Japanese society in terms of "Japanese national character," "Japanese culture," and "Japanese uniqueness." Thus after the loss of the empire, the emperor was made to symbolize the continuity of Japanese tradition and the unity of Japanese national culture. Some conservative intellectuals like Watsuji Tetsurô valued the new definition of the Japanese emperor; they implicitly, or even unwittingly, served as ideologues for the U.S. Occupation Administration and produced an argument that justified the new emperorism on the basis of cultural nationalism.[7]

At the same time in the United States, Japan experts and anthropologists such as Ruth Benedict were involved in the production of a similar culturalist argument about Japanese national character during the war.[8] After Japan's defeat and under the Allied Powers' occupation administered by the United States, these two trends of culturalism reached a remarkably effective synthesis in the legitimization of the new emperorism. Area studies of Japan were thus instituted as an interdisciplinary field in American higher education, with the unmistakable mandate to legitimate the new emperorism. Of course, what was at stake in the legitimacy of the emperor as far as the U.S. policymakers were concerned was an effectual government of an occupied territory, that is, a novel modality of colonial governmentality. The effects of such a culturalist endorsement of the new emperorism are surprisingly lasting. I do not think that even today, after more than a half century, the Japanese public and political elites have liberated themselves from the shackles of such culturalist rhetoric.

As Takashi Fujitani suggested in his reading of Edwin O. Reischauer's "Memorandum on Policy towards Japan" of September 1942, which he discovered at the National Archives in Maryland, the Japanese national tradition and the unity of Japanese culture were clearly considered as part and parcel of the modality of colonial governmentality for the occupation of Japan.[9] Ten months into the war in the Pacific, Reischauer proposed to use the Showa emperor as a puppet of the U.S. Occupation Administration after Japan's surrender. The U.S. policies were collective works, and it is preposterous to attribute them to the genius of a young scholar of Oriental studies. I never argue that the memorandum prepared by Reischauer, who is regarded as one of the founding fathers of area studies in higher education in the United States after the Second World War and who later became ambassador to Japan (1961–66), single-handedly laid the foundation for the postwar U.S. policies toward Japan and Northeast Asia. His memorandum, however, is extremely informative in depicting the overall design of postwar U.S. policies toward Japan, including the endorsement of *kokutai* (the national body). In retrospect, we realize not only that Reischauer was consistent in his subsequent postwar publications, but also that almost all of his proposals were implemented in one way or another in U.S. policies toward Japan and Northeast Asia after the war.

From the late 1940s onward, the legitimacy of the postwar emperor served as a central topic around which knowledge production not only about Japan but also East Asia in general was systematically organized. The newly installed Japanese emperor—in the guise of the continuity of a tradition—was symbolic in more than one respect. Surely he was symbolic because he was deprived of all the juridical entitlements endowed him by the Meiji Constitution. He was, however, also symbolic because he represented the entire domain of cultural politics in which knowledge—historiography, cultural anthropology, literature, linguistics, and so forth—was produced and reproduced to replace the integrationist logic of a multiethnic nationality by the exclusionary logic of ethnic singularity. Consequently there gradually emerged a certain bilateral international complex of academic and journalistic activities and collective fantasies that worked powerfully to justify and legitimate the postwar emperorism along with U.S. policies toward Japan and Northeast Asia. Interestingly, while Japan represents Asia in this discourse, the viewpoints of other Asian countries—not only former Japanese colonies such as Korea and Taiwan but also China and the Southeast Asian countries occupied by Japanese troops—are entirely excluded. In its unity as a discursive formation, this complex of academic and journalistic activities and collective fantasies is neither American nor Japanese, since it is bilateral and transpacific. Within this discourse of postwar emperorism, there are a few important points that its design clearly delineated.

First, Emperor Hirohito had to be forgiven all his war responsibilities because otherwise he would be useless as a puppet leader to be manipulated by the U.S. Occupation Administration and to rule the Japanese population under U.S. hegemony. In his 1942 memorandum, Reischauer claimed that Hirohito could be like Pu Yi of Manchukuo, who symbolized the dynastic continuity of Manchukuo under Japanese colonial rule. He added that Hirohito had the potential to be much more effectual than Pu Yi as a puppet, since the mystification of the emperor had already been deliberately achieved by the prewar Japanese state.[10] In other words, hegemony was much more systematically and coherently constructed for the effective performance of the puppet in Japan proper, in the late 1940s and afterward, than in Manchukuo in the 1930s.

Second, now deprived of its annexed territories, the Japanese people should be allowed to preserve their sense of national tradition and culture. As Watsuji argued consistently from the 1920s and throughout the war years—his culturalist argument manifested a strong racist tendency, very close to that of the German National Socialists[11]—the Japanese people should achieve their cohesion as a nation in terms of the organic wholeness of their national culture and the continuity of their national history; the Japanese must regard themselves as uniquely homogeneous. Here is where the two schools of culturalism, the Japanese ethnic nationalists and the U.S. National Character Studies scholars, found common ground, despite their diametrically opposed intents,[12] and embraced each other, so to speak. Watsuji argued most successfully that the emperor's political significance consisted in his aesthetic function of making Japanese people feel unified, in giving them a sense of togetherness without any concrete content. There was no need to define the emperor as an embodiment of the general will or to seek his political function in his ability to direct state policies.[13] Hence he should be deprived of all legislative, executive, and judicial authority. At that point the meaning of the term *kokutai* changed: the institution of emperor was no longer the embodiment of sovereignty but rather of nationality under popular sovereignty. As a matter of fact, an analysis of the institution of emperor gives us a new perspective about nationality, a perspective that suggests a need to redefine the notion of sovereignty in terms of pastorate in the direction of biopolitics.[14]

Third, as Takashi Fujitani has stressed, U.S. policymakers had to take racial problems into account as part of their "ideological warfare" in domestic as well as international politics during World War II.[15] As a matter of fact, many American area specialists believed they had to continue to fight their ideological warfare well into the 1960s.[16] As a devoted U.S. patriot, Reischauer was seriously worried that the historically infamous treatment of U.S. residents of non-European ancestry, anti-Asian immigration legislation, and particularly the internment of U.S. citizens and residents of Japanese ancestry in concentration camps during the war, could lend support to the Japanese cause in East Asia.[17] He thus confirmed the anxiety widely shared in the United States at the beginning of the Pacific War. The anxiety was far from groundless.

In response to the increasing sense of national emergency in the late 1930s and the outbreak of the war in the Pacific, the United States government attempted to build conformity among its citizens. But according to Marc Gallicchio, "instead of closing ranks as in World War I, blacks continued to battle for their rights as American citizens." It is well known that such African American intellectuals as W. E. B. Du Bois and Marcus Garvey often expressed support of Japan's policies in China in the 1930s and tended to view Japan as a power to counterbalance white racism. Japanese mass media too depicted some African American intellectuals as potential allies of Japan, and Du Bois participated in their publicity campaign by visiting Manchukuo in China, and Japan. According to Gallicchio, African Americans saw the international crisis as an opportunity to overturn racism at home. They "stepped up their rhetorical attacks on colonialism and racism in international affairs. In these tense circumstances many government officials came to view the rising campaign of African American protest and agitation as a sign of disloyalty. Black Americans' intellectual and emotional attachment to Japan added to this misperception and convinced Japanese, Chinese, and U.S. officials that in the event of war, African Americans in large number would oppose their own government."[18] A series of directives concerning the internment of Japanese Americans, advocated by U.S. secretary of war Henry L. Stimson, and ordered by President Franklin D. Roosevelt, reflected the policymakers' fear of mutinies within the United States. As George Lipsitz illustrated, during World War II in the United States, "racial segregation in industry and in the army kept qualified fighters and factory workers from positions where they were sorely needed, while the racialized nature of the war in Asia threatened to open up old wounds on the home front."[19]

Not surprisingly, Reischauer warned his audience in the Department of War to whom his memorandum was addressed with these words: the "point I wish to make has to do with the inter-racial aspects of the conflict in Asia. Japan is attempting to make her war against the United Nations into a holy crusade of the yellow and brown peoples for freedom from the white race."[20] The Japanese attack on White Americanism and white supremacy could well invoke universal sympathy with Japan's justification of its policies in Asia and the Pacific. Japan's rhetoric of universalism could in fact undermine Anglo-American justification for the United States' and Britain's colonial presence in East Asia and the Pacific. Therefore, Reischauer concluded, the United States must appear more universalistic than Japan and open to all races in order to win the ideological war against Japan. Almost simultaneously, the ideologues of the Japanese Empire put forth more or less the same argument for racial and ethnic equality among the peoples under Japanese colonial rule; Japan too was extremely anxious about the possibility of mutiny among the minorities of its empire at war.

We know the truism that imperialism without universalism is an oxymoron. To emphasize the empire's commitment to the universalistic and multiethnic principle, the Japanese government's condemnation of racist policies, and "the integration of ethnic groups according to the Imperial Way,"[21] the ideologues of the Greater East Asian Co-Prosperity Sphere repeatedly issued statements and recited old maxims and idioms. These included "Emperor gives *equal mercy to every subject* without the slightest discrimination among different ethnic groups within the Empire," and "Every person who wishes to reside on a permanent basis in the territory of this new nation is equal and should be able to enjoy rights to be treated as equal, regardless of whether he be of the Han, Manchu, Mongolian, Japanese, Korean or any other ethnicity."[22] These are variations of the statutory idiom "equal benevolence to every subject" (*isshi dôjin* in Japanese; *yi shi tong ren* in Chinese), meaning that every subject of the nation is entitled to equal mercy or benevolence in the gaze of the one and only sovereign, an expression widely known in China to have come from Christian missionaries. At the time of the Meiji Restoration, the new Japanese state adopted this four-character idiom expressing the basic principle of the new polity, and from 1868 until 1945 the Japanese state continued to use it to confirm its legislative authority.

A number of publications, such as Shinmei Masamichi's *Race and Society*, Takata Yasuma's *On Nation,* and Kôsaka Masaaki's *Philosophy of the Nation*, offered systematic philosophical and social scientific critiques of racism and ethnic nationalism as part of the state's "ideological warfare" (*shisô-sen*) against Anglo-American colonialism, communism, and ethnic nationalisms.[23] (It is significant that Watsuji Tetsurô, who was among the few intellectuals consistently arguing against the idea of Japan as a multiethnic nation and who repeatedly made racist statements about the Jews and the Chinese from the late 1920s until the defeat, produced the most lasting cultural nationalistic justification of the U.S. policy concerning the postwar new emperorism.)[24] It is obvious, however, that the critique of racism was needed for a number of political reasons: the Japanese government and military had to compete with the colonial powers of the United States, Britain, and the Netherlands for popularity among peoples in Asia, and therefore had to appeal to Asian peoples' abhorrence of Euro-

American racism; and a large number of young people had to be recruited or drafted from the colonized populations of Korea and Taiwan to serve in the Japanese military and industry because of the shortage of labor and the increasing military casualties. Just as Secretary Stimson was afraid that the Japanese and the Communists would instigate rebellion by blacks, so too Japanese leaders were haunted by the possibility of mutiny among the colonized.[25]

In view of ideological struggles carried out domestically as well as internationally between the Anglo-American and Japanese imperialisms, a number of American intellectuals from different racial and political backgrounds, from Pearl Buck, to Rayford W. Logan, to Edwin Reischauer, had to think seriously about how American racism would look to Asian eyes.[26] In Reischauer's careful consideration of the ramifications of American racism in Asia, the unequivocally racist aspect of U.S. nationalism was all the more clear in his overtures about the strategic need to disavow racism in the United States. Of course, it would be hard to evade a charge of naiveté to presume that either Reischauer or his Japanese counterparts were primarily apprehensive about the abolition of racial discrimination within their respective empires. Perhaps neither of them could imagine what it would be like if racism were genuinely overcome, for only those who are in the midst of the struggle against racism can envision the world beyond racism. What they clearly shared was the recognition that governmental acceptance of racism and ethnic nationalism was absolutely counterproductive to the management of their respective empires and ideological warfare. They insisted, therefore, that their policies had to be cloaked in an aura of universalism, regardless of how unreal or contradictory such a universalism may have been in concrete historical situations. Nevertheless, it is misleading to attribute U.S. or Japanese universalism to a cynical reason in their colonial politics, for racism was not complementary to the universalism of the U.S. or Japanese state; as Étienne Balibar clearly stated, racism was supplemental to their universalism.[27] Also, the antiracist rhetoric would eventually result in the removal of certain racist and discriminatory legislation. Even Reischauer's antiracist rhetoric cannot be treated merely as a case of false consciousness.

Fourth, far from denoting the beginning of an extensive public critique of racism associated with Japanese imperialism, the installment of the new emperorism marked the waning of the antiracist argument in Japan. The U.S. Occupation Administration deliberately censored not racist but antiracist utterances and publications in postwar Japan, since the denunciation of Anglo-American imperialism and Dutch colonialism almost always premised the general critique of white supremacy during the war. It goes

NAOKI SAKAI · 252

without saying that such a repression of the critique of racism was also a convenient measure for the Japanese government, which had to discard the population of its former colonies and the minority population inside Japan proper, such as the resident Koreans and Taiwanese.[28] The majority of the newly redefined Japanese nation did not object to censorship of the critique of racism either; because the atrocities committed by the Japanese during the war were often racist in nature, the censorship could in fact help them overlook their own colonial shame and war responsibility.

Neither the disclosure of war crimes committed by the Japanese military nor the loss of the empire created opportunities for the Japanese nation to reflect on the system of social discrimination and colonial hierarchy in the everyday life in prewar Japan and its annexed territories.[29] It seems that decolonization meant no more to the Japanese than the abandonment of colonial territories and their population, and that it did not give rise to occasions for them to reflect on the colonial power relations inherent in their modality of national identification. In short, decolonization in the sense of the fundamental transformation of Japanese identity never took place, perhaps, until the 1990s, and to the extent that the Japanese were unaffected by decolonization, they remained colonizers "in spirit" even after the loss of the empire.[30]

For the former colonizers, decolonization covers a wide range of issues, from individuals' feelings of guilt and self-esteem, the deprivation of social prestige and economic privileges, the loss of colonial entitlements, the redefinition of nationality, to the form of government. The dissolution of the empire affected every individual in Japan. As its result, some lost their Japanese nationality and gained a new one; others lost their nationality and became stateless. For those who retained nationality, however, an emphasis on the interiority of their lives seemed to insulate them from the external devastation caused by the defeat. The colonizer status had endowed them with an exaggerated sense of pride and arrogance, but for the majority, including those returning from the former annexed and colonized territories, the loss of the empire did not seem to cause a crisis of personal integrity. They were, however, severely affected by other events: the loss of family members, economic deprivation, unemployment, and homelessness.

For one reason or another, the effects of decolonization on the individual were kept to a minimum. An international division of labor was established between the United States and Japan in which the United States remained in charge of uniting various ethnic and racial groups under the banner of universalism, while Japan gave up an active role in this integration. Japan's defeat and subsequent loss of the empire were perceived to be a return to the original state rather than decolonization. The phrase "the second opening to the West" (*daini no kaikoku*) rather shamelessly posited the original Japan as making another fresh start, just as it had done one century earlier. In other words, the Japanese were to be content with their naturalized status, with what they had been before the empire, as if they were returning to their ethnic essence, whereas the Americans would seek to transcend and transform the racial and ethnic particularities so as to create a new subjectivity within the premises of their nationalism. Thus emerged a new transpacific division of ideological labor: the United States continued to legitimate its polity in terms of universalism, while Japan served as the United States' particularistic counterpart.

The Meiji Constitution defined the emperor as the supreme commander of the Japanese military forces, and in his name the war in Pacific Asia was fought and many atrocities were committed by Japanese troops. To redefine the status of the emperor as the symbol of the unity of the Japanese nation and its culture while overlooking his war and colonial responsibility would in due course relieve the Japanese nation of its war responsibility, as many analysts have shown. Under the Meiji Constitution, every important policy, including the declaration of war, was legislated and implemented as an order by the sovereign, the emperor. After the emperor was pardoned, how could one possibly prosecute his subjects, who at least in theory followed his command even in their brutality and inhumane acts? What the U.S. Occupation Administration sought in his place was a few scapegoats such as Tôjô Hideki and a small number of militarists;[31] no doubt Japanese conservatives and many wartime leaders wholeheartedly welcomed such a decision. From the viewpoint of the Occupation Administration, the International Military Tribunal for the Far East (the so-called Tokyo War Crimes Tribunal) was held as a public procedure of legitimization in order to officially exempt the emperor and the overwhelming majority of the Japanese from further investigation into their war responsibility. It has been argued that the Tokyo War Crimes Tribunal was a failure in its historical significance because, generally speaking, the prosecutors did not deal with the racist and sexist atrocities committed under colonial and imperialist policies in East Asia. In short, they did not pursue the possibilities inherent in the idea of "crimes against humanity" (the so-called class C war crimes) for fear that accusing the Japanese leadership of such crimes could easily return to haunt the Allied Powers, particularly the United States. The American hostility toward the idea of crimes against humanity, which more recently most characteristically defined the Bush administration's stance toward international justice, was initiated at the Tokyo War Crimes Tribunal.

Six decades later such a political settlement has produced a situation in which an increasing number of Japanese have shown little remorse for the

Japanese imperialist maneuvers in Asia during the 1930s and early 1940s.[32] At the same time, they are somnolently happy with the new U.S. strategic arrangement in East Asia, except when they are occasionally prodded by incidents such as the English-language publication of *The Rape of Nanking* and the U.S. congressional resolution condemning the Abe Shinzô administration's attitude toward the Comfort Women issue.[33] It is true that an overtly anti-American rhetoric is sometimes used by those populist nationalists, not to mention those self-proclaimed realist nationalists who boast of their technocratic rationality, but they can never take issue with the postwar U.S. occupation policies that released the Japanese from their war responsibility and colonial guilt. While claiming to be victims of American domination, they scarcely pay attention to the victims of Japanese aggression. By leading the movement to censor the topic of Comfort Women in Japanese high-school history textbooks and public television broadcasting, Abe Shinzô was well known for his open dismissal of Japanese war responsibility and sex slavery.[34] He seemed to believe his jingoistic stance was implicitly endorsed by the United States. During his official visit to Washington, D.C., in May 2007, Abe personally apologized to President George Bush and U.S. House leaders for the treatment of the Comfort Women—but not to the surviving Comfort Women themselves, who had been demanding that the Japanese government officially acknowledge its responsibility. Considering that Abe is of the same lineage as Kishi Nobusuke, about which Abe is unflinchingly proud, it would be no surprise to find he was convinced of a secret concord between U.S. anticommunism and the Japanese imperialist lineage as symbolized by the Yasukuni Shrine, where executed class A war criminals—Kishi was one of the surviving ones—are enshrined.[35] Abe's self-confidence collapsed as soon as this assumption was contradicted. After the loss of the general election for the House of Councilors, and passage of the U.S. congressional resolution concerning the Japanese government's attitude toward the Comfort Women in July 2007, it only took a month for Abe Shinzô to abruptly resign his premiership.

It is, however, misleading to presume that Abe's behavior during his official visit to the District of Columbia was aberrant and that he betrayed the Japanese public. Given the structure of transpacific complicity between the United States and Japan, within whose framework the Liberal Democratic Party had been dominant in Japanese politics for more than a half century, the Japanese public—not all of it, of course—expected Abe, the LDP president, to act the way he did, and they endorsed him to a considerable extent. How, then, should we understand the structure of transpacific complicity?

The notion of nationality (*kokutai*) played a decisive role in the process by which sovereignty was handed over from the prewar Japanese state to the U.S. Occupation Administration. The preservation of national history and of the putative unity of national culture, which helped to conjure up the feeling of nationality, was thus an exceedingly effective means to keep the occupied population, first, under direct U.S. rule, and then indirectly complicit with U.S. domination. The most ironic and interesting aspect of the postwar relationship between the United States and Japan can perhaps be found in the fact that the United States effectively continued to dominate Japan by endowing the Japanese with the grounds for their nationalism. It is through the apparent sense of national uniqueness and cultural distinctiveness that people in Japan were subordinated to U.S. hegemony in East Asia.

Some sentimental reactionaries such as Etô Jun have argued that the U.S. Occupation Administration deprived the Japanese people of their right to narrate their own national history.[36] Abe's rhetoric can be seen as an extension of this sort of nationalist argument, although his was an embarrassingly crude and conceited complaint. Such rhetoric only serves as a kind of international coquetry (whose sexist undertone is best depicted by the film *M. Butterfly*), and a kind of *amae* (the infantile attitude of dependency) in which, with a display of self-pity, the disadvantaged (Japan) solicits the attention and sympathy of the advantaged (the United States).[37]

Contrary to Etô's assessment, the U.S. Occupation Administration deliberately allowed the Japanese to maintain their sense of cultural and historical continuity; it helped nurture the desire of the Japanese to narrate their own self-serving story/history. What seems to be a fatal deficiency in Etô and sentimental nationalists like him is their investment in an anachronistic assumption that takes the ideals of the nineteenth-century European nation-state for granted, namely, that a nationalism seeking a nation's autonomy is *external* to the imperialism dominating the affairs of that nation. Supposedly Japanese territoriality is respected by the United States, except that U.S. military bases exist in Japan and that U.S. military personnel are treated according to the terms of the United States–Japan Status of Forces Agreement.[38] Yet each time a U.S. soldier rapes a local female,[39] it becomes glaringly obvious that the status of forces agreement guarantees U.S. military personnel the privileges of extraterritoriality.[40] According to the cartographic imagination, U.S. imperial nationalism is external to Japanese nationalism. So from the outset Etô put aside the logical possibility that U.S. imperial nationalism and Japanese nationalism could be co-possible and internal to one another; he dared not examine the logically available option that Japanese nationalism itself can accommodate U.S. imperial nationalism, or even serve as its instrument. What must be called into question is the assumption of *externality* between an imperial nationalism and a nationalism, of an externality between a colonial domination and an anticolonial nationalism against colonial maneuver. Already, in the 1930s, had not some ideologues for the East Asian Community—which was later called the Greater East Asian Co-Prosperity Sphere—advocated the Japanese policy of embracing Chinese nationalism as a necessary component of Japan's transnational hegemony? The advocates desperately sought ways to construct a Japanese transnational hegemony that also appeared anticolonial. In this respect the ideological maneuvers adopted by the U.S. Occupation Administration in Japan should not have been particularly innovative or surprising.

Yet there is one feature that has become conspicuous since the 1980s, even though it is not easy to talk definitively about the end of the cold war in East Asia. Militarily the United States is overwhelmingly dominant, but economically or politically the United States no longer maintains the exceptionally prestigious status it once enjoyed. No single country would dare to oppose the United States militarily, not only because it monopolizes military high-technology and weapons but also because, Chalmers Johnson claims, it maintains a network of military bases in South Korea, Japan, Okinawa, and virtually everywhere in the world.[41] In such circumstances, national states are forced to enter complementary relations with the United States, even if it is increasingly obvious that a U.S. military advantage does not necessarily convert into economic, diplomatic, or other advantages. The classic concept of colonialism does not apply in this respect either.

In the 1950s, American wealth was just beyond the reach of people in East Asia. Today, some Japanese, for instance, do not feel poor at all when they visit the United States. Soon an increasing number of Koreans will share the same sentiment. Even though the restructuring of export markets and transnational divisions of labor have yet to be elaborated upon among the countries in Northeast Asia, there is a growing sense that Northeast Asia can be a large economic region. In the wake of the electoral victory of Japan's Democratic Party, the new prime minister Hatoyama Yukio finally agreed to the vision of "the East Asian Community," to which the LDP prime ministers had been hesitant to respond despite proposals from China, South Korea, and some countries in Southeast Asia during the last decade.[42] I do not know how realistic the idea of an East Asian Community is today, but it is possible to conceive of coordinating the industrial and trade policies of Northeast Asian countries. The economy of Northeast Asia would be relatively independent of U.S. policies if such a community should be actualized.

Traditionally the U.S. leadership is afraid of such a community. What it feared most in the 1950s and 1960s was that Japan would join China and South Korea, thereby forming a relatively autonomous regional unity. Today such a unity would be similar to the European Union, although I do not think this can easily be accomplished. U.S. hegemony is crumbling, but we do not know what will replace it. Consumerism, which used to lure masses in East Asian markets toward the American lifestyle, Hollywood films, and American fashions, no longer symbolizes specifically American dreams; it simply projects the fantasy of transnational capital. Consumerist luxury continues to bait, but it is no longer necessary to attribute a genitive "American" to luxury.

During the cold war, the imminent threat of communism could rationalize many things and justify the continuing presence of the U.S. military, but today, except for North Korea, a potential conflict in the Taiwan Strait, and possibly international terrorism, I cannot think of any immediate reason why the United States must maintain such massive military installations and personnel in Northeast Asia. It is possible to explain it in terms of protecting U.S. political and economic interests, but such an explanation would not justify but rather disclose the colonial nature of the U.S. military presence; of course, this is the last explanation the U.S. government would accept. International terrorism is a convenient reason, but I'm not sure it justifies the United States keeping the huge naval force and port facilities of the Seventh Fleet and the ports of Yokosuka and Sasebo. I wonder how the United States would legitimate its military presence without North Korea or tension between the two Chinas. Arguably the strategy of a preemptive strike was an attempt to remedy the increasingly obvious absence of U.S. legitimacy in the region. We have now moved into the state of eternal war for the sake of sustaining U.S. military domination. But how long can the United States continue to find justification for its military presence in Afghanistan? The United States collective security system in East Asia seems to be in a crisis of its legitimacy as the cold war structure wanes.

Perhaps after the global network of military bases, the structure of transpacific complicity was best manifested in knowledge production. What we must come to terms with is the institution of area studies, in which, strangely enough, the distinction between the West and Asia has been rigorously maintained throughout the postwar period, despite such complicity between Japan's nationalism and the United States' imperial nationalism. The rhetoric of Japanese culturalism has been predominantly obsessed with the image of Japanese distinctiveness, but such rhetoric was produced only in contrast to some fantastic image of Western culture. The image of Japan's ethnolinguistic unity was sustained with a view to some imaginary observer positioned outside the organic whole of the Japanese nation. And this imaginary observer, in being habitually referred to as the West, often symbolizes U.S. hegemony.

Modern politics has appealed to the idea of nationality as the basis for its legitimacy and has constituted internationality as relationships among the state sovereignties, each of which is hypothesized to represent its own nation as an ethnolinguistic unity. To this extent, the modern world has embraced the hypothesis that the national state ought to be able to have as its own substratum the unity of an ethnos or race, and continue to seek an international order in which class struggles within each nation-state can find some solution in interstate competition for territorial appropriation. Consequently the world was a forum of colonial competition where peoples and regions without state sovereignty were subjugated to the rules of more powerful states. National sovereignty was thus rendered equivalent to national independence. Imagined as an order regulating the configuration of the nation-states in which each monopolizes the sovereignty in its own territory, however, this international order underwent many crises in the twentieth century. Toward the end of the last century, an increasing number of states finally retreated from the task of pursuing this ideal international order; they seem to have moved to a new kind of governmentality, which we often talk about in terms of globalization.

The emergence of this new governmentality, however, did not necessarily lead to the disappearance of the nation-state. In this new element, not only are people more enthralled by their ethnolinguistic unity and their nationalism, but it seems that the institution of the nation-state is revived anew within it. Accordingly, it is utterly misleading to diagnose our era in terms of a conflict between global civil society and nationality, between borderless global capitalism and self-defensive local solidarity, between general globality and a particular ethnic locality. Not surprisingly, a critique of globalization is frequently displaced by concerns for such misguided problematics as how to protect a nation against the movements of transnational immigration.

The new governmentality virtually reduces humanity to nationality and is most violently effectual through national humanism, which defines a human being as one with unambiguous nationality or ethnicity. It establishes the relationship of complicity with each nation-state and thereby deprives that nation-state of sovereignty. Rather than being an expression of the state's assertiveness, jingoistic nationalism is symptomatic of the decline of state sovereignty. Therefore, while it induces police surveillance of national borders, each state is endowed with less and less initiatives with which to observe a social contract, such as the articles of the constitution. The fate of the postwar Japanese Constitution is probably the best testimony to the fact that, already in the 1950s, the complicity of the United States and Japan followed the embryonic logic of this emerging governmentality.

It is no surprise that such a contractuality as basic human rights is less and less respected not only in what used to be called the Third World but also in the European Union, North America, and liberal capitalist states in Northeast Asia. A biopolitical national symbol such as emperorism serves most effectively in this context precisely because Japanese nationalism was established as a mode of transpacific complicity between the United States' domination and Japan's subordination, a mode best exemplified by the scenario of *Madama Butterfly*, in which both the dominating and the dominated are dependent on one another in a relationship of transference.

In the steady evaporation of *externality* between colonial maneuver and anticolonial resistance, because of which anticolonial nationalism is no longer effectual, the distinction between the military force and the police force has gradually diminished. Characteristically, Japan's Self-Defense Forces (*Jieitai*) were originally formed at the outbreak of the Korean War in 1950 as the Supplementary Police Forces (*Keisatsu Yobitai*), by order of the U.S. Occupation Administration, to defend U.S. military facilities and personnel within Japan. In 1952 the Supplementary Police Forces were renamed the Security Forces (*Hoantai*), and then in 1954 the Self-Defense Forces. Thus the military forces named Self-Defense Forces were created to defend not the Japanese people from external threats but U.S. bases from Japanese rebels. In January 2007, without a change in the constitution, the Self-Defense Agency (*Bôeichô*) was promoted to the status of the Ministry of Defense. The operation of military forces was still prohibited by the constitution, so the executive branch of the government took upon itself the task of defense. Therefore, constitutionally there ceased to be a distinction between the police force that maintains the judiciary and executive functions of the state within the subject population, and the military force that solves conflicts arising from outside the subject population. Does the end of this divergence mean that Japan's military forces will be used as an extension of the police force, neglecting the basic distinction between the domestic territory and the international space outside the state sovereignty?

In its relation to the movements of those who do not conform to the univocal taxonomy of nationality and ethnicity and who are therefore placed outside the new definition of humanity, sovereignty cannot but be executed according to the logic of the police, no matter whether persons at issue reside inside or outside the national territory. It goes without saying that the target of police operations is not an enemy but a rebel. Then, with the evaporation of externality, the systemic struggle between center and periphery itself is placed in complicity.

Hence, it is not enough simply to speak of structural complicity such as that among elite classes whose members give extorted consent to the U.S. sovereign police while using anti-Americanism as a tool to achieve their own domestic ends regarding Japan's "parasitic" nationalism. It is also necessary, however, to speak of the kind of complicity found in the schema of cofiguration in translation, which enables the nationalist appropriation of ethnolinguistic identity.[43] Japanese uniqueness or particularism is continually reproduced cofiguratively in its transferential relation to U.S. universalism. It is of no surprise that U.S. area experts have fixatedly been attempting to prove Japan's particularism in contrast to the United States' universalism in the last half century.[44] For this reason, Japanese nationalism has constituted itself at the behest of the United States' imperial nationalism. It is no accident that, in the United Nations and in Asian regional politics, the Japanese government almost always has to behave as if it were America's servant. Yet this docility toward the colonial master does not spell the absence of anti-Americanism in Japan or aspirations for Japan's independence. On the contrary, paradoxically it shows that Japanese nationalism is based on the Japanese people's acceptance of the order of the new governmentality and of the new type of colonial subordination.

The assessment I present here is not limited to the case of Japan after the loss of its empire but is just one instance in which the sense of ethnic and national identity is invoked to exemplify how nationalisms in different countries aid and abet each other. It may appear strange that the United States and Japan, the largest and second (or third) largest national economies in the world, still recognize each other in such a colonialist manner. This instance, however, only shows a new emerging configuration in which a nationalism in the periphery reinforces rather than interrupts the neocolonialist complicity between the imperial center and a subordinate nation-state, the relation between U.S. nationalism and global security.

Since the Peace Treaty of San Francisco, Japan has held nominal sovereignty, but from the 1950s it was understood by both American and Japanese leaders that Japan would remain subordinate to the United States, even after its independence. Japan would not be treated overtly as a colony, but the Japanese state could neither exercise its territorial sovereignty over the U.S. military bases nor conduct international policies in contradiction to U.S. policies. In these historical circumstances, the conservative forces, the remnant of which Abe Shinzô clearly represents, achieved the overall control of polity. Their power base is in Japan's complicity with the United States. If this complicit relationship collapsed, they would lose their power base. They are aware that the Japanese state will face an increasing number of social conflicts that it cannot deal with. The state sovereignty is visibly waning, just as in any other state. Repeatedly Japanese LDP leaders had to indicate to the U.S. leadership that Japan would not incline toward China or Korea to form something like the East Asian Community. Visits to the Yasukuni Shrine are emblematic to convey the interstate message that Japan would choose the United States rather than China or South Korea.

Prime ministers Koizumi Ichirô and Abe Shinzô visited the Yasukuni, and their visits invoked strong reactions in China and South Korea. Domestically it was an effective way to appeal to Japanese jingoist sentiment. Nevertheless, as I have argued, this sort of nationalism instead reinforces Japan's colonial conditions. The more jingoistic Japanese leaders are, the more dependent on the United States are Japan's foreign policies. In this paradoxical sense, Japanese nationalism today is an ideology of colonial dependency. The decline of nation-state sovereignty gives rise to a new colonial dependency, as well as a jingoistic nationalism.

Evidently the contradictions of transpacific complicity are too obvious for the conservative camps to continue to obscure; it is a matter of time before the structural subordination of Japan to the United States has to be openly addressed in Japanese politics.

What has been postponed in this structure of complicity is the process of decolonization, the process in which individuals gradually learn how to form new social relations that are not premised on the legacies and vanities of colonialisms. Yet, are the Americans and Japanese capable of discarding their national pride, that is, their colonialist conceit?

Notes

1. Following the devastation of the First World War, the birth rate fell in countries such as France, and anxiety over the demographics spread throughout Europe. The anxiety reached a peak during the interwar period.

2. See Yuki Tanaka, *Japan's Comfort Women: Sexual Slavery and Prostitution during World War II and the U.S. Occupation* (London: Routledge, 2002).

3. John Dower, *Empire and Aftermath: Yoshida Shigeru and the Japanese Experience, 1978–1954* (Cambridge, MA: Council on East Asian Studies, 1979), 464–65. Michael Schaller, *Altered States* (New York: Oxford University Press, 1997), 69.

4. See Kun Ho Park, "Betonamu senso to 'higashi ajia no kiseki'" [Vietnam War and "East Asian miracle"], in *Globalization Studies* (Tokyo: Heibonsha, 2003) 1:80–120.

5. The system of bureaucracy based on the sovereignty of the emperor has been called

the emperor system; this term was coined by Marxists in the 1920s. Although censored by the state until the end of the Asia Pacific war, this analysis became widely accepted after the war. There are, however, two shortcomings in their analysis. The first is a developmental teleology implicit in the term "emperor system." It is understood as a form of absolutism, comparable to something like Russian czarism, characterized as an already surpassed stage in the development of capitalism. The second is ahistoricality, a lack of historical awareness, concerning the constitution of the national community. Just like the Liberals, the Marxists failed to historicize the existence of the Japanese nation and instead assumed that it had been there before the constitution of the modern nation-state. In respect to regarding the nation as a natural given, the Marxists were no different from the nationalists; after all, they were Marxist nationalists.

6. For Watsuji's xenophobia and racism, see Naoki Sakai, *Translation and Subjectivity: On "Japan" and Cultural Nationalism* (Minneapolis: University of Minnesota Press, 1998), esp. 110–14.

7. Ibid., chaps. 3 and 4.

8. As many have already pointed out, culturalism was also the most prominent feature of the United States' efforts during the war to characterize the Japanese nation; the most famous effort is Ruth Benedict's *The Chrysanthemum and the Sword: Patterns of Japanese Culture* (1946; reprint, Boston: Houghton Mifflin, 1989). For historical evaluations of U.S. national character studies, see C. Douglas Lummis, *A New Look at "The Chrysanthemum and the Sword"* (Tokyo: Shohakusha, 1982); and Mari Yoshihara, *Embracing the East* (Oxford: Oxford University Press, 2002).

9. Takashi Fujitani, "Reischauer no kairai tenno-sei kôsô" [Reischauer's design of a puppet emperor system], *Sekai*, March 2000, 137–46. Edwin O. Reischauer, "Memorandum on Policy towards Japan," September 14, 1942, with materials collected by War Department General Staff, Organization and Training Division, G-3, concerning "Enlistment of loyal American citizens of Japanese descent into the Army and Navy," December 17, 1942, 291.2, Army-AG Classified Decimal File 1940–42, Records of the Adjunct General's Office, 1917–, RG 407, entry 360, box 147, National Archives at College Park, MD. For the entire memorandum, see the March issue of *Sekai* at the Iwanami Web site, http://www.iwanami.co.jp/sekai/.

10. According to Reischauer, "[in Japan] we shall have to win our ideological battles by carefully planned strategy. A first step would naturally be to win over to our side a group willing to cooperate. Such a group, if it represented the minority of the Japanese people, would be in a sense a puppet regime. Japan has used the stratagem of puppet governments extensively but with no great success because of the inadequacy of the puppets. But Japan itself has created the best possible puppet for our purposes, a puppet who not only could be won over to our side but who would carry with him a tremendous weight of authority, which Japan's puppets in China have always lacked. I mean, of course, the Japanese Emperor" ("Memorandum on Policy towards Japan").

11. Cf. Sakai, *Translation and Subjectivity*, esp. 117–52.

12. Yoshihara, *Embracing the East*.

13. See Watsuji Tetsurô, "Kokutai henkô-ron ni tsuite: Sasaki hakushi no oshite wo kou" [On the modification of the national body: Requesting an instruction from Dr. Sasaki] (1947), in "Kokumin tôgô no shôchô" [The symbol of national unity], in *Watsuji Tetsurô zenshû* (Tokyo: Iwanami Shoten, 1962), 14:313–96.

14. The institution of emperor was created as a sort of pastorate during the Meiji period (1868–1912). It must not be confused with what I suggest by the new governmentality. The pastoral power at issue, however, must be distinguished from the pastorate of Oriental antiquity—Egypt and Israel—and from the Christendom of medieval Europe as discussed by Michel Foucault, *Security, Territory, Population: Lectures at the Collège de France, 1977–1978*, ed. Michel Senellart, trans. Graham Burchell (New York: Palgrave, 2007). It is modern in the

sense that it is mediated by the technology of mass reproduction. I conducted more detailed analyses of the Japanese institution of the emperor and nationality in a recent publication, "The Body of the Nation: The Pastorate and the Society of Sympathy," in *Biopolitics, Ethics, and Subjectivation*, ed. J. L. Deotte, Alain Brossat, Joyce C. H. Liu, and Yuan-horng Chu (Paris: L'Harmattan, forthcoming).

15. Fujitani, "Reischauer no kairai tenno-sei kôsô,"143.

16. Reischauer's *Wanted: An Asian Policy* (New York: Knopf, 1955) is an early example. You may also find a number of typically jingoistic declarations in Robert N. Bellah, "Values and Social Changes in Modern Japan," *Asian Cultural Studies*, no. 3 (1962): 13–56.

17. As to Japan's ideological goal, Reischauer wrote, in "Memorandum on Policy towards Japan": "[Japan's propaganda] has apparently met with a certain degree of success in Siam and the colonial lands of southeastern Asia and even in a few circles in China. If China were to be forced out of the war, the Japanese might be able to transform the struggle in Asia in reality into a full-scale racial war." For an analysis of area studies on East Asia during the cold war, see my essay, Naoki Sakai, "'You Asians': On the Historical Role of the West and Asia Binary," *South Atlantic Quarterly* 99, no. 4 (Fall 2000): 789–818.

18. March Gallicchio, *The African American Encounter with Japan and China* (Chapel Hill: University of North Carolina Press, 2000), 103.

19. George Lipsitz, *The Possessive Investment in Whiteness* (Philadelphia: Temple University Press, 1998), 193.

20. According to Reischauer, "[we] have also unwittingly contributed to Japan's dangerous propaganda campaign. The removal from the West Coast of the American citizens of Japanese ancestry along with the Japanese aliens was no doubt a move made necessary by immediate military considerations, but it provided the Japanese with a powerful argument in their attempt to win the Asiatic peoples to the view that the white race is not prepared to recognize them as equals and even now continues to discriminate against them" ("Memorandum on Policy towards Japan").

21. Murayam Michio, *Daitôa kensetsu-ron* [Construction of greater East Asia] (Tokyo: Shôkô Gyôsei Shuppan-sha, 1943).

22. Rescript to the population of Korea, 1917 (author's emphasis); and the Manchukuo Declaration of Independence, 1932.

23. Shinmei Masamichi, *Jinshu to shakai* (Tokyo: Kawade Shobô, 1940); Takata Yasuma *Minzoku-ron* (Tokyo: Iwanami Shoten, 1936); and Kôsaka Masaaki, *Minzoku no tetsugaku* (Tokyo: Iwanami Shoten, 1941).

24. During the war Watsuji continued to adhere to the ideal of pure blood and opposed the multiethnic principle of the Greater East Asian Co-Prosperity Sphere by taking a stance similar to that of Nazism. See Sakai, *Translation and Subjectivity*, chap. 4. Also interesting is the fact that Watsuji was often celebrated as representative of Japanese thought in Japanese studies in the United States and western Europe. Cf. Robert Bellah, "Japan's Cultural Identity: Some Reflections on the Work of Watsuji Tetsurô," *Journal of Asian Studies* 24, no. 4 (1965): 573–94; Augustin Berque, *Vivre l'espace au Japon* (Paris: Presses Universitaires de France, 1982); and Augustin Berque, *Le sauvage et l'artifice: Les japonais devant la nature* (Paris: Gallimard, 1986).

25. Since the Independence Movement of 1919 and the genocide of the Korean residents in the aftermath of the Kanto earthquake in 1923, the Japanese leadership was preoccupied with a possible mutiny of the colonized. We must not forget that to integrate the Koreans into the Japanese military meant giving them arms. In due course the Japanese army had to carefully distribute soldiers from Korea in such a way that they would never constitute the majority. See Higuchi Yûichi, *Kôgun heishi ni sareta chôsenjin* [Koreans who were made the emperor's soldiers] (Tokyo, 1991), 89–93.

26. One can find exemplary arguments in the following work: Pearl Buck, *American*

Unity and Asia (New York: John Day Company, 1942); and Rayford W. Logan, *What the Negro Wants* (Chapel Hill: University of North Carolina Press, 1944).

27. Let us go back, one more time, to the arguments that today we grant the status of classics: Étienne Balibar and Immanuel Wallerstein, *Race, Nation, Class—Ambiguous Identities* (New York: Verso, 1991); and Étienne Balibar, "Racism as Universalism," in *Masses, Classes, Ideas*, trans. James Swenson (New York: Routledge, 1994), 191–204.

28. Edwin Reischauer was also involved in the postwar treatment of Korean residents in Japan. See Reischauer's foreword to Edward G. Wagner, *The Korean Minority in Japan, 1904–1950* (New York: International Secretariat, Institute of Pacific Relations, 1951).

29. What is noteworthy, in view of the scale of the war that was fought for fifteen years on the Asian continent and in the Pacific, are the small number of war criminal prosecutions in comparison with those in Europe. Cf. Hayashi Hirofumi, *BC kyû senpan saiban* [Prosecutions of class B and C war criminals] (Tokyo: Iwanami Shoten, 2006), 38.

30. Of course, there were important exceptions. In literature, a number of works were published in which the defeat and the decolonization as they affected individuals were described, analyzed, and historicized. Among the writers of these volumes are Takeda Taijun, Ôoka Shôhei, Tamura Ryû'ichi, Kim Shijon, Morisaki Kazue, and Shimao Toshio. Although the problem of war responsibility (among intellectuals, literature, religions, and philosophy) was a central topic in postwar Japanese thought, decolonization was never seriously confronted by Japanese intellectuals in the social sciences and political thought until the 1990s.

31. The crimes committed during the Asia Pacific war by those who were prosecuted as war criminals are usually classified as class A (crimes against peace), class B (war crimes by customary definitions—the Hague and Geneva conventions), and class C (war crimes against humanity). A total of 27 Japanese political, military, and government leaders—7 of whom were actually executed—were prosecuted in class A, and 5,700 Japanese nationals—inclusive of those from the annexed territories—were prosecuted in class B. Class C, however, was not applied to the Japanese (Hirofumi, *BC kyû senpan saiban*). Edwin Reischauer, in "Memorandum on Policy towards Japan," argued for the pardoning of Emperor Hirohito:

> The possible role of the Japanese Emperor in the post-war rehabilitation of the Japanese mentality has definite bearing upon the present situation. To keep the Emperor available as a valuable ally or puppet in the post-war ideological battle we must keep him unsullied by the present war. In other words, we cannot allow him to be portrayed to the American people as the counterpart of Hitler and Mussolini in Asia or as the personification of the Japanese brand of totalitarianism. General reviling of the Emperor by our press or radio can easily ruin his utility to us in the post-war world. It would make the American people unprepared to cooperate with him or even to accept him as a tool. And naturally it would make the Emperor himself and the men who surround him less ready to cooperate with our government. During the past several months there has been considerable use of the name Hirohito as a symbol of the evil Japanese system. With the post-war problem in mind, it would be highly advisable for the government to induce the news-disseminating organs of this country to avoid reference to the Emperor as far as possible and to use individuals, such as Tôjô or Yamamoto or even a mythical toothsome Mr. Motto (in uniform!) as personifications of the Japan we are fighting.

32. See Satoshi Ukai, "The Future of an Affect: The Historicity of Shame," *Traces* 1 (2001).

33. The most noteworthy publication among the Japanese rightists was Iris Chang, *The Rape of Nanking: The Forgotten Holocaust of World War II* (New York: Basic Books, 1997). Carol Gluck provides a concise summary of the politics of memory concerning Chang's book and Comfort Women; see Carol Gluck, "Operation of Memory: 'Comfort Women' and the World," in *Kindai nihon no bunkashi* [Cultural history of modern Japan] (Tokyo: Iwanami Shoten, 2002), 8:191–234.

34. See *Bangumi wa naze kaizan saretaka, NHK ETV jiken no shinsô* [Why was the program distorted? The hidden truth of the NHK ETV incident] (Tokyo: Impaction Inc., 2006).

35. See Abe Shinzô, *Utsukushii kuni e* [Toward a beautiful country] (Tokyo: Bungei Shunjû, 2006). Abe cites Kevin Doak, an American Japan expert known for his anticommunism and antimodernity, to endorse Koizumi's and Abe's visit to the Yasukuni Shrine. Perhaps he regards Japan experts such as Doak as representative of U.S. public opinion (74). The endorsement is mutual and illustrates the typical structure of United States–Japan complicity that was anachronistic by 2006. Doak also writes for *Sankei Shimbun,* the right-wing newspaper, endorsing Koizumi's and Abe's visits to the Yasukuni Shrine and their jingoistic views. Cf. Kevin Doak, in *Seiron* [Voice], September 2006, no. 345, 82–89.

36. Etô Jun wrote a series of articles about the censorship exercised by the U.S. Occupation Administration. See Etô Jun, "Wasureta koto to wasuresaserareta koto" [What we forgot and what we were made to forget], *Shokun,* April, May, June, August, September, and October 1979; and Etô, *Tozasareta gengo kûkan* [Closed language space] (Tokyo: Bungeishunjû sha, 1989).

37. *M. Butterfly* (David Cronenberg dir., 1993) is outstanding because of the allegorical implications it expresses. This film, based on the stage play of the same title, is also evocative of the emotive structure of knowledge production in area studies. *Amae* is often translated as "dependency" and derives from its verb form, *amaeru.* It became a well-known psychoanalytical term through its use in Takeo Doi, *Amae no kôzô* [The anatomy of dependence: The key analysis of Japanese behavior] (1971), trans. John Bester (Tokyo: Kodansha International, 1981). Doi argued, in an analysis of the verb *amaeru,* that the word discloses the behavior of a person attempting to induce an authority figure, such as a parent, spouse, or teacher, to take care of him. The verb is applied descriptively to the behavior of a person in an interpersonal relation. The person of *amae* may beg or plead, or alternatively act selfishly, while secure in the knowledge that the caregiver will forgive. Doi's argument has a strong culturalist orientation.

38. The Status of Forces Agreement is an abbreviation of the "Agreement under Article VI of the Treaty of Mutual Cooperation and Security between Japan and the United States of America, Regarding Facilities and Areas and the Status of United States Military Forces in Japan." The agreement was originally promulgated in 1952 and re-signed in 1960.

39. Of course, this behavior occurs not only in Japan but also in other countries that accommodate large U.S. military bases.

40. Rapes by American soldiers are reported almost routinely in Okinawa, where some 70 percent of the U.S. military facilities in Japan are concentrated. Because of the extraterritoriality enjoyed by American military personnel in Japan, it is difficult for Japanese police to prevent American soldiers from committing crimes in Japan.

41. Chalmers Johnson, *The Sorrows of Empire* (New York: Metropolitan Books, 2004).

42. The idea of the East Asian Community in the 1930s requires a chapter of its own. After the Malaysian government's initiative in 1990, there have been a number of proposals for the East Asian Community. Most explicit among the intellectuals who advocate the formation of the East Asian Community are Kang Sangjung, resident Korean political scientist in Japan, and Chen Kuanhsing, literary critic in Taiwan.

43. See Naoki Sakai, the introduction to *Translation and Subjectivity.* Also see Naoki Sakai and Jon Solomon, "Introduction: Addressing the Multitude of Foreigners, Echoing Foucault," and "Appendix: Sovereign Police, Global Complicity: Addressing the Multitude of Foreigners," in *Translation, Biopolitics, Colonial Difference,* ed. Naoki Sakai and Jon Solomon, Traces series (Hong Kong: Hong Kong University Press, 2006) 4:1–35, 333–36.

44. Cf. Naoki Sakai, "Imperial Nationalisms and the Comparative Perspective," *Positions: East Asia Cultures Critique* 17, no. 1 (2009): 159–207.

PART III

NINE

War in Several Tongues

Nations, Languages, Genres

Wai Chee Dimock

Where exactly to draw the lines around American studies? Should the field be nation-based, matching the jurisdiction of the territorial state, beginning and ending within its recognized borders? Is the adjective "American" fully self-sufficient, able to stand on its own, giving us an archive, an analytic prism, and a research program that can sustain a forward momentum, a web of relations opening into the world?

NATION AS CONTAINER

Janice Radway, in her presidential address to the American Studies Association in 1998, raises all of these questions and answers with a resounding no. She proposes a name change for the association for just that reason. A field calling itself "American" imagines that there is something exceptional about the United States, manifesting itself as "a distinctive set of properties and themes in all things American, whether individuals, institutions, or cultural products."[1] This premise of exceptionalism translates into a methodology that privileges the nation above all else, affirming it as a conceptual foundation, a criterion of membership underwriting and regulating an entire intellectual field.[2] The latter can legitimize itself as a field only because the nation does the legitimizing. Disciplinary sovereignty and territorial sovereignty go hand in hand. Against this conflation of nation and field, Radway proposes a rigorous decoupling, a deliberate emphasis on the *noncoincidence* between the two. The nation has solid borders; the field, on the other hand, is fluid and amorphous, shaped and re-shaped by emerging forces, by "intricate interdependencies" between "the near and far, the local and the distant." In short, the "Americanist" field, as a domain of inquiry, needs to be kept clearly distinct from the nation as a jurisdictional regime. Its vitality resides in a carefully maintained and carefully theorized zone, a penumbra intervening between it and the conceptual foreclosure dictated by its name. That penumbra makes the field open rather than closed: "It suggests that far from being conceived on the model of a container—that is, as a particular kind of hollowed out object with evident edges or skin enclosing certain organically uniform contents—territories and geographies need to be reconceived as spatially situated and intricately intertwined networks of social relationships that tie specific locales to particular histories."[3] Radway's challenge to the "container" model turns the United States from a discrete entity into an open network, with no tangible edges, its circumference being continually negotiated, its crisscrossing pathways continually modified by local input, local inflections. These dynamic exchanges suggest that the American field has never been unified and will never be.[4]

Still, though not self-contained, the nation remains procedurally central for Radway: it is a first-order phenomenon, a primary field of inquiry. If it is no longer a "hollowed out object" filled with contents unique to it and homogenized within it, it remains an object so foundational to American studies that it might even be said to be the field's *disciplinary subject*. Conceptually front and center, this subject signs its name into the length and breadth of the field, delimiting its scale and scope. The field is its bildungsroman, so to speak, coterminous with its life span, its jealously guarded borders and chronology.

Can American studies ever free itself from this subject? Can it partake of other networks, constitute itself out of other relations? It is helpful here to have the perspective from an adjacent field—history—where the protocol of the discipline has been under a different kind of scrutiny. Prasenjit Duara's *Rescuing History from the Nation* is a case in point. Duara's avowed purpose is "to decouple the deep, tenacious, and . . . repressive connection" between an intellectual discipline and a territorial regime. The latter is not only that—territorial—but ephemeral for just that reason. For "the rapidity with which nations are being formed, destroyed, and reformed" makes them the shakiest of foundations. Rather than forcing history inside this ill-behaved and demonstrably unreliable container, Duara makes a plea for a different mapping of the discipline, leaving room for a different kind of subject: "My principal argument is that national history secures for the contested and contingent nation the false unity of a self-same, national subject evolving through time. . . . Within this schema, the nation appears as the newly realized, sovereign subject of History, embodying a moral and political force that has overcome dynasties, aristocracies, and ruling priests and mandarins, who are seen to represent merely themselves historically."[5] Nations are fabricated things, with an identity all too prominent but no less spurious. They are not natural subjects, even though some of us make them look as if they were, as if each were some kind of personality, with a "national character," attributes individualized at any given moment, and a sovereign self-sameness maintained across time. The Chinese nation—a deceptively unified name given to a vast array of languages and cultures—is a spurious subject of just this sort. Even apart from this glaring example, however, all fields of history—and indeed all fields of the humanities—tend to personify the nation in some way, attributing to it an origin, a date of birth, and a story of growth and development.[6] Personification of this sort turns a territorial unit into the prime agent of history. It turns scholars into partisan specialists, trained to do no more than show how that agent works. And, for American studies, it leads to this automatic assumption—to study the United States, we need go no farther than the United States—surely a tautology if ever there is one.

MULTILATERAL WAR

Tautologies come at a cost: anything that fails to replicate their shape tends to disappear into the woodwork. National biographies thus impose a weighted kind of bookkeeping, telling us what counts and what does not, "which people and cultures belonged to the time of History and who and what had to be eliminated."[7] The erasures and distortions are considerable. Rather than accepting these as necessary casualties, and rather than taking the nation as the default unit, it is worth exploring alternate landscapes that contest this mode of census taking. This task may be one of the most critical now facing the field.[8] How to pry history away from the self-centeredness of the territorial state? What genres of writing would emerge? And what would a multilateral world truly look like?

I address these questions through the phenomenon of war, a favorite subject of national biographies, and one especially susceptible to unilateral accounts. To avoid these almost congenital pitfalls, what kind of alternate archives do we need to put together? How many languages should we consult or hold ourselves accountable for? And what is the scale of this undertaking, what kind of time frame and geographical coordinates do we need to build a platform different from the customary reach of American studies? At the risk of being schematic, I propose three words to make up a conceptual grid for this endeavor: multinational, multilingual, and multigeneric. Let me flesh these out a bit more.

First, even though most of us would probably always be looking at war only from one side, which is to say, through a national lens, there is no reason to assume that the material we look at should be defined exclusively by this lens. In fact, it makes sense to construct an archive that is self-consciously broader, representing the point of view of more than just one player. Once we've made this decision, our archive will have to open up, will have to become less partisan, and more truly experimental, proceeding along pathways that are empirically generated rather than preassigned, and following them even if they take us to unlikely places.

Second, even though most of us from English departments would probably always be reading about war in just one language, there should be no automatic assumption that this one language would suffice, that it could encompass the full range of pertinent material. On the contrary, it seems reasonable to assume that, on such a contested subject, many linguistic windows would open up, pointing to many texts, many bodies of evidence, beyond what is available in English. Without unrealistic hopes about our linguistic competence, it is possible to acknowledge these diverse languages and the life worlds revolving around them, and to do so in full recognition of the problem of access. These languages are beyond most of us in more than a technical sense. And that is precisely the point. To realize just how hard it is to get to them, to have some idea of what our native tongue cannot convey, is surely one of the most powerful intellectual jolts we can get. At the same time, it must be said as well that the English language is actually more supple, more open to new input, and therefore more rich and various, than we usually give it credit for. Its experiment with other languages—quoting, translating, and playing with various accented foreign words—suggests that what we are dealing with is not a flat landscape but a layered formation, with two or more languages stacked on top of one another. Multilingualism flourishes even on a monolingual platform. Needless to say, this is especially interesting in the context of war, when these different linguistic layers could be pulling in opposite, partisan directions.

Finally, if one of the challenges in thinking about war is to give some sense of a vast and shadowy field beyond the default language, one of the most helpful concepts to highlight this fact is the concept of genre. After all, genres are historically (and perhaps by their very nature) multilingual, with ample representation across all human tongues, across all the world's populations. It is impossible to count the number of languages that inhabit the genre of epic, or lyric, or, most obviously, the novel. To map the phenomenon of war against the linguistic diversity of genres is to come up with a rich and, to some extent, emerging landscape, not predictable ahead of time, and perhaps not even populated by objects that we can easily classify.

It is this rich and emerging landscape that I explore through the concept of migration. And migration, in this context, can be understood in more ways than one. First, I am obviously interested in the variation across languages, the changing face of war as it moves from tongue to tongue.

Second, even as we look at these cross-lingual trajectories, by and large a horizontal movement, we may also want to think about a vertical movement that accompanies it: a percolating action, going up and down, and going back and forth between the high and the low. This kind of migration allows for a continual exchange, a continual "streaming," between different levels of cultural elevation, between canonical works and popular genres. It suggests that Brownian motion is central to our field, and that it does not make sense to look at works only on one level. In the context of war, this means that we have to be especially alert to what I call the "quantum possibility" of foreign words: they don't always just move sideways into another language but can make a leap, jump to a different tonal register, morph from highbrow to lowbrow.

Finally, given this combination of up-and-down movement with cross-lingual movement, a third kind of migration comes to the foreground as well. It is the one I focus on the most, namely, the migration from poetry to prose, or, more specifically, the citational presence of epic and lyric in contemporary fiction. This embedded poetry is of course put to work in a different way, sometimes enlarged and sometimes miniaturized, and showing us not only the different sides to a war but also the different scales on which war can be witnessed. This kind of movement suggests that the standard division of the curriculum into poetry and prose might be unduly limiting, blinding us to the continual *breakdown* of that dividing line, a breakdown generating new and unclassifiable works. What I propose, then, is a more fluid, multigeneric continuum, as the bare minimum for the explosive subject of war, one that allows poetry and prose to commingle, and that invites us to think about switchability and scalability as crucial dynamics in human conflict.

As it happens, many of these questions are already being dramatized in *Inglourious Basterds*, Quentin Tarantino's film that opened across the United States in August 2009. This film is a self-professed hybrid, a cross between the revenge war genre and the spaghetti western. Its chief protagonist, Hans Landa, a Waffen-SS officer, also turns out to be a walking example of multilingualism, moving effortlessly from German to French, English, and Italian. Although it is debatable whether the film is casting a parodic eye on nationalism or simply trading in its refracted currency, it gives a vivid demonstration of what the terrain of war looks like when it is remapped in linguistic and generic terms. Using this example as a reference point, both negative and positive, I take the remapping one step further. One kind of alternative history already emerges in Tarantino's film; I want to see what other kinds may emerge if other popular genres—say, science fiction—are thrown into the mix.

ALIEN SPACE

Science fiction, of course, has always been a multigeneric, and indeed mul-
timedia, phenomenon. It is not just text based but also a strong presence
in film and television. It has other advantages as well, especially when it
comes to the subject of war. Because this genre is not bound by the actual
outcome of history, not bound by the standard account of winners and losers, heroes and villains, it is free to assign blame in more complex ways.
Science fiction only has one leg in the "real" world, the world empirically
reported by our senses. Its other leg is quite literally somewhere else, off to
a space-time that is in no way a mirror image of the world as we know it—
because the whole point of science fiction is to depict an alien space, one
that violates, in some fundamental way, the condition we call "normal."
Darko Suvin says that science fiction is a literature of "cognitive estrangement."[9] The estrangement can begin with futuristic technologies and then
extend to the entire semantic field, bending and shifting all our customary
moorings. Science fiction is antinaturalistic in this sense: it does not allow
any version of the "natural" to naturalize itself. It has a switch mechanism that engages the world counterfactually, turning its "objective" coordinates into an otherworldly landscape, a virtual platform where business
as usual breaks down, where the ordinarily invisible rules of everyday life
are suspended and rendered visible by that suspension. This antinaturalistic impulse suggests that, of all prose genres, science fiction might be the
one that is most akin to poetry. In fact it might be seen as a long-distance
cousin of epic, a genre that also has a crucial antinaturalistic dimension,
routinely sending its protagonists into virtual spaces, populated by gods,
demons, monsters, and other creatures who are not exactly "normal."

This essay is not the place to lay out a full-blown theory about science
fiction and epic. What I do instead is take a short cut and look at one particular example that wears its poetic genealogy on its sleeve: the novel *Inferno* (1976), by the Hugo Award–winning team of Larry Niven and Jerry
Pournelle.[10] The book is dedicated to Dante, so we know right away that
this is science fiction with a pedigree. And the pedigree is not just orna-
mental; it is structural, reproducing the same, dual-protagonist structure
of Dante's *Inferno*. Dante does not go through hell by himself. He is accompanied by someone else, a companion, a guide—Virgil—referred to sometimes as the *maestro*, master, and sometimes as the *duca*, leader.[11] Niven and
Pournelle repeat this structure. Their protagonist, Allen Carpentier, also
has a companion, a guide, by name of Benito. And one of first things these
two do together is to talk about Dante's *Inferno*.

I remembered then. "Dante's *Inferno*?"
Benito nodded, his big square jaw heaving like a
broaching whale. "You have read the *Inferno*, then.
Good. That was the first clue I had to the way out of
here. We must go down—" (22)

Who is this Benito? That turns out to be the central mystery in Niven and
Pournelle. Bits of information are given to us along the way. We found out,
just now, that Benito has a big square jaw jutting out. We are told that he
speaks "with an accent: Mediterranean; Spanish perhaps, or Italian" (15).
He seems to know Dante's *Inferno* very well; it also seems that, when alive,
he was used to giving commands.

The secret is revealed at the end of the book, when the two compan-
ions get to the very bottom of hell, the Bolgia of the Evil Counselors. The
sinners here are those public figures who used their power of persuasion
to push through evil policies; as punishment, they have been turned into
tongues of flame that burn even as they speak:

"Come down!" one of the flames called to Benito.
It was eerily compelling. That thrumming voice. The
tip of the flame wavered, turned to me. "Throw him
down, you, if you're an American! That's Mussolini!
Benito Mussolini!"
Jolted, I turned to Benito. He shrugged.
Mussolini?
Another voice thrummed from the pit. "You *are*
American. I know your accent. Do you understand?
That's Mussolini! Throw the bastard down here where
he belongs!"
"Who are you?"
"Does it matter? I approved the firebombing of
Dresden." (188)

The genealogy linking Niven and Pournelle's *Inferno* back to Dante's *Inferno* is indeed a world genealogy, because World War II turns out to be the
subtext. But it is not the official, naturalized version of World War II. Instead, it is a version turned on its head, its coordinates completely switched
around. In this version, Winston Churchill is not the hero who saved the
world. He is the villain who is guilty of a heinous war crime, who approved the firebombing of Dresden. Niven and Pournelle have put him
into the very bottom of hell. It is Benito, Benito Mussolini, who is a second
Virgil, a dependable guide, someone who, in this rewriting of Dante's *In-*

ferno, has a second chance, a chance to vindicate himself and redeem himself for posterity.

ALTERNATE HISTORIES

To understand this switch, we need a multigeneric history of the world. This history would include not only epic and science fiction, but also other, newly genre-bending books, such as *Human Smoke* by Nicholson Baker. Baker, always known as an author of unclassifiable works, has recently written another one that is even more of a surprise: a big book, 566 pages, titled *Human Smoke,* on World War II.[12] Another surprise is that, although the book is about World War II, it actually ends on December 31, 1941, well before the war ends. And it ends with these words: "I dedicate this book to the memory of Clarence Pickett and other American and British pacifists. . . . They failed, but they were right." Clearly this is not your usual history of the war. Instead, it is something like a counterfactual mediation, giving voice to those who wanted the war not to have happened, and casting aspersion on those who made that impossible. Churchill is foremost among that group. To see how this impossibility crystallized into a hard fact, Baker goes back to World War I, to Churchill's decision, as the First Lord of the Admiralty, to run a blockade of Germany. He had justified that action with these words: "The British blockade treated the whole of Germany as if it were a beleaguered fortress, and avowedly sought to starve the whole population—men, women, and children, old and young, wounded and sound—into submission."[13]

Churchill's philosophy is a philosophy of victory at all costs, a philosophy of total war. It treats the whole of the Germany as one killing field, making no distinction, as he says, between civilian populations and military personnel, between those who are sick and wounded and those are doing the actual fighting. This was a winning strategy for him, so it is not surprising that, going into World War II, he would want to have a replay of this macro-rule of engagement. Just as he had once been a staunch proponent of the naval blockade, he would now be a staunch proponent of aerial bombardment. Aerial bombardment is the literal enactment of the bird's-eye view. From that distance, and on that scale, of course it was impossible to tell the civilians from the military, and indeed the point was not to. In World War II, the norm of combat, for Great Britain no less than for Germany, was to raise indiscrimination to an art, to destroy whole cities, whole populations, as tiny dots that could be wiped out on a large canvas. To the extent that this action could be understood as criminal, Hitler certainly had no monopoly; Churchill had a liberal share of it as well.

Niven and Pournelle's *Inferno* seems to have anticipated Baker's *Human Smoke*. The cumulative weight of these two would in turn point to a new genre, something like "alternative histories of World War II," a genre that is now almost reaching critical mass, thanks to a spate of new work by British historians, many of whom are seeing Churchill in the same light as he was once seen by many of his contemporaries, including E. D. Morel and Sir Basil Bartlett, as "a personal force for evil," "inflammatory," "unscrupulous," and "surrounded by corpses."[14] Niven and Pournelle's *Inferno* would not be out of place in that scholarly company. It is science fiction, to be sure, but it *could* wear other labels quite comfortably. Switchability, in other words, seems to be a capability built into every text, activated whenever we put it in a new kinship network. And there is no reason to limit that kinship network to English. Indeed, given the crucial Dante genealogy for Niven and Pournelle, it seems especially important to go outside the English-speaking world, to consult archives in Italian. One such archive is the over 6,000-page, seven-volume biography of Mussolini by the distinguished Italian historian Renzo De Felice, published between 1965 and 1998. According to this massive research, Fascism as a movement was historically very different from Fascism as a regime, and in both stages needs to be distinguished from the German National Socialism.[15] Mussolini was by no means a fool, a knave, or a lackey of Hitler's. He was instead a tragic figure, someone whose horrendous end was not so much a foregone conclusion as a cruel perversion of the radical syndicalism that he had championed in his early career.[16]

Niven and Pournelle may or may not have looked at that archive. For them, however, there is an easier way to give Mussolini a second chance, a chance to insert himself into a new narrative. The kernel of that narrative is planted in a direct link between him and Virgil. It is a direct link, but to recognize it, we need to make another switch: we need to bracket English and, for a second, think in another language, using whatever primitive Italian we have at our disposal. In Italian, the *Duca* that was Virgil has simply morphed into the *Duce, il Duce,* that is Mussolini. And the switch is more than just a switch to another language; it is, even more fundamentally, a switch in allegiance. This is World War II told from the other side. For most Anglo-American readers, this is alternative history with a vengeance, a complete rewriting of the official story, even as it rewrites the outcome of Dante's *Inferno*.

This kind of switch suggests that literature is indeed a percolating field, full of upheavals and reversals. The movement of the heart is part of that dynamics. This switch in allegiance is probably not something we would feel comfortable about. It is literally an alienation of affection, turning patriotism into a face strange and scary. Science fiction, a genre traditionally inhabited by aliens, is no doubt a logical place for this alienation to happen. It achieves this effect by resurrecting a genre we may not expect it to—a poetic genre, more ancient, more honored, but also antinaturalistic and without apology, because for it this is simply a matter of convention. Taking the relation between these two as a nontrivial path of generic migration, I look at one other work that may also serve as a way station, Kurt Vonnegut's *Slaughterhouse-Five*.[17]

Slaughterhouse-Five is most famous, of course, as an antiwar novel. Vonnegut, after all, minces no words about where he stands: on the title page, he identifies himself as a "fourth-generation German-American," and ten pages into the book, he tells us that this is a "book about Dresden. It wasn't a famous air raid back then in America. Not many Americans know how much worse it had been than Hiroshima, for instance. I didn't know that, either. There hadn't been much publicity" (10).

What most of us tend to forget, though, is that *Slaughterhouse-Five* is also a science fiction novel, complete with time travel and trips to an alien planet, with its protagonist, Billy Pilgrim, sometimes being transported by a flying saucer to a planet named Tralfamadore, 446,120,000,000,000,000 miles from earth, and sometimes being hurtled back twenty years and finding himself once again a POW, in Dresden, just when that city was firebombed by the British Bomber Command. Why is the story of Dresden once again the stuff for science fiction? Is there something about this genre that makes it especially hospitable not only to mass catastrophe but also to an alternative history growing out of that catastrophe? And if this alternative history calls for a backward journey to Dante's *Inferno* for Niven and Pournelle, is there another epic that is being revisited by Vonnegut?

As it happens, Billy Pilgrim's hometown, the place where he grew up and where he comes back to live, is called Ilium, so there's no way to look away from this particular epic lineage. And the *Iliad* seems to be the logical template for the destruction of Dresden in *Slaughterhouse-Five*. After all, isn't Homer's epic about the destruction of a city, a city that it identifies not by its Greek name, Troy, but by its Trojan name, Ilium?

Well, the answer is actually no. The destruction of Troy is certainly on everyone's mind, and there is plenty of blood and gore in the *Iliad*, but, like Nicholson Baker's *Human Smoke*, Homer's epic also stops short, cutting off the narrative well before what readers would call the "real" ending. It ends not with the massacre of the Trojan population but with a much smaller event, on an entirely different scale: the burial of Hector:

> Then they collected the white bones of Hector—
> all his brothers, his friends-in-arms, mourning.
> They placed the bones they found in a golden chest,
> shrouding them round and round in soft purple cloths.
> They quickly lowered the chest in a deep, hollow grave
> and over it piled a cope of huge stones closely set,
> then hastily heaped a barrow, posted lookouts all around
> for fear the Achaean combat troops would launch their attack
> before the time agreed. And once they'd heaped the mound
> they turned back home to Troy, and gathering once again
> they shared a splendid funeral feast in Hector's honor,
> held in the house of Priam, king by will of Zeus.
> And so the Trojans buried Hector breaker of horses.[18]

The burial of Hector can take place only because Achilles has granted the Trojans a truce. The truce will end soon, however, perhaps sooner than Achilles had said, which is why the burial has to be done hastily, with sentries posted all around. Still, it is a proper burial for Hector; his bones are wrapped in purple cloths and put in a golden chest, and there is a funeral feast afterward in Priam's house. These small details are important, and, at least for now, they seem to keep the large-scale catastrophe at bay. The telling of that catastrophe is left to another genre. It is a task Euripides will take up in his three Trojan tragedies, *Hecuba, Andromache,* and *The Women of Troy.* Epic, unlike tragedy, is haunted by the knowledge of catastrophe but nonetheless insists on being an antistructure. It stays shy of its fully scripted but also never-arrived-at "real" ending, offering us instead an alternative moment, a miniaturized moment, an almost counterfactual stopping of time, allowing the human need to mourn to come to the foreground, and to do so on the smallest possible scale.

Kurt Vonnegut chooses to do this as well in *Slaughterhouse-Five.* For a book that bills itself as being about Dresden, there is actually very little about the city when it is destroyed. And for good reason. Because the American POWs are held in a meat locker at the slaughterhouse, they are safe, and when the high-explosive bombs fall, all they can hear are the footsteps of giants walking and walking (177). When the firestorm finally subsides, all the POWs can see is that Dresden is "like the moon now, nothing but minerals" (178), with no organic life left. All of this, in just a couple of paragraphs. Then the novel leaves the year 1945 abruptly behind, jumping ahead twenty years as Billy Pilgrim is transported by his involuntary time-travel, transported back to his hometown, Ilium.

Ilium is Vonnegut's hometown as well, not least in the antistructure of time that his novel inherits from the epic. Rather than proceeding "normally," which is to say, in a sensible chronological sequence, time is acting here as if it were out its mind, as if it had been driven crazy by the terrible event that it could not bear to look upon. Here is what Vonnegut says: this novel "is so short and jumbled and jangled ... because there is nothing intelligent to say about a massacre. Everybody is supposed to be dead, to never say or want anything ever again" (19). Because those who are killed by the firebombing are forever silent, what they went through must also remain a void, a space emptied of language. It is almost as if the catastrophe were some kind of black hole, sucking everything in, but releasing nothing, letting nothing out. Science fiction is the appropriate genre to represent this black hole—but representing it in two ways: as a void, and also as a tiny space outside of that void, a brief arrested moment outside of that destructive orbit. True to its epic template, *Slaughterhouse-Five* is marked both by an unstoppable calamity and by some small details that allow it to rescale that calamity and to perform its mourning on that basis. One such rescaling happens shortly after the destruction of the city, when Billy Pilgrim is left alone in a horse-drawn wagon, sunning himself while the other POWs go in search of souvenirs among the charred bodies. This moment is actually a happy one for Billy; he is snoozing away. But then something happens:

> Now his snoozing became shallower as he heard a man and a woman speaking German in pitying tones. The speakers were commiserating with somebody lyrically. . . . Billy opened his eyes. A middle-aged man and wife were crooning to the horses. They were noticing what the Americans had not noticed—that the horses' mouths were bleeding, gashed by the bits, that the horses' hooves were broken, so that every step meant agony, that the horses were insane with thirst. The Americans had treated their form of transportation as though it were no more sensitive than a six-cylinder Chevrolet. (196)

The bleeding mouths of the horses and their broken hooves are registered on the same scale as the purple cloths and golden chest that attend Hector's burial. It is the same scale on which Billy hears the "lyrically" pitying tones of the German couple. This lyrical couple "made Billy get out of the wagon and come look at the horses. When Billy saw the condition of his means of transportation, he burst into tears. He hadn't cried about anything else in the war" (197).

The emotional release here suggests that the black hole is not all, that the void is not all, that there is an antistructure running counter to its structure of mass extermination. Vonnegut even has a name for it: lyric. *This* genre has never been absent, not in the *Iliad*, and not in *Slaughterhouse-Five*. The epic can switch into this alternative genre, just as it can switch into another language, and over onto another side. This is the other face of war, history told from the other side—history that will never make its way into any military report, or into any standard account of World War II. It is left to a science fiction novel, deviating flagrantly from the national frame (as it also does from empirical reality), to capture this truth that would otherwise have vanished without a trace. This is what American studies looks like when it is allowed to be both less than American and more than American, when it is reconstituted as a genealogy of sorrow that takes in the whole world: multilingual, multinational, and multigeneric.

Notes

1. Janice Radway, "What's in a Name? Presidential Address to the American Studies Association," November 20, 1998, *American Quarterly* 51 (March 1999): 1-32, quotation at 4.

2. See also Michael Kammen, "The Problem of American Exceptionalism: A Reconsideration," *American Quarterly* 45 (March 1993): 1-43.

3. Radway, "What's in a Name?" 10, 15.

4. For important collections that affirm the multicultural nature of the United States, see, for instance, David Palumbo-Liu, ed., *The Ethnic Canon: Histories, Institutions, and Interventions* (Minneapolis: University of Minnesota Press, 1995); Avery F. Gordon and Christopher Newfield, eds., *Mapping Multiculturalism* (Minneapolis: University of Minnesota Press, 1996); Rob Wilson and Wimal Dissanayake, eds., *Global/Local: Cultural Production and the Transnational Imaginary* (Durham, NC: Duke University Press, 1996); David Palumbo-Liu and Hans Ulrich Gumbrecht, eds., *Streams of Cultural Capital* (Stanford: Stanford University Press, 1997); Lisa Lowe and David Lloyd, eds., *The Politics of Culture in the Shadow of Capital* (Durham, NC: Duke University Press, 1997); and John Carlos Rowe, ed., *Post-National American Studies* (Berkeley: University of California Press, 2000).

5. Prasenjit Duara, *Rescuing History from the Nation: Questioning Narratives of Modern China* (Chicago: University of Chicago Press, 1995), 4.

6. For two important critiques of this nation-based humanities, see Geoffrey Galt Harpham, "Between Humanity and the Homeland," and Thomas Bender, "The Boundaries and Constituencies of History," both in *American Literary History* 18, no. 2 (Summer 2006): 245-61 and 267-82, respectively.

7. Duara, *Rescuing History from the Nation,* 5. For a discussion of the way the nation aggregates *out* subnational peoples and cultures, see my article, Wai Chee Dimock, "Scales of Aggregation: Prenational, Subnational, Transnational," *American Literary History* 18, no. 2 (Summer 2006): 219-28.

8. For alternate geographies, see, for instance, Sheila Hones and Julia Leyda, "Geographies of American Studies," *American Quarterly* 57 (December 2005): 1019-32; and Donald E. Pease, "The Extraterritoriality of the Literature for Our Planet," *ESQ* 50 (2004): 177-221. For alternate histories, see especially Thomas Bender, ed., *Rethinking American History in a Global Age* (Berkeley: University of California Press, 2002).

9. Darko Suvin, *Metamorphoses of Science Fiction: On the Poetics and History of a Literary Genre* (New Haven: Yale University Press, 1979).

10. Larry Niven and Jerry Pournelle, *Inferno* (New York: Pocket Books, 1976). All page references to this edition are in parentheses in the text.

11. In *Inferno* 1:85, for instance, Dante addresses Virgil: "Tu se' lo mio maestro e 'l mio autore" (You are my master and my author). In *Inferno* 3:94, Dante writes: "E 'l duca lui: 'Caron, no ti curcciare'" (And my leader: "Charon, do not torment yourself").

12. Nicholson Baker, *Human Smoke: The Beginning of World War II, the End of Civilization* (New York: Simon and Schuster, 2008).

13. As quoted ibid., 4.

14. Geoffrey Wheatcroft, "Churchill and His Myths," *New York Review of Books*, May 29, 2008.

15. Needless to say, Renzo De Felice's own work has also come under considerable criticism, especially by Giulano Troccaci, Paolo Alatri, and Nicola Tranfaglia. For accounts of his place in Italian historiography, see Michael Ledeen, "Renzo De Felice and the Controversy over Italian Fascism," *Journal of Contemporary History* 11 (1976): 269–83; Borden Painter, "Renzo De Felice and the Historiography of Italian Fascism," *American Historical Review* 95 (1990): 391–405; Emilio Gentile, "Renzo de Felice: A Tribute," *Journal of Contemporary History* 32 (1997): 139–51.

16. James A. Gregor, *Young Mussolini and the Intellectual Origins of Fascism* (Berkeley: University of California Press, 1979).

17. Kurt Vonnegut, *Slaughterhouse-Five* (1969; reprint, New York: Dell, 1991). All page references to this edition are in parentheses in the text.

18. Homer, *The Iliad*, trans. Robert Fagles (New York: Penguin, 1990), 614.

TEN

Neo-Orientalism

Ali Behdad and Juliet Williams

In his preface to the twenty-fifth anniversary edition of *Orientalism*, Edward Said bemoans the fact that since the publication of his seminal book in 1978, nothing has changed in the way European and American representations of the Middle East depict "the contemporary societies of the Arab and Muslim for their backwardness, lack of democracy, and abrogation of women's rights."[1] Indeed, the "general understanding of the Middle East, the Arabs, and Islam," he argues, has considerably worsened, at least in the United States, since the publication of *Orientalism*. He writes, "In the United States, the hardening of attitudes, the tightening of the grip of demeaning generalization and triumphalist cliché, the dominance of crude power allied with simplistic contempt for dissenters and 'others' has found a fitting correlative in the looting, pillaging, and destruction of Iraq's libraries and museums" (xviii). Said is right, of course, about the continued misrepresentations of Arab and Muslim people in Western media and by politicians and political pundits, for, as he observes, even a cursory glance at the shelves of bookstores in the United States reveals how they "are filled with shabby screeds bearing screaming headlines about Islam and terror" (xx). At the same time, Orientalist stereotypes pervade everyday journalism about the region. Consider, as just one example, the following statement by Jeffrey Fleishman, a *Los Angeles Times* staff writer, in a recent story titled "Pursuing Happiness behind the Veil" about the American wife of a Saudi man:

> For American women married to Saudi men, such is life in this *exotic, repressive and often beguiling* society where *tribal customs* and *religious fervor* rub against oil wealth and the tinted-glass skyscrapers that rise Oz-like in the blurry desert heat. This is *not* a land of the 1st Amendment and voting rights; it is a kingdom run by the strict interpretation of Wahhabi Islam, where *abayas* hang in foyers, servants linger like ghosts, minarets glow in green neon and, as a recent court case showed, a woman who is raped can also be sentenced to 200 lashes for un-Islamic behavior."[2]

The nakedly Orientalist claims of this journalist are too obvious to need further elaboration, but it is worth noting in passing that the article does not offer its readers any clue as to why American women, who can benefit from the privileges of the First Amendment, choose to live in such a repressive society. Nor does the story mention the U.S. government's fierce political and military support of the Saudi monarchy, especially during the two Bush administrations.

Yet in spite of such unabashed and unrefined forms of Orientalist representation, one may take issue with Said's claim that nothing has changed in representations of the Middle East in the West, particularly in the United States, during the past three decades. In this essay, we explore a phenomenon we call "neo-Orientalism"—a mode of representation that, while indebted to classical Orientalism, engenders new tropes of othering. Although predominantly a North American phenomenon, neo-Orientalism is not limited to the United States; nor is it merely produced by Western subjects. On the contrary, not only do Middle Eastern writers, scholars, and so-called experts participate in its production, but they play an active and significant role in propagating it. Second, unlike its classical counterpart, neo-Orientalism entails a popular mode of representing, a kind of *doxa* about the Middle East and Muslims that is disseminated, thanks to new technologies of communication, throughout the world. Finally, we designate this mode of representation as *neo* rather than *new* in order to signal the continuity between contemporary and traditional forms of Orientalism. Although the term "neo-Orientalism" designates a shift in the discourse of Orientalism that represents a distinct, and in ways novel formation, it nonetheless entails certain discursive repetitions of and conceptual continuities with its precursor. Like its classical counterpart, for example, neo-Orientalism is monolithic, totalizing, reliant on a binary logic, and based on an assumption of moral and cultural superiority over the Oriental other. To put the point more aphoristically, neo-Orientalism should be understood not as sui generis but rather as a supplement to enduring modes of Orientalist representation.

Focusing for the most part on memoirs by Iranian women recently published in English, we sketch some of the salient features of neo-Orientalism in the United States. First, whereas classical Orientalists were commonly male European savants, philologists, established writers, and artists, neo-Orientalists tend to be ordinary Middle Eastern subjects whose self-proclaimed authenticity sanctions and authorizes their discourses. Contemporary neo-Orientalists are not, however, merely "native informants" or "comprador intellectuals" as Hamid Dabashi and others have suggested,[3] but rather Middle Eastern women and men who use their native subjectivity and newfound agency in the West to render otherwise biased accounts of the region seemly more authoritative and objective. Second, in contrast to classical Orientalism's apparent privileging of philological, cultural, and formalistic concerns over ideological ones, neo-Orientalism is marked by an unapologetic investment in and engagement with the politics of the Middle East. Neo-Orientalists such as Azar Nafisi not only maintain political affiliations with neoconservative institutions such as the Paul H. Nitze School for Advanced International Studies (SAIS), but in their writings as well they pointedly criticize Islamic governments and unapologetically advocate regime change in Iran and other countries in the region. Third, in contrast with classical Orientalism, neo-Orientalism is characterized by an ahistorical form of historicism. While claiming to be attentive to historical changes in the Middle East, neo-Orientalists tend to misrepresent important aspects of recent events in the region while denying the neo-imperialist relation of the United States to the Middle East. Fourth, unlike the "will to knowledge" of classical Orientalism,[4] a journalistic pretense of direct access to truth and the real dominates the current form, as neo-Orientalists deploy superficial empirical observations about Muslim societies and cultures to make great generalizations about them. Fifth, the neo-Orientalist discourse is marked by a redeployment of the trope of the veil as a signifier of oppression. Whereas in classical Orientalism, the veil functioned as a metonymy for the harem, portrayed as a mysterious and inaccessible space of eroticism and lusty sexuality, in neo-Orientalist discourse the veil has been refashioned once again into a symbol of Muslim women's oppression and lack of civil rights and liberties.

In this essay we develop our account of the constitutive features of neo-Orientalism through an analysis of several recently published memoirs by Middle Eastern writers. We then explore the way in which neo-Orientalism perpetuates, develops, and enables gender stereotypes foundational to the Orientalist representational vocabulary. We conclude by considering the distinctive challenges and possibilities available for resisting the cultural ascent of neo-Orientalism

ORIENTAL SUBJECTS, OCCIDENTAL DISCOURSES

In his controversial and much-debated essay "Native Informers and the Making of the American Empire," Hamid Dabashi lambastes what he calls the "comprador native intellectuals" whose role is "to package [the atrocities taking place in their countries of origin] in a manner that serves the belligerent empire best: in the guise of a legitimate critic of localized tyr-

anny facilitating the operation of a far more insidious global domination—
effectively perpetuating (indeed aggravating) the domestic terror they purport to expose" (5). Although one may readily agree with Dabashi's general
point that the such actors "feign authority, authenticity, and native knowledge" as the basis for their participation in the public discourse, Dabashi's
discussion of native informers nonetheless risks exaggerating the inten-
tionality of these authors' complicity with U.S. imperialism by overlooking their agency as self-promoting, if not always self-made, immigrants
who have capitalized on the post-9/11 thirst for knowledge about Muslim
societies to empower themselves and realize their ambitious desires. The
Web page of Roya Hakakian, the author of *Journey from the Land of No:
A Girlhood Caught in Revolutionary Iran*, provides a representative example
of such self-promoting, immigrant entrepreneurship.[5] On the site, she pro-
claims herself an authority on Iranian society and human rights and provides a long list of media appearances, past and future lectures, press releases, and professional affiliations to buttress her credentials as an expert.
Crass though it may be, Hakakian's Web page suggests that far from being
a mere cog or tool in the imperial machinery, she is an ambitious first-
generation immigrant more interested in promoting herself and her work
than in "justifying the imperial designs of the U.S." as Dabashi has it.

What is lacking in Dabashi's political analysis of Azar Nafisi and other
native informers, and what we briefly discuss here by way of elaborat-
ing our argument about the emergence of neo-Orientalism, is a consideration of the distinctive discursive strategy whereby these writers claim
authenticity and authority. Consider the following passage from Nafisi's
Reading Lolita in Tehran: "Those of us living in the Islamic Republic of
Iran grasped both the tragedy and absurdity of the cruelty to which we
were subjected. We had to poke fun at our own misery in order to survive.
We also instinctively recognized poshlust—not just in others, but in ourselves. This was one reason that art and literature became so essential to
our lives: they were not a luxury but a necessity. What Nabokov captured
was the texture of life in a totalitarian society, where you are completely
alone in an illusory world of false promises, where you can no longer differentiate between your savior and your executioner."[6] Neo-Orientalist
authority is an *experiential* form of authority, an authority construed and
claimed not only through having lived in the Middle East but also by having a "feel" for this particular society as a Middle Easterner, a kind of native sense of the people, their culture, and political situation. In contrast to
her Western readers who are being informed about the region, Nafisi here
portrays herself and the women of her reading group as capable of grasping the underlying ethos and neuroses of Iranian culture.

An appeal to experiential authority is prevalent in all the recent memoirs by Middle Eastern writers.[7] To cite another example, in the first pages of *Journey from the Land of No*, Hakakian quickly distinguishes herself from the Americans who speak or write about Iran by describing them as either "the misinformed, who think of Iran as a backward nation of Arabs, veiled and turbaned, living on the periphery of oases and fairly represented by a government of mullahs; and the misguided, who believed the Shah's regime was a puppet government run by the CIA, and who think that Ayatollah Khomeini and his clerical cabal are an authentic, home-grown answer to unwarranted U.S. meddling" (11). In spite of having left Iran soon after the 1979 revolution as a young teenager and never having returned, Hakakian nonetheless fills the pages of her memoir with an account of "what life was like for women after the country fell into the hands of Islamic fundamentalists who had declared an insidious war against them," seen from "the eyes of a strong, youthful optimist who somehow came up in the world believing that she was different, knowing she was special" (back flap of the book cover). The invocation of first-hand experience of Iranian culture by Hakakian and many other young Iranian authors living in America, such as Gelareh Asayesh, Azadeh Moaveni, and Afschineh Latifi, to claim interpretive authority smacks of a crude form of identity politics in which ethnic or racial identity is considered to be in and of itself constitutive of knowledge about a particular ethnicity or race. As a memoir each book claims to be a unique account of a specific Muslim society, and the authors lay claim to knowing and understanding the region and its most common religion—a knowledge that far exceeds their actual contact or experience. In short, in these memoirs claims of experience are made in spite of a lack of concrete perception—the usual basis upon which claims of experiential authority are presumed to lie.

The passages from Hakakian's and Nafisi's memoirs quoted earlier also provide examples of the second characteristic of neo-Orientalism, namely, an unapologetic investment in the politics of the region. In both of the quoted passages, the authors quickly join their personal observations with statements about the political situation in Iran. Unlike traditional Orientalists who maintained at least the pretense of objectivity and scholarly disinterest in current affairs, neo-Orientalists perceive of their discourses as political engagements aimed at liberating the region from tyrannical regimes. Although we would not dispute that many if not most Middle Eastern regimes today justifiably could be labeled oppressive in terms of their disregard for a range of civil rights widely regarded as basic in the West, nor would we take issue with the feminist claim that the personal is the political, we nonetheless find the convergence of personal observations and political statements in these narratives symptomatic of the ideological bent in neo-Orientalist discourse. *Reading Lolita in Tehran* is particularly remarkable as an example of neo-Orientalism's investment in politics. As the subtitle of the book (*A Memoir in Books*) suggests, Nafisi's text interlaces old-fashioned literary criticism of novels by such canonical Western writers as Nabokov, Fitzgerald, James, and Austen with her own and her students' commentary about living in postrevolutionary Iran. Whether discussing literary texts or reflecting on the everyday practices of Iranians, Nafisi frequently interjects overtly political commentary into her remarks. Consider, for example, the following passage in which she is discussing Fitzgerald's *The Great Gatsby* and commenting on Gatsby's imagination:

> What we in Iran had in common with Fitzgerald was this dream that became an obsession and took over our reality, this terrible, beautiful dream, impossible in its actualization, for which any amount of violence might be justified or forgiven.... When I left the class that day, I did not tell them what I myself was just beginning to discover: how similar our own fate was becoming to Gatsby's. He wanted to fulfill his dream by repeating the past, and in the end he discovered that the past was dead, the present a sham, and there was no future. Was this not similar to our revolution, which had come in the name of our collective past and had wrecked our lives in the name of a dream? (144)

In spite of the fact that Nafisi considers *The Great Gatsby* "a non-political novel," ridiculing one of her students, Mr. Nyazi, for considering it an expression of American materialism and consumerism, she ironically uses her interpretation of the novel to wage a political attack on the Islamic government of Iran (129). Now, one can be more forgiving, even approving, of Nafisi's appropriation of the literary text for political critique, as Steven Mailloux and Susan Friedman have done by claiming that "where you are *does* matter in reading Western classics," were it not for the fact that, as John Carlos Rowe cogently reminds us, "written by an Iranian immigrant educated and living in the United States and published only in English for Anglophone readers, *Reading Lolita in Tehran* primarily relies on its location within the United States."[8] Indeed, to our knowledge, none of the memoirs by Iranian immigrants in the United States, or for that matter works by other Middle Eastern American authors such as Khaled Hosseini's *The Kite Runner*, Yasmina Khadra's *The Swallows of Kabul*, and Saira Shah's *The Storyteller's Daughter*, have been either translated or published in the Middle East, a fact perhaps owing to the complicit and contradictory nature of their political claims and critiques. That such neo-Orientalist texts are produced, published, and disseminated mainly in the United States and western Europe suggests that their authors' investment in politics must be understood not as an oppositional demand for human rights or democracy by a subaltern subject but in relation to the neo-imperial interests and interventions of the United States in the region. By this we do not mean that such works constitute "the *locus classicus* of the ideological foregrounding of the U.S. imperial domination at home and abroad," as Dabashi has claimed (3). Rather, these neo-Orientalist texts and their authors have been promoted in part to advance what Dag Tuas-tad, following Paul Richards, calls "the new barbarism thesis," that is, "explanations of political violence [in the Middle East] that omit political and economic interests and contexts when describing violence, and present violence as a result of traits embedded in local cultures [of the region]."[9] Political critique in the works of neo-Orientalists such as Nafisi or Haka-kian provides the moral authority that the United States government seeks to pursue its neo-imperial interests and interventions in the Middle East. This is not to suggest that such native intellectuals are being "actively re-cruited to perform a critical function for the militant ideologues of the U.S. Empire," as Dabashi speculates (5). Instead, the post-9/11 craving of the general public in the United States for "authentic" and "expert" informa-tion about Islam and the Middle East, combined with the market calcula-tions of commercial publishers, create a fertile ground for the prolifera-tion of neo-Orientalist discourses, discourses that, in enabling the general consensus about what Muslim societies and people are, prove useful to neoconservative elements in the U.S. government in pursuit of their impe-rialist projects in the Middle East—for example, the intimate relationship between Paul Wolfowitz, Bernard Lewis, and Azar Nafisi. True, some of these intellectuals like Nafisi have been recruited by conservative insti-tutions such as SAIS, the Hoover Institution, and the Smith Richardson Foundation, but most of those whom Dabashi calls "comprador native in-tellectuals" are self-made and self-promoting Middle Eastern immigrants who have found a publishing niche in a cottage industry to gain fame and fortune.

JOURNALISM, HISTORICISM, AND THE NEO-ORIENTALIST REGIME OF TRUTH

Crucial to native intellectuals' complicit investment in and critical en-gagement with the politics of the Middle East are what we have termed ahistorical historicism and the claim to journalistic truth, two of the most important discursive tropes of neo-Orientalism. One of the most salient features of neo-Orientalist discourse is an apparent tendency to histori-cize social and cultural practices in the Middle East. Consider the following passage in which Nafisi explains to her American readers the issue of veiling in Iran:

> From the beginning of the revolution there had been many aborted attempts to impose the veil on women; these attempts failed because of persistent and militant resistance put up mainly by Iranian women. In many important ways the veil had gained a symbolic significance for the regime. Its reimposition would signify the complete victory of the Islamic aspect of the revolution, which in those first years was not a forgone conclusion. The unveiling of women mandated by Reza Shah in 1936 had been a controversial symbol of modernization, a powerful sign of the reduction of the clergy's power. It was important for the ruling clerics to reassert that power. (112)

On the surface, this passage provides a compact history of unveiling and veiling in Iran. But read against the actual historical accounts of how the first Pahlavi king forced women to unveil and the postrevolutionary government-imposed mandatory veiling, Nafisi's remarks are anything but historical. A substantial discussion of veiling in Iran is beyond the scope of this essay, but we recall here a few basic facts by way of demonstrating the ahistorical form of Nafisi's historicism. First, as Parvin Paidar has documented,[10] Reza Shah's forceful and compulsory unveiling of women was not only resisted by most Iranian women whose access to education and socialization was ironically curtailed due to the Shah's decree, but it also maligned independent socialists, liberal nationalists, and feminists who were fighting for women's rights at the time as puppets of the tyrannical regime. Although couched as the signifier of modernization, the unveiling of women was a calculated measure by the dictatorial king to undermine the power of the clergy in Iran. The passage also makes it seem that the veil was a new imposition from above, disavowing the fact that the second Pahlavi, Mohammad Reza Shah, had to lift the compulsory unveiling soon after his inauguration as king in 1941 due to the strong public opposition, a move that enabled women to wear again the hijab in public spaces. In fact, during the second Pahlavi regime, most women in Iran, with the exception of a small minority in Tehran and a few other major cities, wore chador, the traditional full-length outer garment worn by Iranian women, a garment whose origin dates back to the pre-Islamic Achaemenid rulers, who imposed it to protect their wives and concubines from the public gaze. Moreover, Nafisi's passage leaves out that what enabled the imposition of mandatory veiling by the Islamic government of Iran were profound cultural and religious notions of modesty and piety among Iranian women, without whose consensus mandatory veiling would have been difficult, if not impossible.

The ahistorical historicism finds its most problematic expression in the way recent memoirs by Iranians depict prerevolutionary Iran. Consider the following example from the first section of Hakakian's memoir, titled, "Historical Note," in which she describes the late-Pahlavi Iran: "There indeed was an Iran perfectly at peace and on its way to a great future. The nation's annual growth rate was roughly double the average of other third world countries, and per capita income was on the rise; so were student population and life expectancy. Education and health had improved. The infant mortality rate, malnutrition, endemic diseases, and illiteracy had been reduced" (5). This passage provides a glimpse into the way the historical claims of these memoirs romanticize, and indeed misrepresent, prerevolutionary Iran as a modern and progressive society unburdened by religious backwardness and repression by a clerical regime. Some, like Nafisi, even distort historical facts by, for example, claiming that "when I was growing up, in the 1960s, there was little difference between my rights and the rights of women in Western democracies" (261). Others with less conservative credentials, such as Moaveni and Hakakian, make references in passing to the shah's brutal intelligence service, SAVAK, or to Jimmy Carter's support of the tyrannical regime, but these references are quickly pushed aside as the authors dwell on the repressive aspects of the Islamic Republic. None, however, entertains the idea that, after the revolution, the quality of life indeed became better in certain respects for many rural and working-class Iranians. In addition, the neo-Orientalists either repress or turn a blind eye to some of the important changes that have occurred since the revolution. For example, as Roksana Bahramitash, using the data from the *World Development Indicator*, reminds us, "infant mortality dropped from 131.20 in 1975 to 25.50 in 1999; life expectancy at birth increased from 49 for men and women in 1960 to 70 for men and 72 for women by 1999; and the illiteracy rate for young women declined considerably, from over 55 percent in 1970 to 8.7 percent by 1999."[11] Our intent here emphatically is not to offer a defense of or an apology for the policies of the Islamic government of Iran, but rather to draw attention to the ways in which neo-Orientalists disavow certain historical facts in their narratives, which purport to be authentic and objective representations of the Middle East. That one reviewer of Nafisi's book ventures to speculate that *"Reading Lolita in Tehran* is probably the best introduction to Iran to be found anywhere,"[12] demonstrates the uncritical reception of neo-Orientalist discourses as factual representations in the United States and more broadly in the West.

Akin to ahistorical historicism is the claim to journalistic truth that underscores the political project of neo-Orientalism. To be sure, some of the recent memoirs about the Middle East are written by journalists such as Azadeh Moaveni and Christopher de Bellaigue, who use their experiences as reporters in Iran to tell their stories. But the journalistic will to knowledge is less a function of professional credentials than a discursive tendency that permeates virtually every account of life in the Middle East. Some of the passages quoted earlier may have already demonstrated what we have in mind in highlighting this tendency, but let us consider another example, by Bellaigue, to briefly elaborate this trope:

> Why, I wondered long ago, don't the Iranians smile? Even before I first thought of visiting Iran, I remember seeing photographs of thousands of crying Iranians, men and women wearing black. In Iran, I read, laughing in a public place is considered coarse and improper. Later, when I took an oriental studies course at university, I learned that the Islamic Republic of Iran built much of its ideology on the public's longing for a man who died more than thirteen hundred years ago. This is the Imam Hossein, the supreme martyr of Shi'a Islam and a man whose virtue and bravery provide a moral shelter for all. Now that I'm living in Tehran, witness to the interminable sorrow of Iranians for their Imam, I sense that I'm among a people that enjoys grief, relishes it. Iran mourns on a fragrant spring day, while watching a ladybird scale a blade of grass, while making love. This was the case fifty years ago, long before the setting up of the Islamic Republic, and will be the case fifty years hence, after it has gone.[13]

This opening paragraph of *In the Rose Garden of Martyrs: A Memoir of Iran* by Christopher de Bellaigue offers an example of the way a journalistic form of empirical knowledge enables the regime of neo-Orientalist truth. Beyond his own initial intuition, or the photographs he had seen before his trip, or even his Persian studies at Cambridge, it is Bellaigue's observation as a journalist in Iran that substantiates his claim about Iranians' culture of mourning. Like the notion of experience discussed earlier, empirical observation constitutes not only authority but truth. It is from having witnessed the Ashura rituals in Iran that Bellaigue is able to make truth claims about the pathos of Iranian society. Individual observation here allows the neo-Orientalist to postulate his subjective claims as self-evident and to extract the truth about a society. Here the cultural dynamics of a complex historical experience is effaced in the service of a neo-Orientalist regime of truth. What is remarkable, indeed disturbing, is the leap from a specific observation or encounter in Iran to an enormous generalization about its culture. More symptomatically, Bellaigue goes on to make assertions about the unchanging quality of Iranian culture, depicting it as a premodern, if not primitive, society incapable of changing its melancholic pathos. In sum, journalistic empiricism allows the neo-Orientalist to get to the heart of Middle Eastern societies, grasp their essential characteristics, and finally produce a generalized and generalizable cultural theory.

THE MONOLITHIC REPRESENTATION OF THE VEIL AND THE MULTIPLE MEANINGS OF HIJAB

The cover of Nafisi's *Reading Lolita in Tehran* depicts two Iranian women who appear to be reading a forbidden Western novel. The image apparently is meant both as a reference to the young women of Nafisi's clandestine reading group and as an expression of the book's thematic concern with the liberatory power of reading Western classics in a totalitarian society. Yet what this cropped image covers is the truth about what these young women are actually reading, namely, a newspaper article about President Khatami's election in which they had participated. This example underscores neo-Orientalism's strategic mystification of the veil, that is, of what happens when the veil is discussed outside of its historical and cultural context. The cropped picture not only emblematizes the way neo-Orientalism effaces the agency of Muslim women in the region and beyond, but it also offers a visual representation of the way the obsession with the veil masks the complexity and multiple meanings that attach to the Islamic notion of hijab. Above all, as Fatima Mernissi, Parvin Paidar, and Maryam Poya have demonstrated,[14] far from being agency-less victims of an inherently misogynistic culture, Muslim women have been able to fashion alternative forms of agency to live and work under Islamic patriarchy. Indeed, contrary to Nafisi's portrayal of Iranian universities as strongholds of Islamic fundamentalist men, over 60 percent of university students are women. One of the crucial omissions of *Reading Lolita in Tehran* and other such memoirs is the fact that the Islamic government of Iran passed a law requiring that at least 50 percent of student enrollment in certain fields be allocated to women. More ironically, the mandatory veiling policy in Iran removed any remaining objection by traditional and religious families to allowing their daughters to attend schools and universities. Again, the point is not to defend the veil but to demand a reckoning with unexpected and ideologically ambiguous aspects of the practice.

In spite of such developments in postrevolutionary Iran, the issue of the veil has become a *topos obligé* among neo-Orientalists, a "constant obsession" to use Nafisi's own words (167). Even a cursory glance at the covers of recent memoirs by Middle Easterners—and, ironically, at the covers of books critical of them, such as Dabashi's *Iran: A People Interrupted* or Fatemeh Keshavarz's *Jasmine and Stars: Reading More Than Lolita in Teh-*

ran—reveals the fixation with the veil any time the issue of Muslim female identity is raised. To cite a textual example, Moaveni, in her volume *Lipstick Jihad,* includes a whole chapter titled "I'm Too Sexy for My Veil" in which she argues: "Though most women in modern-day Iran might not consider the veil their highest grievance, they knew it symbolized the system's disregard for women's legal status in general. Mandatory veiling crushed women's ability to express themselves, therefore denying them a basic right."[15] Without exception, the issue of the veil is discussed as a literal and symbolic expression of how women are utterly oppressed in Islamic societies. Although an in-depth analysis of how Islamic patriarchy engenders and perpetuates Muslim women's oppression *would be* a worthy scholarly project, the preoccupation with the veil speaks not so much to the desire to dismantle oppression as to the profound Islamophobia in the United States and the West. In neo-Orientalist discourses, the veil is always constructed in terms of a binary between freedom and oppression, secularism and religion, modernity and tradition, and democracy and tyranny. As a signifier of Muslim women's oppression and religious backwardness, the veil has come to serve as a crucial site for constructing and reaffirming a hierarchical and "civilizing" relationship between the West and Muslim societies. Put otherwise, the veil sanctions a paternalistic and neo-imperial relation between the West and Muslim societies by enabling a discourse of rescue. Thus, in the name of feminism and concern for women's rights, neo-Orientalist representations of the veil mobilize a consensus about the oppressive and undemocratic nature of Islam and the need to liberate Muslim women, and more broadly Muslim societies, from tyrannical fathers, husbands, and regimes.

RESISTING NEO-ORIENTALISM

It can hardly escape notice that the preponderance of the memoirists we have discussed above are women,[16] a fact that underscores the profoundly gendered nature of neo-Orientalism. Observers long have noted that Orientalism itself is a thoroughly gendered phenomenon in which women are classically positioned as oppressed subjects in dire need of liberation by the West, while men are depicted in ways that emphasize excessive sexuality and a fidelity to the irrational, violent forces of fundamentalist religiosity.[17] Within this rigid dichotomy, the quintessential "good Muslim" is by definition female. Given the unsympathetic depiction of masculinity at the heart of both the Orientalist and the neo-Orientalist projects, the mere possibility of a male memoirist threatens to contradict, and thereby subvert, the very stereotypes that undergird the genre in the first place, so it is hardly surprising that female voices dominate the field.[18] Particularly in the post-9/11 era, as a mass market has emerged for books that promise to shed light on why "they" hate "us" so much, it is similarly predictable that authors who validate existing preconceptions about gender roles in "the Islamic world" have proven easy and even quite satisfying to digest by consumers in the West.

Acknowledging the pivotal role that 9/11 has played in securing the success of neo-Orientalist memoirs, we nonetheless worry about the tendency of the now-ubiquitous rhetoric of pre- and post-9/11 periodization not only to obscure continuities between the present era and Orientalisms of the past, but also to occlude the significance of other, contemporaneous cultural forces that also have been instrumental in generating the mass appeal of the neo-Orientalist memoir. One overlooked but particularly important factor to consider has been the shift in the United States toward disclosure as a dominant mode of social relations—a shift evident not only in the rhetoric of the war on terror, which encourages the willing surrender of civil rights for the supposed security of surveillance, but also in the ascendance of reality TV and other tell-all genres to a position of pop culture dominance.[19] Neo-Orientalist memoirs can be viewed as part of a much larger movement within U.S. popular culture toward cultural forms that center on the drama and potential for scandal common to works based on the principle of personal revelation.

The ascendance of popular genres centering claims of "reality" and "authenticity" poses special challenges to those who would contest both the specific claims and the broader ideological effects that such works produce. In the age of "truthiness,"[20] recourse to the charge of false consciousness seems not only antiquated but politically suspect, as democracy is understood to require not merely political self-determination but equal participation in knowledge production as well (think Wikipedia). From this standpoint, reality genres—including memoirs—become virtually impervious to critique. Neo-Orientalist memoirists capitalize on both the moral authority and the special immunity they enjoy as presumptive survivors of patriarchal and religious oppression; by centering survivor subjectivity, these works straddle the form of the memoir and the testimonial in a way that subtly installs authenticity over factual accuracy as the standard by which recollections are judged.

In this moment, then, it may not be enough simply to identify the many ways in which distorted and brazenly ideological accounts of "the Muslim world" find ready acceptance as authoritative accounts in mainstream political discourse and in popular culture. What is needed is a way to challenge the authority of the native Orientalist, which, in contesting the epistemic privilege claimed by the native informant, does not recapitulate the long history of silencing the non-Western other, thereby reinscribing precisely the gendered dynamics that animate our critique of neo-Orientalism in the first place.[21] One possible approach is suggested by Marjane Satrapi, the author of the graphic memoir *Persepolis*, which recently was made into an Academy Award–nominated animated film. Satrapi is intentionally absent from the list of authors we have been considering because we believe her oeuvre presents in many ways an original and artful challenge to the neo-Orientalist tendencies pervading the works we have discussed here. Consider the following excerpt from an interview with Satrapi presented by Deborah Solomon in her "Questions for" column, which appears weekly in the *New York Times Sunday Magazine*:

> SOLOMON: You're a Muslim, yes?
>
> SATRAPI: I'm not a religious person at all.
>
> SOLOMON: Your books denounce Islamic fanaticism, particularly as it curtails the rights of women. Is that your main theme?
>
> SATRAPI: Oh, no, not at all. I don't consider myself as a feminist but more a humanist.
>
> SOLOMON: Still, in your work, you are constantly contrasting your love of food, smoking and sensual pleasures with the acts of self-denial demanded by the mullahs, like wearing a chador.
>
> SATRAPI: It's a problem for women no matter the religion or the society. If in Muslim countries they try to cover the woman, in America they try to make them look like a piece of meat.
>
> SOLOMON: Are you suggesting that veiling and unveiling women are equally reductive? I disagree.
>
> SATRAPI: We have to look at ourselves here also. Why do all the women get plastic surgery? Why? Why? Why should we look like some freaks with big lips that look like an anus? What is so sexy about that? What is sexy about having something that looks like a goose anus?[22]

The relationship between cultural disavowal and critical authority reflected in this quotation stands in stark contrast to the memoirs we have examined in the preceding sections. In those works, disavowal plays an essential role in establishing the credibility of the author to a Western audience; disavowal is one of the most prominent strategies neo-Orientalist memoirists deploy to mark the distinction between the native Other and the native informant. In this way, disavowal—understood as the act of renouncing what may be regarded as foundational aspects of the native culture—enables the neo-Orientalist memoirist to speak authoritatively about her native land, while enjoying the trust and sense of common perspective accorded to Western insiders. Satrapi deploys the strategy of disavowal quite differently, however, for she disavows a personal relationship with Islam in order to authorize a critique not of her native country but of the *West*. In other words, rather than disavowing Islam to allay the suspicion that she might be more like "them" than like "us," Satrapi claims membership in the "we" of the West in order to authorize an indictment of the sexism she has encountered outside of the Muslim world.

In considering Satrapi's deployment of the strategy of disavowal, it is important to note that she disavows not just Islam but feminism as well (in favor of humanism), presumably to emphasize her distance from those who have allowed a campaign for universal women's rights to be co-opted by an Orientalist, imperialist agenda. To be sure, when the long-ignored plight of Afghani women is exploited to justify military invasions and occupations across the Middle East, one may understandably conclude that the concept of feminism has been so thoroughly distorted by misappropriation as to be irredeemable. In abandoning the possibility of other feminisms, however, Satrapi forms an alliance with those who would be all too happy to see the feminist project dismissed altogether—for in the liberal, imperialist imaginary in which equal rights for women in the West have already been attained, the contingent resuscitation of feminism to justify imperialist occupations abroad has been carefully contoured to ensure that feminism is only allowed "over there."

In the end, what is the critical purchase or the political value in distinguishing neo-Orientalist discourses from their traditional counterparts? Our goal in attempting to delineate certain characteristics of an otherwise amorphous phenomenon called neo-Orientalism is twofold. On the one hand, in trying to describe neo-Orientalism we seek to challenge the post-Orientalist pretense prevalent in the West today, a perspective implicit in recent works by Middle Easterners and others in the United States and Europe to speak outside of and beyond the Orientalist tradition. In spite of the persistent, indeed intensified, vilification of Islam and Muslims throughout the West, scholars and intellectuals, politicians and political pundits continue to insist that Said's *Orientalism* wrongfully dismisses Western scholars of Islamic societies and cultures as agents of European colonialism.[23] The Middle Eastern writers and intellectuals we have discussed here further corroborate this position by implicitly reaffirming Orientalist stereotypes while claiming a post-Orientalist imagination in their representations. Our notion of neo-Orientalism provides a critical framework both to make sense of the challenge posed by the emergence of these historically unprecedented memoirs and novels by Middle Easterners, and to mediate between the relevance and enduring insight of Orientalist critique in the face of such examples of women from the Middle East speaking for and representing themselves.

At the same time, our notion of neo-Orientalism is meant as an extension of Orientalist critique. The indisputably unprecedented proliferation of memoirs and novels by Middle Easterners is a disturbing reminder that Orientalist perceptions of the region continue to enable neo-imperial relations of power. Yet what the recent representations of the Middle East make evident is that Orientalism is not a single and unchanging entity whose totalizing impulse leaves little room for discursive and ideological transformations. Orientalism always entails rearticulations of otherness to ensure its cultural hegemony in the face of complex political and social change. As a result, Orientalist critique must be understood as a discursively flexible and perpetually revisionist project, a project that remains attentive to changes in representations of alterity, interrogates its own political and theoretical assumptions, and reconsiders its critical strategies and tactics. Orientalist critique is, in short, an ongoing project that requires continual reevaluations of what constitutes an effective political critique and careful reexamination of the idea of engaged scholarship.

Notes

1. Edward Said, preface to the 25th anniversary ed. of *Orientalism: Western Conceptions of the Orient* (New York: Penguin, 2003), xix.

2. Jeffrey Fleishman, "Pursuing Happiness behind the Veil," *Los Angeles Times*, January 14, 2008, A1 (emphasis added).

3. Hamid Dabashi, "Native Informers and the Making of the American Empire," *Al-Ahram*, June 1–7, 2006, http://weekly.ahram.org/2006/797/special.htm.

4. See Ali Behdad, *Belated Travelers: Orientalism in the Age of Colonial Dissolution* (Durham, NC: Duke University Press, 1994).

5. Roya Hakakian, *Journey from the Land of No: A Girlhood Caught in Revolutionary Iran* (New York: Crown, 2004). Hakakian's personal Web page is http://www.royahakakian.com/.

6. Azar Nafisi, *Reading Lolita in Tehran: A Memoir in Books* (New York: Random House, 2003), 23.

7. We borrow the term "experiential authority" from James Clifford, who uses it to describe how authority is constructed in twentieth-century ethnography. See Clifford, "On Ethnographic Authority," in *Predicament of Culture: Twentieth-Century Ethnography, Literature, and Art* (Cambridge: Harvard University Press, 1988), 21–54.

8. Steven Mailloux, "Judging and Hoping: Rhetorical Effects of Reading about Reading," in *American Reception Studies: Reconsiderations and New Directions*, ed. James Manchor and Philip Goldstein (New York: Oxford University Press, 2008); Susan Stanford Friedman, "Unthinking Manifest Destiny: Muslim Modernities on Three Continents," in *American Literature and the Planet*, ed. Lawrence Buell and Wai Chee Dimock (Princeton: Princeton University

Press, 2007); and John Carlos Rowe, "Reading *Reading Lolita in Tehran* in Idaho," *American Quarterly* (2007): 258.

9. Dag Tuastad, "Neo-Orientalism and the New Barbarism Thesis: Aspects of Symbolic Violence in the Middle East Conflict(s)," *Third World Quarterly* 24, no. 24 (2003): 591. Although here Tuastad uses the term in the context of the Middle East, he borrows the term from Paul Richards. See the latter's *Fighting for the Rain Forest: War, Youth and Resources in Sierra Leone* (Oxford: James Currey, 1996).

10. Parvin Paidar, "Feminism and Islam in Iran," in *Gendering the Middle East: Emerging Perspectives*, ed. Deniz Kandiyoti (Syracuse: Syracuse University Press, 1996), 51–68.

11. Roksana Bahramitash, "The War on Terror, Feminist Orientalism and Orientalist Feminism: Case Studies of Two North American Bestsellers," *Critique: Critical Middle Eastern Studies* 14, no. 2 (Summer 2005): 233.

12. *Travel Book Review*, May 24, 2007, http://roadjunky.com/article/720/reading-lolita-in-tehran-by-azar-nafisi.

13. Christopher de Bellaigue, *In the Rose Garden of Martyrs: A Memoir of Iran* (New York: HarperCollins, 2004), 1.

14. Fatima Mernissi, *Beyond the Veil: Male–Female Dynamics in Modern Muslim Society* (Bloomington: Indiana University Press, 1987); Parvin Paidar, *Women and the Political Process in Twentieth-Century Iran* (Cambridge: Cambridge University Press, 1995); and Maryam Poya, *Women, Work, and Islamism* (London: Zed Books, 1999).

15. Azadeh Moaveni, *Lipstick Jihad: A Memoir of Growing Up Iranian in America and American in Iran* (New York: Perseus Books, 2005), 170.

16. The most notable recent memoir about Iran written by a man is Christopher de Bellaigue's *In the Rose Garden of Martyrs*, which we discussed earlier. Bellaigue is a British journalist who covers Iran for the *Economist* and who lives in Tehran with his Iranian wife.

17. See the helpful discussion of "gendered Orientalism" in Minoo Moallem, *Between Warrior Brother and Veiled Sister: Islamic Fundamentalism and the Politics of Patriarchy in Iran* (Berkeley: University of California Press, 2005).

18. See Mahmood Mamdani, *Good Muslim, Bad Muslim: America, the Cold War and the Roots of Terror* (New York: Random House, 2004), for an illuminating discussion of the recent history of the development of these gendered stereotypes in the U.S. popular imaginary.

19. See Juliet Williams, "Privacy in the (Too Much) Information Age," in *Public Affairs: Politics in the Age of Sex Scandals*, ed. Paul Apostolidis and Juliet Williams (Durham, NC: Duke University Press, 2004), for an account of the development of privacy as a legal right and a cultural value in the United States. For an especially trenchant analysis of the dynamics of exposure in reality TV in particular, see Mark Andrejevic, *Reality TV: The Work of Being Watched* (Lanham, MD: Rowman and Littlefield, 2004).

20. "Truthiness" was selected as the 2006 Word of the Year by the *Merriam-Webster Dictionary*, following popularization of the term by Stephen Colbert on his satirical news show *The Colbert Report*.

21. See Gayatri Spivak, "Can the Subaltern Speak?" in Cary Nelson and Larry Grossberg, eds., *Marxism and the Interpretation of Culture*, 271–313 (Champaign Urbana: University of Illinois Press, 1988), for the classic statement of this dilemma.

22. Deborah Solomon, "Questions for" column, *New York Times Sunday Magazine*, October 21, 2007.

23. A representative example of this claim is in Robert Irwin, *Dangerous Knowledge: Orientalism and Its Discontents* (New York: Overlook Press, 2006). Irwin calls *Orientalism* "a work of malignant charlatanry in which it is hard to distinguish honest mistakes from willful misrepresentations" (4).

ELEVEN

American Studies in Motion

Tehran, Hyderabad, Cairo

Brian T. Edwards

TEHRAN (FEBRUARY 2007)

It's Friday in February in downtown Tehran. I'm taking advantage of the day off from the seminar I'm teaching to catch up with unfinished work from home. I feel guilty to be spending a few hours secluded away, when it was so difficult to get the visa to come here. The windows in my apartment are closed; it has been chilly and damp with the occasional dusting of snow. For the past few minutes I can hear the muffled tones of midday prayers across the street on the campus of the University of Tehran. My Persian isn't good enough yet to understand the sermon, but I can pick out a number of words that I know from Arabic. *Estiqlal, enqalab.* Independence, revolution. *Israel* several times. These are difficult times in Tehran, with UN deadlines expiring, aggressive talk coming from the United States, and President Ahmadinejad ever strengthening his resolve to push forward the nation's nuclear program. "Like a train without brakes or reverse gear," he announces, and the phrase makes it into papers around the world (February 25, 2007). "They need a stop button," Condoleezza Rice retorts. From here the word "button" sounds ominous, perhaps a reference to the United States' own nuclear power. About a week ago (February 19), the USS *John C. Stennis* pulled into the Gulf of Oman to remind Iran that "all options are on the table," as U.S. Democrats and Republicans alike keep saying publicly. Rumors run through the city that an American attack is imminent. "The Japanese embassy has announced that the U.S. will attack Tehran this evening," goes one. The students speak of psychological terrorism. Finally, I know what they mean.

The cleric giving the sermon is hitting his stride. His voice gets faster and louder. I move to the window, open it, and stick my head out to listen. The crescendo is exhilarating and intimidating. It builds and builds and then gives way to that shockingly familiar but ever-foreign chant: *Marg bar Amrika! Marg bar Amrika!* (Death to America!). I feel the chill of danger tingle across my skin. The speaker has his public fully with him; it joins in. The anxiety provoked by the roar of the crowd is enhanced by the fact that I can't see what is going on. All I can see from my window is 16 Azar Street, empty save a woman walking alone. *Marg bar Amrika!* Is that the cheer of a thousand voices—or ten thousand?

I decide to go see for myself. I'm dressed appropriately in muted colors (bright clothing stands out as flashy in Tehran). I remove my U.S. passport from my pocket and my dollars, and stash them in a closet. I chuckle at myself. Am I really expecting to be stopped and stripped—to be exposed as an American? If so, why am I going outside?

As I walk the perimeter of the campus and beyond, prayers are always audible, broadcast through audio speakers strung to poles. On the east side of campus, Qods Street, men on prayer rugs spill out of the university gates, several hundred deep. Some sit on the curb dangling their feet into the open storm drains, while others spread their carpets on the pavement. But another block east and the streets are empty again. A string of buses and sleeping drivers await the return of the crowd. I consider entering the campus to get closer to the source of the sermon and guess that I'd have a decent chance of being let in. When I get to the southern gate, however, I look at the security, the metal detectors, and decide to let it go. I want to get back to my apartment anyway, back to writing.

I head back to 16 Azar and start up the street. A police officer calls to me to stop. Sixteen Azar, the west perimeter of campus, is reserved as the women's entrance to Friday prayers. That is why it had been so empty, I realize. I must wait another hour or so. I walk a short block west to En-qalab Square, where the huge pulse of traffic circulates ceaselessly, apparently oblivious to Friday prayers, and then up Kargar Street, from which I think I might sneak back to my apartment via one of the back alleys. Here there's more action: people are in popular restaurants, and some food shops are open. But every alley is either guarded or roped off. I head up to Laleh Park.

The sounds of the service are getting faint. The park is pleasant, despite the chill. Families are out. A father and his teenaged daughter are playing badminton without a net. She is good. Smaller kids run around the playground. A young boy climbs a ladder into the hatch of a faux army helicopter, then slides down out its mouth. In spite of the military play structure, life in the park does not seem that different in Tehran from Chicago. I do a big circle, then make my way back to the edge of the park and stop in one of the shops at the southwest corner. A year ago, in this same shop, I found several books by Tony Robbins, the American motivational guru, in Persian translation. Today my eye is caught by giant Shrek books, two-by-three-foot illustrated soft covers, retelling the animated Dream-

Works film and its sequel in both Persian and grammatically suspect English. I buy the two Shrek books for my kids and head back. People are spilling out of campus. My street is open again.

Sixteen Azar Street is named to commemorate the date in 1953 when three students of the Tudeh (communist) Party were killed by the shah's police. The students were protesting Vice President Nixon's trip to Iran, less than four months after the CIA-sponsored overthrow of Mohammad Mossadegh, the democratically elected hero who had made the geopolitical mistake of nationalizing the Iranian oil fields. When Nixon came to Tehran in a show of solidarity with the shaky shah, the students threw stones at his car from the rooftops of university buildings. The day, December 7 on the Western calendar, is called Students' Day. I walk down 16 Azar, holding my two giant Shrek portfolios. I pass a hamburger shop, a cybercafé, a tailor, and a bookshop before heading down the alley where my apartment is located.

The next day, Saturday, is the beginning of the new week. The University of Tehran is given back to the university for the business of education, and I'm back in class for the fourth meeting of my seminar. It is my second trip to Iran in the last fourteen months. I am the guest of the Institute of North American and European Studies, where I am teaching a two-week graduate seminar on research methodologies in American studies. Many intellectuals in Tehran don't know of the institute yet, even some who teach at the University of Tehran. The institute occupies its own small building in central Tehran, across Laleh Park from the main campus. Created in 2005, the institute launched its first degree program in early 2006. There are already two cohorts of M.A. students working their way through four semesters of course work. When I returned to teach another such seminar in February 2009, I met the fourth cohort. By the time this volume is published, a sixth will have matriculated.

The idea of my coming to teach at the institute emerged in December 2005, when I gave several lectures in Tehran (on globalization and culture, diaspora, American literature, and U.S. Orientalism) at both the School of Humanities and the School of Social Sciences. My hosts were the two key men in the new institute. One, a social scientist, had done work on Muslim communities in the United Kingdom and on globalization and urbanism. The second, a literature specialist with a Ph.D. from England and a dissertation on British literary Orientalism, would be his deputy. Despite his training in British literature, the latter had the advantage of having grown up in Ohio until 1979, when his father, a prominent physician, wanted to join the revolutionary project. This deputy, M——, is almost exactly my age (I was born in 1968), and our points of reference growing up in the United States cross over in many ways. We reminisce about Wacky Packs, old Reese's Peanut Butter Cup commercials, and the lineup of the Cincinnati Reds of the late 1970s. Both he and his boss are *seyyeds*, that is, people who can trace their lineage back to the Prophet. Both are charismatic, although in different ways. When the director, who wears his clerical robes and turban on campus, speaks to me in his calm and yet passionate way about what he calls a "culture of peace," I feel as if I am in the presence of a kindly Catholic priest. In between frequent interruptions by students and his cell phone, he discusses the difference between a "culture of peace" and a "culture of war" and how, ironically enough, the United States is much more effective in making its case to Iranians within a "culture of peace." With his deputy, who wears a suit and button-down shirt to campus and does not cover his head, I feel less at a remove, despite his unsparing critique of the confluence of Western hegemony, media, and academia. It's his wisecracking humor and pop cultural references that put us in the same universe.

When I was here last, the institute was an idea that had started to be a reality. These men had persuaded the chancellor of the university to fund a center for studying the United States (Canada and western Europe were part of the larger plan, but clearly lag behind in implementation). Given the importance of the United States, they argued, Iran could not afford to be without its own academic expertise on American history and society. A center dedicated to North America could train young men and women who could move on to jobs in government, academia, and civil society with an understanding of that country whose force, both political and cultural, was undeniable. Then they won the internal debate that the "culture people" were better suited to create such a center than the political scientists, who wanted to pursue an area studies model. They argued for interdisciplinarity as a greater means to understanding. After the election of former Tehran mayor Mahmoud Ahmadinejad to the presidency in June 2005, the university community held its collective breath to see which way the wind would blow. Ahmadinejad would replace the chancellor of course, but he was not able to get his man in the post. The man he did appoint to lead the university did not cancel the plans to fund the new Institute of North American and European Studies.

Although the institute still had funding, it didn't have anyone, save a couple of people who had trained or lived in the United States, to teach the courses. M——, the deputy, traveled to the United States (the director's visa was denied), where he met with representatives of prominent Middle East studies programs on the East Coast. In the post-9/11 era, with their own faculty and programs under siege as being overly sympathetic to their object of study, the representatives didn't know whom in American studies to recommend. He met with people in American studies at universities in New York and Washington, D.C., but they couldn't figure out who would be interested in going to Iran. He learned quickly something that surprised him but shouldn't have: that American studies programs and Middle East studies programs in the United States are entities that rarely meet. And although one may find some Middle East studies faculty who would come to the University of Tehran, it is difficult to convince most Americanists to travel outside the United States to develop their own understanding of their field and where it is going.

Still, this deputy director made enough of an impression, apparently, that someone suggested to the leadership of the American Studies Association (ASA) that the organization invite him to attend the annual meeting that year in Washington, D.C. The ASA paid for him to come and gave him free registration and money for a hotel, and it didn't ask him to do anything other than roam the corridors of those opulent hotels. The invitation was meant, of course, as an effort to break out of the exceptionalism of the ASA and, particularly after the 2003 invasion of Iraq, as an effort to engage more directly with the Middle East and its scholars. There were, however, neocolonial overtones in inviting a person, who in the French colonial period would have been called an *évolué*, to the imperial center to stroll the hallways and stay at its own expense at a hotel that cost $200 a night (the discounted conference rate), when the salary of a deputy director of an institute was something like $1,000 a month. More to the point, the topics that this director found himself learning about, as he made his way through the hallways of this grand hotel, were so esoteric as to be of no help to him in planning how to teach himself American studies so that he could teach his students. He would stay for a few moments at each panel, trying to relate it to the needs of the institute he was building back home, before he staggered on to the next.

The ASA is a decidedly left-leaning organization, and the overwhelming majority of American studies scholars would hardly think of their participation in an ASA meeting in Washington, D.C., as pertaining to an imperial project. When the ASA takes its turn in D.C., I feel a more concerted attempt to "talk truth to power" and a more profound sense at times of how futile that is. Indeed it was not long before the meeting in question that the putatively "liberal" *New Republic* attacked the scholars associated with the cutting edge of the American Studies Association as participating in what the writer Alan Wolfe called "anti-American studies" (February 2003). Wolfe would have loved the detail of the Iranian being invited to the ASA, and surely would have used it as an example of the perfidy and double dealing of the so-called new American studies. To the Iranian scholar, however, who was feeling increasingly out of his element, the obsessions of American studies scholars on the minutiae of their history and the idea that he might be able to relate to that scholarship were hardly anti-American or antagonistic to the U.S. state. Rather, what he heard as he drifted in and out of sessions was, from his perspective, so thoroughly caught up in the ideology of American exceptionalism as to be untranslatable outside the United States. Nonetheless, he continued to approach American scholars, with considerable charm and persistence, and ask them to come teach for a couple of weeks at his institute.

When I was in Tehran a month later, coming to the institute by a completely different route, a textbook arrived and an anthology, donations of extra desk copies from two American scholars. He was appreciative.

The past several years have seen a small boom in the creation and development of American studies programs in North Africa and the Middle East. Some programs have benefited from funds or personnel supplied indirectly by the U.S. State Department (such as through the Fulbright Program) and some have formal affiliations with U.S. institutions. Many of the most interesting programs, however, such as the one in Tehran, have been initiated fully outside the directives of the United States. Not surprisingly, there are starkly different conceptions of what "American studies" might mean. These differences were evident at a meeting I attended in Beirut just before Christmas 2005, on my way back from Tehran, held at the newly endowed Prince Alwaleed bin Talal bin Abdulaziz Alsaud Center for American Studies and Research at the American University of Beirut. Participants from American studies programs in a dozen countries in the Middle East struggled with the question of how to manage local perceptions of the United States, their own political anger at the Bush administration, and traditions of Americanist scholarship (or the lack of them) in the region.

Since 2005, I have been visiting and sometimes teaching short seminars at American studies programs in six countries in North Africa, the Middle East, and South Asia. The trajectories are as different as the histories of those cities and countries. In some places, these programs call themselves American studies, but in others they do not, often for strategic reasons. None of them is in any sustained dialogue with American scholars of the field, nor do they necessarily want to be, as those exchanges are often essentializing (such as when Arab scholars come to the United States on the Fulbright's new exchange called Direct Access to the Muslim

World), or the trips end up offering little practical guidance for their projects back home.

As American studies circulates beyond the hemisphere, and when that circulation is considered in the myriad ways that we have seen in this volume, how might we understand something like American studies in Tehran? In Hyderabad? In Cairo?

In Tehran, at least, something quite different is happening than the expansion of an exceptionalist model. The British scholar Paul Giles has described that model as the "magic circle between text and context." Its seductive power, and thus its persistence, Giles argues, has been to "hold in suspension those conditions whereby the progressivist formulas of American studies would—naturally, as it were—underwrite a rhetoric of emancipation."[1] The Tehran institute has its shortcomings, to be sure, but it has broken that magic circle. Whatever else the Tehran "Americanists" have to contribute to scholarly discussions within American studies, that break—that interruption—should be of some interest to the field at large.

In the seminar room, we are discussing the film *Casablanca*. For A——, it clearly represents the beginning of American internationalism, when America thought it could sit there at the center of things and tell everyone what to do, turn a blind eye to corruption, as Rick does in the Café Américain. A—— says this from across the seminar table and looks a bit resigned. She is wearing a beret over her hijab, and her jeans and combat boots suggest an individualistic, "alternative" perspective. Here, however, nearly all the class agrees with her. I am trying to provoke a discussion and almost plead for dissent. Finally, B——, who is dressed more conservatively, without a strand of hair showing (and a white wimple under her black hijab that reminds me of a nun who taught my Sunday school class for years), raises her hand. She sees it differently. For her, *Casablanca* is a beautiful love story and universal in its appeal. Hers is a lone voice. A third student, a woman, C——, turns the discussion to the recent film *Babel*. Now several hands shoot up. Across the board, the students object to *Babel* as the pinnacle of Islamophobia. I admit to them I haven't yet seen it. When I left home, it was in my online rental queue, still awaiting its release on DVD. One young woman promises me a copy tomorrow. I beat her to it. That evening, I pick up high-quality copies of *Babel*, along with *Borat*, *The Good Shepherd*, and the latest Bond film, all of which are still in the theaters back in the United States. I pay about two dollars for each. The students tell me that I got ripped off. Next time, I go to Haft-e Teer Square for my DVDs and pick up all the contenders for this year's Academy Awards for one dollar each.

After class, I mention the *Marg bar Amrika* incident to a couple of the students with whom I have started to develop a rapport and tell them, in a joking, insiderish way, the story with which I have begun this chapter. We are sitting in a café called Godot on Enqalab Street in central Tehran. From my experience elsewhere in the Middle East, I expect them to apologize, to be embarrassed. Not at all. One, D——, jumps in quickly. "But you call us the 'Axis of Evil,'" she says. "Why should we mind it if people call you *Shaytan-e Bozorg* [Great Satan] or say '*Marg bar Amrika*'?" Hamid Dabashi has written recently that Bush's "Axis of Evil" speech was perhaps the "second most damaging thing the United States has done against the cause of democracy in Iran."[2] (The first was the overthrow of Mossadegh.) "Don't you realize," I say, "that rejection of President Bush's rhetoric is a rallying call around which Americans define themselves as oppositional?" No one is convinced. The conversation takes many turns, some predictable, others not. What the students perceive and misperceive about American culture, however, is always interesting and at times, dare I say, profound. How could it be otherwise?

As I look at the assignments these students have written before my arrival and the topics that they propose for their master's theses, present concerns clearly orient their interest in U.S. history and culture. This approach is not necessarily a problem. Why should they study American culture and history the way Americans do? Whether these students trace religious imagery in American presidential rhetoric, Islamophobia in contemporary Hollywood, or public diplomacy and "soft power," and whether the texts they draw on are from the Internet, donated desk copies of U.S. history textbooks, or books from the impressive library the institute has been building on its own, the students' hunger to understand American society seems to emerge from a sense of despair at the disconnect between their projects, pursued passionately, and the object they are studying, which has little regard—in both senses of the word—for them. As they look at American media, whether it be CNN or rebroadcasts of Jon Stewart, or the oppositional Persian-language programs beamed in from the Iranian diaspora in L.A.'s "Tehrangeles," or as they listen to American political rhetoric or watch Hollywood films, they are struck by what seems to them a fundamental misunderstanding of Iran and an imperial arrogance on the part of Americans. Their disconnect—and the trade sanctions that are the major source of that separation—clearly inhibits their ability to contextualize or fill in their understanding of many aspects of U.S. history and society. Nonetheless, they have the ability to see through the lenses of ideology that shield many Americans (myself included) from perceiving the collusion of, say, CNN, the liberal Hollywood that makes films such as *Babel* or *300*, and, during the first decade of the 2000s, the Bush administration. They also, however, are often blocked from fuller comprehension of American society by some of these presentist concerns.

There is in Tehran, it becomes apparent, no innocent way to approach America as an object of study. As opposed to the famous American Studies Research Centre in Hyderabad, India, for example, which I visited in late 2006 and where for nearly four decades Indian scholars of American literature, history, sociology, and politics built, on their own ground, an impressive tradition of academic expertise on the United States, in Iran there is neither a tradition of American studies scholarship nor the ability yet to create one dispassionately. There is no uncontaminated starting point. The present is overdetermined. It cannot be easily undone. Just as 16 Azar Street, the street where I am staying, names Students' Day through an always already oppositional relation to the United States, the engagement with American history and culture is from the start marked. Whether this is the ideal way to break what Giles derided as the magic circle inhibiting American studies is ultimately irrelevant. But, in Tehran, broken it is.

HYDERABAD (DECEMBER 2006)

I had come to Hyderabad, in the southern Indian state of Andhra Pradesh, to try to learn something about the American Studies Research Centre (1962–99). I do not work otherwise in South Asia, but given that the development of American studies programs in the Middle East and North Africa is a mostly recent affair, I thought it important to visit this major center, which emerged from an era that seems to haunt our own. My access to Hyderabad would be limited, I knew, since I speak neither Telugu nor Deccani (as the Hyderabad dialect of Urdu, the other principal language of the region, is called), nor indeed Hindi, the national language. However, the vestiges of English as colonial language in use across the country—and as global language of the post–American Century era— would facilitate my interactions both at the university and in the street. This very easiness tends to make me uneasy and had motivated my language study in Arabic and Persian/Farsi, as well as French and Spanish, years earlier. But even comparatists must move beyond the familiar.

On arrival in South India, I was surprised to see how many people from the first of my three flights were still traveling with me, although we had left O'Hare two days before. The IT revolution has made Hyderabad a major destination for business travel; also, Chicago has a significant Hyderabadi population, whose shops and businesses dominate Devon Avenue on the far north side of the city. American Airlines began nonstop flights from Chicago to Delhi; on Air India you can fly "direct" to Hyderabad, with only a stop in the capital city. None of these changes has anything to do with the American Studies Research Centre (ASRC) but everything to do with "Tech City," a striking neighborhood of glass buildings on the other side of this crowded city of five million.

I had read of the demise of the ASRC, but the information I found was sketchy. The ASRC, I knew, had been around since the early 1960s, but late in the Clinton administration it had disappeared from view. U.S. funding for this bilaterally funded research center, I would learn, was pulled out in 1998, one of the many victims of a consequential back room deal between Madeleine Albright and Jesse Helms which dismantled the USIA and consolidated the cultural arms of the government within the State Department, in return for an agreement from Helms on abortion rights laws, a chemical warfare treaty, and back payment of UN dues.[3] On the Internet, I found news releases about the creation of a center for international programs at Osmania University; the center, which emerged from ASRC's ashes, seemed a shift from American studies to a global perspective, which intrigued me. As usual in such situations where I know no one, I contacted scholars directly, introduced myself from afar, and asked if I could visit at my own expense (avoiding official state sponsorship and the questions it provokes), offering to give a talk if desired, and suggesting some topics (Globalizing American Studies, American Orientalism, and the like). My e-mails reached a dynamic senior scholar named Kousar Azam, a leading figure in Indian American studies. Professor Azam welcomed me, and before I knew it, she had scheduled four talks for my visit to Hyderabad, at the two universities in the city, and one at the ASRC—or Osmania University Centre for International Programmes (OUCIP), as it was now called. Just before my departure from the United States, I received a surprising e-mail from Professor Azam. My lecture, she informed me, had been redesignated as the inaugural for the relaunching of the American studies program at OUCIP. The balance in participant observation had quickly tilted from observation (my goal) toward participation. Then another e-mail let me know that despite my efforts to avoid the imprimatur of the U.S. state, I would be introduced by Frederick Kaplan, the consul for public affairs at the U.S. consulate in Chennai. Kaplan, she wrote, would fly in at 11:00 a.m. and leave by 3:30 that afternoon. His short turnaround was the first sign of what was to come.

There are several ways to tell this story, and one may be the co-opting of the work of a non-state-sponsored American cultural actor by the United States, which is what I felt was happening to me.[4] As soon as I arrived in Kousar Azam's office in Hyderabad, however, I realized what she had in mind. She was trying to attract back U.S. funding for the defunct ASRC. The path that had led from the ASRC to the current OUCIP was not one with which she seemed to agree. From the aging structures and aging scholars populating the center's reading rooms, it was clear that the vitality of the place had gone elsewhere. In 1999, having lost its funding, ASRC first became the Indo-American Centre for International Studies (IACIS), then in 2001 the Inter-University Centre for International Studies. As Azam wrote me, "All this was done to attract funding from possible sources after the termination of its funding by the U.S. government." Then the UGC, a regional administrative body, asked Osmania University to take over the facility and the library, and reopen it as OUCIP. "It was decided that the new Centre should be open for multiple disciplines with a scope for seeking funding from multiple sources—unlike the former ASRC that had only one single specialization and a single funding." Thus the move to "inter- and multidisciplinarity" and a broader interest in "international themes and participation including Globalization Studies."[5] The language of globalization was coming from engineering, IT, and the business school—coming from Hyderabad, that is. The American studies crowd was scrambling to keep up.

Hyderabad, meanwhile, with Tech City booming, and as a city with an important Muslim Indian population, had attracted the renewed interest of the U.S. Department of State. With the U.S. embassy in Delhi, and with consulates in Kolkata, Mumbai, and Chennai, the State Department was planning (as would be announced by the public affairs officer during the inaugural) to open a consulate in Hyderabad.[6] This huge resource in American studies, seven years after the funding had been cut, it became clear, might be of interest.

Kaplan's visit was much anticipated, and the Indian directors of the OUCIP (all with primary interests in American studies) were ready to show the public affairs officer their impressive but crumbling structure. Its reading room, its massive American studies library, its microfilm and video viewing rooms, and its collections of four decades of American studies dissertations (and its now defunct *Indian Journal of American Studies*) were spread over multiple rooms and floors. Across the street, the business school of Osmania University—the College of Commerce and Business Management—was new and outfitted with journals and computer centers, but here we were housed in a decaying structure, the guest rooms for the visiting scholars of the past were empty and dusty, the journals subscriptions were mostly halted, and no new books had been bought since 1999. The OUCIP presented a starkly different picture than did the business, technology, and engineering programs at Osmania University—or than Tech City.

Despite his hosts' anticipation, Kaplan showed up late, having decided he preferred to visit the famous Charminar monument. At OUCIP there was barely time for a cup of chai and a quick walk through the center before we had to take our places for the inaugural. His presence attracted several Indian newspapers, and write-ups appeared in three dailies the next day.

In his official remarks, Kaplan spoke the familiar language of bilateral friendship with a slight twist. His examples, translated to make reference to the city of Chicago and Northwestern University, included intriguing references to the digital age that had put Hyderabad and the United States into virtual communication, which was somewhat at odds with the very grounded structure in which we were standing.[7] Noting the eleven-and-a-half-hour time difference between Chicago and Hyderabad, he pointed out, for example, that a late-night emergency room doctor in Chicago would find it easier and more efficient to e-mail an x-ray to Hyderabad to be read, where it was the middle of the day, rather than to go down a couple of floors in his own building in the middle of the night.[8]

The awareness of the realities of the digital age and the focus on their novelty is typical of the U.S. State Department's public diplomacy efforts in the post-9/11 era. The State Department is arguably thinking more about the fact that cultural production is spread by the new media technologies of the present than American studies scholars are, and it has been doing so for longer, despite the former's complete misunderstanding of what Arjun Appadurai has called the "disjunctures" in the global cultural economy.

In my lecture, I spoke of the circulation of American cultural production off its usual pathways, what I called the "ends of circulation." I suggested that in the post-9/11 moment there was a shared logic in the cultural and public diplomacy machinery wherein U.S. culture was imagined to speak simply to foreign audiences. This logic I will call here the logic of broadcasting, that is, the project was simply to broadcast or spread American culture, on a logic borrowed from marketing (be it jazz tours during the cold war or mockumentaries about Muslim bliss in America in the early 2000s). To demonstrate the errors of this logic, I gave the example of the *Porgy and Bess* tour to the Soviet Union in the mid-1950s. Referring to Kate Baldwin's discussion of this tour in the Soviet archive, in her analysis of Paul Robeson's career in the Soviet Union, I suggested that the Soviets, as much as they enjoyed the putative "freedom" of the musical structure, saw evidence of the racial discrimination at the heart of the American enterprise and thereby frustrated the very logic by which the State Department had granted visas to African American performers for the tour.[9] This point would have both policy implications (which the public affairs officer heard) and research implications, which I directed to the Indian academics.

When I finished, Kaplan, who, please recall, had to rush to a plane to get home to Chennai, indicated that he would like a minute to reply. He politely berated me. Picking up on the *Porgy and Bess* incident, he offered his own anecdote. Recently, he said (and it must have been in the previous three months since he was new to his post), the U.S. consular staff had discussed screening the film *The Color Purple* in Chennai. A staff debate ensued, he told, and one of his colleagues on the public affairs staff, "who happens to be an African American," as he put it, argued against the screening, expressing the worry that *The Color Purple* would give a bad impression of American race relations to local residents.[10] The point of his anecdote was twofold: to show that these days the State Department was no dupe, that the post-9/11 moment was not the same as the cold war; and to indicate that there were African American workers in positions of importance at the U.S. consulate in Chennai. Their presence was apparently to speak simply to this Indian audience.

Having made his point, he apologized and left the room, offering no time for questions or discussion. The thirty people in the room all looked at each other. A senior scholar raised his hand. "We saw *The Color Purple* a long time ago, and showed it in our classrooms. What are they worrying about?" The U.S. officer's ignorance of Indian cultural realities was underlined by his failure to engage in discussion or dialogue with his Indian audience. His early departure is the paradigmatic example of "broadcasting" a message and expecting (hoping?) that it will be received as sent without bothering to engage in dialogue. His misapprehension of American studies too—by which I mean not only Kaplan's misapprehension but that of the entire state apparatus from which this individual emerges—is of intersecting interest.

Among my other lectures while I was in Hyderabad was a visit to an English classroom where I was asked to survey and discuss twentieth-century literature of the United States. The room was filled with undergraduates. This was the least formal of my talks, and in some ways the most instructive, particularly compared to my experiences in North Africa and the Middle East, where I had often encountered a tension between the popularity of American popular culture and anger about U.S. policies, especially since the 2003 invasion of Iraq. So when it came to the question and answer period, perhaps I could be forgiven for mishearing the question asked by a charismatic young man, completely blind, whom I had noticed being led to the classroom by a classmate. "I think America is a terrible thing," I heard him say. I began formulating a response—what should I say? I started by asking him to say more about how it was a terrible thing.

The students began to laugh at my mistake. "No, a *terrific* thing," he and they chimed together. The students, it turned out, were particularly fascinated with American literature, but not the American literature, even in all its diversity, that I had discussed. They wanted to discuss literature by Indian writers resident in the United States, such as Jhumpa Lahiri and Kiran Desai, who were then getting a lot of attention. This work, to them, was America—the America of the Indian diaspora. And they were riveted. (As a professor of American studies pointed out to me the next day, much cutting-edge literary theory in the United States was a product, in his view, of intellectuals among the Indian diaspora living in the United States—he named Gayatri Spivak, Arjun Appadurai, Homi Bhabha, and Gauri Viswanathan. I had to give him that.)

Similarly, at a workshop I gave titled "American Studies Now" for the faculty at the various Hyderabad campuses (the subject and title suggested by my hosts), I was surprised by the enthusiasm for American studies approaches and the optimism of most of my hosts for the disentanglement of the field from its cold war origins. A comment made by the dean of the business school struck me particularly. Charming and enthusiastic, R. K. Mishra warned the audience of Indian historians and literary scholars that the discipline of Management had not played a role in American studies in Hyderabad, despite the influence of American culture on global understandings of business and management. He went on to suggest that his own students would benefit greatly from a better comprehension of American culture and history as they attempted to learn "management," a product of the American ethos. His comment recalled for me the blind student. Because I had been busy fielding questions and moderating the discussion, I later asked Professor Azam for her notes on the event. She e-mailed them to me some weeks later. Her summary of the event was telling: "Most participants agreed that pursuit of American Studies will not only keep the radical content of American Revolution alive but will also promote freedom and democracy as universal norms. There was a consensus that American Studies had moved beyond its cold war origins and need not be viewed as part of US Government cultural diplomacy."[11] Professor Azam had been there the day when the American public affairs officer had spoken.

Two methodological questions emerge from the experience in Hyderabad. First, why does attention to circulation matter—what would reading texts in circulation, emphasizing their motion over their meaning, look like? Second, what is a multisited American studies? For some time I have been troubled by the institutional space between cultural production and material "politics," and have tried to send out warning signals about the work that Americanist analysis can—and cannot—do.[12] For me this type of analysis requires a continual awareness of the institutional chasm separating the work of academic critique and foreign policy. On the one hand, I understand that consumption may indeed be where politics is located in the circulation of goods.[13] On the other hand, I am struck by the impermeability of state political institutions (even reflective ones, which I think do exist within the U.S. State Department) to critiques such as these. That does not mean to give up. More important is being aware of that institutional chasm.

The argument about the logics of cultural diplomacy is, I hope, clear enough: cultural diplomacy "after the American Century" misses the lessons about the digital age that it has made explicit and even invoked.[14] The mention of the debate in the Chennai embassy about showing *The Color Purple* just an hour after a discussion of the digital scanning of x-rays for e-mail analysis should not seem tenable to the public affairs officer. And yet of course it does. Much of this disconnect is precisely because of the power of institutions and the ways in which they are constituted and replicate themselves. The sensitivity to the circulation of American cultural products and cultural forms—their recoding, their public jumping, the various "ends of circulation" they locate—unwrites the nationalistic narrative about digital technologies seamlessly bringing India and the United States together by frustrating the logic on which the narrative of cultural diplomacy relies. Critical attention to these forms in circulation tried to show how the meeting of American studies and globalization studies that seemed to vex scholars at the ASRC may be brought together. As the public affairs officer left the room at OUCIP, however, the Indian news media followed *him*, and not of course *me*. The articles in the Indian dailies the next day highlighted his announcement of funds allocated, of the plans for the new consulate. My inaugural lecture, which I was concerned might be co-opted by the presence of the U.S. state, was mentioned only in a phrase, full stop.

CAIRO (MARCH 2009)

Cairo is both ancient and young. It is ancient, as everyone reading this knows, because of millennia of layered cultural histories and traditions. The Pyramids rise over the southwest border of the city, in Giza, not too far from the largest state university, Cairo University. Egypt's population is young: the median age is under 25; more than 60 percent are under the age of 30 by most estimates, with about one-third under the age of 14. To walk around the campus of Cairo University, bursting at the seams, is to feel the energy and the frustrations of yet another generation whose members have grown up under the political state of emergency that has ruled the land without interruption since Hosni Mubarak's ascension to the presidency in 1981. That the massive amount of foreign aid the United States has contributed to Egypt has helped keep Mubarak in power is not lost on most Egyptians. Still, the colonial regime that is most immediately present for most is the former British Empire, which brought English language, literature, and culture to educated Egyptians. In this sense the similarities to India are instructive. Yet in Cairo, the dismay toward the United States as a political entity goes far beyond what I encountered in print or in person in Hyderabad. Circulated through the remarkable rise in Arab satellite television and news stations such as al-Jazeera and al-'Arabiyya, the rhetoric of the Bush administration from late 2001 until the end of 2008 was perceived as fundamentally hostile to Muslims in most of the Arab world, a rhetoric reaffirmed by the revelations of torture of prisoners at Abu Ghraib, with decidedly anti-Islamic extravagances. In Egypt, as in other Arab countries friendly to the United States such as Morocco and Tunisia, the very binarism suggested by President Bush in 2001—"with us or against us"—had turned those who had admired the United States into bitter even if sometimes reluctant critics of American hypocrisy.

As I prepared to travel to Cairo in March 2009, I was returning to a city I had visited with some frequency over the previous year. I was also traveling to a city where I knew the language (Arabic).[15] This time I was the official guest of Cairo University on a project planned by my Egyptian hosts and at their invitation, jointly funded by the Binational Fulbright Commission in Egypt (BFCE) and Cairo University. The fact that my visit to consult on the development of an American studies program at Cairo University was initiated by Egyptian scholars softened my discomfort about receiving partial funding from the U.S. state. Since the geopolitical context had changed substantially since the two episodes described earlier in this essay, however, I was less adamant in my refusal of any funding from the U.S. state. I was, after all, traveling during the hopeful early moments of the Obama administration. That election, I knew from a visit to Cairo a few months earlier in the immediate aftermath of Barack Obama's victory, had changed the Egyptian conversation about American culture and its international reach.[16]

Egypt, like India and Iran in important ways, has some real claim to "exceptional" status. Egyptians have a distinct sense of their Arabness, one that negotiates the peculiar relationship of ancient Egyptian culture to contemporary Egypt and the centrality of Egypt in twentieth-century pan-Arab thinking. After the various perceived failures of the national project since 1967, Egyptians frequently lament the status of their nation in both high and popular culture, in the latter case in such best sellers as Galal Amin's *Whatever Happened to the Egyptians?* (in Arabic, 1998; in English, 2000) and Khaled al-Khamissi's episodic reportage *Taxi* (2007). But as the largest Arab nation in the world, with a distinctive dialect of Arabic (the only Arabic dialect that truly travels, though Lebanese Arabic has made recent challenges because of the increased popularity of its music and satellite channels), and the largest and longest tradition of national cinema and television with a recognizable national style, Egyptians have some claim to exceptionalist status—they certainly feel that they do.

What does it mean to be "exceptional" or exceptionalist in Egypt, when compared to American "exceptionalism"? One clue to an answer was uttered in Nebraska, on the Santee Sioux Reservation, to an Egyptian scholar from Upper Egypt. This dynamic junior scholar had come from Sohag, in the Egyptian south, to Chicago to pursue research on Native American studies at the Newberry Library. After several weeks in the archives, in late 2004, she had taken it upon herself to visit the Sioux Reservation in Nebraska. She was struck, she told me later, by a comment she heard there from an elderly Sioux: "What the Bush administration is doing to you Arabs now," the gentleman said, "they did to us 200 years ago." In Nebraska, with a status in the United States comparable to that of Sohag in Egypt, a connection was forged between Egyptian American studies and Native American studies.[17]

On previous visits to Cairo in 2005 and 2008, I had lectured widely in Cairene universities, from the elite American University in Cairo to lower-tier state universities, funded privately either through my university or a grant from the Carnegie Corporation of New York. I had been curious to learn more about the state of American studies in Egypt. What I had learned then surprised me, though it was not yet scientific: as Egyptian undergraduates, graduate students, and junior faculty turned toward American literature and culture, which they were doing with increasing frequency, they were drawn much more to what U.S.-based Americanists would call "ethnic" literatures than to the mainstream canonical figures recommended by senior Egyptian literature scholars (for example, Fitzgerald, Hemingway, T. S. Eliot, and Updike, to pick those most frequently mentioned to me). Subfields such as Latina/o studies, Native American studies, Asian American studies, and African American studies had captured the attention of the younger generation of English students and scholars. There had not yet been in 2005, 2008, or 2009 a collective awareness of what seemed to me so common as to be an identifiable trend. But the turn had made its way into the syllabi of American literature (or "American civilization") surveys at schools such as Cairo University, which had begun to include texts from these minority literary traditions.

Still, what was called "American studies" at Cairo University meant two things, with two constituencies, that recalled the debate at the University of Tehran, though with a different trajectory and a different outcome. First, a group operating out of the political science department had created an American studies concentration with decidedly area studies aims. Close to President Mubarak's administration, the political scientist leading this group focused on the United States explicitly as a political entity. Second, fueled by the energy of a handful of young professors in the English department who were attending to international discussions about American studies in the United States and elsewhere, a small group in the otherwise British-focused department was attempting to open up the curriculum to admit more than the cursory semester on American literature. This latter cohort had created a lecture and workshop series called the American Studies Circle, supported in part by the BFCE, where faculty could discuss their work or invite visiting lecturers. Unlike in Tehran, where American studies brings together the humanities and the social sciences (including political economy), and where the political science department lost in its bid against the more humanistic and interdisciplinary American studies program, in Cairo the two exist simultaneously, alternatively in tension and in mutual exclusion from one another. Still, among the faculty of the English department, the interest in Cairo about the development of American studies in Tehran (and its history in India) was strong, just as in India there had been much interest in what was happening with the field in the Middle East.

The election of Barack Obama of course offered an opportunity for the English department Americanists to bring together both aspects of American studies. If the Egyptian American studies curriculum had begun to establish itself as one of "difference"—difference of American culture from British culture, difference and oppositionality of ethnic Americans from white Americans, both of which were projects dear to postcolonialist Egyptian scholars' hearts—Obama's rise in the United States put the difficult questions that Egyptians were now asking about the United States at the forefront of the American civilization classroom.

As I returned to Cairo University in March 2009, a new course packet in American literature had just been created and distributed to students in the fourth-year undergraduate American literature course. The course pack ended with two provocative texts that had been published almost simultaneously with its creation: Obama's inaugural address and an article by Hua Hsu titled "The End of White America?" in the January/February

2009 issue of the *Atlantic Monthly*. When I arrived in Cairo, the course had just begun, so the students had not yet grappled with these texts. But their placement at the end of a syllabus that began with essays on ethnic American literatures (including articles on Jewish American writers and Arab American writers) suggested the direction of the course.

In Alexandria a few days later, in the shadow of the newly reopened and spectacular Bibliotheca Alexandrina, I lectured to a large class of students and faculty in American literature. This group was well read—at Alexandria University the American literature curriculum was more extensive than that in Cairo, with a two-semester survey divided between the third and fourth years of the English major. Still, it was a traditional syllabus by the standards of the more multicultural syllabus now generally in use in the United States, one that moved essentially from John Smith to Arthur Miller (there were some interesting interruptions, however, from Native American oral narratives to Langston Hughes, which reflects, I think, the influence I had observed beginning in 2005). Seeking to turn the energy and the friction between American popular and political culture into a discussion, I asked the students how many of them had ever read an American novel before coming to Alexandria University. No hands. Then I asked them how many had ever seen an American film. Laughter. How many had heard hip-hop music? Even more laughter. I don't think a single hand was not raised in response to either of the two final questions. After my lecture on tensions within twentieth-century American literature around questions of race, ethnicity, and empire, the questions from the students were all about Obama. How had he possibly been elected? Did this show that America had resolved its problem with race? If Obama could win the presidency, why were Americans still so racist in their attitudes toward Arabs?

Rather than see these Egyptian students' response to Obama's victory as a simple acceptance of America's victory over its history, as a reinscription of exceptionalism, both Egyptian students and those nonuniversity Cairenes I spoke to outside the university expressed what they believed was a division of the U.S. state from American culture and found a way to place (aspects of) Obama in both. This response was as true at the more prestigious state institutions, such as Cairo University and Alexandria University, as it was at the second- or third-tier regional campuses I visited—such as University of Minufiya, a two-hour drive from Cairo (though only seventy kilometers away), where several students told me they had never ventured even as far as Cairo itself. On both elite and peripheral campuses, the familiarity with American popular culture overwhelms what Dilip Gaonkar and I have called, in our introduction to this volume, the "vernacular tradition" of American studies. As scholars in Cairo and Alexandria develop American studies syllabi and curricula, they must confront the ways in which their students' understanding of "America" is mediated by American popular culture.

Eventually what will emerge in Cairo—and is already emerging in Tehran—is an American studies without its vernacular tradition. The pieties about the centrality of the vernacular tradition of American studies simply do not obtain in Cairo or Tehran, and decreasingly so in Hyderabad. We may wonder if there is a deeper politics that underlies this development. To be sure, the lack of resources that might create the conditions for the development of a fuller curriculum is part of the cause. In Cairo, however, as in Tehran and Hyderabad, such an American studies cannot be anything than what it is—and what it is becoming. Whereas U.S. area studies programs seem to impart a *civilizational* explication of foreign cultures and societies—an impulse exaggerated in American media—in these new American studies programs, the American *present* is overwhelming. The American past is relatively invisible to ordinary eyes.

What the experience of engaging with American studies in Tehran, Hyderabad, and Cairo suggests, then, is that the archive of American studies itself has to be radically reconfigured for the field to be relevant in the twenty-first century. The way American history, literature, and society are perceived, interpreted, and reconfigured outside the United States, and the problems and possibilities that emerge from engagement with those who bring an outsider's regard to the trajectory of the United States, must be considered by the field at large. In order to understand this perception, not only will comparative, multilingual American studies work be a prerequisite, but the circulation of scholars of "America" along multiple pathways will be necessary. And although this understanding will require scholars of all nationalities at times to stagger around looking for common ground, as our Iranian colleague did at the ASA in Washington, D.C., and as I did during Friday prayers in Tehran under the threat of U.S. attack, or in Hyderabad while the American Studies Research Centre was trying to regain U.S. funding, or in Cairo in the wake of President Obama's victory, doing so may lead to a greater future for a field in need of one.

Notes

The first section of this chapter originally appeared, in slightly different form, as "American Studies in Tehran," *Public Culture* 19, no. 3 (2007): 415–24. I presented a shorter version of the Hyderabad section in June 2008 as part of a plenary lecture at the Futures of American Studies Institute, Dartmouth College, organized by Donald Pease.

1. Paul Giles, *Virtual Americas: Transnational Fictions and the Transatlantic Imaginary* (Durham, NC: Duke University Press, 2002), 263.

2. Hamid Dabashi, *Iran: A People Interrupted* (New York: New Press, 2007), 203.

3. See Wilson P. Dizard, Jr., *Inventing Public Diplomacy: The Story of the U.S. Information Agency* (Boulder, CO: Lynne Rienner, 2004).

4. A similar situation occurred in 2007, although on a much more elevated plane, to a group of Iranian artists and American members of a Washington NGO called Meridian. Meridian, in the interest of intercultural exchange, sponsored a large exhibition of contemporary Iranian art in DC, only to be told at the eleventh hour that the secretary of state Condoleezza Rice would be opening the event (Meridian apparently received funds from the U.S. State Department). The introduction by Secretary Rice complicated matters back in Iran for the Iranian artists represented in the show and immediately shifted the collaboration from one between individuals and an NGO to one between individuals and the U.S. state.

5. While "retaining its rich resources in different aspects of American Studies and International Relations," she added. Kousar Azam, personal communication, November 12, 2006.

6. Indeed, a U.S. consulate in Hyderabad was opened subsequently. Ribbon cutting on consular operations was on March 24, 2009. In April 2009, the U.S. consulate in Hyderabad donated nearly $300,000 for American studies books and materials to OUCIP. http://hyderabad.usconsulate.gov/events091109.html. In September 2009, a major gift of books to the OUCIP library collection was announced by the U.S. consulate. The gift, from "the Asia Society and the Confederation of Indian Industry, with the assistance of the U.S. Consulate General in Hyderabad," constituted "thousands of new books . . . most . . . on American studies topics." http://hyderabad.usconsulate.gov/pr41710.html.

7. He also spoke of an Indian American success story from Hyderabad, the invocation of diaspora.

8. I had had my own mirror experience when my wife, at nearly 10:00 p.m. Chicago time across the world, called Best Western's domestic 800 number to try to help me out of the dismal university guest house where I was lodged (without phone or Internet access of my own). She was seamlessly transferred to a call center in Hyderabad, where, despite the reluctance of the call center worker (who was forbidden to mention where he was located), she got hotel advice for Hyderabad.

9. See Kate A. Baldwin, *Beyond the Color Line and the Iron Curtain: Reading Encounters between Black and Red, 1922–1963* (Durham, NC: Duke University Press, 2002), chap. 4.

10. My colleague in Istanbul, the communications scholar Nezih Erdogan, has shown how in the 1950s, the USIA and the Turkish state both censored Hollywood films and kept them from being screened in Turkey for much the same reason. See Nezih Erdogan and Dilek Kaya, "Institutional Intervention in the Distribution and Exhibition of Hollywood Films in Turkey," *Historical Journal of Film, Radio and Television* 22, no. 1 (2002): 47–59.

11. Kousar J. Azam, "Notes on 'American Studies Now'—A Roundtable at OUCIP, 12th December 2006," personal correspondence, January 1, 2007.

12. See my article, Brian T. Edwards, "Sheltering Screens: Paul Bowles and Foreign Relations," *American Literary History* 17, no. 2 (2005): 307–34.

13. This insight is inspired by Arjun Appadurai, "Introduction: Commodities and the Politics of Value," in *The Social Life of Things: Commodities in Cultural Perspective*, ed. A. Appadurai (New York: Cambridge University Press, 1986), 3–63.

14. I expand on this point in my forthcoming book *After the American Century: American Culture in Middle Eastern Circulation.*

15. This statement requires some clarification. "Arabic" refers generally to the formal language (called Modern Standard Arabic in American classrooms, and *al-'arabia al-fosha* in the Arab world) used in literature, media, university lectures, and official speeches. Modern

Standard Arabic is no one's birth language, and the language of Egypt is accurately described as Egyptian Colloquial Arabic, or ʿ*ammiyya*. Having spent a decade and a half working and occasionally living in Morocco, I was fairly fluent in Moroccan Colloquial Arabic. But Moroccan Arabic is useless in Egypt, where it is considered incomprehensible, and the two are as different as Spanish and Portuguese. Although I have become more proficient in Egyptian Colloquial Arabic since my Fulbright trip, at that time my abilities in the dialect were limited.

16. Shortly after my Fulbright trip, President Obama made a major address at Cairo University in June 2009, in which he laid out a vision of a new American attitude toward the Middle East. I returned again to Cairo soon after the June address (twice in summer 2009) and encountered increased popular enthusiasm for the president in the wake of this speech.

17. Joanna Brooks, a professor of African American and Native American literature at San Diego State University, tells me that this comparison is a common one in Native American circles. Much satire has come from Native Americans who imagined an overlap between acronyms for the Bureau of Indian Affairs and a Bureau of Iraqi Affairs, according to Brooks. Following up on her comment, I found a great deal of Native American humor playing on this topic. See http://64.38.12.138/boardx/topic.asp?ARCHIVE=true&TOPIC_ID=1053; also see *Cherokee Phoenix* staff writer Travis Snell's essay "Bureau of Iraqi Affairs?" *Native Press*, http://www.thenativepress.com/essays/rants2.html.

KATE BALDWIN is associate professor of rhetoric and director of the American Studies Program at Northwestern University. Her book *Beyond the Color Line and the Iron Curtain: Reading Encounters between Black and Red, 1922–63* was published by Duke University Press in 2002. Her current book project is titled *Cold War Hot Kitchen*.

ALI BEHDAD is professor of English and comparative literature and chair of the Comparative Literature Department at the University of California, Los Angeles. He is the author of *Belated Travelers; Orientalism in the Age of Colonial Dissolution* (Duke University Press, 1994) and *A Forgetful Nation: On Immigration and Cultural Identity in the United States* (Duke University Press, 2005). He is completing a volume tentatively titled *Contact Visions: On Photography and Orientalism, 1840–1910*.

WAI CHEE DIMOCK is the William Lampson Professor of English and American Studies at Yale University. Among her recent publications are *Through Other Continents: American Literature across Deep Time* (Princeton University Press, 2006); a collaborative volume, *Shades of the Planet: American Literature as World Literature* (Princeton University Press, 2007); and a special issue of *PMLA*, coedited with Bruce Robbins, "Remapping Genre" (October 2007). She is also a consultant for an educational television series, *Invitation to World Literature*, funded by the Annenberg Foundation and produced by WGBH, and a frequent contributor to a related Facebook forum, "Rethinking World Literature."

BRENT HAYES EDWARDS is a professor in the Department of English and Comparative Literature at Columbia University. He is author of *The Practice of Diaspora: Literature, Translation, and the Rise of Black Internationalism* (Harvard University Press, 2003), which was awarded the John Hope Franklin Prize of the American Studies Association. With Robert G. O'Meally and Farah Jasmine Griffin, he coedited *Uptown Conversation: The New Jazz Studies* (Columbia University Press, 2004). Edwards is coeditor of the journal *Social Text* and serves on the editorial boards of *Transition* and *Callaloo*. He is currently working on two book projects: a study of the interplay between jazz and literature in African American culture, and a cultural history of "loft jazz" in downtown New York in the 1970s.

BRIAN T. EDWARDS is an associate professor of English, comparative literary studies, and American studies at Northwestern University, where he also co-chairs the Middle East and North African studies working group. He is the author of *Morocco Bound: Disorienting America's Maghreb, from Casablanca to the Marrakech Express* (Duke University Press, 2005). He is completing a book titled *After the American Century: American Culture in Middle Eastern Circulation*, based on research in Morocco, Egypt, Lebanon, and Iran, for which he was named a 2005 Carnegie Scholar. Edwards has lectured widely in the Middle East, North Africa, South Asia, and Europe and has been a visiting faculty member at the University of Tehran and the École des Hautes Études en Sciences Sociales (Paris). He was a Fulbright Senior Specialist in American Studies at Cairo University, Giza, in 2009. In 2008–9, funded by a New Directions Fellowship from the Andrew Mellon Foundation, he trained in anthropology and Middle East studies at the University of Chicago.

DILIP PARAMESHWAR GAONKAR is an associate professor in rhetoric and public culture and the director of the Center for Global Culture and Communication at Northwestern University. He is also the codirector of the Center for Transcultural Studies, an independent scholarly research network concerned with global issues. He is closely associated with the journal *Public Culture*, currently serving as the executive editor. Gaonkar has two sets of scholarly interests: rhetoric as an intellectual tradition, both its ancient roots and its contemporary mutations; and global modernities and their impact on the political. In the former area he has written "The Idea of Rhetoric in the Rhetoric of Science," which was published along with ten critical responses as a book, *Rhetorical Hermeneutics* (edited by Alan Gross and William Keith; SUNY Press, 1995). In the latter categories, he has edited a series of special issues of *Public Culture*, including "Alternative Modernities" (2001), "New Imaginaries" (2002), and "Cultures of Democracy" (2008).

BRIAN LARKIN examines the materiality of media technologies and their role in the formation of colonial and postcolonial urban experience in Nigeria. He has published on media circulation, piracy, and intellectual property, and on religious mediation and the enchantments of technology. He is the author of *Signal and Noise: Infrastructure, Media and Urban Culture in Nigeria* (Duke University Press, 2008) and a coeditor of *Media Worlds: Anthropology on New Terrain* (University of California Press, 2002). Larkin serves on the editorial board of *Social Text* and on the board of the Society for Cultural Anthropology. He teaches anthropology at Barnard College, Columbia University.

CLAUDIO LOMNITZ works on culture and politics in Mexico and in the Americas. His books include *Evolución de una sociedad rural* (Fondo de Cultura Económica, 1982); *Exits from the Labyrinth: Culture and Ideology in Mexican National Space* (University of California Press, 1992); *Modernidad Indiana: Nación y mediación en México* (Planeta, 1999); *Deep Mexico, Silent Mexico: An Anthropology of Nationalism* (University of Minnesota Press, 2001); and, most recently, *Death and the Idea of Mexico* (Zone Books, 2005). The Spanish-language version of that book was awarded the García Cubas Prize for the best scientific contribution to anthropology and history, and Mexico's Camara de la Industria Editorial (CANIERM) for the best sociological essay. Claudio Lomnitz is currently the editor of the journal *Public Culture* and is the Campbell Family Professor of Anthropology at Columbia University.

DONALD E. PEASE, Avalon Foundation Chair of the Humanities at Dartmouth and founding director of the Dartmouth Institute in American Studies, is the author of *Visionary Compacts: American Renaissance Writings in Cultural Context,* and editor or coeditor of eight volumes, including *The Culture of United States Imperialism, American Renaissance Rediscovered,* and *The Futures of American Studies.* Pease is general editor of the New Americanists series of books published by Duke University Press. His latest books are *The New American Exceptionalism* (University of Minnesota Press, 2009) and the biography *Theodor SEUSS Geisel* (Oxford University Press, 2010).

NAOKI SAKAI is a professor of comparative literature and Asian studies at Cornell University. He has published in the fields of comparative literature, intellectual history, translation studies, and studies of racism and nationalism. His publications include *Translation and Subjectivity* (in English, Japanese, and Korean); *Voices of the Past* (in English and Japanese; Korean forthcoming); *Japan/Image/the United States: The Community of Sympathy and Imperial Nationalisms* (in Japanese and Korean); and *Hope and the Constitution* (in Japanese; Korean forthcoming). He has been working for *Traces, A Multi-Lingual Series of Cultural Theory and Translation,* which is published in Chinese, Korean, Japanese, English, and German (German version forthcoming in 2011), and served as its founding senior editor (1996–2004).

ELIZABETH F. THOMPSON is an associate professor of history at the University of Virginia. She is currently working on two book projects, *Cinema and the Politics of Late Colonialism* and *Seeking Justice in the Middle East.* Her first book, *Colonial Citizens: Republican Rights, Paternal Privilege, and Gender in French Syria and Lebanon,* won awards from the American Historical Association and the Berkshire Conference of Women Historians.

JULIET WILLIAMS is associate professor of women's studies at the University of California, Los Angeles. She is author of *Liberalism and the Limits of Power* (Palgrave Macmillan, 2005) and coeditor, with Paul Apostolidis, of *Public Affairs: Politics in the Age of Sex Scandals* (Duke University Press, 2004). Her research interests lie at the intersection of feminist theory and sociocultural studies. She is currently working on a book titled *Making a Difference: Single-Sex Public Education and the New Science of Sex Difference.*

KARIANN AKEMI YOKOTA is an assistant professor of American studies and history at Yale University. Her book *Unbecoming British: How Revolutionary America Became a Postcolonial Nation* is being published by Oxford University Press. She is currently at work on *Pacific Overtures: America and the Trans-Pacific World of Goods, 1776–1850,* which discusses how the encroachment of the United States into the Pacific shaped the development of American culture and democracy. Yokota's interests include transatlantic and transpacific history, material culture studies, cultural history of the late colonial/Early Republic, and ethnic studies.

INDEX

Bridges, Herb, 203n2
British institutions, as definitive sources of knowledge, 85–86
Bromley, Constance, 164, 180n19, 181n25
Brooks, Cleanth, 12
Brown, Ralph, 108n36
Brown-Guillory, Elizabeth, 142
Bruckner, Martin, 109n37
Brunton, Deborah, 105n2
Buck, Pearl, 251
Buddle, Ann, 106n12
Buell, Lawrence, 112n75
Burke, Edmund, 16
Burke, Kenneth, 43n13
Burroughs, William S., 16
Bush, George W., 3, 22, 75, 78, 254
Bush administration(s), 3–4, 29, 47–48, 50, 52–53, 55–56, 75–77, 241, 253, 284, 305, 308, 315–16
Bush's Axis of Evil, 307
Bush's State of Exception, 2, 4, 51–53, 55–56, 58, 70, 73, 75–80
Butterfield, L. H., 110n56

Cabrera, Luis, 229–30
Cairo, 189–91, 193–95, 314–16, 318–19
Callahan, John H., 131n6, 133n42
Campbell, Edward D. C., Jr., 203n2, 207n72
Capa, Robert, 150n7
capital, 35; transnational, 257
capitalism: American, 27, 178; neoliberal, 79; U.S., 119
Captive Nations Week, 139
Cardoso, Fernando Henrique, 210
Carnegie, Andrew, 216
Carson, David L., 132n22
Carter, Bill, 44n32
Carter, Jimmy, 291
Casablanca (film), 306
Catroux, Gen. and Mme., 192
censorship, 164–67, 174, 178, 181n25, 191, 193, 265n36
Chahine, Youssef, 188
Chang, Iris, 264n33
Chaplin, Charlie, 194
Chaplin, Joyce, 102–3, 112n77
Chatterjee, Partha, 112n81

chemistry, 97–98; America's first professorship, 97
Chen Kuanhsing, 265n42
Cherokees, 77
Childress, Alice, 34, 36, 140–46
Chowdhry, Prem, 203n3
Chrisman, Laura, 111n72
Churchill, Winston, 37, 275–77
cinema, 155–58, 160–62, 167, 169, 177–78, 184, 202; American, 155–208, 306–8, 312; American dominance, 174–75; British, 161, 163; colonial, 159, 165; in colonial India, 171, 181n25; Egyptian, 191; as a social space, 169–74 (*see also* film(s))
cinema-going, in the colonial world, 156, 159
circulation, 5–6, 24, 28, 31, 306, 313; of American cultural products, 311, 314; of images, 28, 162
civil liberties (civil rights), 77, 295
civil rights movement, 5
class conflict, absent in the U.S., 59–60
class struggle, 83n24
Clifford, James, 298n7
Clinton, DeWitt, 225
Clive, John, 106n13
Cohn, Bernard S., 179n2
Colbert, Stephen, 299n20
cold war, 3, 9, 14, 16, 19–20, 34, 38–39, 49, 54, 59–63, 72, 74–75, 77, 127, 140, 150, 242, 256–57, 311–13
Coleman, Peter, 133n39
College of New Jersey (later Princeton University), 33, 84, 96–98
Collet, Anne, 196–200, 202n1
Colonial Film Unit, 178
Colonial Films Committee, 166
colonial rule, 102, 158, 163
colonialism, 55, 57, 62, 70, 79, 102, 126, 172, 177, 210, 218, 249–50, 256; European, 128, 297
Color Purple, The (film), 312, 314
Comas, Juan, 226, 228n25
Comfort Women, 242, 254
Commager, Henry Steele, 16, 60
commodity culture, 157, 161
communications, 156, 162, 177
communism, 250, 257

internationalism: American, 306; anticolo-
nial, 118, 129-30; black, 120; grassroots
version, 216, 219; in Ralph Ellison, 119,
121-22, 125-26
International Military Tribunal for the Far
East. *See* Tokyo War Crimes Tribunal
international relations, 209, 212, 230
Iran, 21-23, 284-98, 300-308
Iraq, invasion of, 74
Irwin, Robert, 299n23
Isenberg, Nancy, 42n11
Islam, 184, 283
Islamophobia, 294, 306-7
Iturbide, Agustín, 210
Ivy, James, 127

Jackson, Jesse, 22
Jackson, Lawrence, 126, 131n10
Jaikumar, Priya, 181n32, 181n33, 181n35,
182n38
James, C. L. R., 111n72
James, Henry, 15-16, 18, 119, 288
Japan: Democratic Party, 241, 243, 256;
Liberal Democratic Party, 241, 243, 254;
Lost Decade, 241; military, 242-44, 246,
251, 253, 259; war responsibility, 244,
252-54, 264n30
Japanese Americans, interred in the U.S.,
248-49
Jarvie, Ian, 179n8, 203n2
Jefferson, Thomas, 3, 64-66, 68-69
Jeffries, Theodore, 110n65
Jennings, Francis, 112n75, 113n84
Johnson, Chalmers, 256
Johnson, James Weldon, 15
Johnson, Samuel, 86, 106n10
Jones, Claudia, 141
journalism, yellow, 222, 229
journalistic empiricism, 293
judiciary, U.S., 66
jurisprudence, British, 113n82

Kadir, Djelal, 2-4, 47-48, 50-58, 70, 74-75,
78-79
Kammen, Michael, 281n2
Kang Sangjung, 265n42
Kansas-Nebraska Act, 65
Kaplan, Amy, 2, 4, 7-10, 14, 26, 53-58, 70, 75,
78-79, 111n75, 137, 139-40

Kaplan, Frederick, 309-12
Kassem, Mahmoud, 208n84
Katz, Friedrich, 215
Kaya, Dilek, 320n10
Kazanjian, David, 113n84
Kelley, Robin D. G., 124
Kerber, Linda K., 42n11
Keshavarz, Fatemeh, 293
Keswick, Maggie, 106n12
Khadra, Yasmina, 288
Khalaf, Samir, 205n31, 206n56
Khalidi, Rashid, 203n4
al-Khamissi, Khaled, 316
Khater, Akram, 208n86
Khomeini, Ayatollah Ruhollah, 287
Khrushchev, Nikita, 34, 136-37, 140, 147,
149-50
kibô-gaku (study of hope in Japan), 240-41
Kim Shijon, 264n30
King, James, 108n35
Kingston, Maxine Hong, 17
Kishi administration, 242
Kishi Nobusuke, 254
Kitchen Aid, 137-39, 143, 149
kitchen debate, between Richard Nixon and
Nikita Khrushchev, Moscow (1959), 23,
34, 136, 140, 149-50
kitchens, as segregated spaces, 140, 145
Klein, Julius, 160
knowledge, as an object of value, 90, 99
knowledge production, 48, 51, 54, 91, 216,
106n7, 247, 257, 265n37, 295
Koizumi administration, 243
Koizumi Ichirô, 261
kokutai (nationality), 245, 247-48, 255
Koppes, Clayton R., 204n21
Kôsaka Masaaki, 250
Kracauer, Siegfried, 158
Krinsky, Emma Cecilia García, 239n40
Krishnaswamy, S., 181n32, 181n33
Kroes, Rob, 81n6
Kuhn, Adam, 105n2
Kuhn, Annette, 180n18
Kyoto treaty, 74

Lahiri, Jhumpa, 313
Lancaster, Sonya, 151n12
Landau, Jacob M., 205n29
Landsman, Ned, 106n13